Creative COLORED

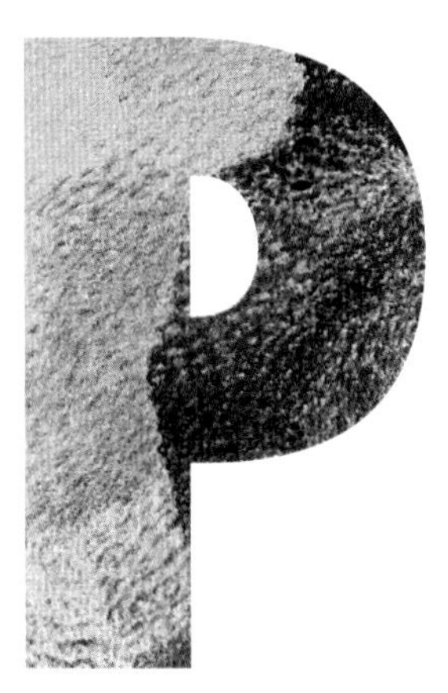

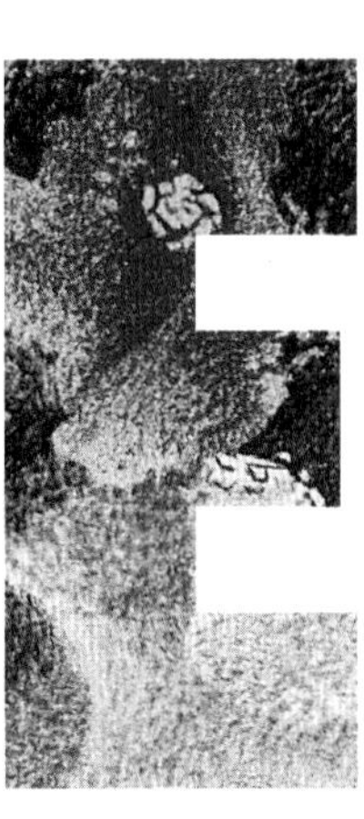

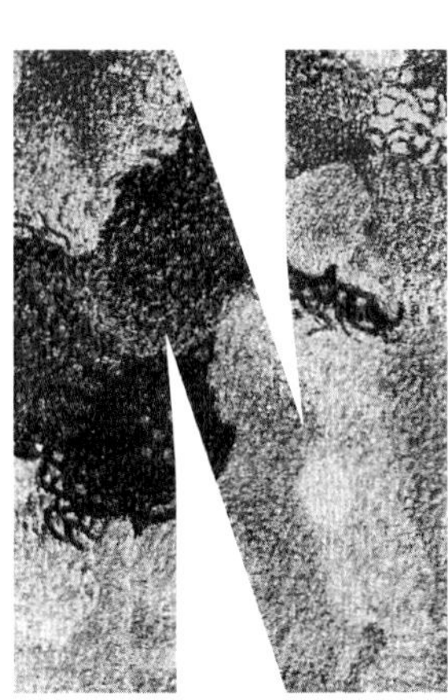

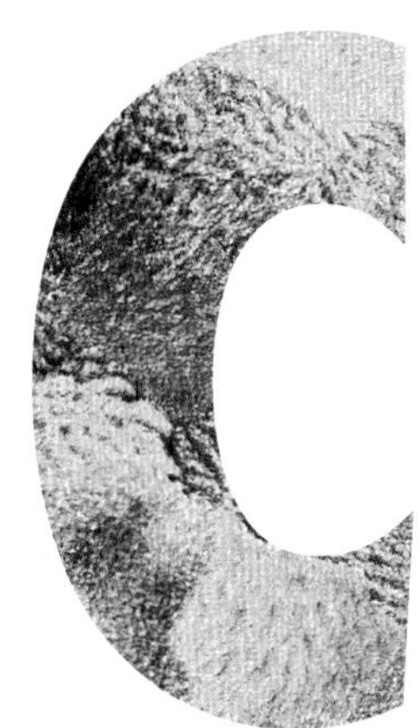

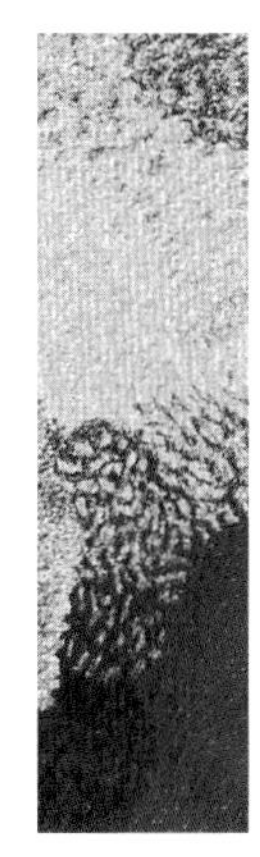

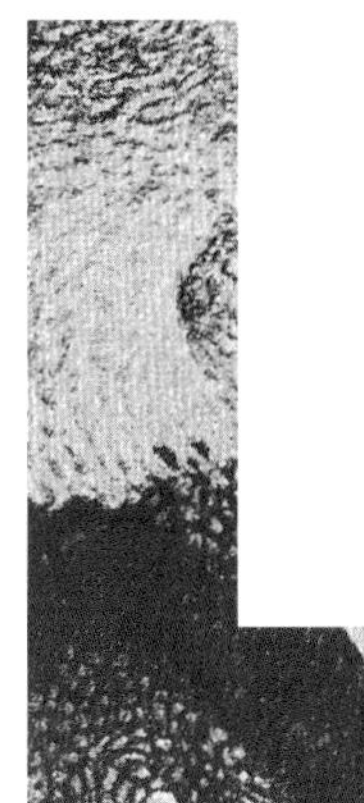

THE STEP-BY-STEP GUIDE

& SHOWCASE

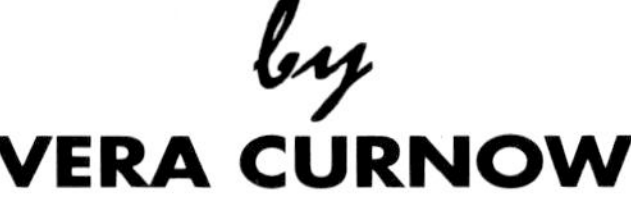

by
VERA CURNOW

Rockport Publishers, Rockport Massachusetts
Distributed by North Light Books, Cincinnati, Ohio

First published in the United States of America by:
Rockport Publishers, Inc.
146 Granite Street
Rockport, Massachusetts 01966
Telephone: (508) 546-9590
Fax: (508) 546-7141

Distributed to the book trade and art trade in the U.S. and Canada by:
North Light, an imprint of
F & W Publications
1507 Dana Avenue
Cincinnati, Ohio 45207
Telephone: (513) 531-2222

Other Distribution by:
Rockport Publishers, Inc.
Rockport, Massachusetts 01966

ISBN 1-56496-141-9

10 9 8 7 6 5 4 3 2 1

Creative Director and Designer
Gary Greene
Gary Greene Artworks
Woodinville, Washington

Photography
Gary Greene
Gary Greene Artworks

Prolab, Inc.
Seattle, Washington

Cover Illustration
Bruce J. Nelson

Cover Design
Laura P. Herrmann

Printed in Hong Kong

This is dedicated to

Angeline La Duca

for more reasons than this book could hold.

ACKNOWLEDGEMENTS

This is not *my* book. It belongs to the Chapter artists who allowed me to look over their shoulder, ask too many questions, and then tell all their creative secrets. Without them and the artists who contributed to the Gallery Sections, this would have been a very short book. While the work of these artists fills the pages, there are other people, perhaps less visible, who are responsible for putting it there, among them the Editors and Production staff at Rockport Publishers, Inc. I would be remiss if I didn't single out the following people for their professional and personal efforts:

SPECIAL THANKS TO...

GARY GREENE, not only for his professional collaboration in every aspect of the book, but also for his bottomless well of patience and kindness and for always being my friend even when it wasn't convenient.

PATTI GREENE for unbegrudgingly doing the long, tedious tasks of making lists and checking them twice and for her nurturing nature and open door policy.

SHAWNA MULLEN for crossing all the t's, dotting the i's and cracking a velvet whip.

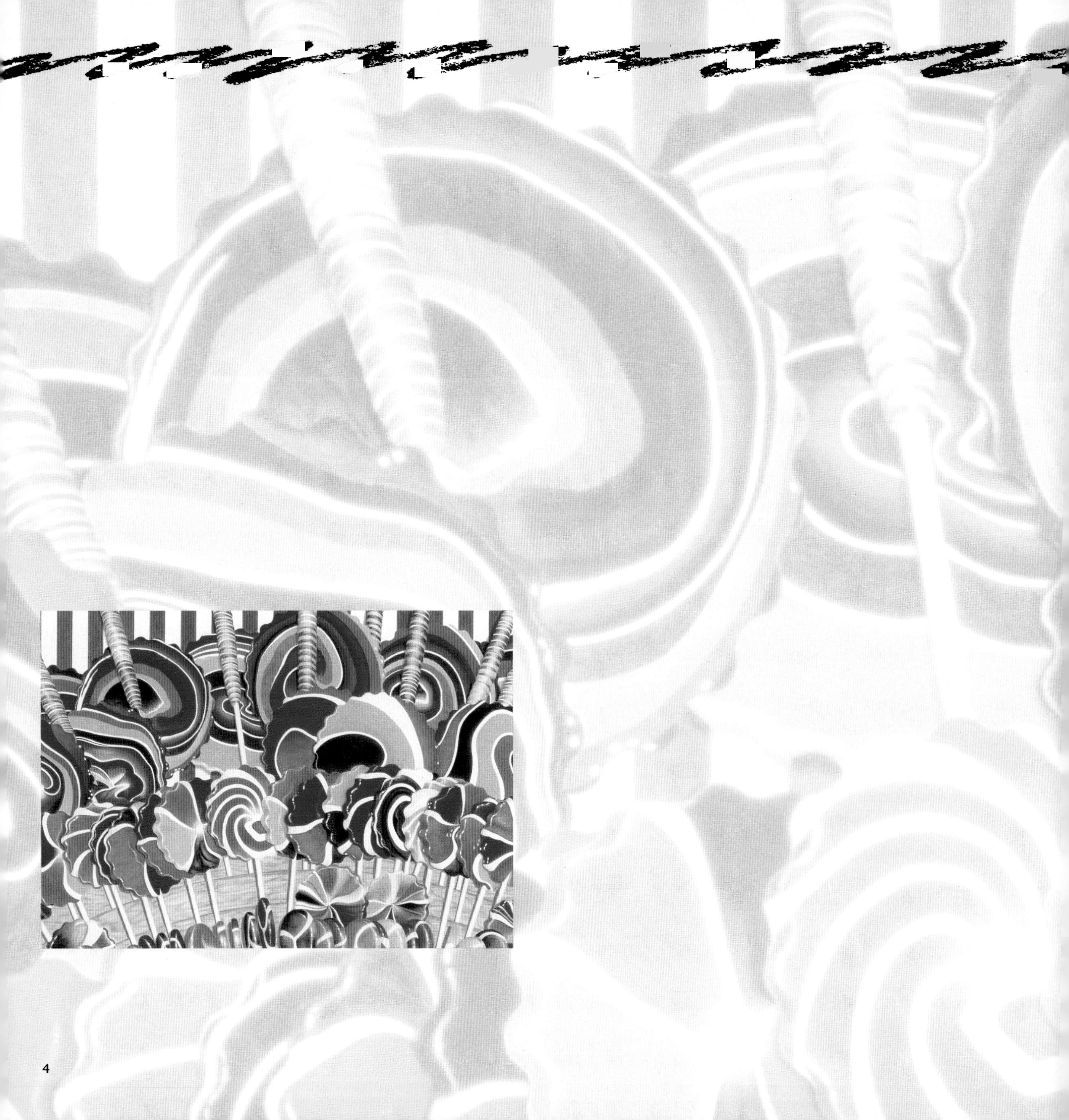

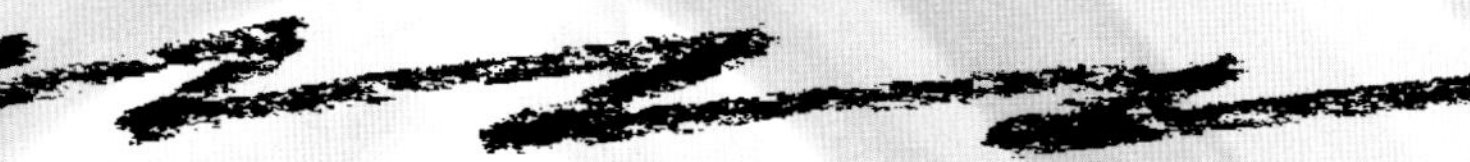

TABLE OF CONTENTS

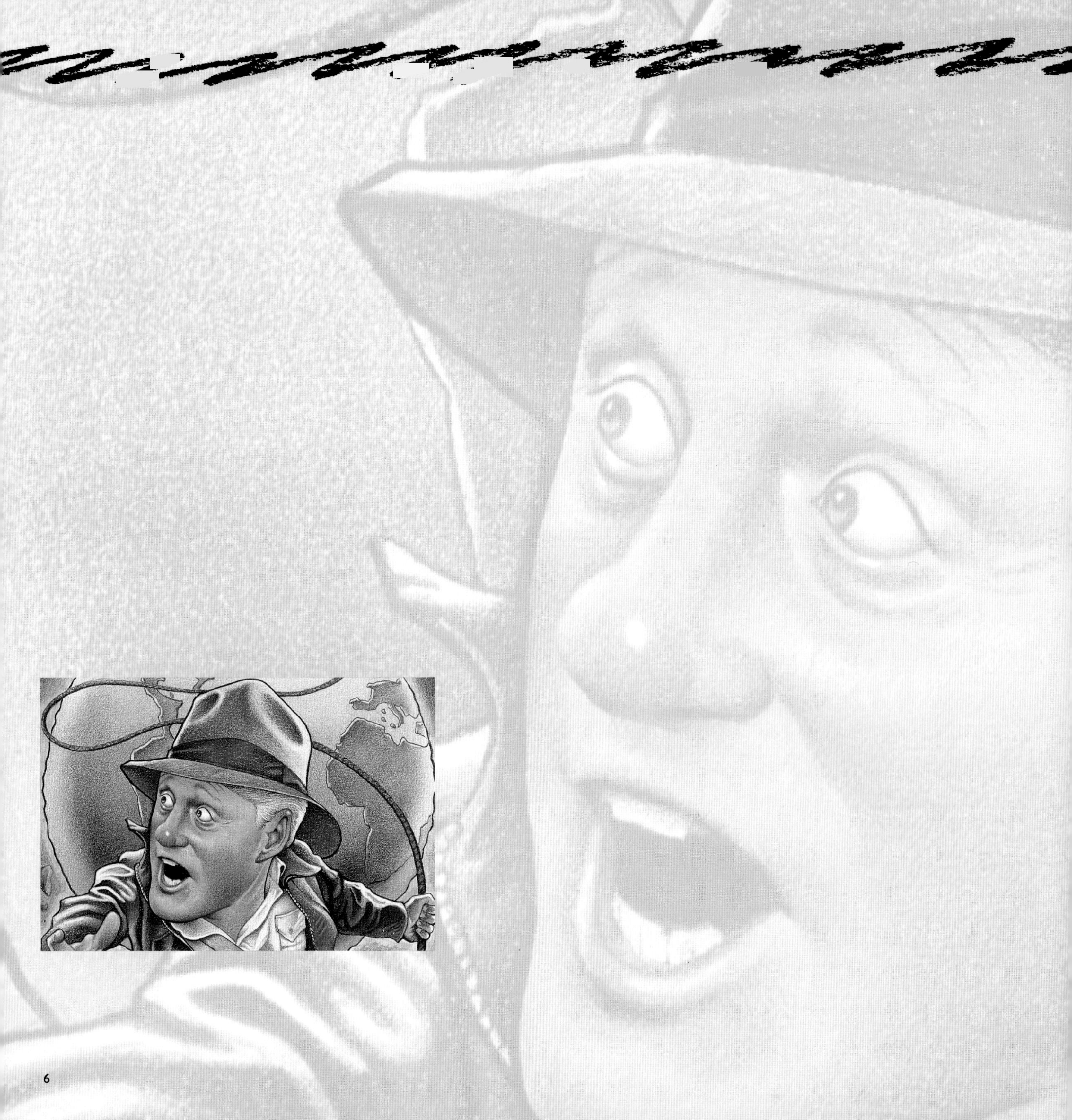

FOREWORD

by Bill Nelson

It is difficult to separate the book Creative Colored Pencil from the book's author, Vera Curnow, but for the sake of this forward I will try. Like the Colored Pencil Society of America, which Vera founded, this book strives – and succeeds – in elevating colored pencil to the realm of fine art.

In a world of coffee table books that never get worn out from use, it is refreshing to find one that will wear out because it actually teaches. Creative Colored Pencil teaches in a variety of ways. Multiple step-by-step demonstrations by some of the best artists in the business are instructive and illuminating. But Vera doesn't stop there (if you knew her you'd already know she wouldn't stop there). There are also sections that present new techniques, new approaches to using mixed media, and highlight creative applications and color. When was the last time you said "I know everything there is to know about color"?

As if this weren't enough, (if you knew Vera you'd already know that it's never enough), there are fantastic gallery sections that follow each chapter and show you what pencil looks like when handled by true artists.

So once again, you can expect to learn a lot from this book. Expect to make notes in the margins and dog-ear the pages. Expect to smudge favorite chapters by consulting them over and over again. Expect dirt and grass on the book's binding, from taking it outside where you're sketching. Just don't expect to leave it on the coffee table.

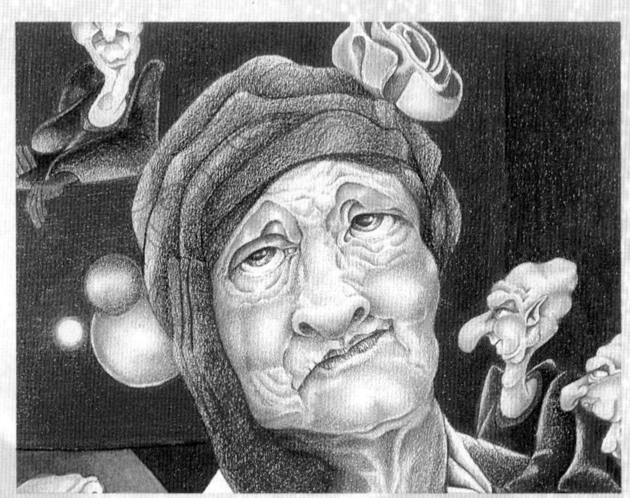

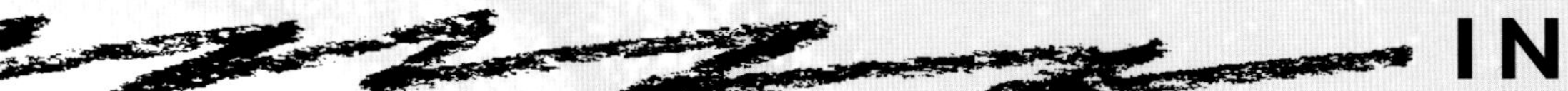

INTRODUCTION

by Vera Curnow

"IT'S ONLY PAPER!" This seemingly simple declaration was made loudly and repeatedly by my friend and art mentor, Mary Ann Beckwith. As an emerging artist, it soon became my mantra. Staring at the pristine whiteness of the drawing surface, I was like a deer caught in the glare of headlights. Wide-eyed and frozen. The responsibility of creatively filling the sanctity of this space intimidated the hell out of me. And then one day, Mary Ann did the unthinkable. Reaching out in front of me, she quickly, purposely, and unceremoniously smudged my illustration board. "Now", she pointed out, "this is used paper — feel free to experiment with it before you throw it out." This incredibly ordinary act of desecration put into perspective how little was at risk in light of what could be gained.

It is with this attitude of experimentation that I'd like you to approach this book. The subject is not about changing your colored pencil style or technique. Its purpose is not to recommend that you work with circular strokes or do photorealism. Its focus is not even on the end result. This book is about creatively approaching the process of working with colored pencils. It is about exploration and discovery not simply of the medium, but in our art as well.

If you are new to colored pencil, learn by what others are doing, but don't be afraid to venture on your own. There is no right or wrong. And remember, this is not about sculpting the perfect scale model of Mt. Rushmore. This is about getting creative effects with a pencil. On the other hand, don't be deceived by the simplicity of colored pencil. It is not a one-dimensional tool when it comes to producing powerful and varied results.

If you are a seasoned colored pencil artist with a finely tuned method of working, take a break. Better yet, break a habit — just this once. Do it for the sake of broadening your scope, changing your perspective, or adding a new spark to your work. Remember how you relied on your instincts and impulses when you didn't know so much about colored pencil? Remember the revelations? Take some time to subliminate what you know and concentrate on what you feel.

If you're looking for a new muse, you must try a path less traveled. Creativity is such an elusive element with subjective interpretations. And that's the way it should be. Anyone who assigns it a specific definition or thinks there should be rules for achieving it is missing the point. It's also not something we "arrive at" and keep. It has to be rediscovered with each new work. That means we have to leave the door to creative possibilities open.

As someone once said,the answers you get will depend on the questions you ask. This is particularly true in creating art. By continually asking the same questions of ourselves and our work, we will always get the same answers — and results. Dyanne Locati's advice to artists says it all, "Don't be predictable." All we have to do is keep asking ourselves,"what if..." and then be daring enough to find out. Even if a painting begins with just a smudge, we know we have nothing to lose because, after all, it's only paper.

Vera Curnow

Litterly Speaking
30 x 16" (762 x 407 mm)
Crescent Illustration Board

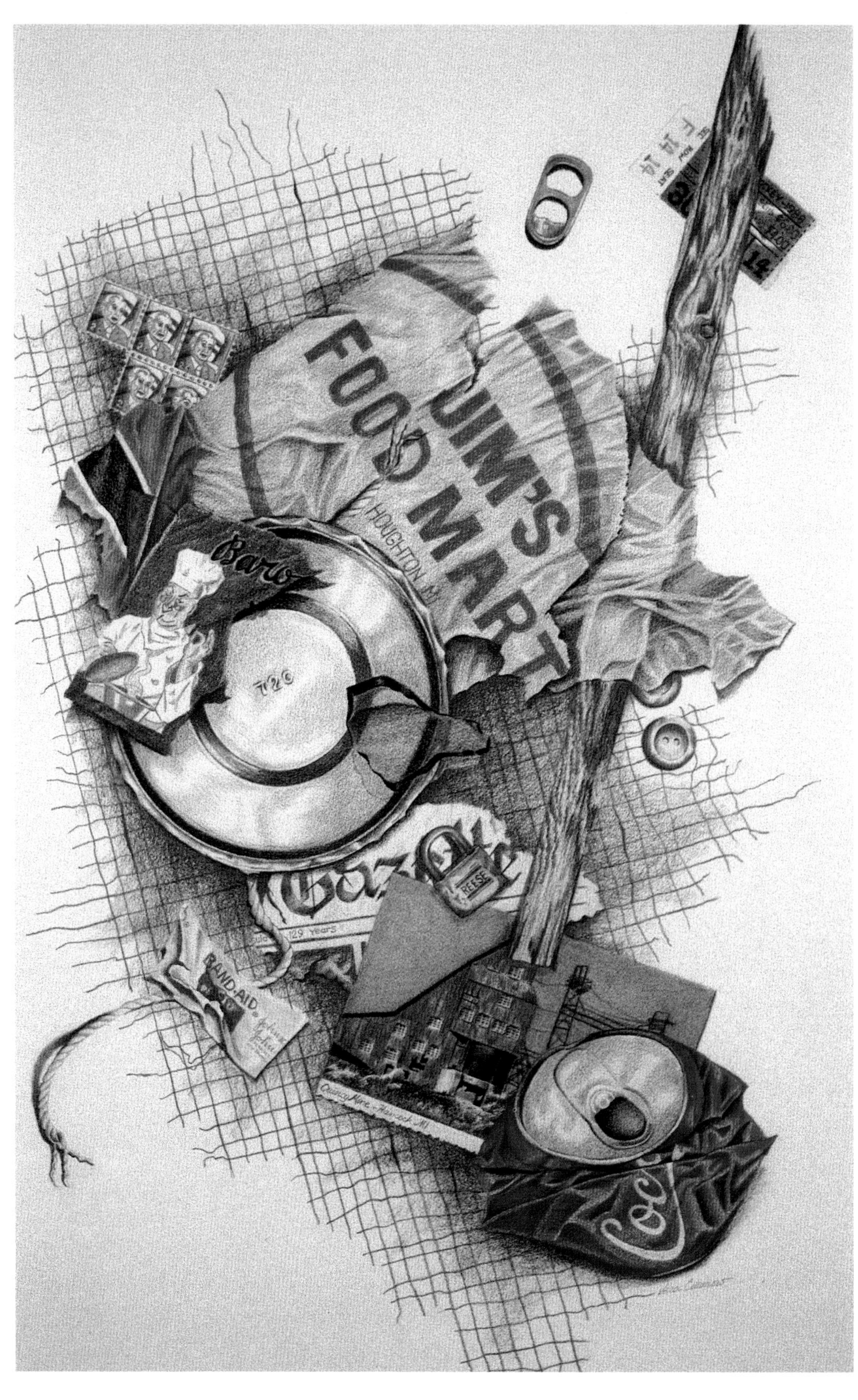

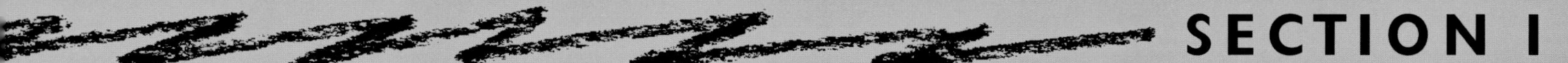

Creative Applications for Professional Results

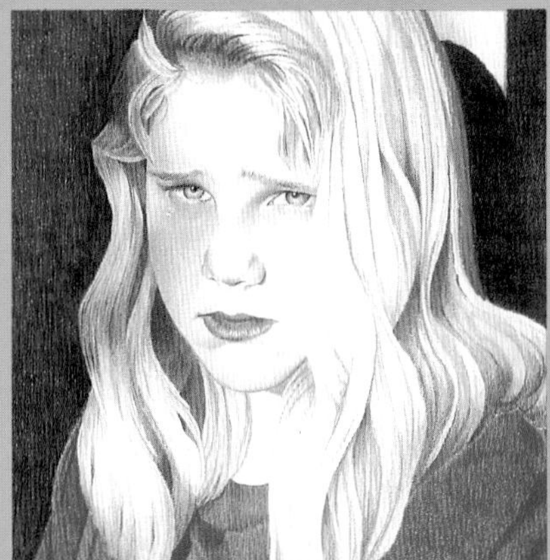

Vertical Strokes to Model Form
Ann Kullberg

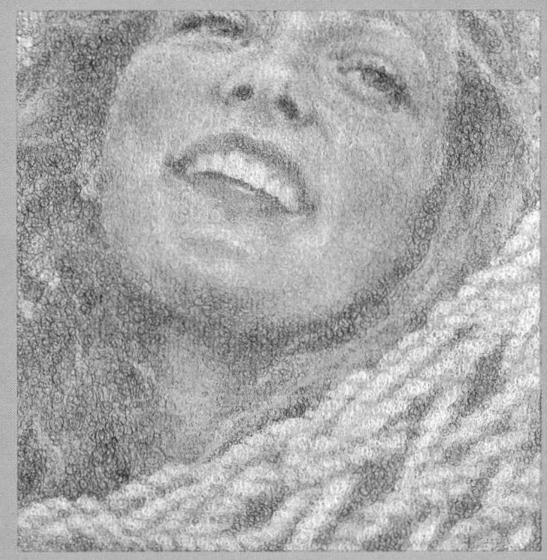

Working In Circles
Maggie Toole

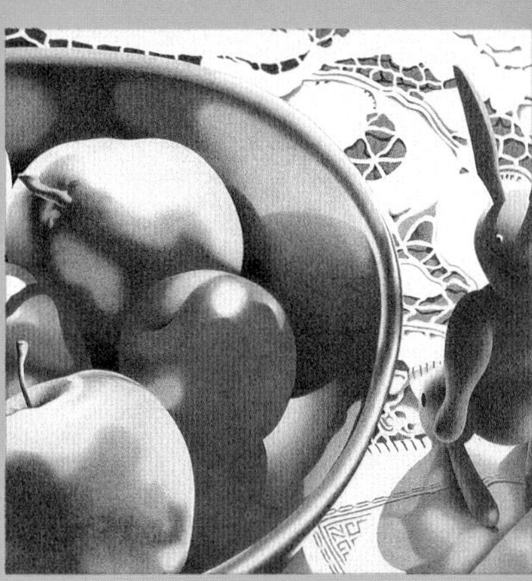

Tonal Quality Goes Beyond the Line
Sherry Loomis

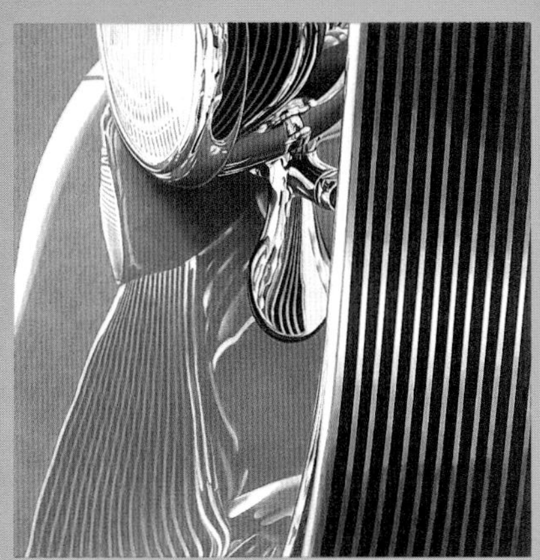

Heavy Burnishing for Realistic Impact
Gary Greene

Let's consider the color Red. Hot, angry, exciting, aggressive. It has a temperature, a mood, and sometimes an attitude. If it had a voice, it would be loud. If it was music, you might hear a trumpet. Since color doesn't work in a vacuum, however, let's consider it in context: red car, red sweater, red flower, or "Is my face red." These red images all differ in form, weight and texture. Artists must convey these differences – from the object's look to its "feel" – not only through color, but just as importantly, through how that color is applied.

It starts with the simplest form of artistic expression: The line or stroke. This is more than a vehicle that transports color. The repetition of this single gesture lays down color while simultaneously creating structure. When left visible, strokes exercise their own characteristics to create direction and tempo. They can illustrate the languid movement of pond water or the velocity of a hurricane. And when they are heavily layered, burnished strokes simulate the fluid color transitions of a painting.

Yes, we work in color. But whether vertical, horizontal, diagonal or circular, strokes play an integral role. After all, if color has a message, the strokes we use serve to deliver it. Explore the possibilities that the techniques in this section provide. Some methods are full of movement and energy, some are placid and serene. Whatever your natural rhythm, try a new tempo in your visual narrative through the creative use of strokes.

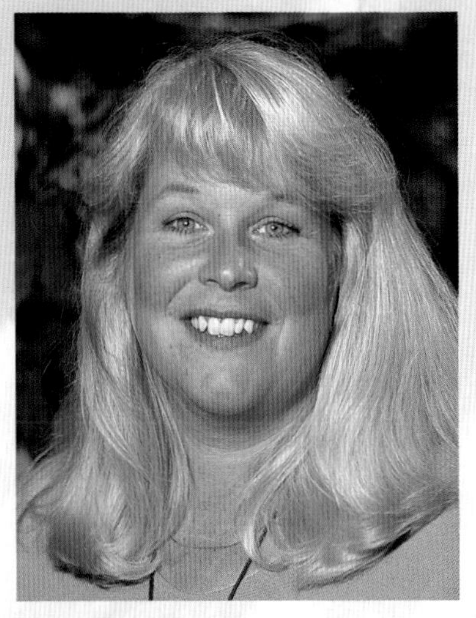

Ann Kullberg

Tokyo-born Ann Kulberg brings a sensitivity to colored pencil artistry that goes back to her childhood. Raised in Japan by Lutheran missionary parents, she experimented with watercolors and pastels at a young age, but didn't devote herself to art until 1987. A self-taught artist and former school teacher, Ann began receiving recognition for her portraiture in galleries throughout the Pacific Northwest. Her work was selected for national greeting cards and has won many exhibition awards. Ann has served as an art juror for art shows and conducts national colored pencil workshops.

CHAPTER 1

Vertical Strokes to Model Form

Vertical lines of equal length layered in horizontal rows? It's difficult to imagine that this could produce anything but a flat field of color. Yet, in spite of these hard, linear strokes, Ann Kullberg's colored pencil portraits sensitively capture form, depth, and light. Without using any horizontal lines, she is able to delicately shape a child's face, model soft fabric folds, or illustrate the texture of any surface – from glass to wicker. The vertical lines themselves are just part of the picture; what makes them effective is the precise way in which they are applied. Never bent. Never diagonal. Each vertical stroke is the product of four important considerations: Pressure, length, distance, and layering.

Varying the pressure of the lines is a vital part in Ann's technique. It allows colors and edges to blend, creating depth and "roundness." Heavy pressure used in dark areas accelerates the process of getting full, rich color. Pressure in light areas may vary from light to medium. Length is determined by the space being filled. In very large areas, Ann works with 3/4 inch vertical strokes. A horizontal line would be rendered in what amounts to miniscule vertical dots.

The vertical lines are placed side by side to create one horizontal row after another. Distance between the lines varies. Dark areas are densely filled with closely placed lines. To blend a shadowed area into a light area, the strokes are gradually placed farther apart. Each area has at least three layers of color. The lightest colors are always applied first. Some areas have as many as 15 color layers.

While Ann's self-developed vertical approach is extremely unique, it doesn't overshadow the exquisite portraits she creates. No vignettes of floating heads in the middle of the paper, Ann anchors her subjects with a backdrop of high-contrast colors and values. The effect is bold and direct. Her paintings take on an illustrative quality that is at once dramatic and believable.

GETTING STARTED
Ann's reference materials include slides and 8 x 10" photographs of her subject. Using a slide projector, she transfers the image onto a vellum finished Rising Stonehenge museum board. This surface erases well and is sturdy enough to accept 20-plus layers. MATERIALS: Soft, wax-based pencils, kneaded eraser, electric pencil sharpener. (Headphones and classical CD's are optional.) The completed work is sprayed with a matte fixative.

PALETTE
BACKGROUND: purple, black, lavender, grayed lavender, raspberry, mahogany red, vermillion, cream, ultramarine, french gray, limepeel, peach, raw umber, jasmine, indigo blue, black. HAIR: deco yellow, canary yellow, goldenrod, pumpkin, burnt ochre, terra cotta, tuscan red, burnt umber, crimson red, black, sunburst yellow, yellow ochre, orange, mineral orange. SHIRT: flesh, scarlet lake, terra cotta, pumpkin, crimson red, tuscan red. SKIN: peach, flesh, jasmine, yellow, ochre, goldenrod, pumpkin, carmine red, clay rose, burnt ochre, raw umber. EYES: PUPIL – deco blue, slate gray, indigo blue, dark brown, umber, black. IRIS – cloud blue, jasmine, lavender, indigo blue. LIPS: peach, carmine red.

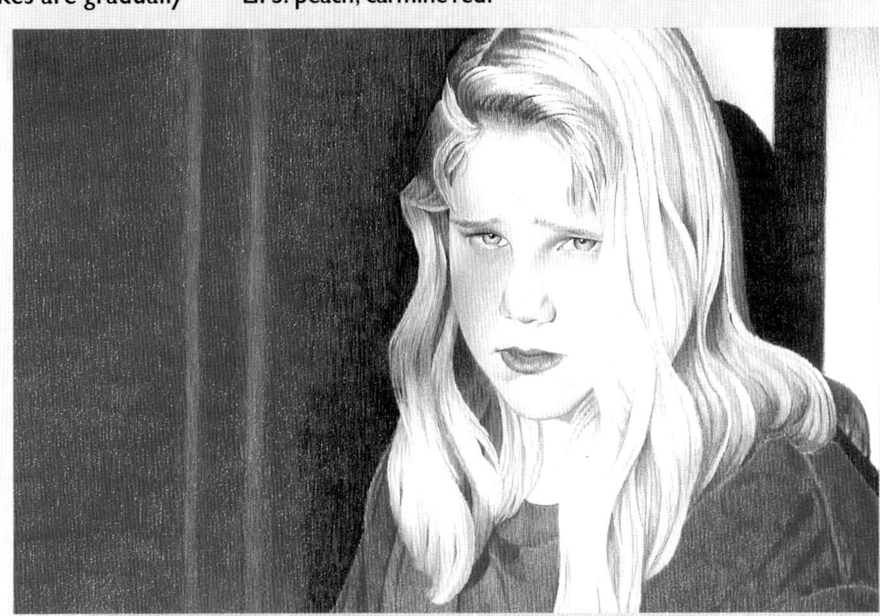

Katy
17 x 25" (431 x 634 mm)

1 Developing the darkest areas first helps to determine what the medium and light values should be. Instead of a dense application of raw black, the darks are built using various colors. For example, the section to the left of the model, which will eventually be blue-black, begins with a base coat of raspberry. Other colors will be added later. The shadow behind the figure is completed here in three layers: purple, then black, then purple again. Heavy pressure is used in the dark areas. The lavender "wash" to the far left and washes on the hair, shirt, and face are done with light pressure. This technique takes less time than traditional layering – Step 1 was completed in two and a half hours.

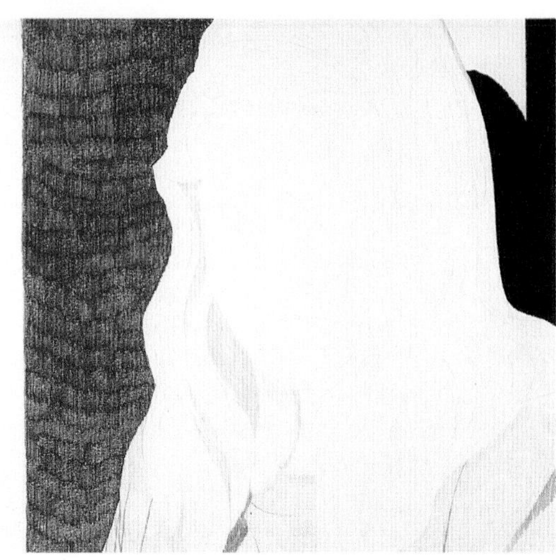

2 The straight vertical strokes are placed close together horizontally (note the eyebrows) working from left to right. In larger areas, the rows are slightly overlapped. The strokes are very visible in the beginning but become less pronounced with additional layering. Varying the pencil pressure helps to blend the layers and creates depth and roundness. The area to the right is layered with gray, light green, peach, raw umber and jasmine, using heavy pressure. This section is now finished. Depth is given to the raspberry background by applying ultramarine with progressively firmer pressure until the darkest area is next to the hair.

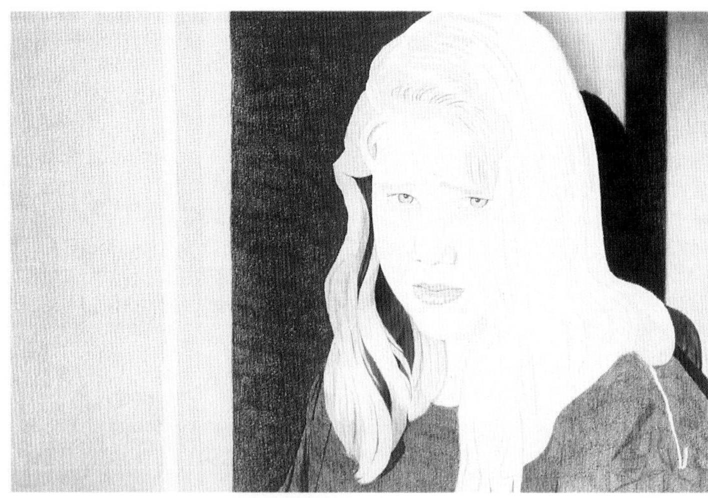

3 The background area to the left is finished after a layer each of indigo blue and black is added over the ultramarine. The shirt, which is also finished in this step, is drawn using eight different colors. Next, the shadow areas of the hair are completed using terra cotta and tuscan red. Yellow, yellow-orange, and mineral orange are applied with light-to-medium pressure in the highlight areas. Note that Ann has invested 11 hours up to this point.

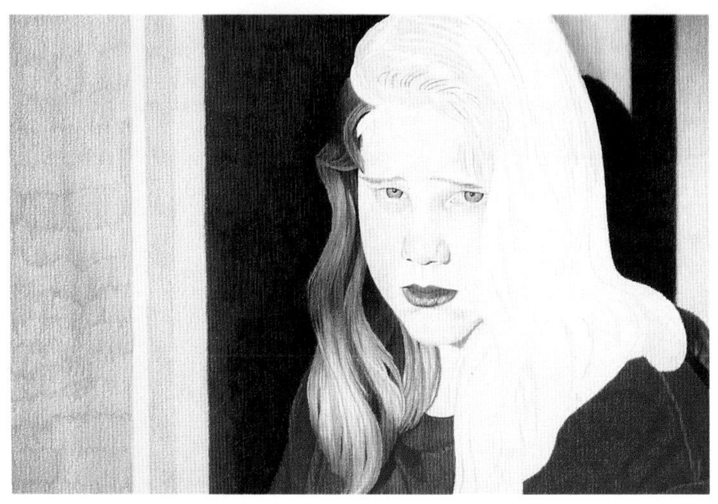

4 The intensity and values used to create the hair color dictate those needed for the face. Ann uses her standard palette for flesh tones (refer to Palette Section) by beginning with the lightest colors first. The values in the face are kept balanced by working back and forth between the highlight and shadow areas. A sharp pencil point is used to apply light to medium pressure while modelling the face.

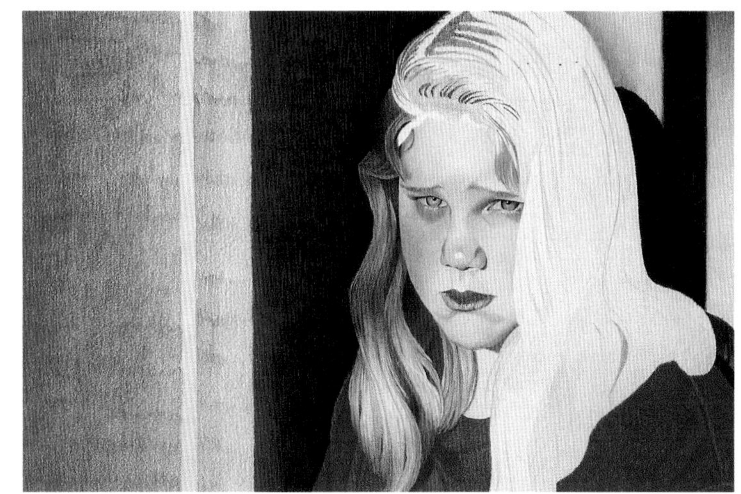

5 The far left side of the background is covered with mahogany red, a lighter pressure is used as the strokes are worked to the right. Then, a layer each of purple and blue is heavily applied to leave a smooth surface. This background section is now finished. The hair is drawn in "sections" as opposed to depicting individual strands. The contrast between the highlights and shadows gives the hair weight and volume. Waves and curls are created by carefully blending light-, mid-, and dark-values into smooth gradations. Remember, the strokes are still straight and vertical; avoid the temptation to contour the lines to the curves in the hair.

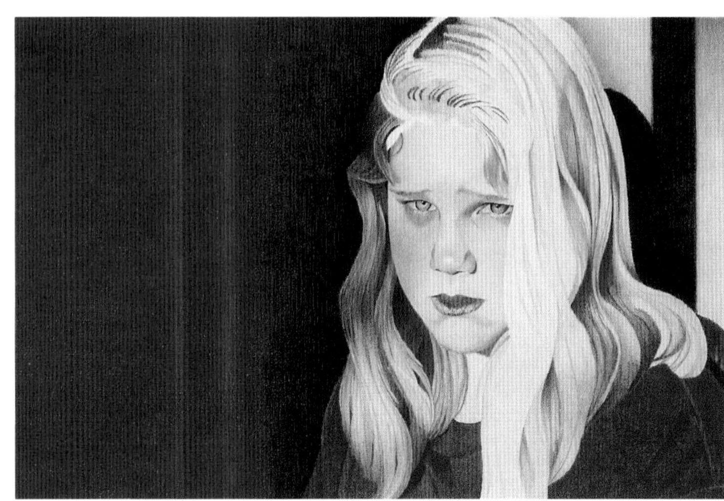

6 The last stage of the portrait is devoted to the skin tones and facial features. Yellow ochre and goldenrod add a glow to the complexion. Adjustments are made to the bottom of the chin and nose, adding red to capture the reflection from the shirt. The eyes, lips, and nostrils are darkened by alternately working from one to the other. Throughout the painting, as each section is completed, the last visible layer of straight vertical lines is accentuated by using a very sharp pencil point. Ann's use of vertical strokes, strong colors and bold composition results in the sensitive portrait of her daughter, *Katy*.

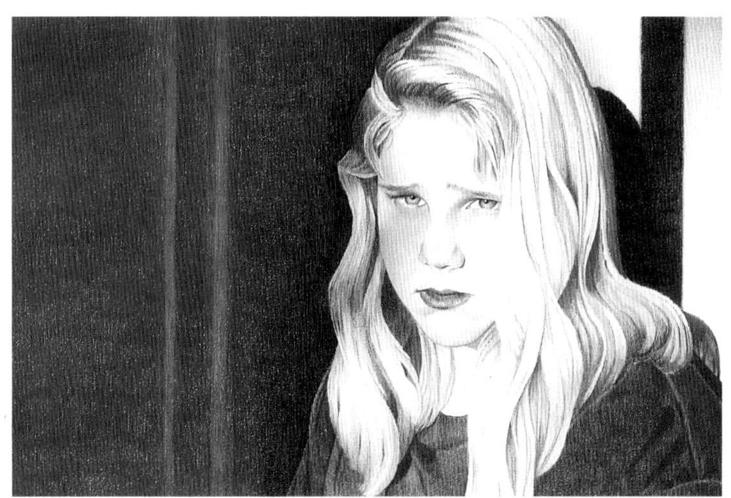

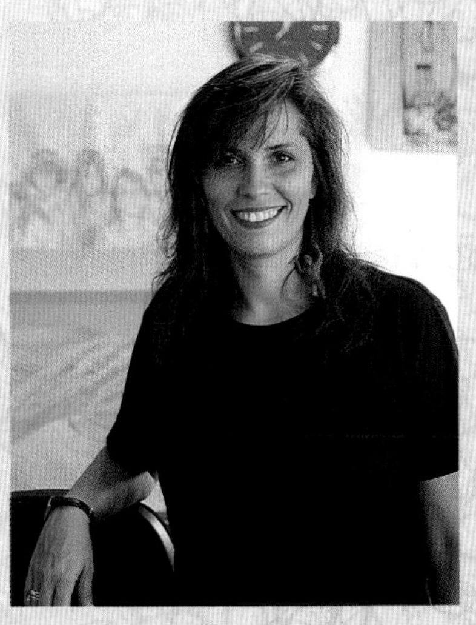

Maggie Toole

Since the sale of her first painting at the age of 15, Maggie Toole's art career has been rich and varied. Her expertise spans a wide range of media including leaded glass, watercolors, and colored pencils. In the past she has worked as a consultant and designer and has run her own business making leaded glass windows. Her colored pencil work has appeared in galleries and received numerous awards in juried exhibitions. It is included in many private and public collections.

CHAPTER 2

Working In Circles

"Whether or not by choice," says Maggie Toole, "I believe that people 'wear' their personalities. And that is what I am really interested in portraying. Capturing the person's likeness just seems to follow."

Maggie does, indeed, take her colored pencil figure paintings beyond the rendered image. Using creative compositions, she places her subjects in a slice-of-life freeze-frame full of energy. And she does it without using any straight lines. Maggie's exceptional technique, which she calls circulism, consists of overlapping thousands of intertwined circles in transparent colors. As many as 75 different colors are used in any given painting. But, their specific hues aren't important at the onset and may easily change as the work progresses. The first concern is to establish the values. Maggie uses strong areas of light and dark to set the mood. In creating these high contrasts, she never uses black and rarely uses white. Layer upon layer of circles in varying sizes, thicknesses, and colors slowly develop values and model form. In addition to the somewhat transparent circles, each work has "movement," created by the underlying pattern of the drawing surface. By working on exotic woods, Maggie incorporates their natural grains into the rhythm of her composition. As the work progresses and circles are randomly placed in no particular sequence, the "puzzle" begins to unfold. Much as in pointillism, the viewer's eye fuses this combination of hues into discernible shapes. The result: a colored pencil painting of figurative realism done entirely in rings of color.

GETTING STARTED

Important Work was done on a one-inch thick pear wood panel that had been sprayed with a thin coat of sanding sealer and was then lightly sanded. Working from reference photographs taken of the model, she drew a loose grid over the photograph and a corresponding grid over the wood's surface. Rather than do a contour drawing of the subject, she simply began drawing circles. MATERIALS: Soft, wax-based pencils, electric pencil sharpener, and kneaded eraser. The finished work was sprayed with a flat coat of clear water-based sealant.

PALETTE

Step 1. Jasmine, burnt ochre, warm silver grey, mineral orange, sand, cool grey, bottle green, grass green, henna, burnt carmine, Step 2. Violet, peach, bottle green, grass green, cinnamon, olive green, peacock blue. Step 3. Periwinkle, aqua marine, flesh, burnt yellow ochre, yellow ochre, olive green, crimson red, forest green. Step 4. Sky blue, greyed lavender, olive green, peach, apple green, copenhagen blue. Step 5. Imperial violet, blue violet, orange, apple green, mahogany red, light blue, yellow ochre. Step 6. Night green, periwinkle, sky blue, jasmine, french grey, creme, cedar green, aqua marine, blue, red, yellow.

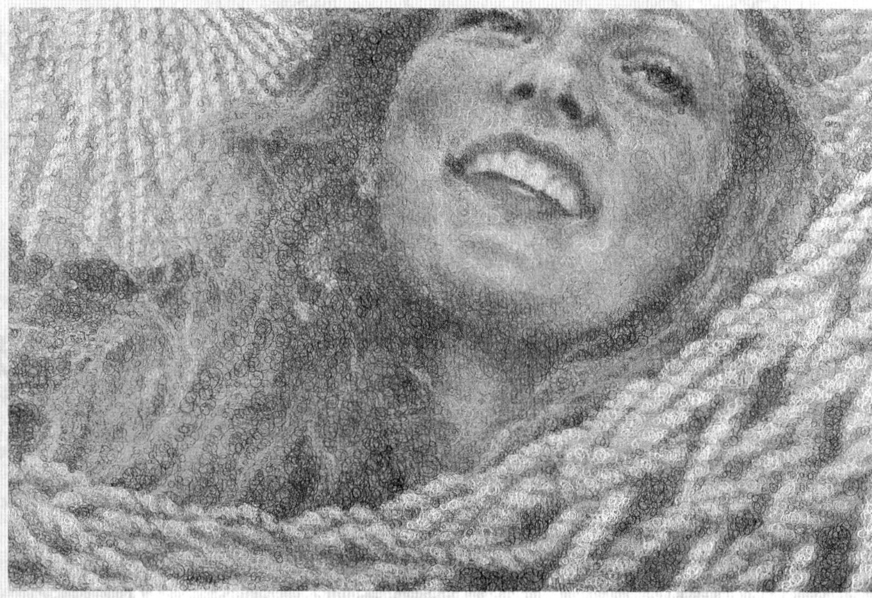

Important Work
20 x 30" (308 x 762 mm)

1 Without making an outline drawing, overlapping circles of varying sizes are lightly drawn over a grid to define shapes and establish values. The lightest values are identified with a medium-light (jasmine) colored pencil. Middle-value areas are marked with burnt ochre, warm silver grey and mineral orange. Bottle green, grass green, henna, and carmine circles are applied in what will be the darkest areas. Since the circles in the lightest areas will eventually get lost, highlights of sand and cool grey are added to serve as markers for when the work progresses. The composition and value patterns are now in place. The work that follows is simply a matter of strengthening and balancing the light and dark areas.

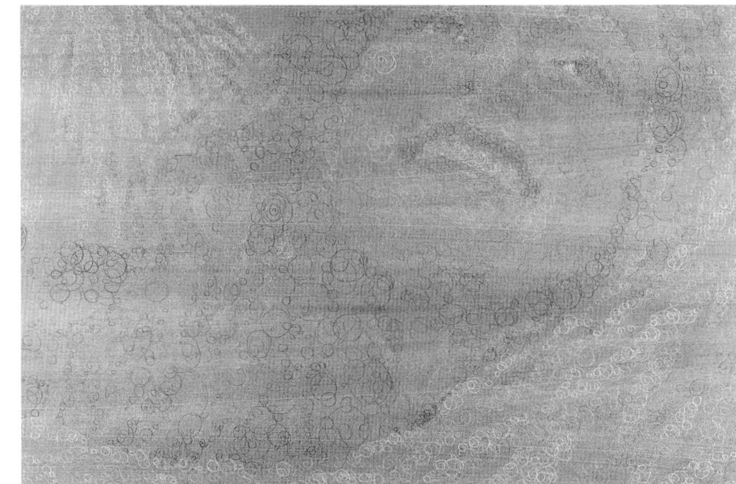

2 This drawing has three main sections: the face, the hair, and the hammock. Every color selected for one section is also applied to some degree in the two remaining areas. This creates color harmony throughout the work. The value contrasts are built slowly by jumping back and forth from light to dark areas. Rather than finishing one section at a time, all areas of the drawing are developed simultaneously. Since the patterns of the hammock are confusing, however, the background (sky) was left untouched so far.

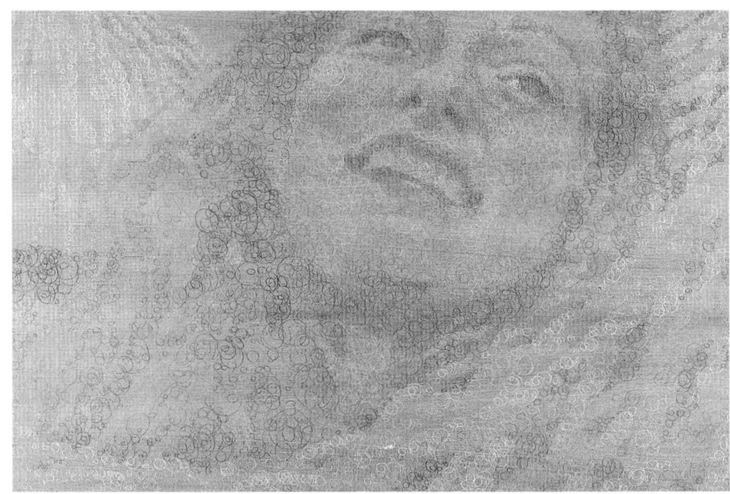

3 From this point on, the overlapping circles are applied with a firmer pressure. After defining the hammock ropes with olive green, periwinkle blue is added to the background and the subject's hair. Shadows and eyes are sparked with aquamarine. Medium flesh circles help model the cheek and lip area and are then added to the hair, sky, and hammock. Cinnamon and olive green circles soften the value transitions in the face and hair. (Stepping back and squinting helps check the perspective.)

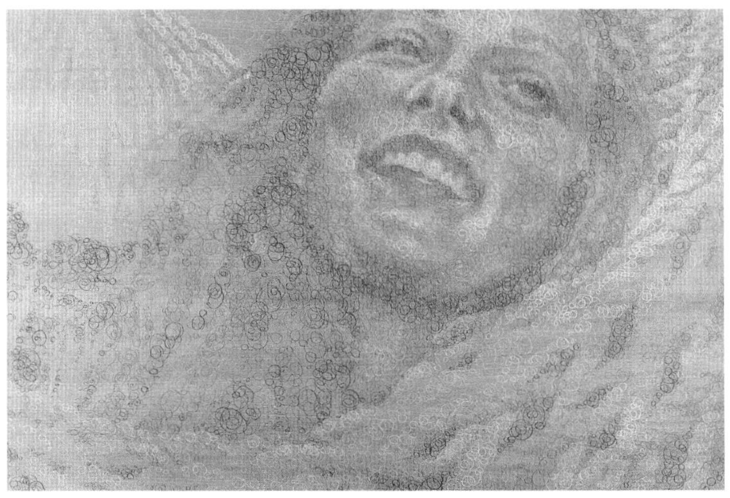

4 If any problems exist, they will usually surface in this stage. Corrections are made to lower the tip of the nose and adjust the width of the left cheek. The lightest sides of the hammock are intensified with sky blue, greyed lavender and peach. These colors also accent the hair and face. Circles of apple green are sparingly added throughout the work to add excitement. Because dark blues have a tendency to bleed into other layers, copenhagen blue is cautiously applied to the eyes, lashes, nostrils and mouth.

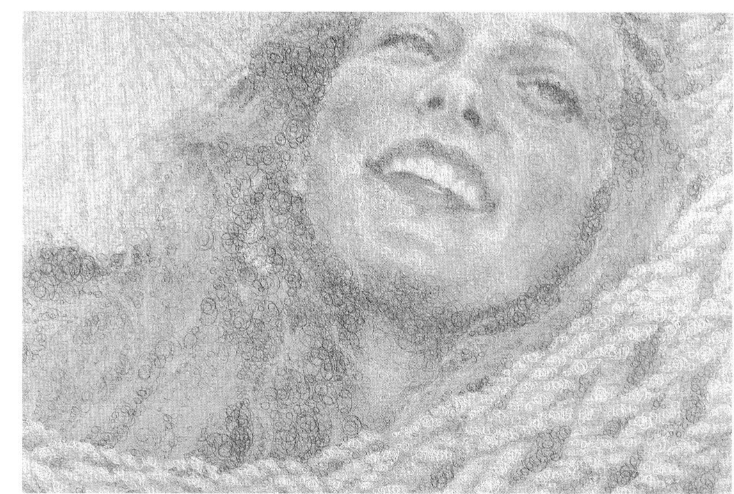

5 At this point, the layers of circles become fairly dense. Color choices and pencil pressure must now become bolder. Imperial violet and blue violet are firmly placed in the hair, lips and eyes. Orange is randomly added to all areas for zest and warmth. Mahogany red circles detail the hair and the darkest shadows of the subject's shirt. Color corrections and value adjustments are continually made as the work progresses.

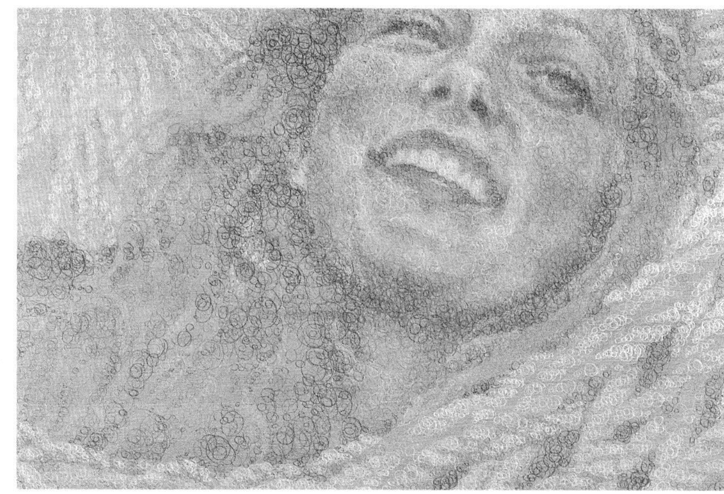

6 This last stage dramatically brings the subject to focus. Details are further defined and value contrasts are intensified. Depth is added to the deepest shadows with night green. The lightest highlights in the foreground hammock "pop" out when white is sparingly applied for the first and only time. Cedar green softens the edges between the very hard darks and the lighter areas. As a final touch, groupings of three overlapping rings – a blue, red and yellow one — are placed in inconspicuous areas throughout *Important Work*. This little trick goes unnoticed yet seems to add a vibrant charge to Maggie's circulism technique.

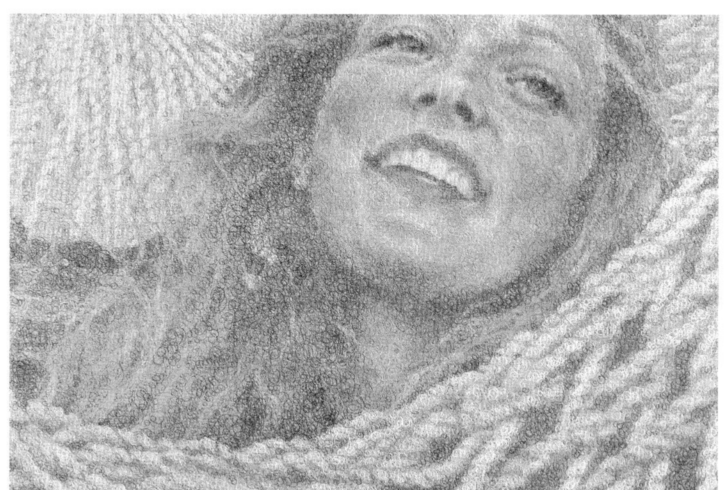

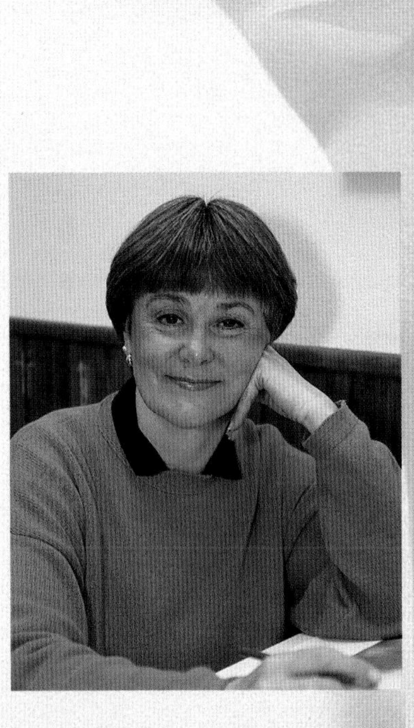

Sherry Loomis

Award-winning artist Sherry Loomis has exhibited in national juried competitions from California to West Virginia. Sherry has had her work published in two books on colored pencil art.

Sherry studied at three California universities and currently shares her knowledge of the colored pencil medium by conducting regional workshops and demonstrations.

CHAPTER 3

Tonal Quality Goes Beyond the Line

No errant fleck of color. No inconsistent stroke. No wavering edge. Just a uniform flow of color harmony and value transitions. The word "perfection" comes to mind. Sherry Loomis' colored pencil paintings are paragons of tonal application. The fluidity of her work is unmarred by even the slightest suggestion of human haste or hestitation. Sherry applies every layer with as little pressure as possible. The dramatic difference between the lightest and darkest areas results from the number of layers applied, not the amount of pressure used. The pressure stays consistent throughout the work. Each color layer is so delicately "feathered" it resembles a finely sprayed mist. While Sherry renders still life arrangements that she has constructed, she maintains that the objects in them are merely backdrops. The real subject of her work is reflected light and how it affects form and color. "Lace, fruit, and silver, in and of themselves, are secondary to the way they interact with light – casting shadows, diffusing color. I capture the drama with abstract patterns of light and shade. Then I add the sparkle and glow." Her first step is the most important. Sherry begins by establishing all the values in the work, known as "chiaroscuro," with a monochromatic underpainting. Since she fully understands the nature of the forms, she doesn't outline the objects. The modulated areas of light and shadow evolve into beautiful definitions of dimension. At this point the "heart" of the painting is captured. All that's left to do is add the color. The key to this technique is sharp pencils, light pressure, and patience.

GETTING STARTED

Sherry photographs her still life arrangement using natural light. The image is enlarged on vellum or tracing paper by using a grid format. The resulting line drawing is then transferred with graphite paper to 3-ply Strathmore plate (smooth) finish Bristol board. MATERIALS: Soft wax-based colored pencils to apply layers; hard, thin colored pencils to define crisp edges; kneaded eraser for lifting; battery-operated eraser to remove substantial pigment if necessary; both hand-held and electric pencil sharpeners; workable fixative is sprayed on the completed work.

PALETTE

90% French gray, cream, beige, lemon yellow, deco yellow, yellow orange, peach, sand, pumpkin orange, mineral orange, spanish orange, terra cotta, light yellow green, chartreuse, spring green, apple green, peacock green, celadon green, marine green, olive green, dark green, cloud blue, copenhagen blue, true blue, indigo blue, poppy red, henna, mahogany red, crimson lake, tuscan red, lavender, grape.

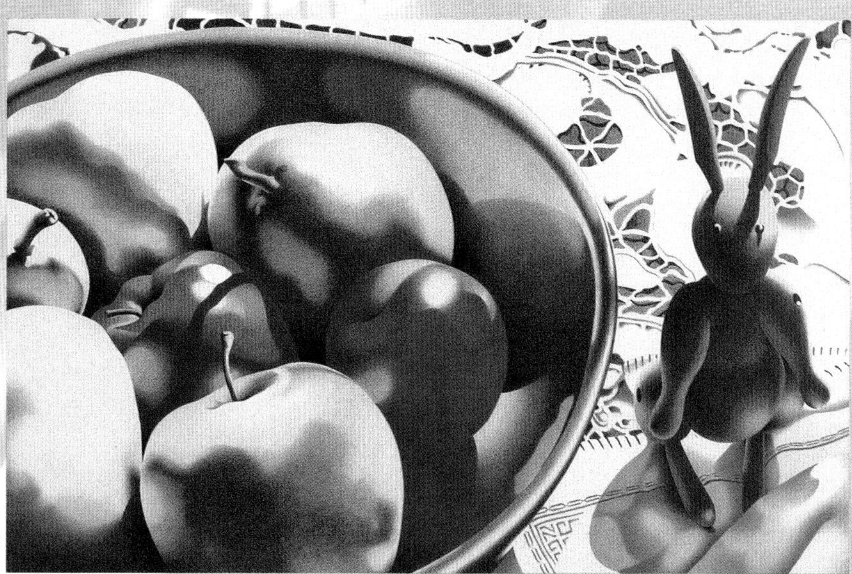

Verismo
17 x 25" (431 x 634 mm)

1 Working over a graphite outline, the shadow areas are defined with a medium-dark, warm grey pencil. A very sharp pencil point is necessary to get the pigment into the tooth of the paper without disturbing its texture. With as little pressure as possible, the strokes are laid in various directions – sometimes by turning the paper for easier access. The dark areas are built slowly by adding more layers – not by increasing the stroke pressure. This photograph shows an application of several layers. The white of the paper is left untouched where the lightest values will be.

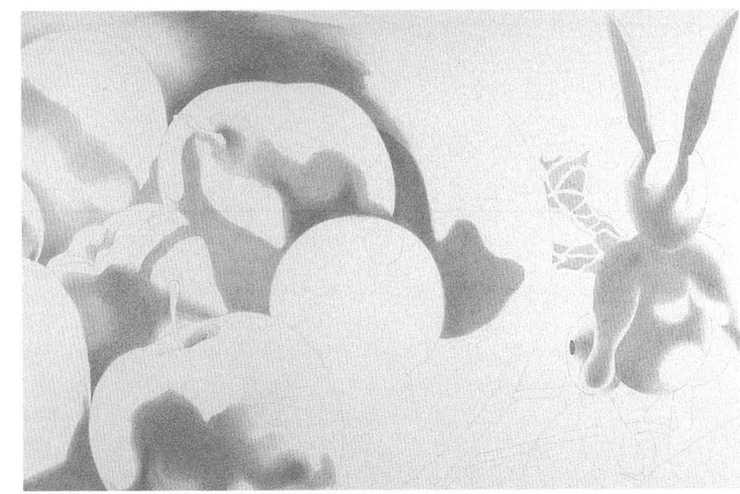

2 Once the value pattern is established, the "modeling" process begins. The very darkest values are developed with additional layers of grey. Strokes are still applied softly with a sharp pencil. The lightest areas remain paper white. The value transition of lights and darks are controlled through the use of hard and soft edges – as in the rim of the bowl. The objects now begin to look three-dimensional. Compare the depth and volume of the bowl of fruit with the flatness of the wooden rabbit and tablecloth. This value underpainting will show through all subsequent layers of color.

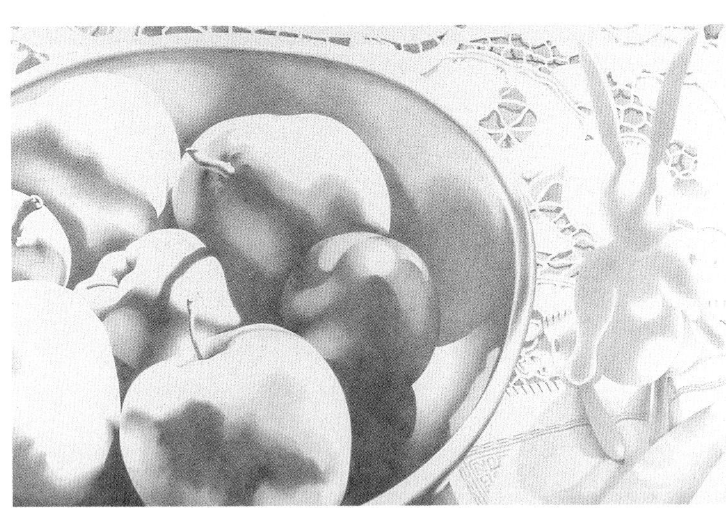

3 Before any local colors are applied, the gray underpainting is prepared. First, a deep purple is laid over the grey shadow areas. Then,depending on the final tone desired, varied combinations of indigo blue, peacock green or tuscan red are applied in some of the smaller areas. This deepens the shadows and produces a warm, rich base tone for the local colors. For example, the apple in the foreground, which will eventually be green, is shown layered with grey, tuscan red, grape and peacock green. Once these intermediate layers are applied, the underpainting is done.

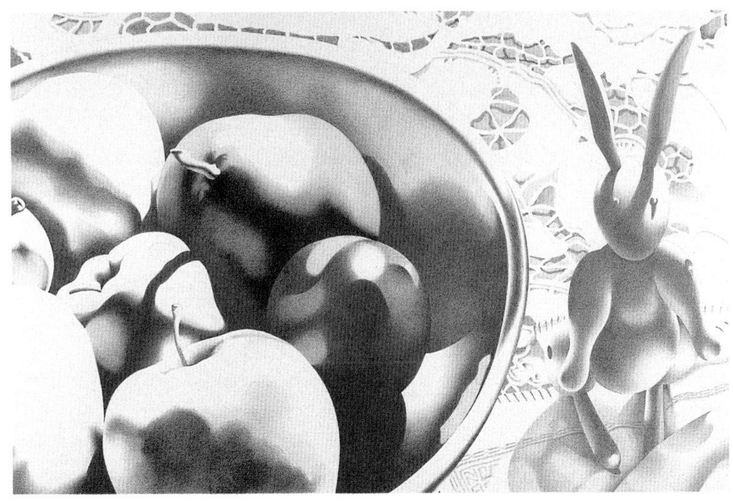

4 Layers of local color are now lightly applied. (Refer to the Palette list on the previous page.) Because the pigments are transparent, it may seem difficult to sufficiently color the darkest shadows. However, resist the temptation to increase the stroke pressure or you will lose the tonal effect. These are not the final colors. And the more colors are mixed and layered, the richer they become. Color is also applied very softly to the white areas where the lightest values will be – only tiny areas of the brightest highlights are left paper white.

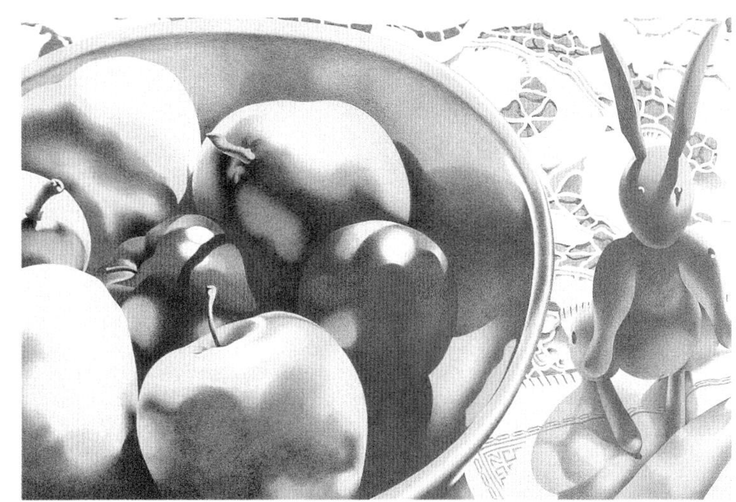

5 The colors need to be strengthened to give the objects more volume. A greater spectrum of hues is added to both the highlight and shadow areas. The color selections are made intuitively – sometimes experimenting with less obvious choices as with the addition of peacock blue in the highlights of the plum. As color shapes overlap within each object, they are blended into subtle gradations. This leaves a smooth color and value transition and contributes to the three-dimensional look.

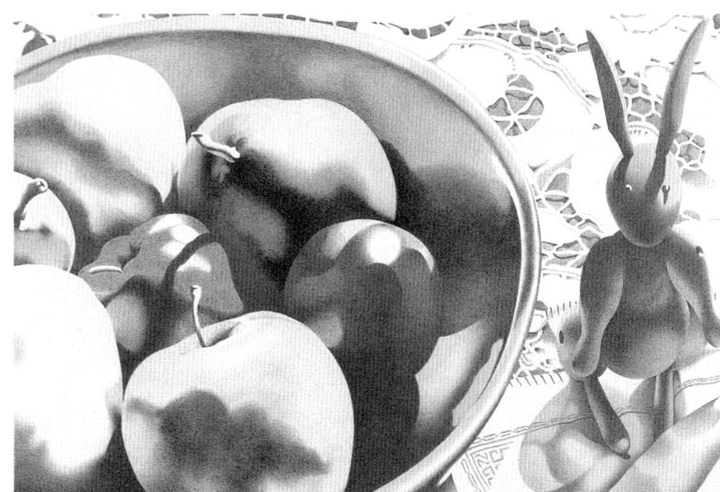

6 The next two procedures add volume and weight to the objects. First, thin hard-lead colored pencils (in colors corresponding to the local color) are used to outline edges that need crisp definition. Some edges require a softer, less exacting border and are left untouched. Then, the perspective is markedly pronounced by deepening the darkest shadows. This is done sparingly in very small areas around the object with a soft, wax-based black pencil. The objects are now sharper and more intense. Notice how the colors glow in Sherry's painting of *Verismo*.

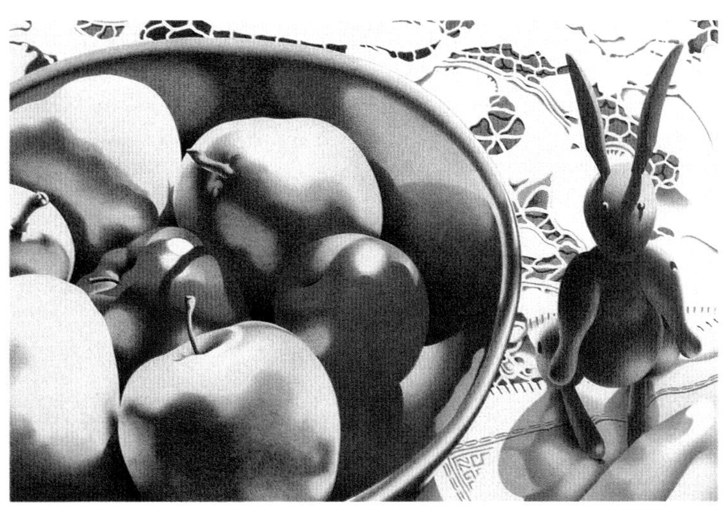

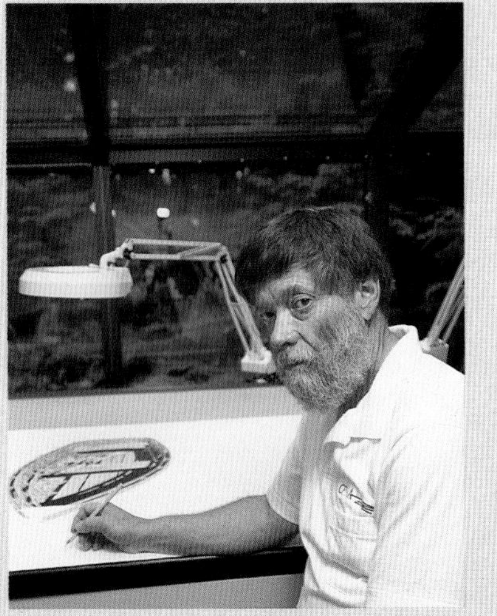

Gary Greene

Nationally-recognized colored pencil artist Gary Greene showed an interest in art at age five, when he copied cartoon characters from comic books. That interest led to greater things, eventually launching him a career in photography, graphic design, and illustration. Along the way he perfected the precise, detailed style for which he is known today. A master of many media, Gary's focus in recent years has been colored pencil. His work has received awards in national exhibitions and has appeared in several publications, including *The American Artist* and *The Artist's Magazine* and on the cover of *The Best of Colored Pencil Book*. Gary conducts colored pencil and photography workshops around the United States.

CHAPTER 4

Heavy Burnishing for Realistic Impact

Look again. This is not a photograph. It is, however, the epitome of photorealism. From perspective to color, every detail rings true. Gary Greene's colored pencil art is meticulously hand-rendered to rival the work of any camera. Ironically, Gary is just as accomplished with a camera as he is with a colored pencil. While his photographs are a source of reference for his colored pencil paintings, he renders the subject matter beyond mere documentation.

With a trained eye, Gary manipulates the reality before him to make a greater artistic impact. His technique uses heavy pressure, or "burnishing," to give the work a painterly appearance. This method of blending and fusing layers of color is usually done with a light colored pencil. Burnishing grinds the color pigment that is left on top of the paper grain into the paper's surface. This abrades the paper's tooth allowing the pigment to smear to a solid, smooth finish.

Gary establishes the first layers of color with a tonal application. using sharp pencils and light pressure. He begins with the darkest shade and works to the lightest shade within the spectrum of the object's local color. He then burnishes these layers of color by using extreme pressure. Gary "obliterates" the grain of the paper for complete color saturation. This combination of color layering and burnishing is done several times. As you can see in *'32 Packard*, burnishing is an excellent method for capturing reflective surfaces such as glass, painted metal, and chrome. Because it creates a shiny surface, it gives the subject a heavy, weighted look and makes colors luminous. Gary's larger, 30 x 40", colored pencil paintings can take more than 400 hours to complete. His devotion is evident. And as he says, "It takes a special kind of 'seeing' and a tremendous amount of understanding to render a subject exactly the way it is." In the process, Gary also allows us to see the subject in a new light.

GETTING STARTED

Gary first determines the painting's composition and values with his camera and then transfers the slide image onto Strathmore 4-ply Museum Board. He does preliminary studies of the subject to graphically refine, delete, or change details as necessary. MATERIALS: Thin hard-lead, soft wax-based, and water-soluble colored pencils, 2B graphite pencil, No. 4 watercolor brush, custom-made plexiglass template, kneaded and electric erasers, electric pencil sharpener. Several light coats of workable fixative are sprayed on the finished work.

PALETTE

Soft Wax-Based Colored Pencils: French Gray in values of 90%, 70%, 50%, 30%, 20%, 10%; white, cream, burnt umber, terra cotta, sienna brown, goldenrod. Thin hard-Lead Colored Pencils: Dark gray, light gray, black. Water-soluble Colored Pencils: Straw yellow, zinc yellow.

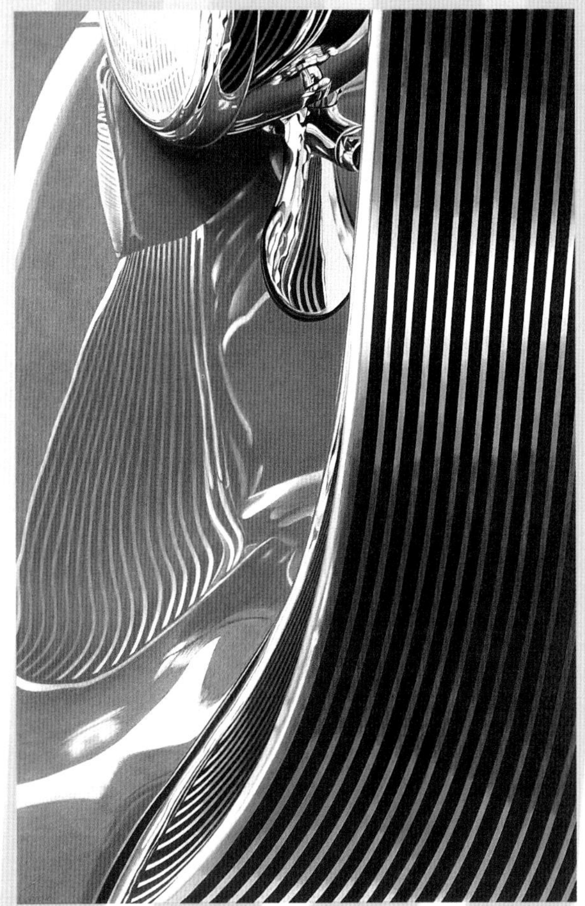

'32 Packard
28 x 18" (710 x 456 mm)

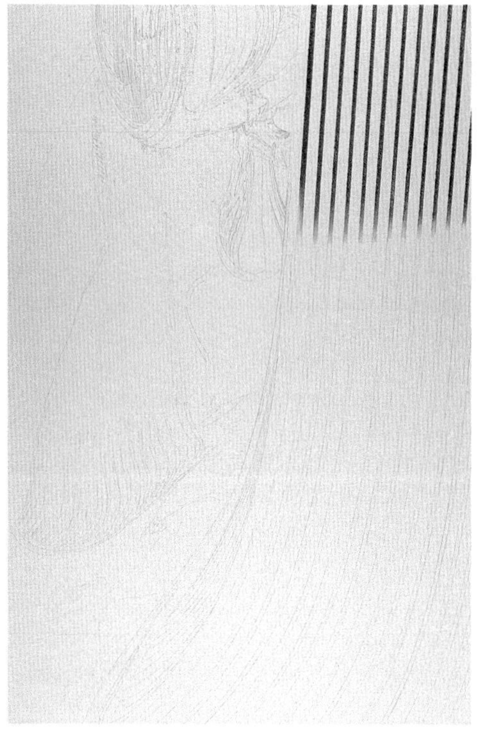

1

A light contour drawing of the subject is done twice. The first line drawing is done with graphite using a cutom-made template. A second line is drawn next to the first with a hard lead colored pencil of the same local color as the subject. The graphite lines are then removed with a kneaded eraser leaving the colored lines intact. The painting progresses section by section. The lightest area of each section is always colored first so that pigment from the darker areas won't be "dragged" into it. The colors themselves, however, are always applied dark to light. No linear strokes are visible.

2

Working downward to the highlighted area of the grill, the chrome bars are layered with the following succession of dark-to-light French gray values: 90%, 70%, 50%, 30%, 20%, 10% and finally white. As the layers are applied, one over the other, each new layer is extended slightly past the previous layer. This gradually blends the value transition from dark to light. The brightest highlight is captured by the white of the untouched paper surface.

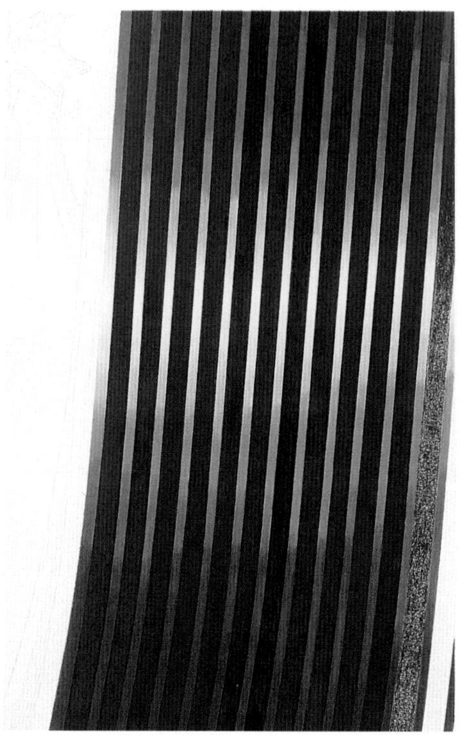

3

A second sequence of French gray layers is applied over the first. This time, however, each layer is applied with increased pressure – or "burnished" – until the value transitions become seamless and the surface is smooth. Compare the granular appearance of the unburnished strip to the far right with the others. Once all the chrome bars are burnished, hard-lead colored pencils and a template are used to true-up the ragged edges left by the soft wax-based pencils. The shadow areas between the bars are done with burnished layers of black.

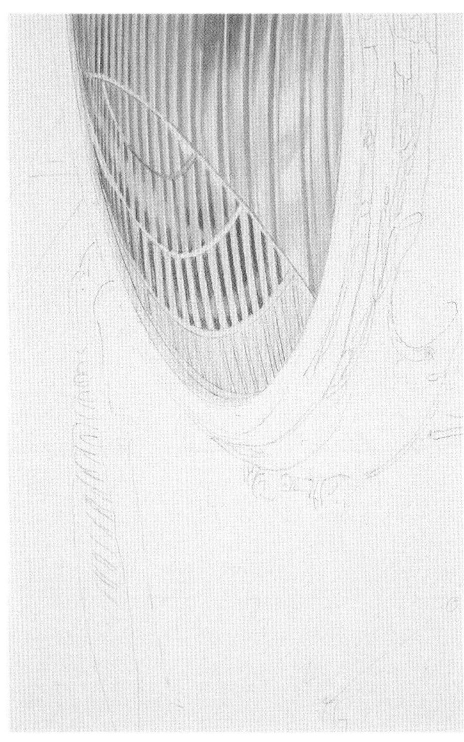

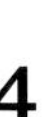

4

The graphite lines in the headlight area are replaced with colored lines using a large ellipse guide. Straw yellow and zinc yellow water-soluble pencils are layered sparingly on the glass. Highlights are left paper white. Using a small amount of water and a brush, the dissolved pigment is spread into a wash and carefully blended into the white of the highlights. When they are completely dry, the highlights are lightened and defined with an electric eraser. The lens area is then burnished and the "ribs" of the glass are defined with the ellipse template and a hard-lead light gray pencil.

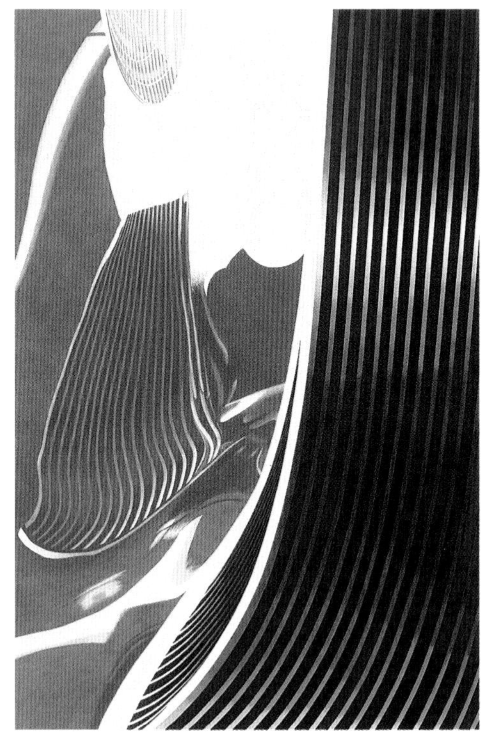

5

The graphite lines are now replaced on the body of the car. Colors are applied using the same process of layering and burnishing. Beginning with the darkest area (the shadow cast by the headlight), the sequence of dark umber, terra cotta and sienna brown layers was applied four times, increasing the pressure with each layer. Mid-value areas, such as the reflections in the headlight and grill, are layered with terra cotta and sienna brown. Lighter values of the body consist of sienna brown, goldenrod and cream layers. The whitest highlights are left paper white.

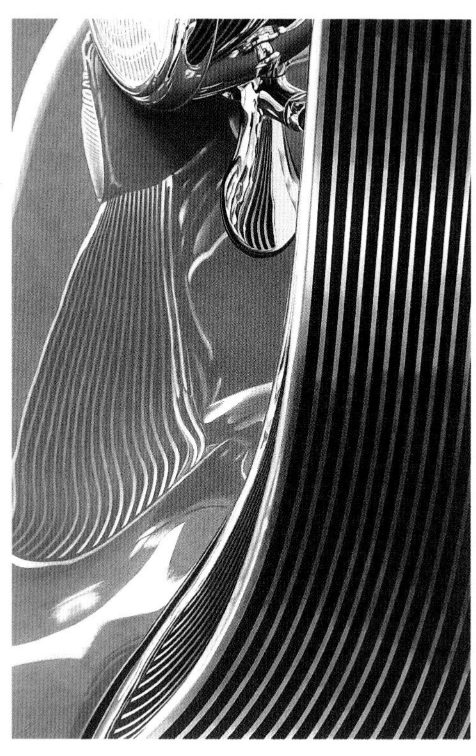

6

Notice how the subtle gradation of dark hues into light model the body contours of the car. Without these blended values, this area would look like a flat field of colored patterns. A word of caution: heavily burnished layers of pigment cause the wax content to form an opaque film, known as "wax bloom," over the paintings surface which dulls the colors. There are various methods of removing this film, but Gary chooses to ignore it until the painting is completed. At the end of the 156 hours that it took to finish *32 Packard*, several lightly sprayed coats of fixative made the colors vibrant again.

1

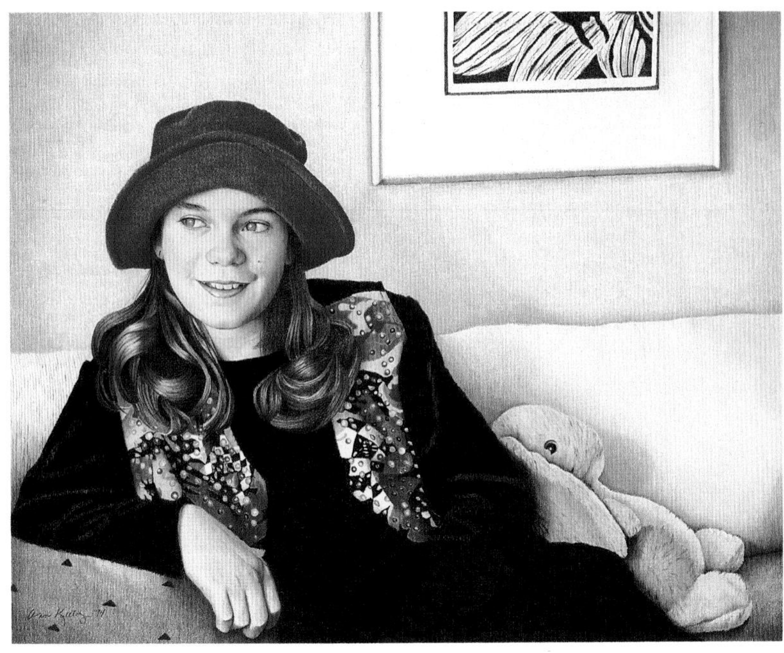

2

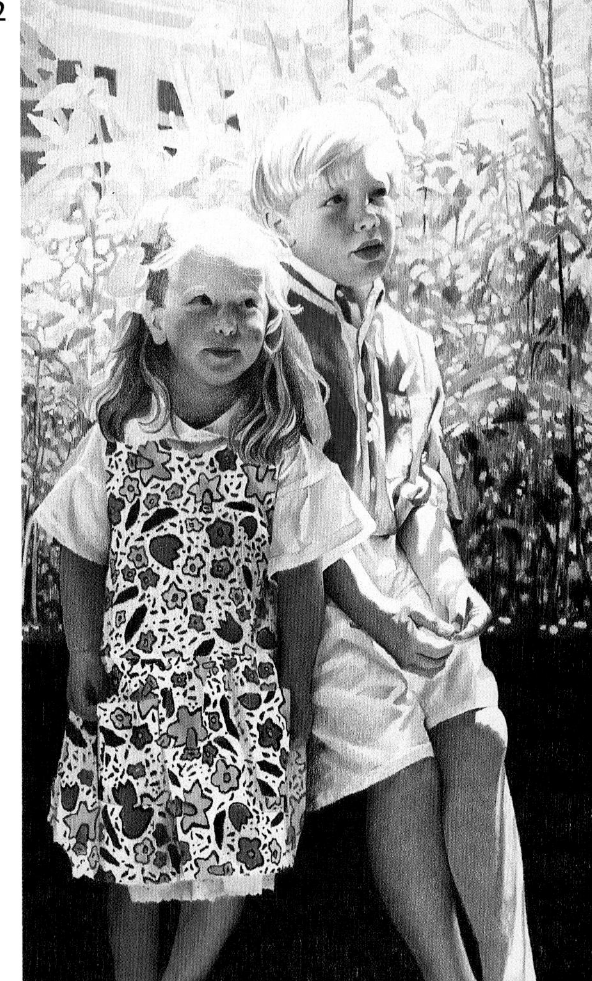

3

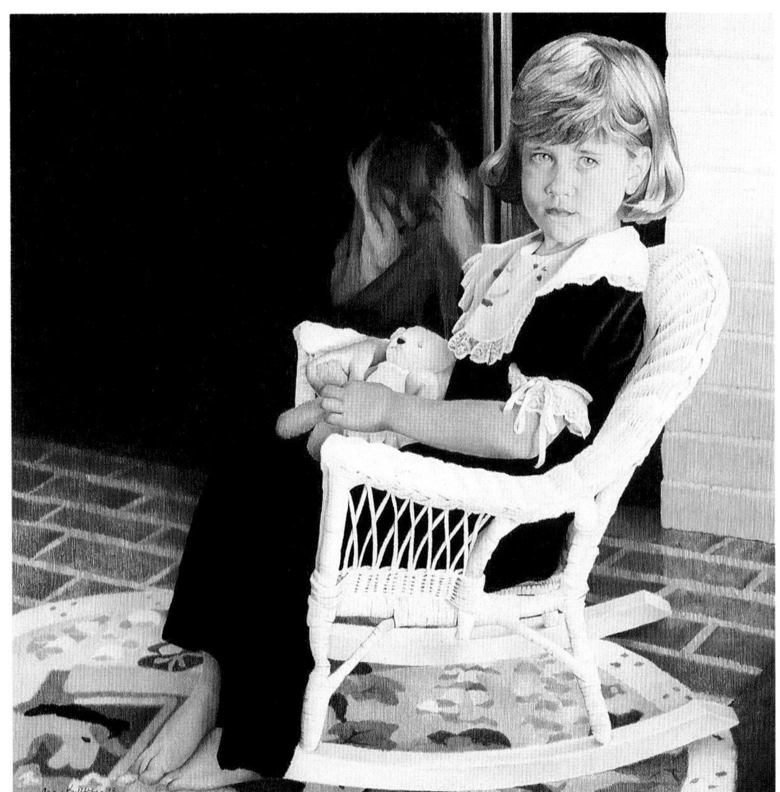

Ann Kullberg

1 *Allison and Friend*
19 x 23" (483 x 584 mm)
Rising Stonehenge Museum Board
Technique: Vertical Strokes

2 *Siblings*
25 x 16" (635 x 406 mm)
Rising Stonehenge Museum Board
Technique: Vertical Strokes

3 *Molly*
26 x 24" (648 x 610 mm)
Rising Stonehenge Museum Board
Technique: Vertical Strokes

1

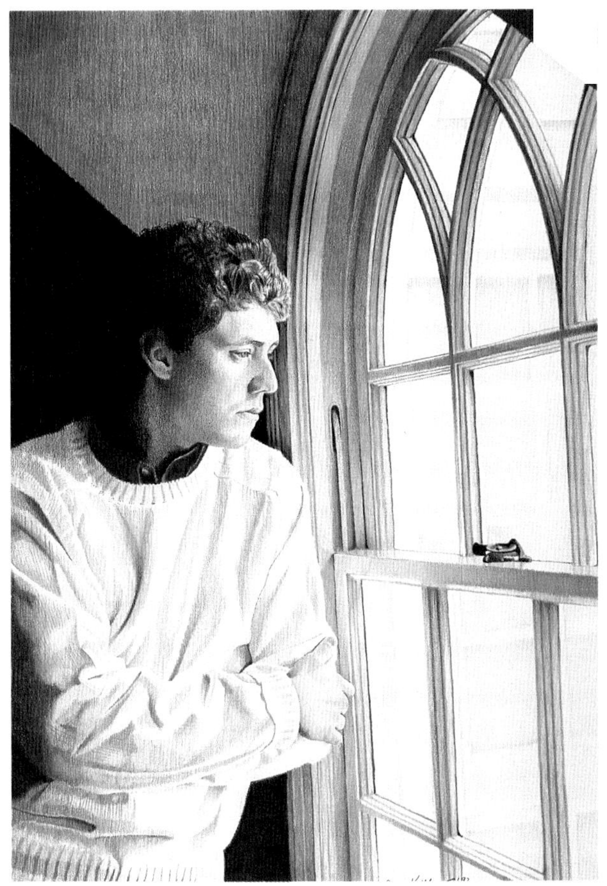

2

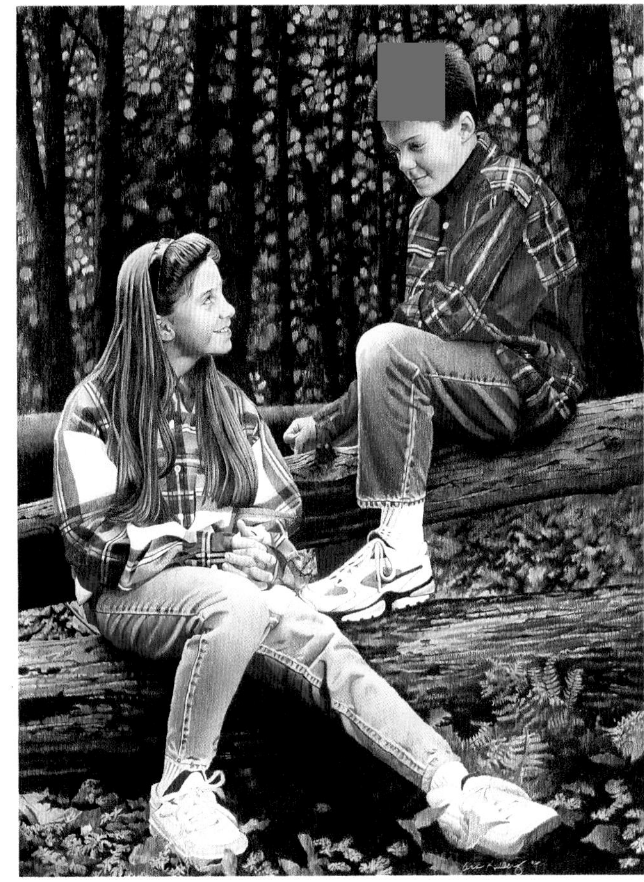

Ann Kullberg

1 *Matt*
22 x 35" (381 x 889 mm)
Rising Stonehenge Board
Technique: Vertical Strokes

2 *October Morning*
22 x 27" (559 x 686 mm)
Rising Stonehenge Board
Technique: Vertical Strokes

3 *Chris*
18 x 27" (445 x 673 mm)
Rising Stonehenge Museum Board
Technique: Vertical Strokes

3

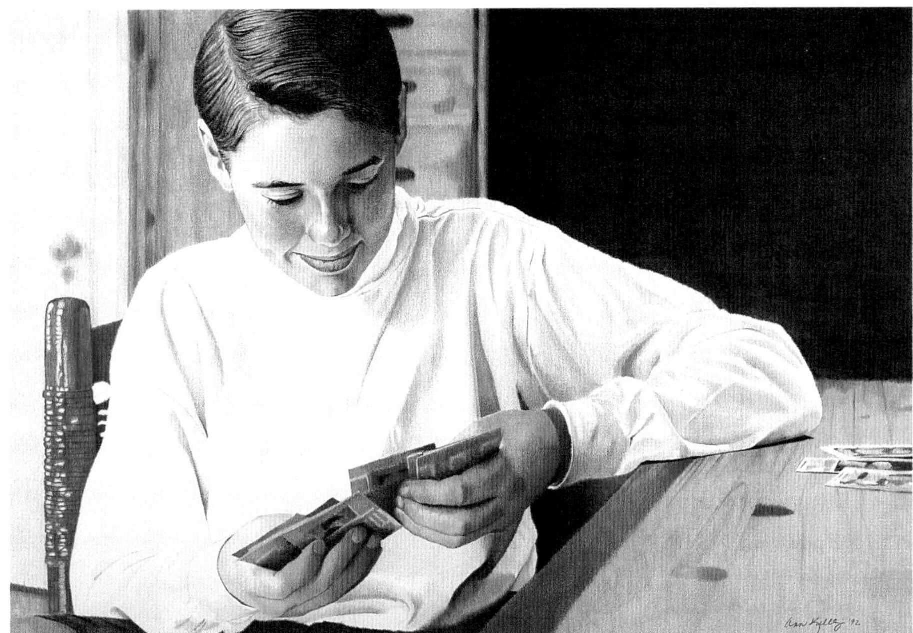

1

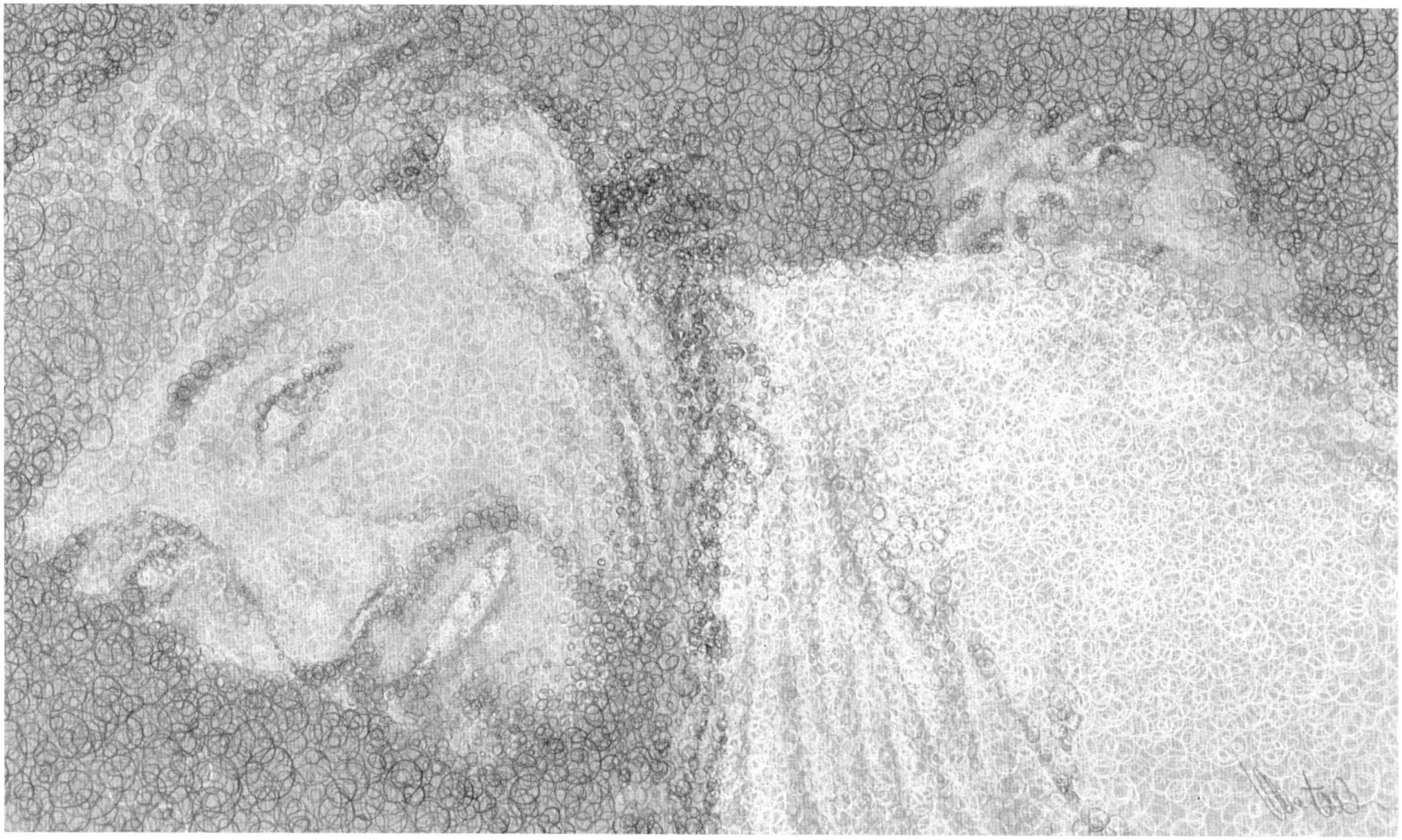

2

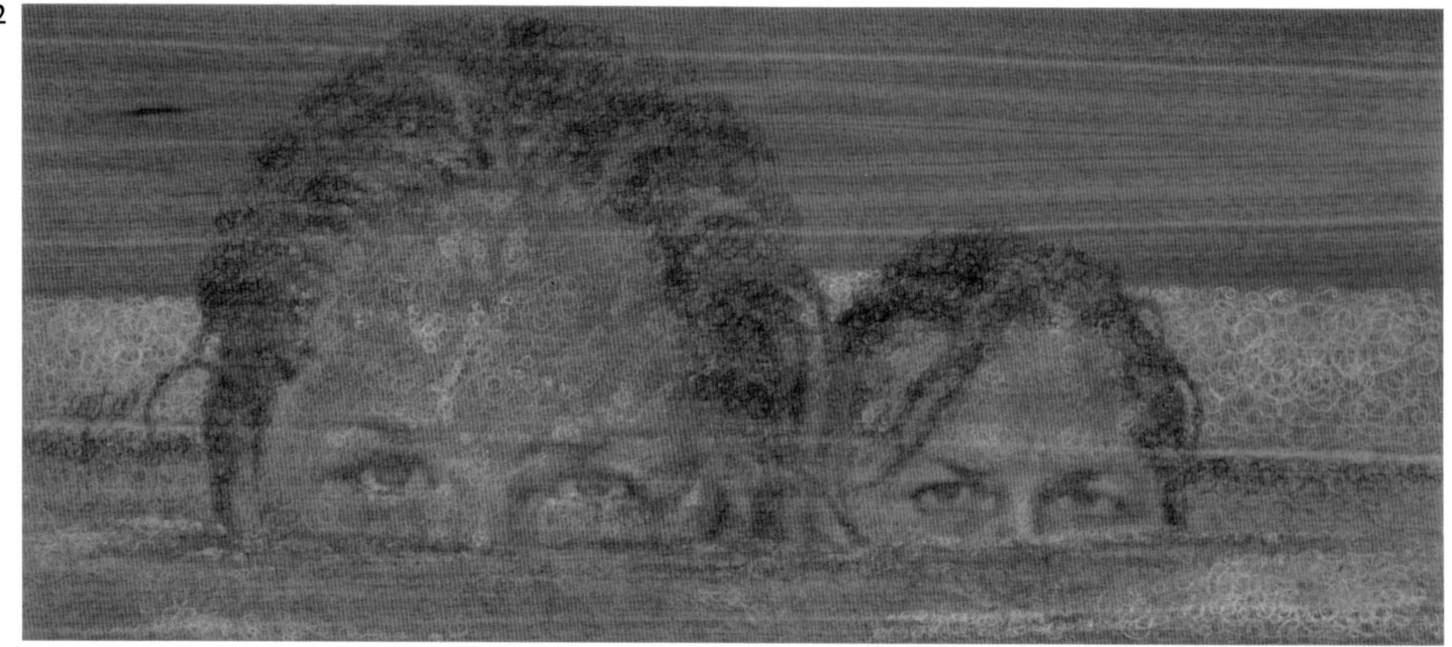

Maggie Toole

1 *Wedding Invitation*
17 x 30" (432 x 762 mm)
Technique: Circular Strokes

2 *Up to Your Eyes In It*
15 x 35" (381 x 889 mm)
Technique: Circular Strokes

3 *Hard As Wood*
22 x 18" (546 x 445 mm)
Walnut Wood Panel
Technique: Circular Strokes

4 *Leading Follower*
26 x 20" (660 x 508 mm)
Romanes Que Paper
Technique: Circular Strokes

5 *Rose Would*
16 x 15" (406 x 381 mm)
Rose Wood Panel
Technique: Circular Strokes

3

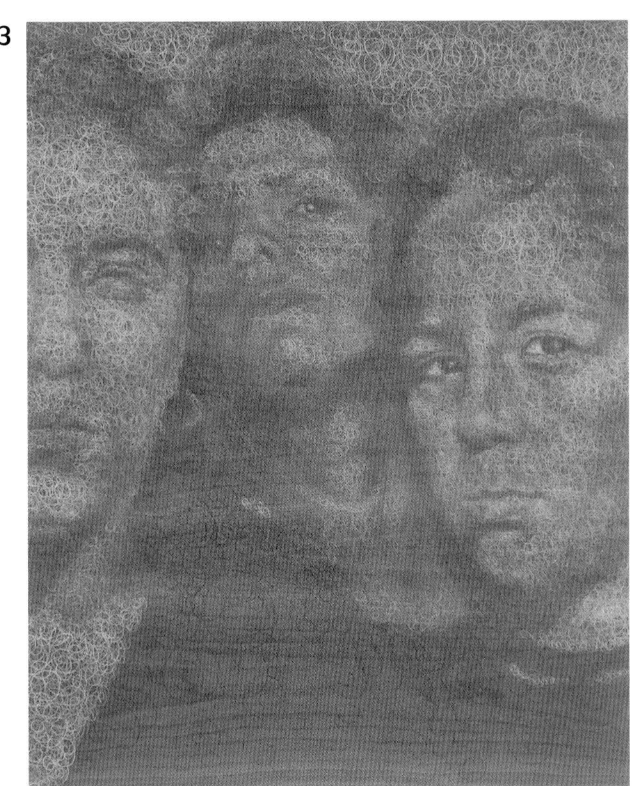

4

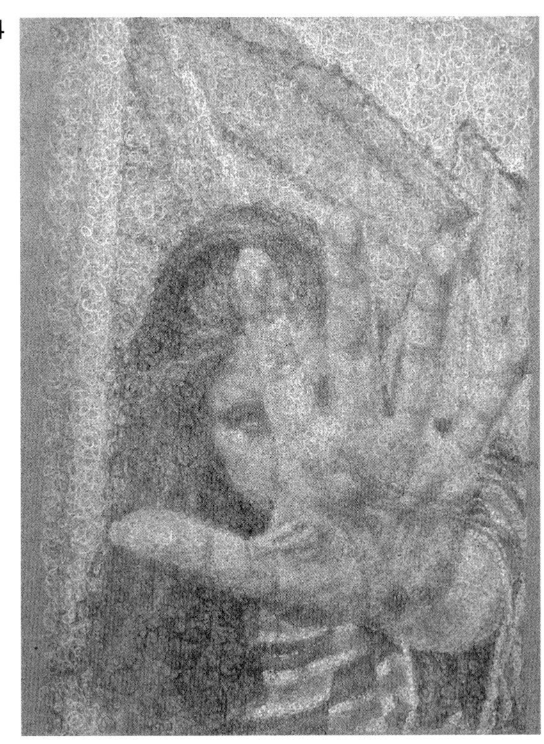

5

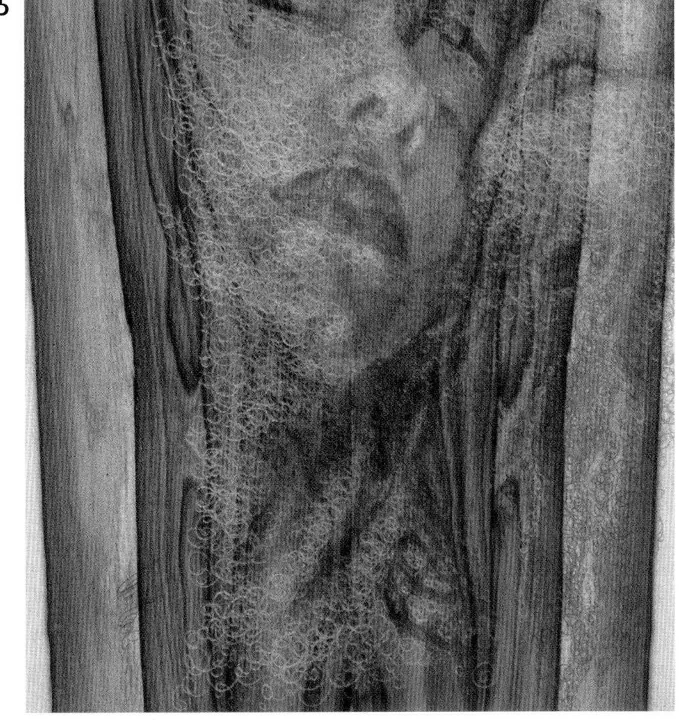

Maggie Toole

1 *Con & Park*
18 x 36" (457 x 914 mm)
Technique: Circular Strokes

Sherry Loomis

2 *Amor*
6 x 6" (152 x 152 mm)
Technique: Vertical Strokes

3 *Blue Candle*
6 x 6" (152 x 152 mm)
Technique: Vertical Strokes

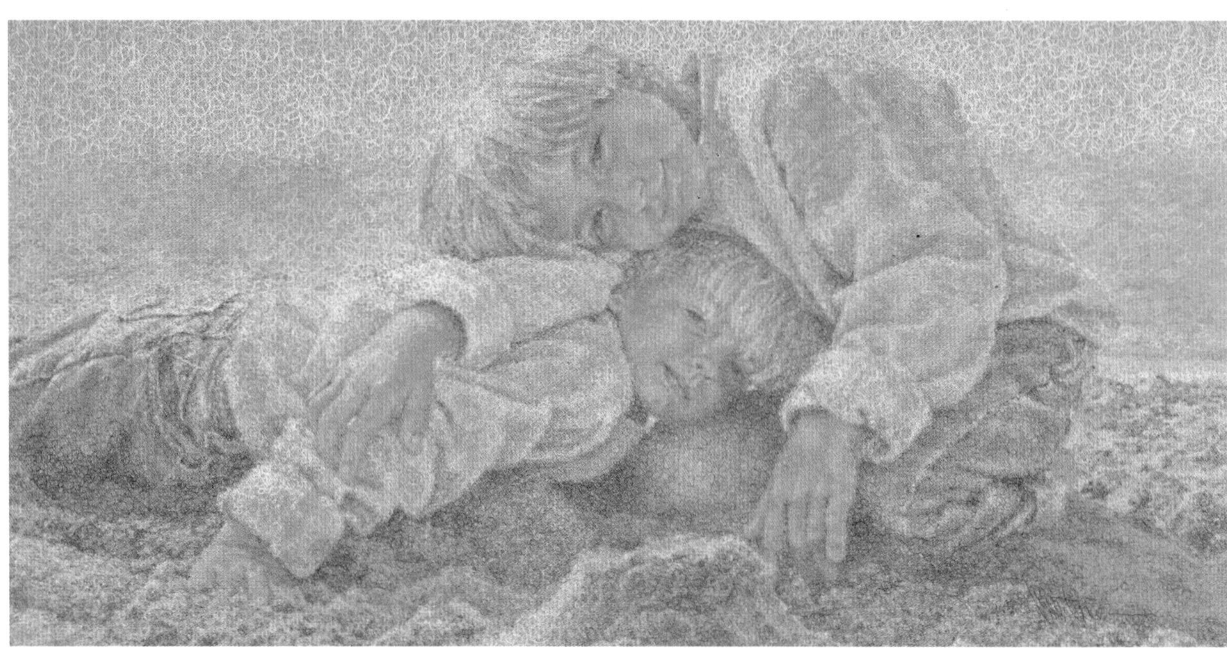

1

2

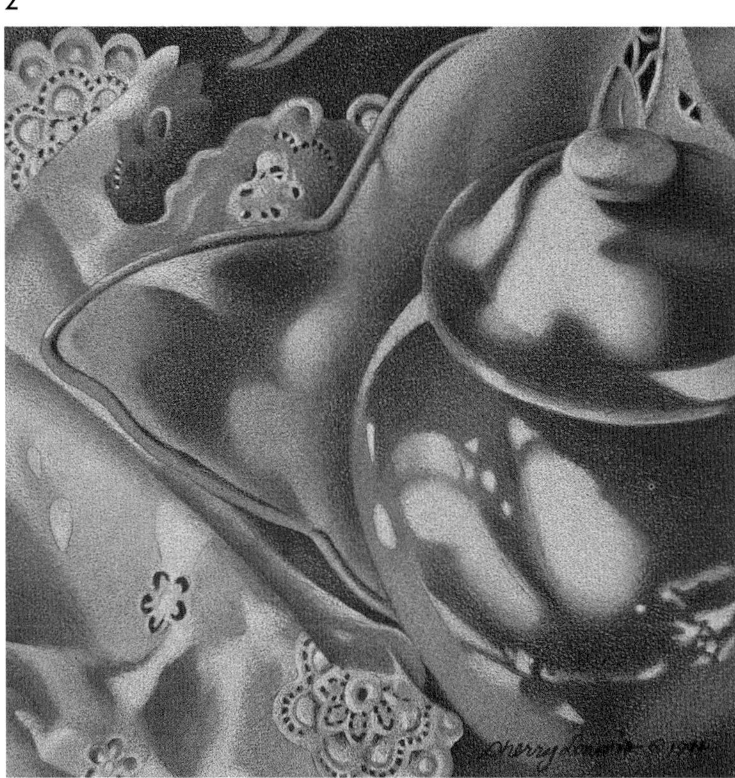

3

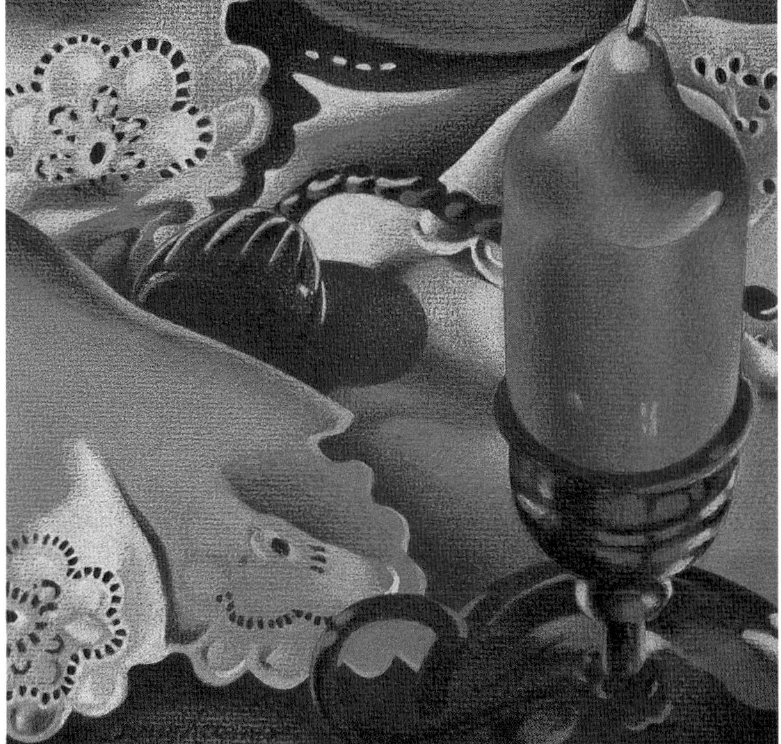

1

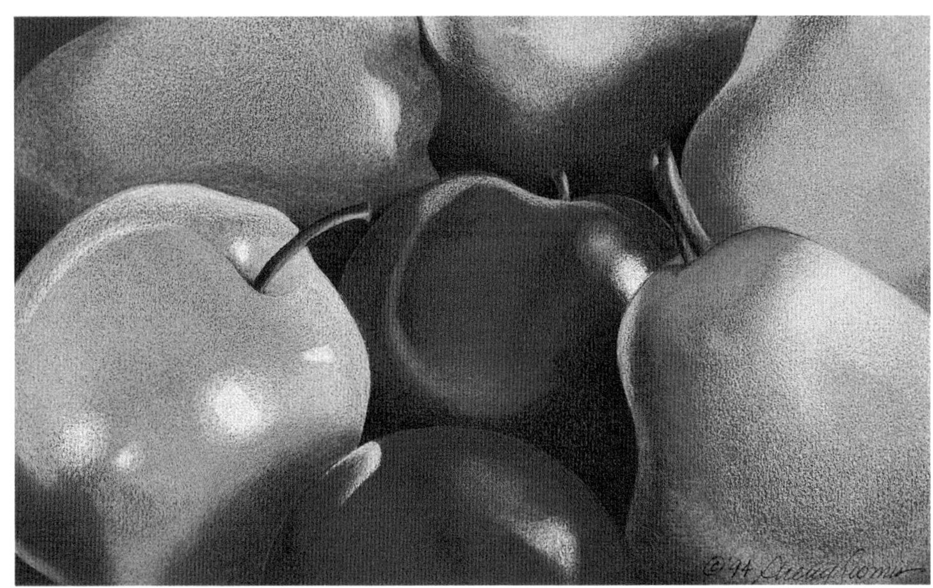

2

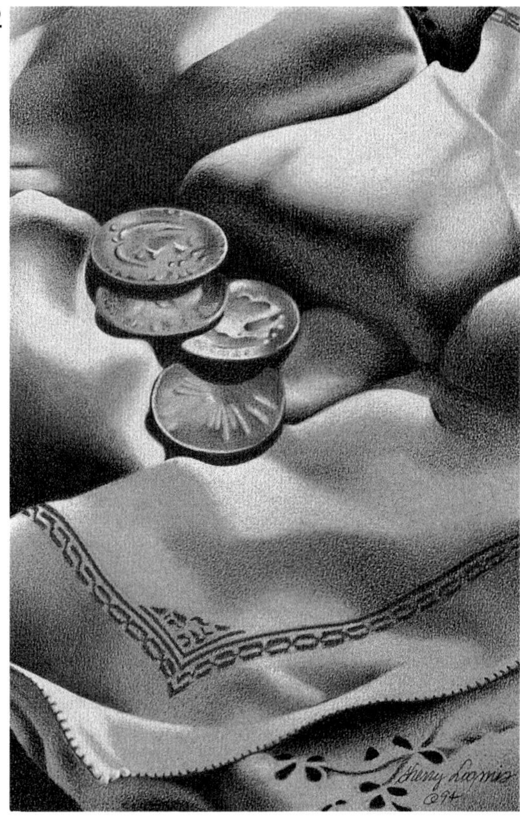

Sherry Loomis

1 *Ambrosia*
6 x 9" (152 x 229 mm)
Technique: Vertical Strokes

2 *Unas Monedas*
10 x 7" (254 x 177 mm)
Technique: Vertical Strokes

3 *No Ordinary Day*
19 x 29" (449 x 724 mm)
Technique: Vertical Strokes

3

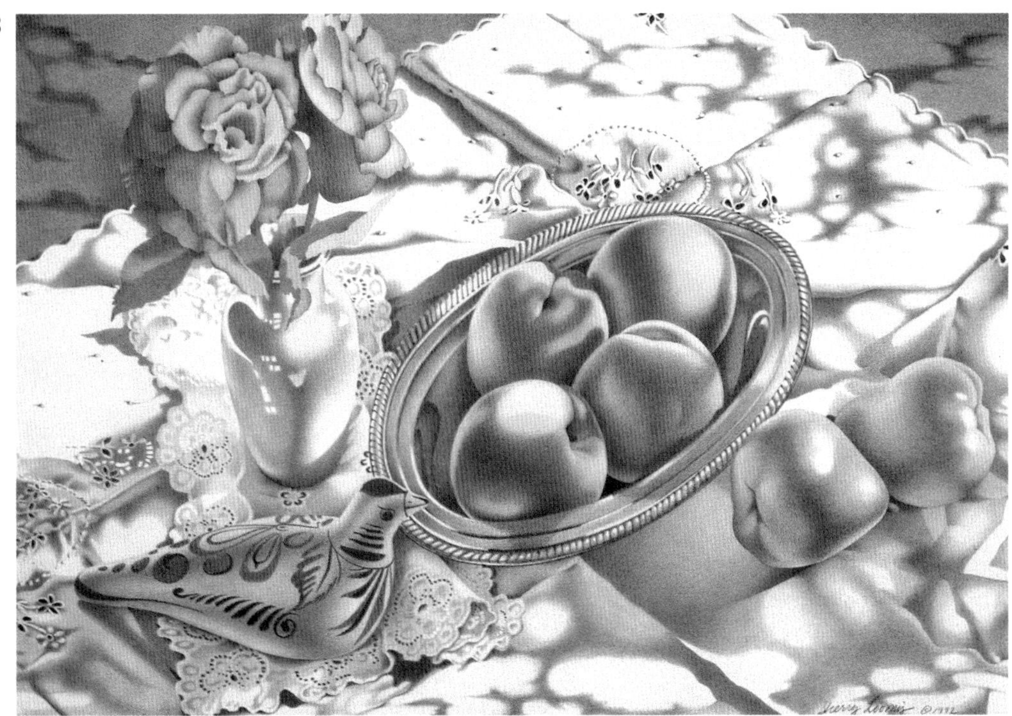

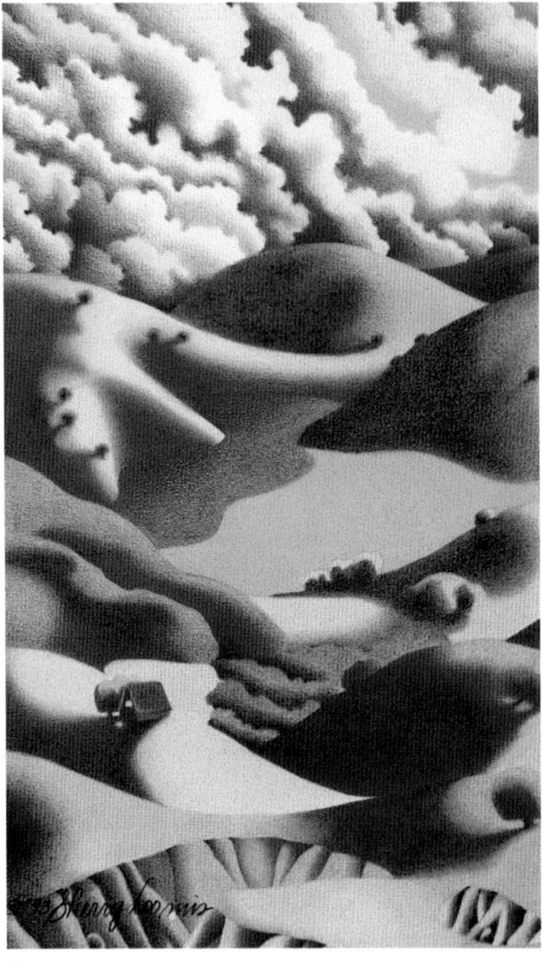

1

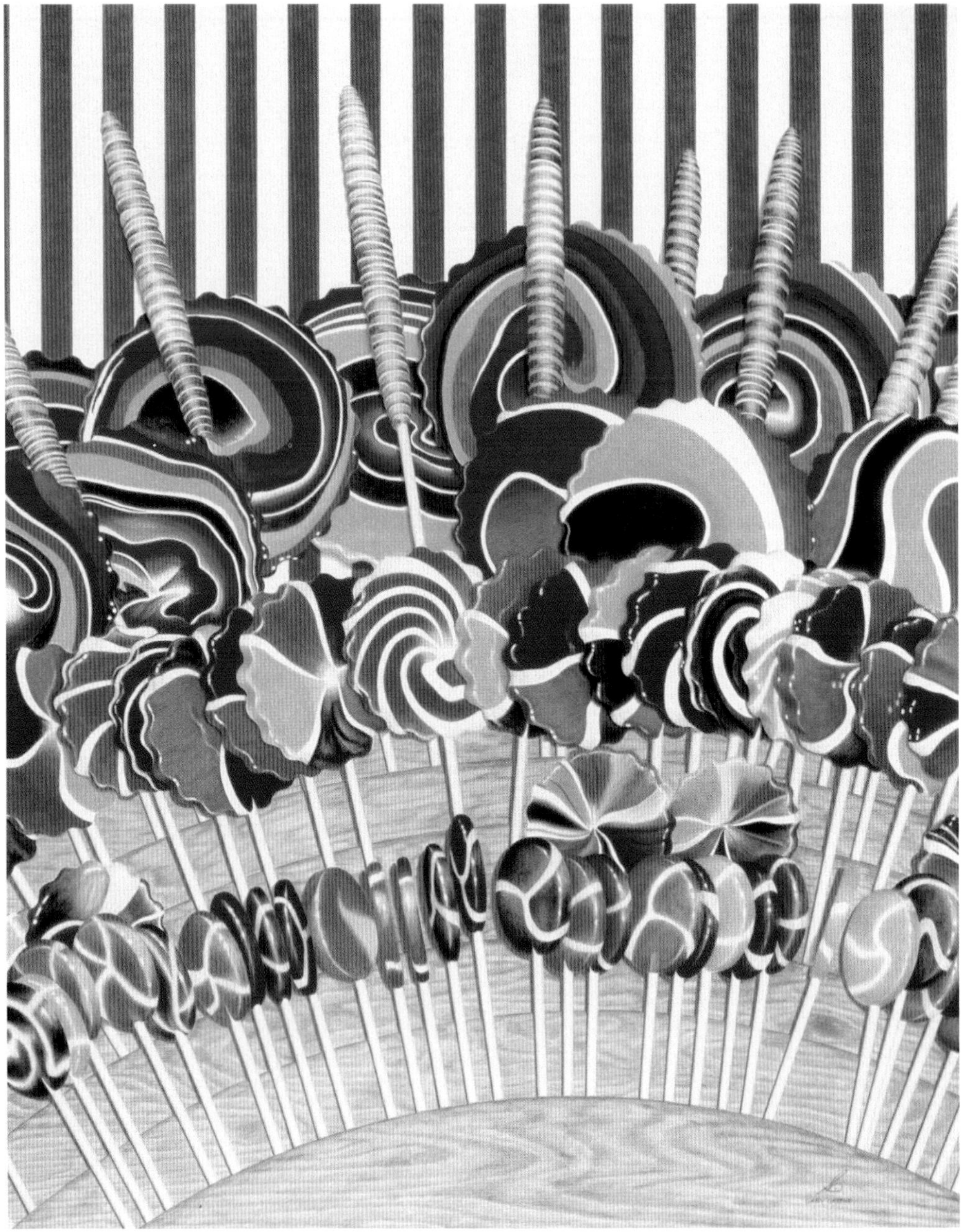

2

Sherry Loomis

1 *Blue Hill*
10 x 6" (254 x 152 mm)
Technique: Vertical Strokes

Gary Greene

2 *I'm Gonna' Git You, Suka'*
29 x 24" (737 x 610 mm)
Strathmore 4-ply Museum Board
Technique: Burnishing, Water-Soluble Color Pencil Underpainting

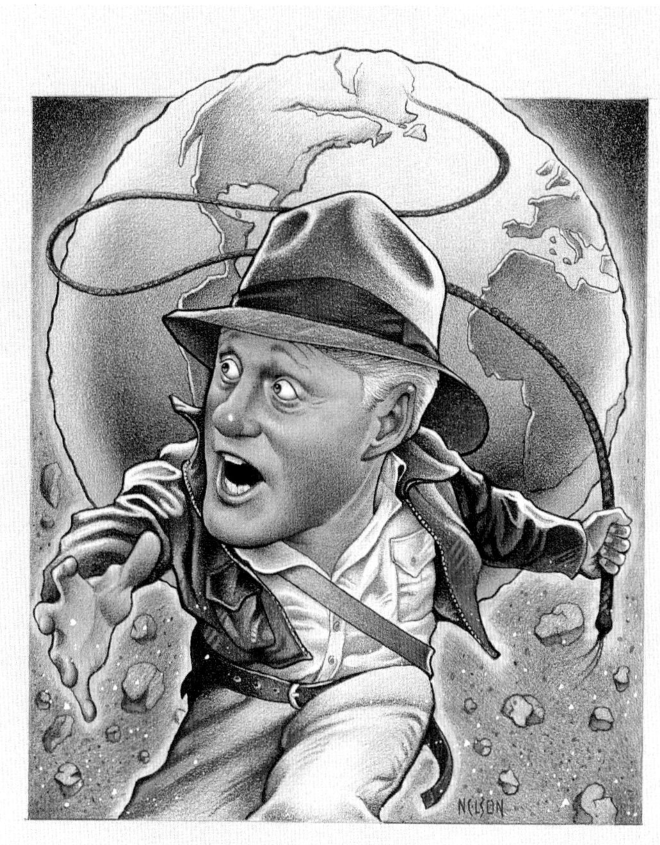

1

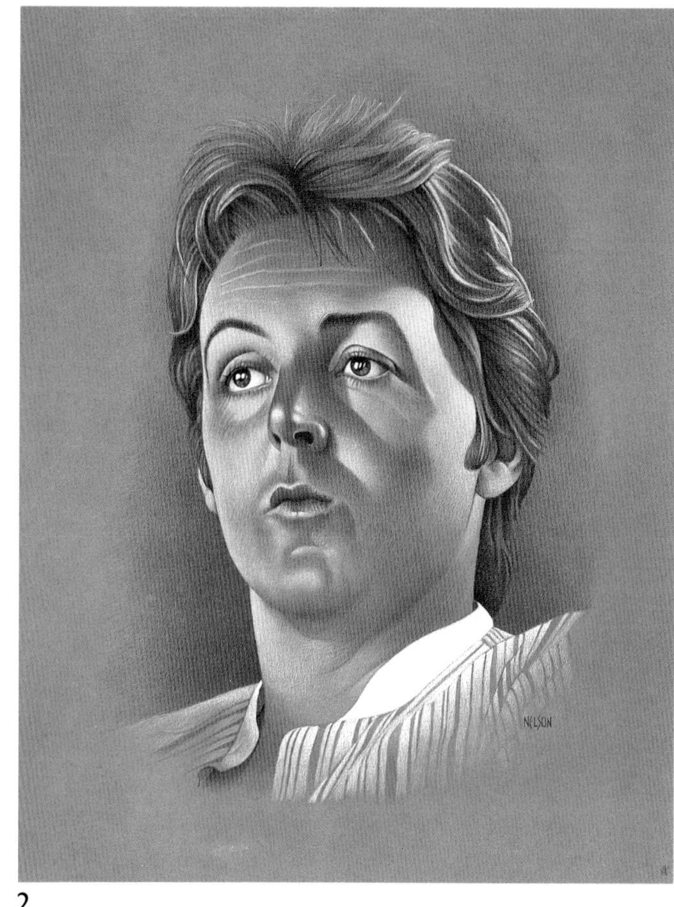

2

Bill Nelson

1 *Clinton As Indiana Jones*
Commissioned by *Time* Magazine
5 x 7" (127 x 178 mm)
100% Rag Crescent Sand Mat Board

2 *Paul McCartney*
Commissioned by *Rolling Stone* Magazine
9 x 12" (229 x 305 mm)
100% Rag Crescent Sand Mat Board

Patti McQuillin

3 *Mean Eddie Greenfish*
11 x 16" (279 x 406 mm)
4-Ply Rising Museum Board
Technique: Impressed

3

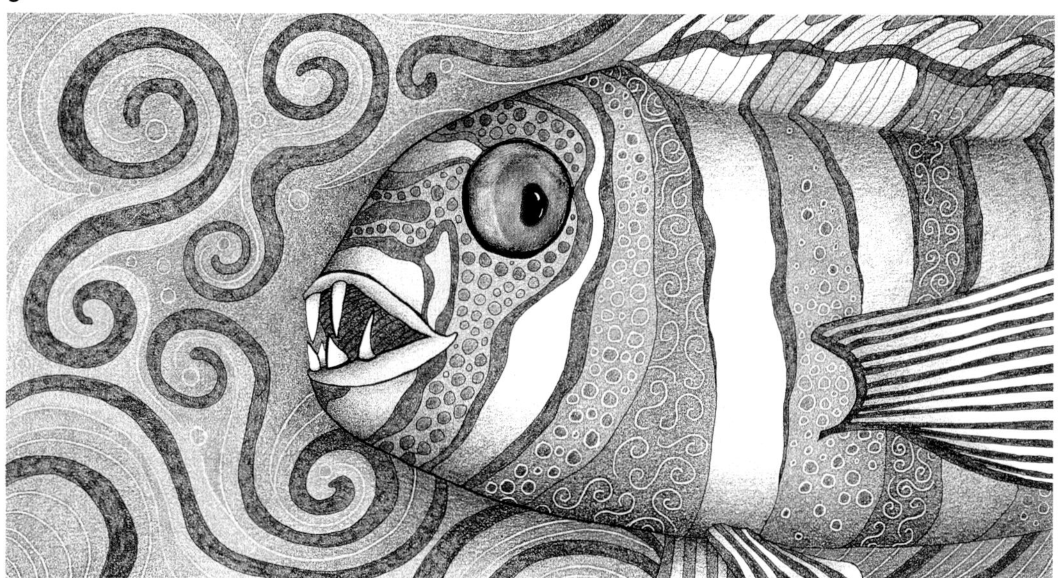

1

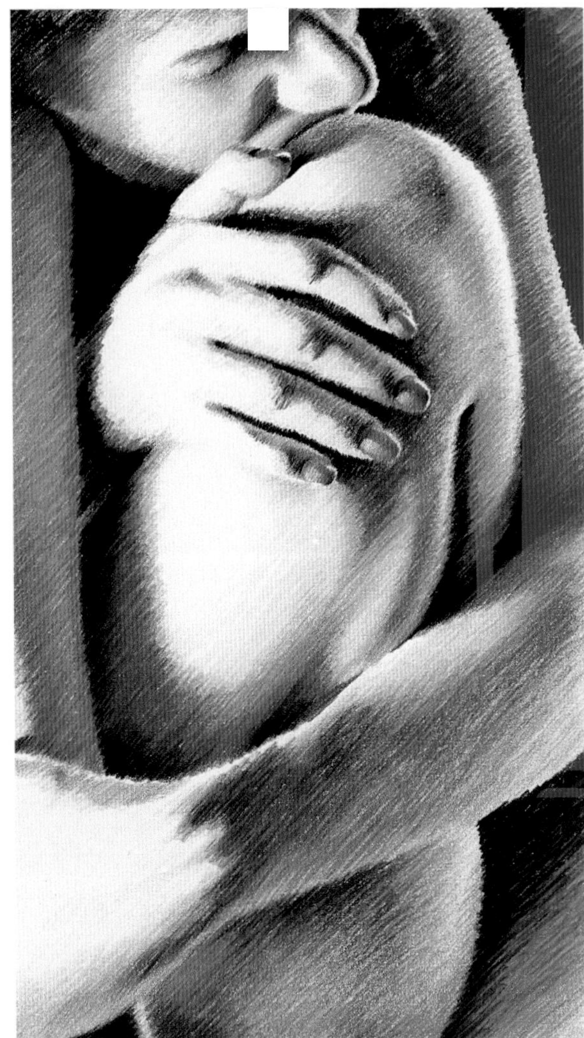

2

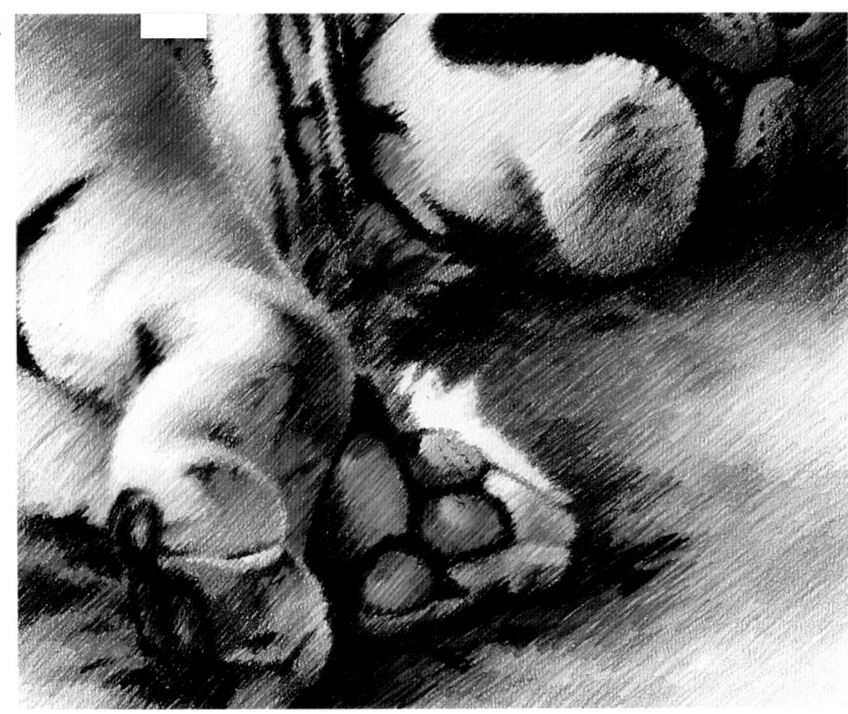

3

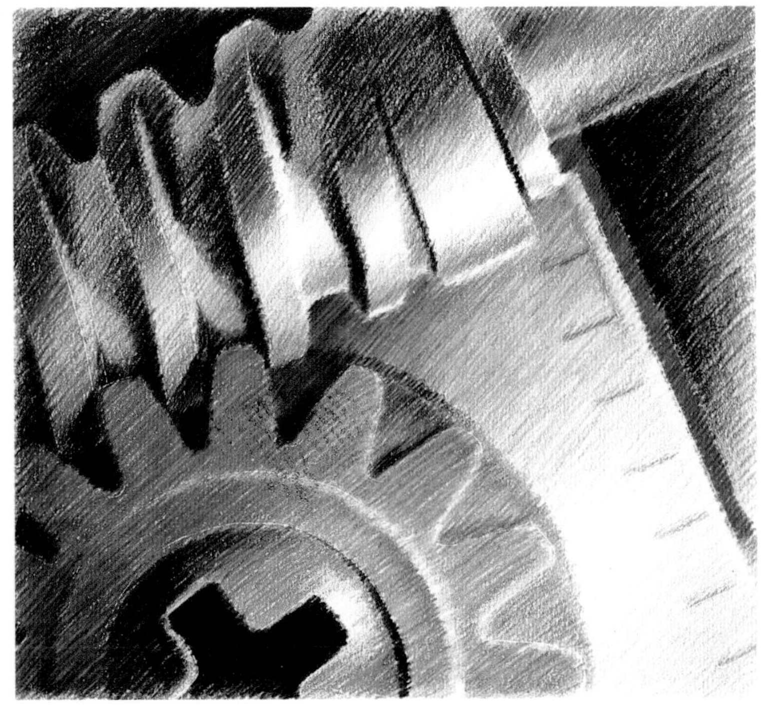

Brent Bowen

1 *Hiding From The Light*
22 x 14" (559 x 356 mm)
Cold Press Bristol Board
Technique: Diagonal Hatched Strokes

2 *Sleeping Tiger Paws*
14 x 20" (356 x 508 mm)
Cold Press Bristol Board
Technique: Diagonal Hatched Strokes

3 *Guitar Close Up*
11 x 11" (279 x 279 mm)
Cold Press Bristol Board
Technique: Diagonal Hatched Strokes

1 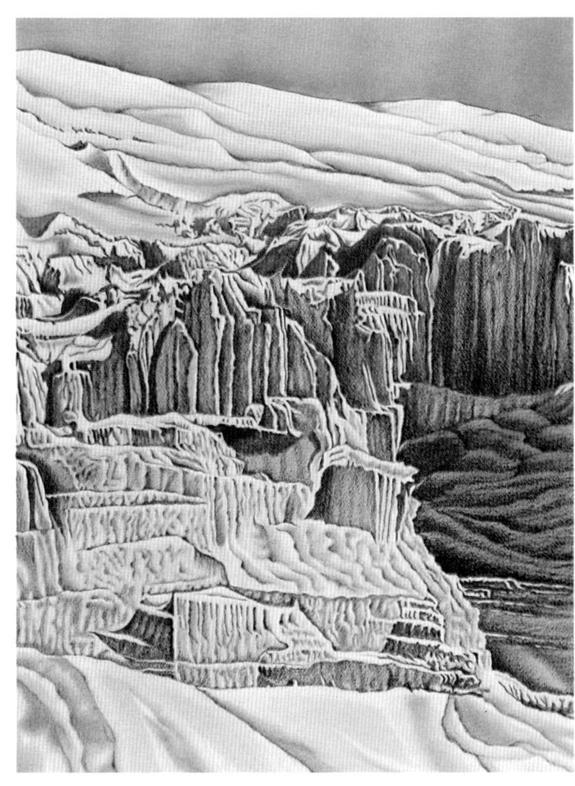

2 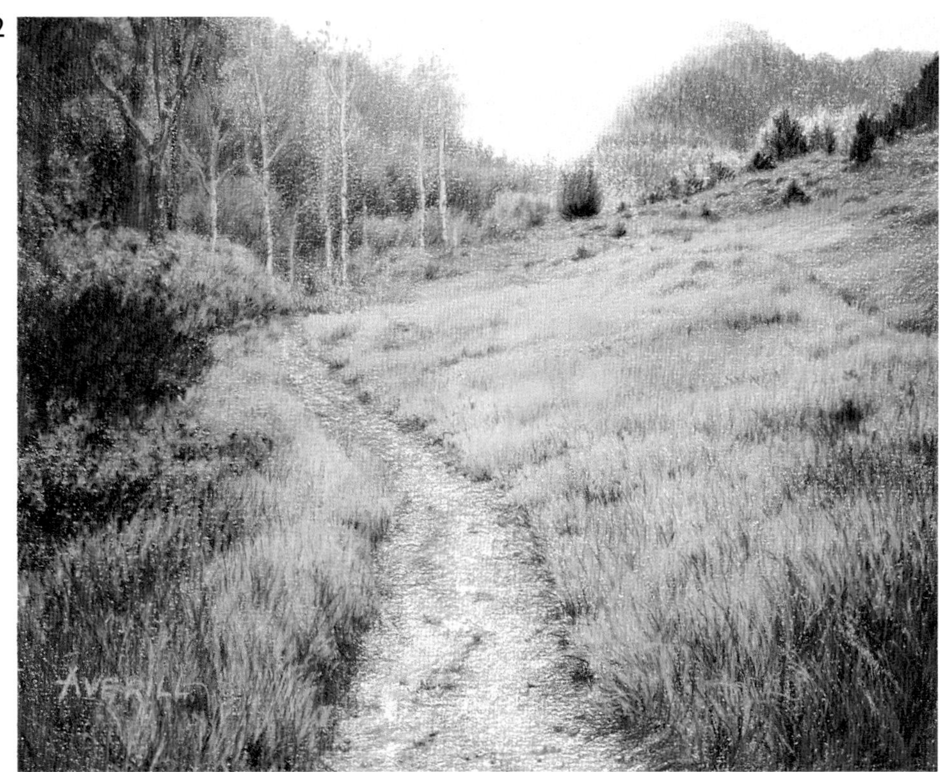

Kristy A. Kutch

1 *Sculptured Dune*
30 x 23" (762 x 584 mm)
Canson Colored Pastel Paper
Technique: Colored Pencil, Watercolor

Pat Averill

2 *This Way*
8 x 10" (197 x 248 mm)
Rising Museum Board

3 *On A Beach*
5 x 9" (133 x 229 mm)
Arches Watercolor

3 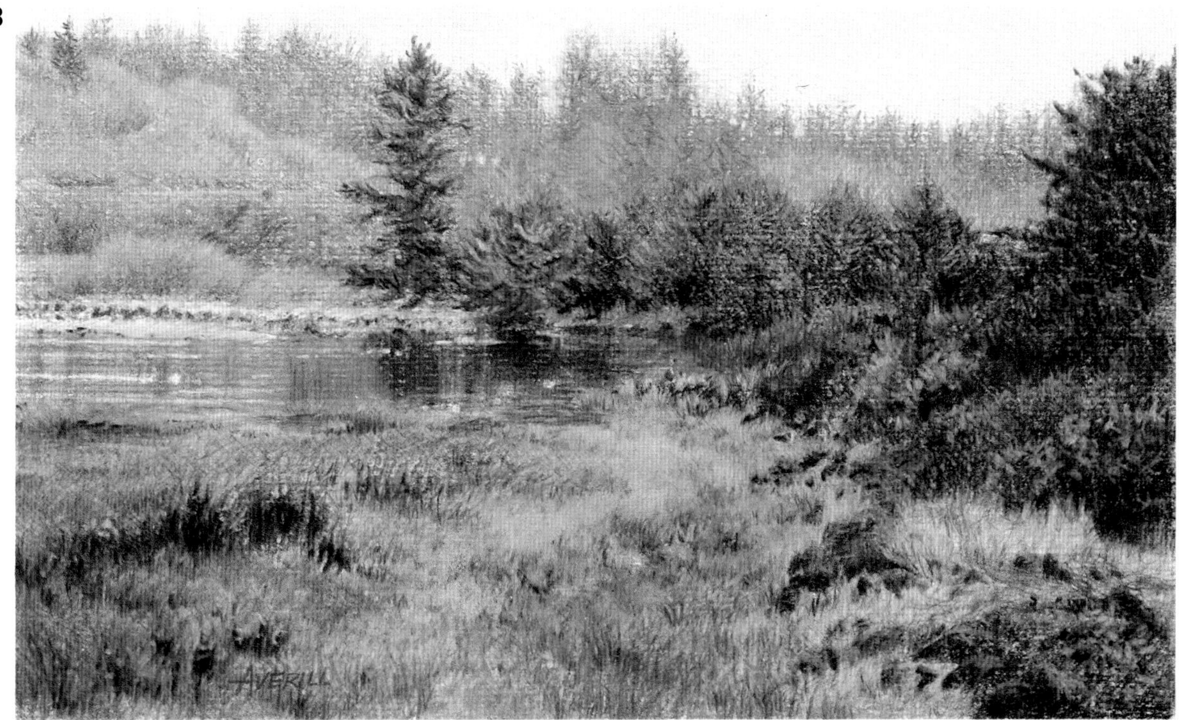

Pat Averill

1 *Friendship*
6 x 9" (140 x 216 mm)
Rising Museum Board

Iris Strpling

2 *Roots*
11 x 14" (279 x 356 mm)
Rising Museum Board
Technique: Impressed

1

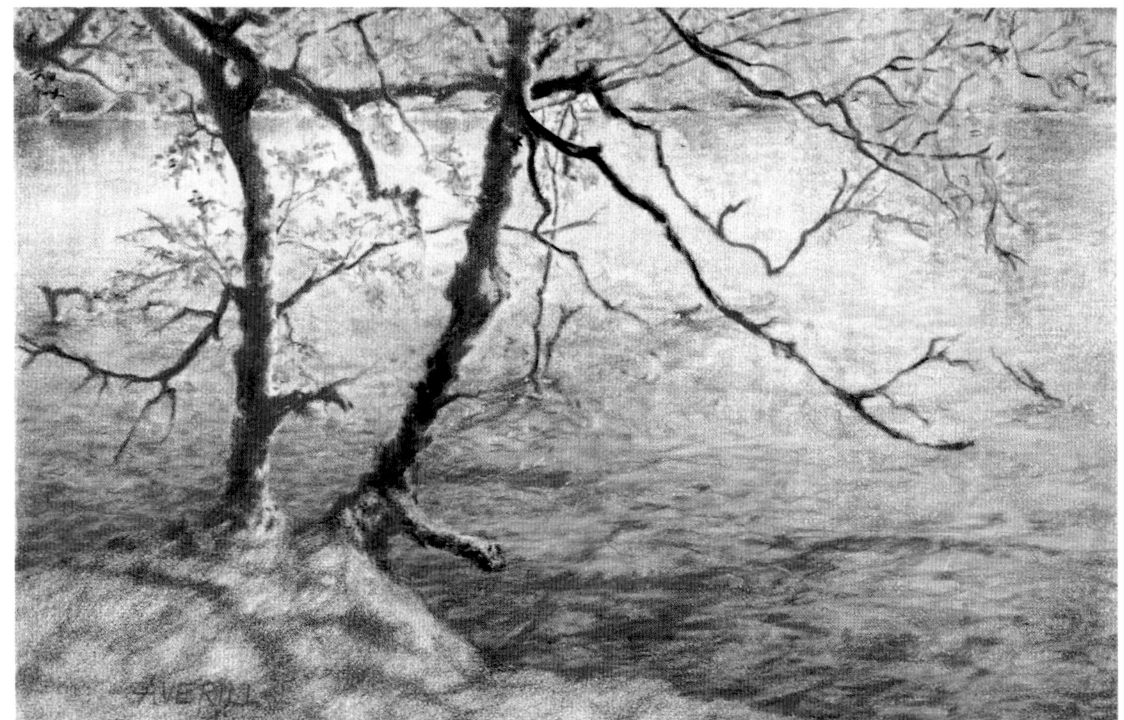

2

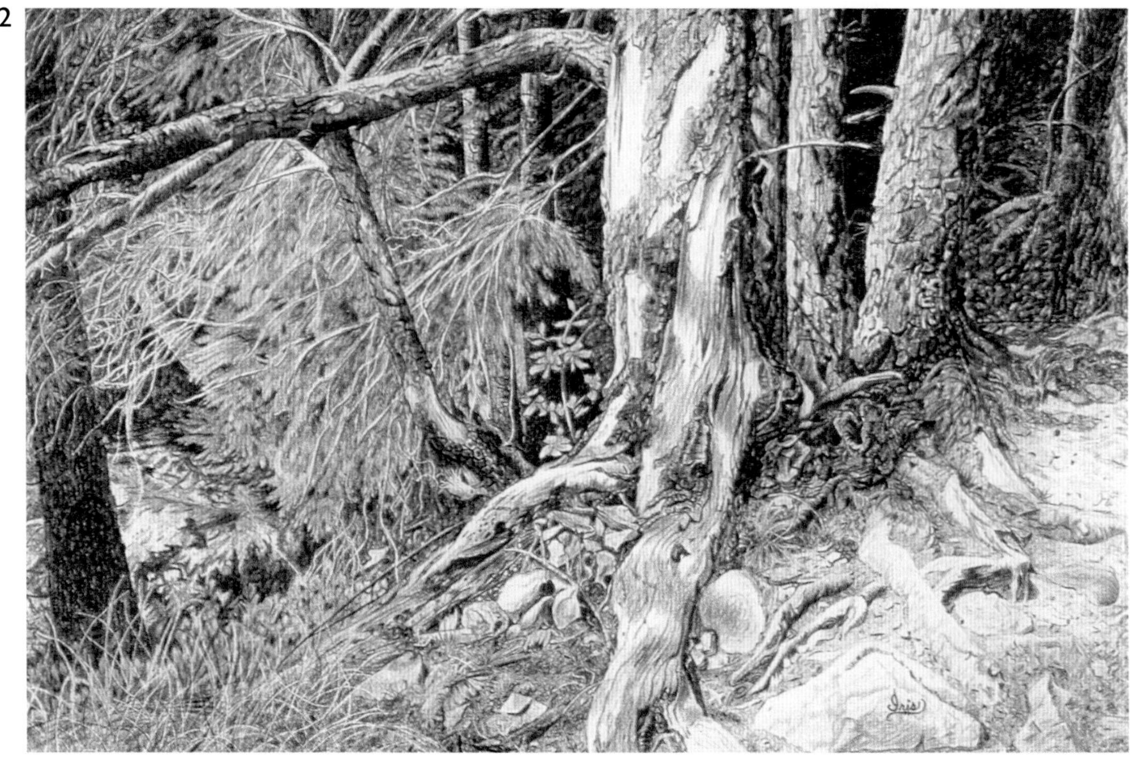

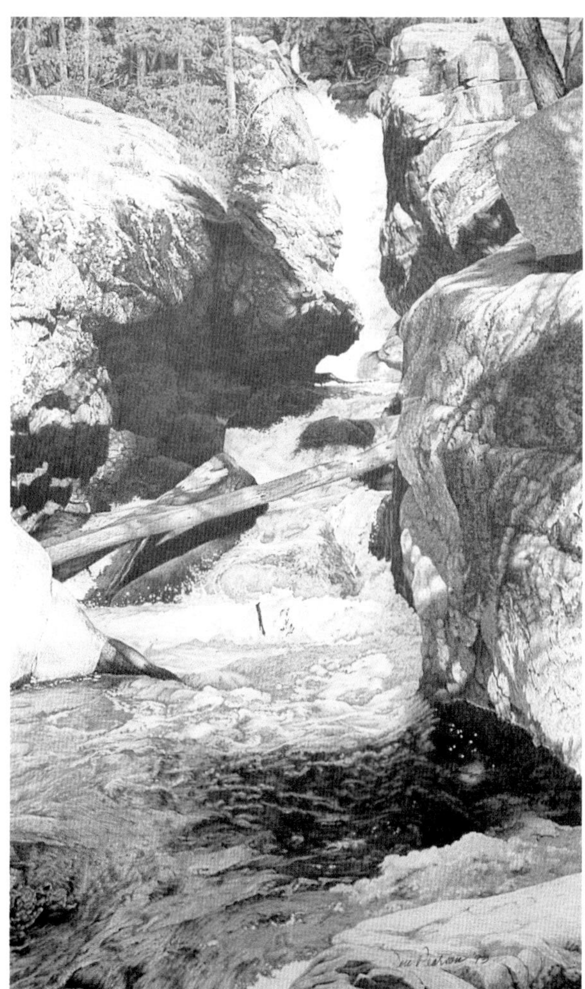

1

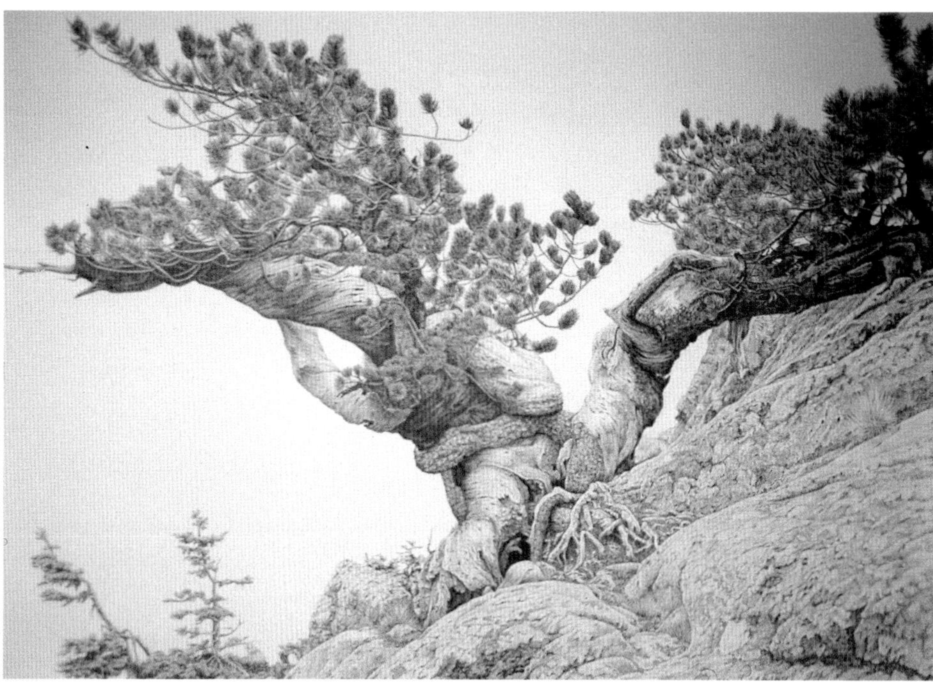

2

Don Pearson

1 *Chasm Falls*
32 x 19" (813 x 483 mm)
100% Rag Crescent Mat Board

2 *Tree At Dream Lake*
16 x 22" (406 x 559 mm)
100% Rag Crescent Mat Board

3 *The Three Stooges*
9 x 12" (228 x 304 mm)
100% Rag Crescent Mat Board

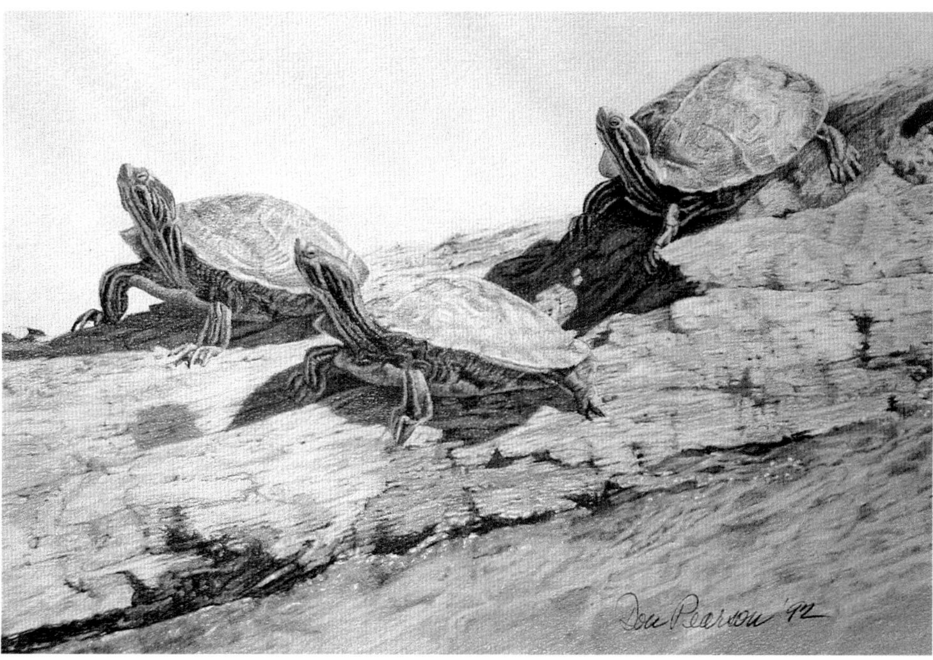

3

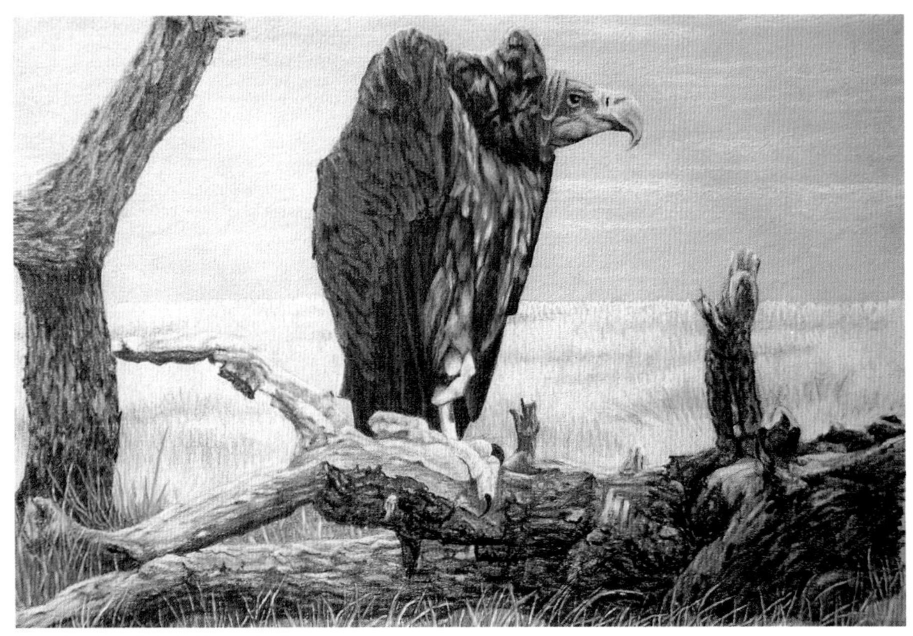

1

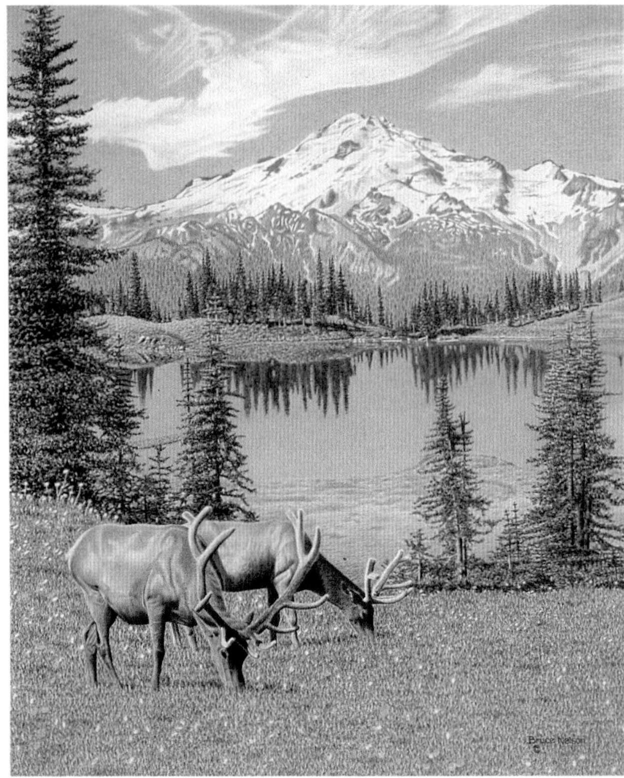

2

3

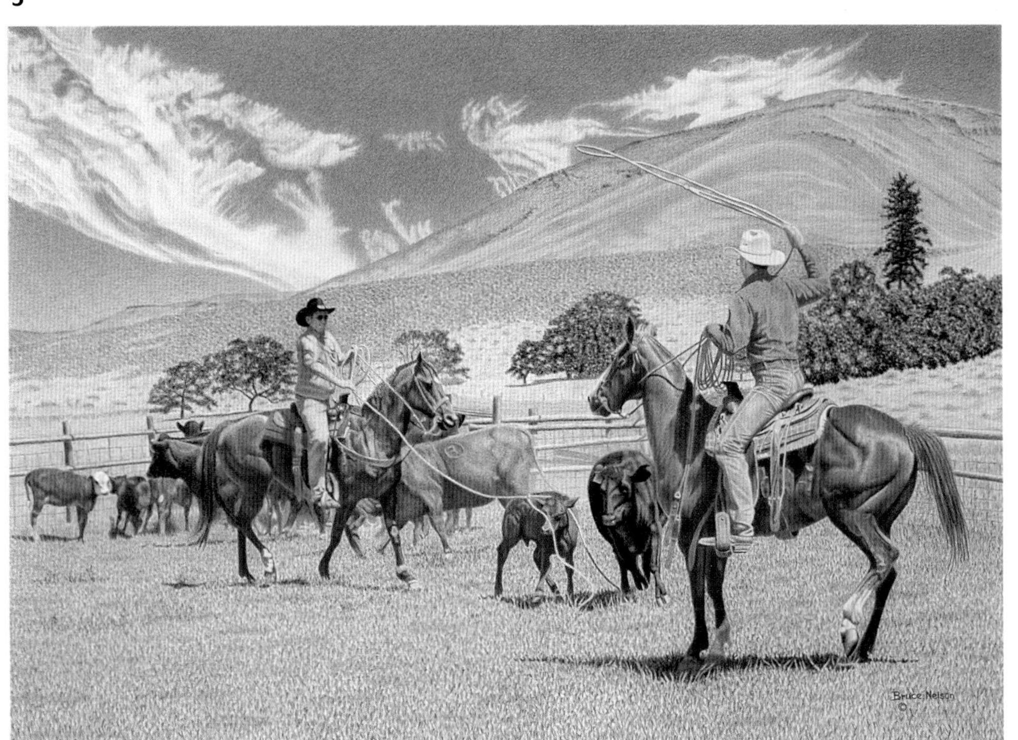

Don Pearson

1 *Patience is A Virtue*
8 x 10" (203 x 254 mm)
100% Rag Crescent Mat Board

Bruce J. Nelson

2 *Morning at Image Lake*
19 x 23" (483 x 584 mm)
Rives BFK Heavy Weight
Technique: Pointillism

3 *Under Western Skies*
18 x 25" (445 x 635 mm)
Rives BFK Heavyweight
Technique: Pointillism

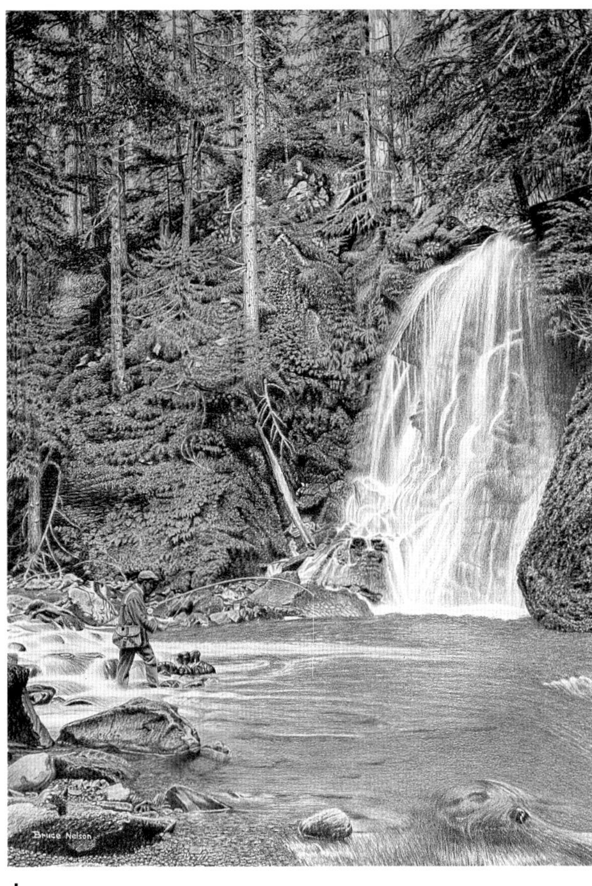

1

Bruce J. Nelson

1 *Mt. Rainier Series # 1*
20 x 16" (513 x 406 mm)
Strathmore Bristol, 5-ply Smooth Surface
Technique: Pointillism

2 *Olymic Idyll*
18 x 24" (457 x 610 mm)
Strathmore Bristol, 5-ply Smooth Surface
Technique: Pointillism

3 *Still Life with Flowers*
14 x 20" (356 x 508 mm)
Strathmore Bristol, 5-ply Medium Surface,
Smooth Side
Technique: Pointillism

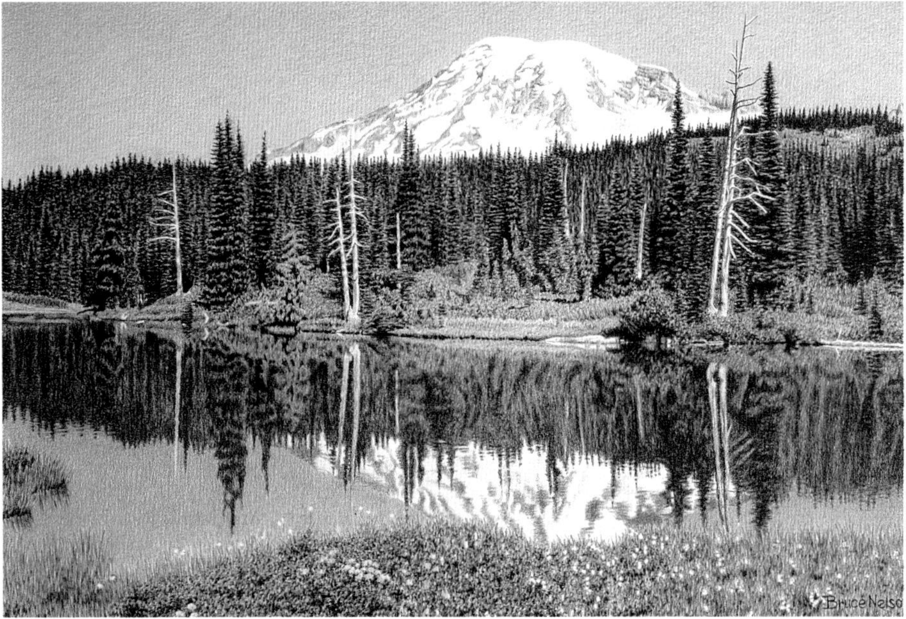

2

3

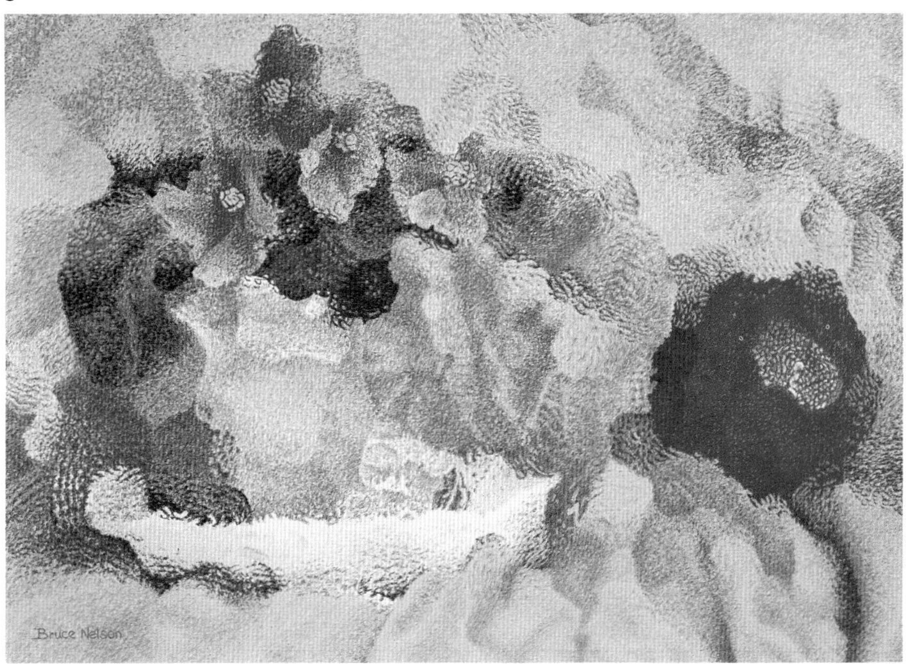

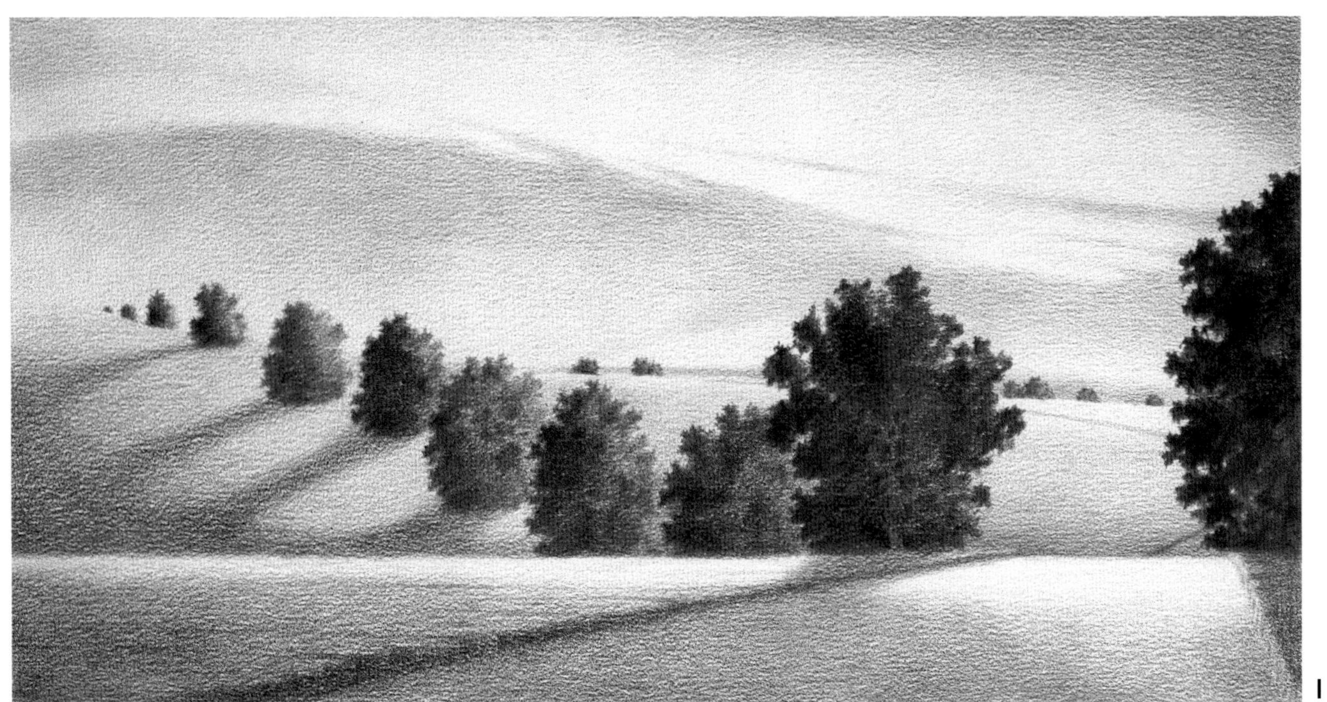

1

2

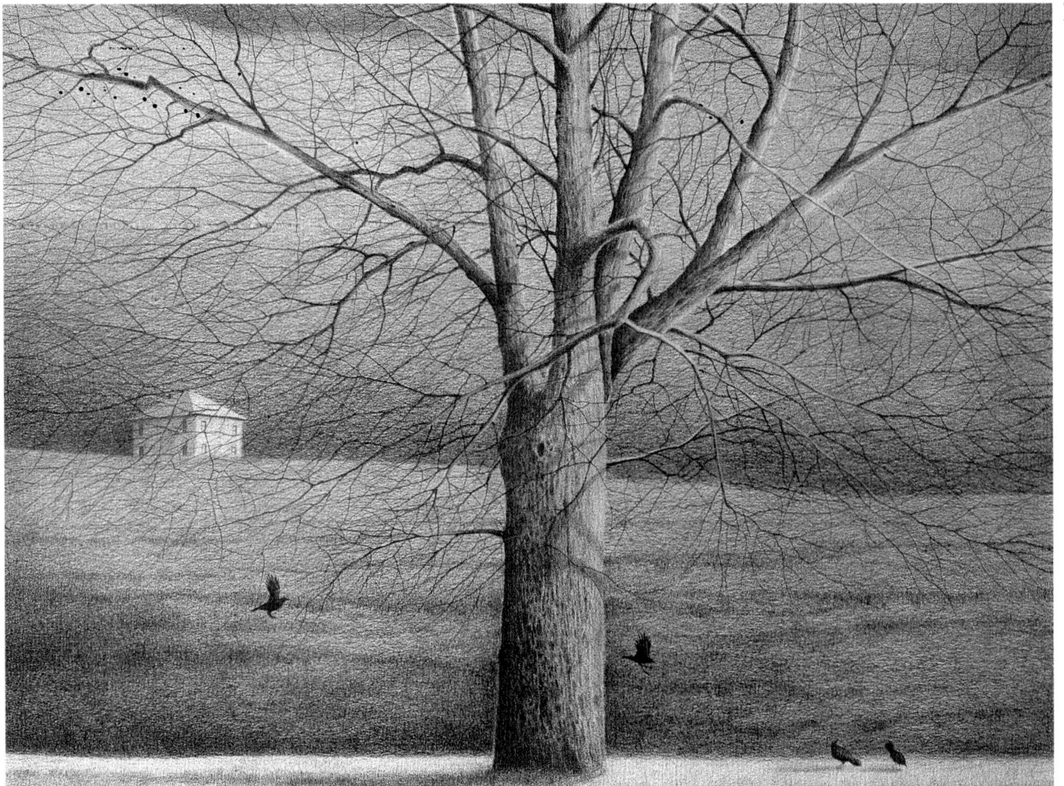

Allan Servoss

1 *At the Tree Line*
18 x 32" (457 x 813 mm)
Canson Paper
Technique: Tonal Application

2 *Landing Sites II*
30 x 40" (762 x 1,016 mm)
Canson Paper
Technique: Tonal Application

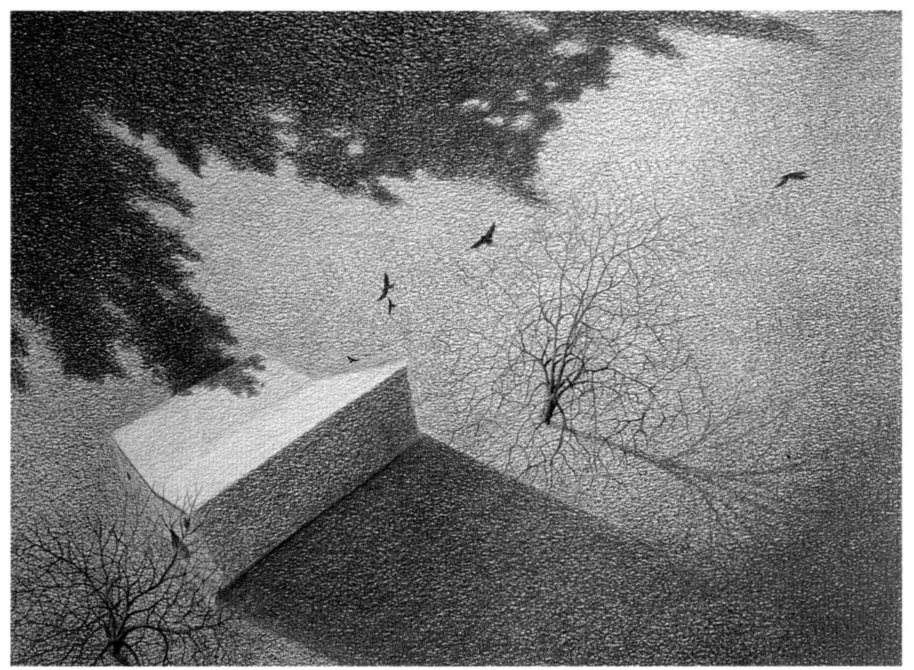

1

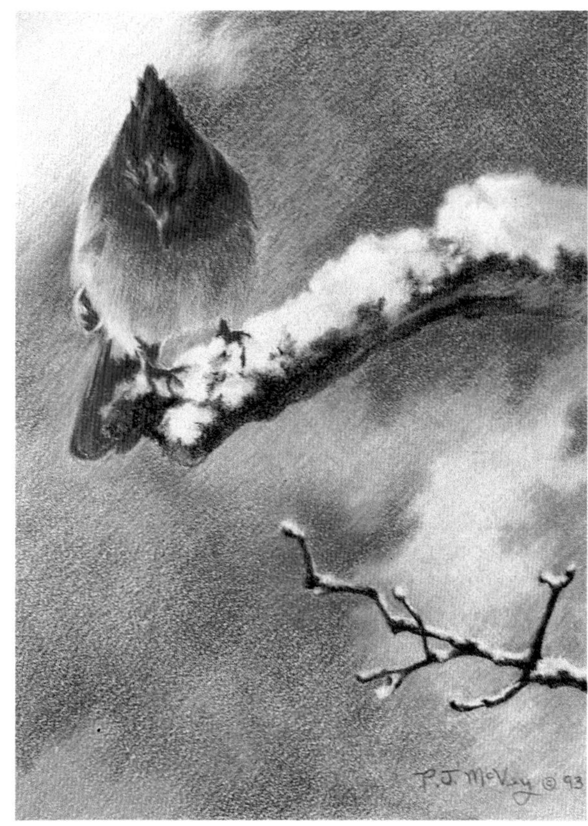

2

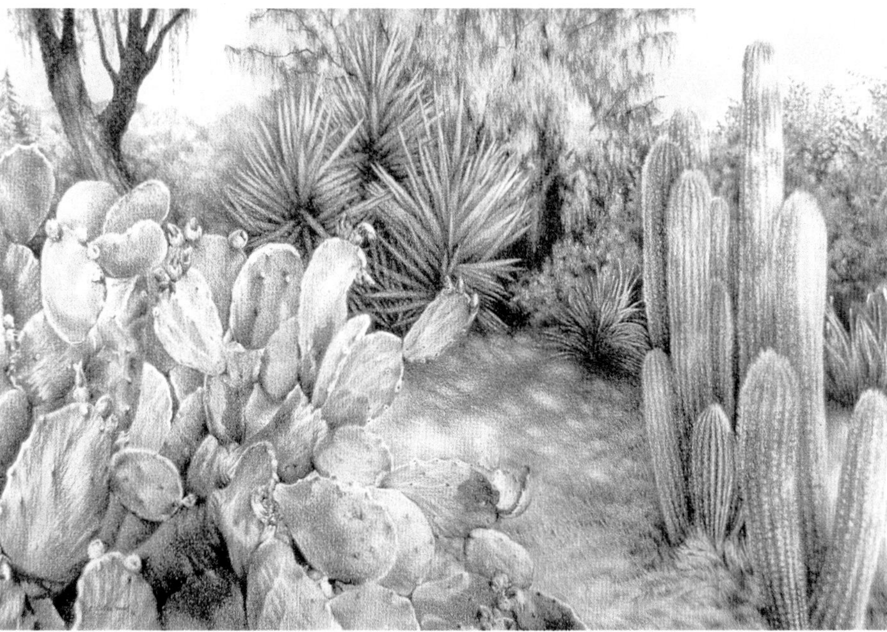

3

Allan Servoss

1 *Condition of Gradual - Descent*
15 x 24" (381 x 610 mm)
Canson Paper
Techniques: Tonal application

Patricia Joy McVey

2 *Snowy Perch, Steller's Jay*
10 x 8" (254 x 191 mm)
Strathmore 580 Regular Surface 106 lb. Paper

Eileen Cotter Howell

3 *Mom's Garden*
35 x 49" (889 x 1,245 mm)
Rough Watercolor Paper

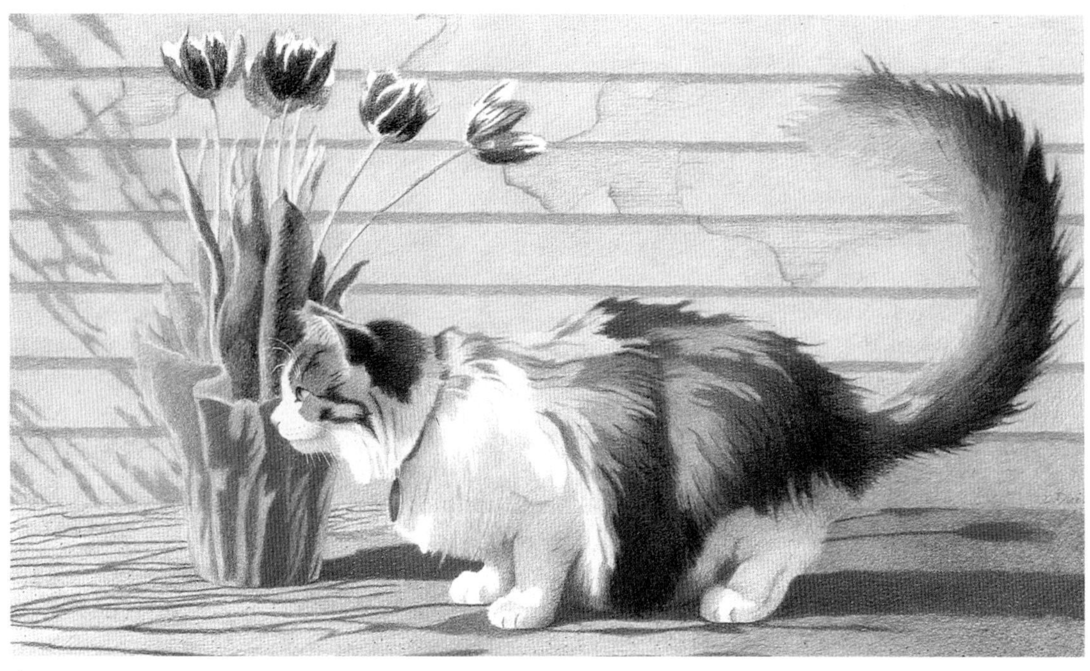

1

Laura Duis

1 *April Afternoon*
10 x 17" (241 x 419 mm)
Rising 2-ply Museum Board
Technique: Impressed Line

2 *Mystical Cat*
12 x 12" (311 x 311 mm)
Rising 2-ply Museum Board
Technique: Impressed Line

Elly Zadlo

3 *Portrait of a Toad*
16 x 23" (406 x 584 mm)
Gray Mat Board

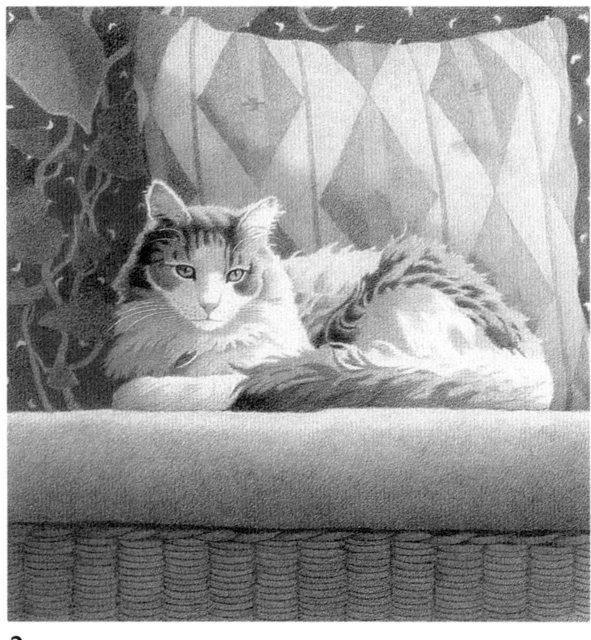

2

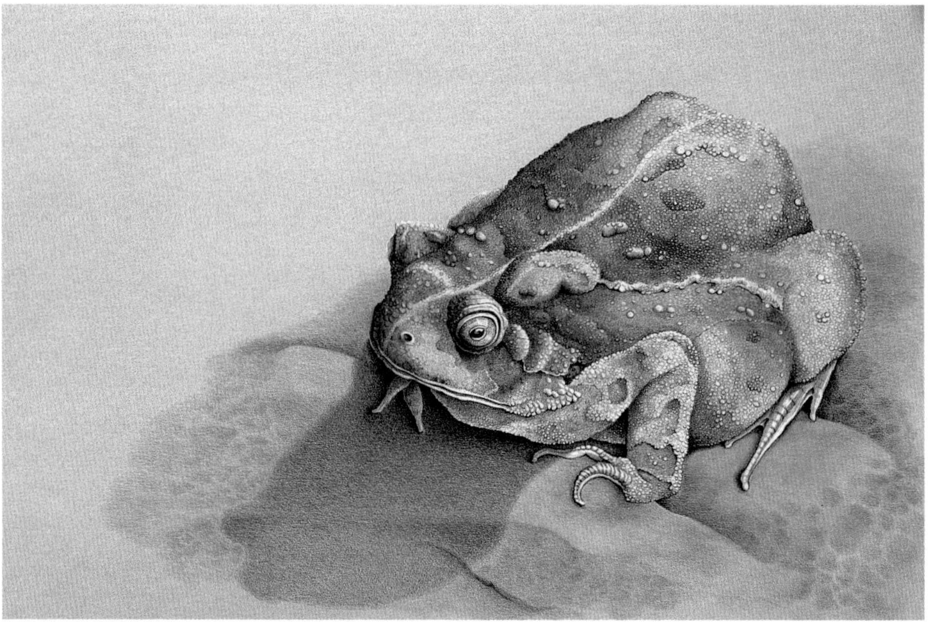

3

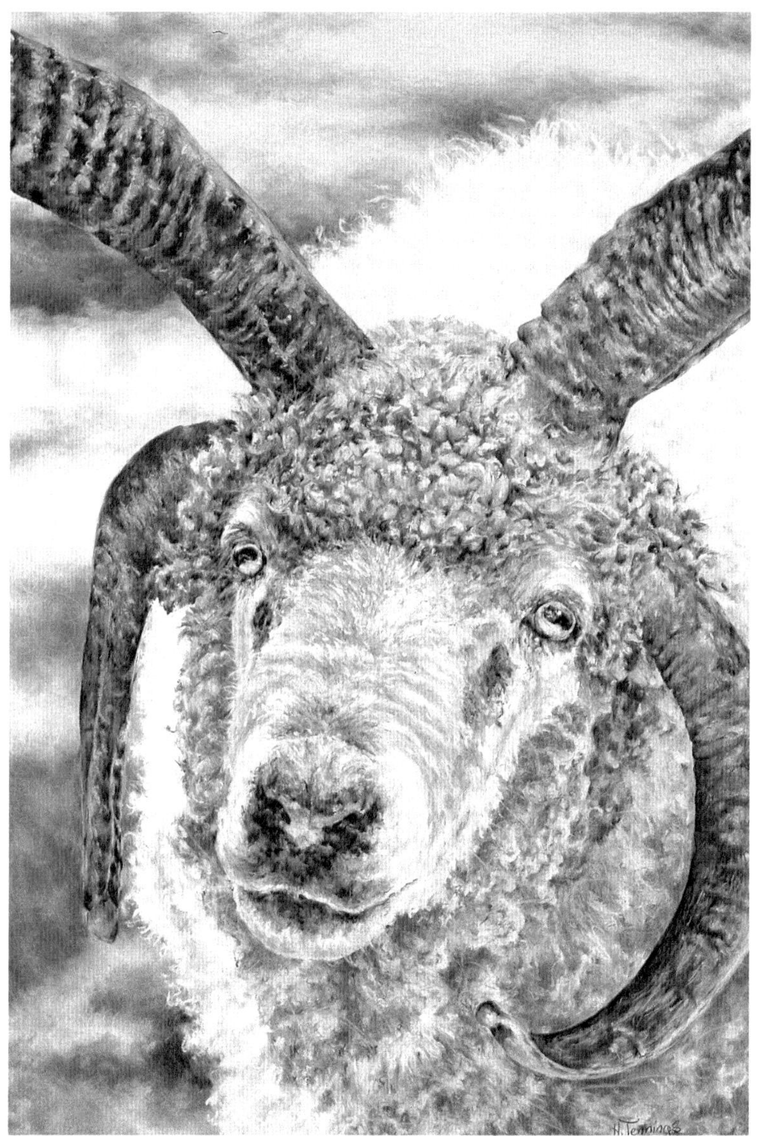

1

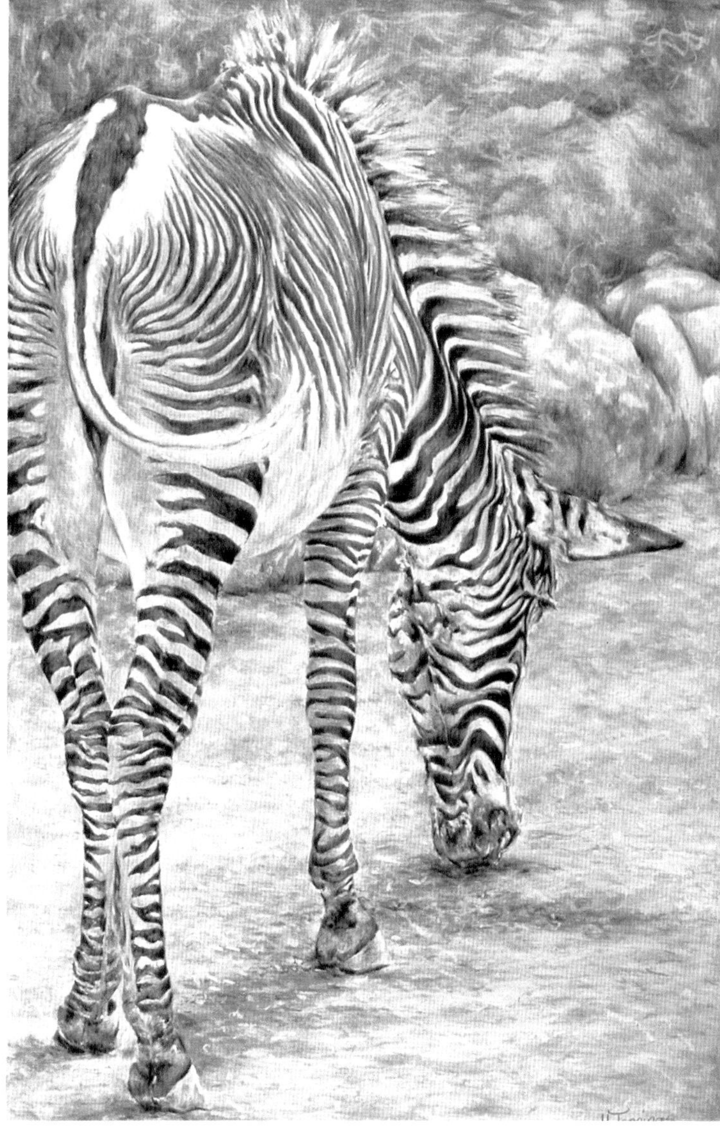

2

Helen Jennings

1 *Speaking Without Words*
23 x 16" (584 x 406 mm)
Strathmore 4-ply Smooth Bristol Board
Technique: Burnishing

2 *A Moment Alone*
18 x 12" (547 x 305 mm)
Strathmore 4-ply Smooth Bristol Board
Technique: Burnishing

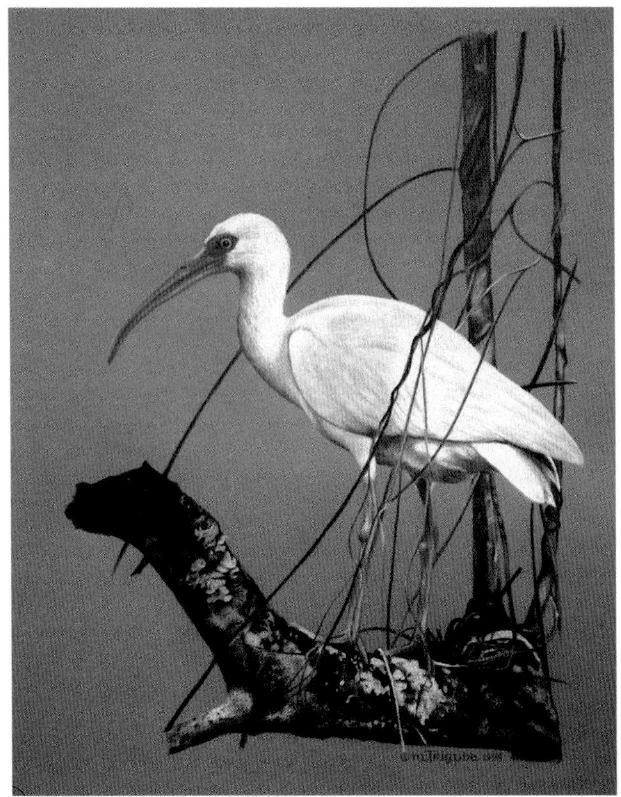

1

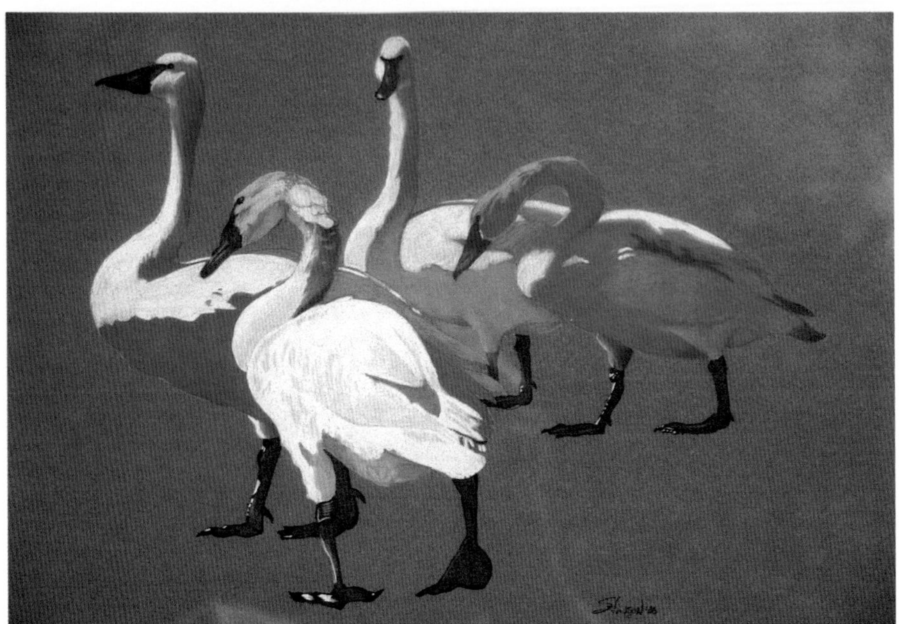

2

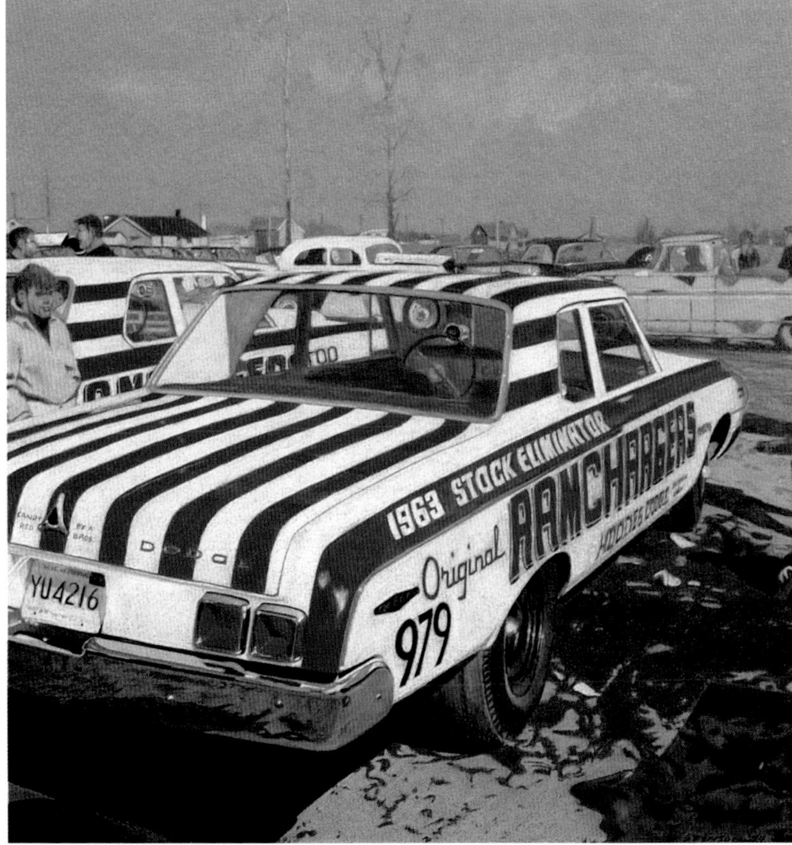

3

Marvin Triguba

1 *White Ibis*
22 x 16" (559 x 406 mm)
Canson Paper
Technique: Burnishing

Bill Stinson

2 *Trumpeter Swans*
9 x 12" (229 x 305 mm)
Crescent Sienna Brown Mat Board

3 *64 Ramchargers at Detroit Dragway*
14 x 13" (340 x 337 mm)
Crescent Sienna Brown Mat Board

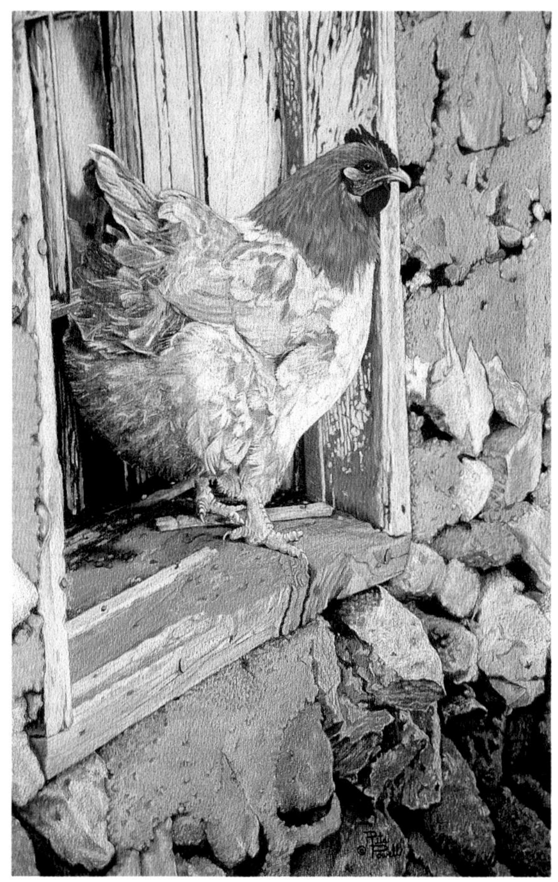

1

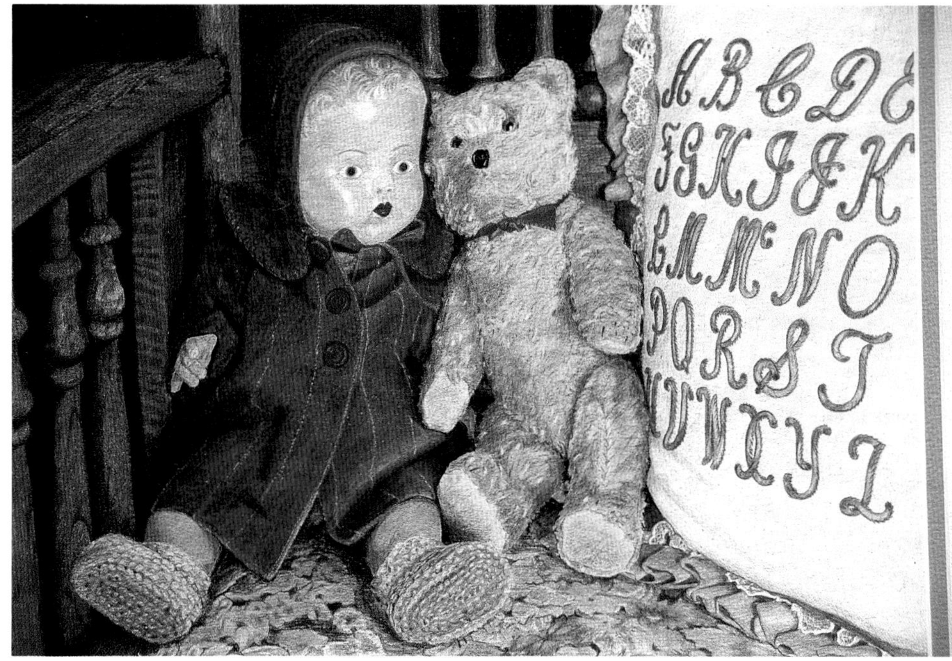

2

3

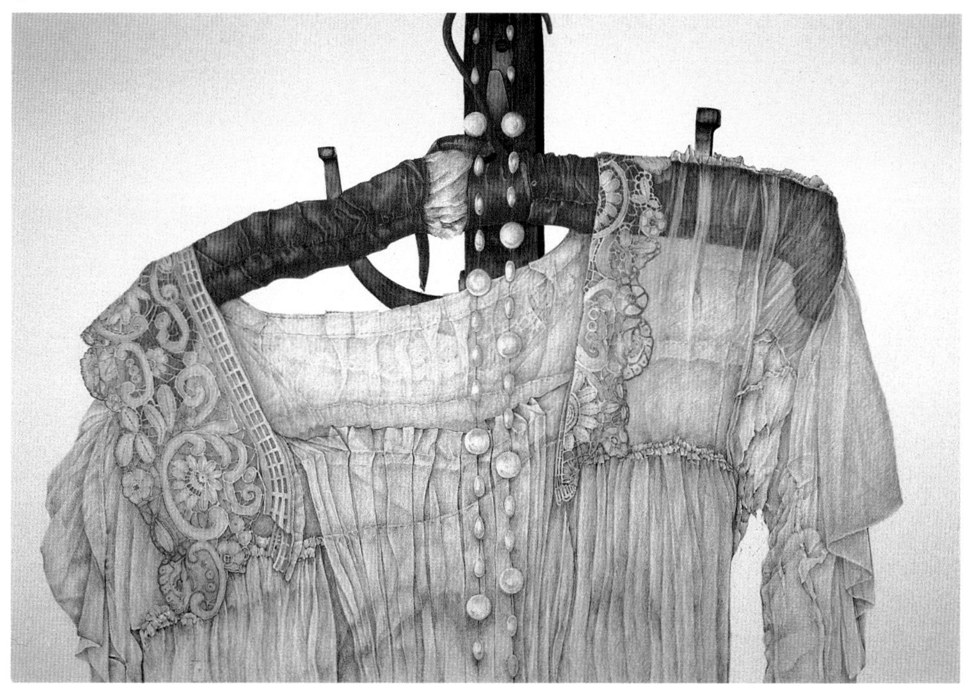

Rita Sue Powell

1 *Chicken In the Window*
26 x 20" (667 x 518 mm)
Strathmore Artgrain Recycled Color Paper-Flannel

2 *Memories at Rest*
20 x 20" (495 x 495 mm)
Strathmore Illustration Board Cold Press, 100% Cotton

Jeanne Lachance

3 *The Bride*
56 x 73" (1,410 x 1,842 mm)
Museum Board
Technique: Colored Pencil, Oil Pastel

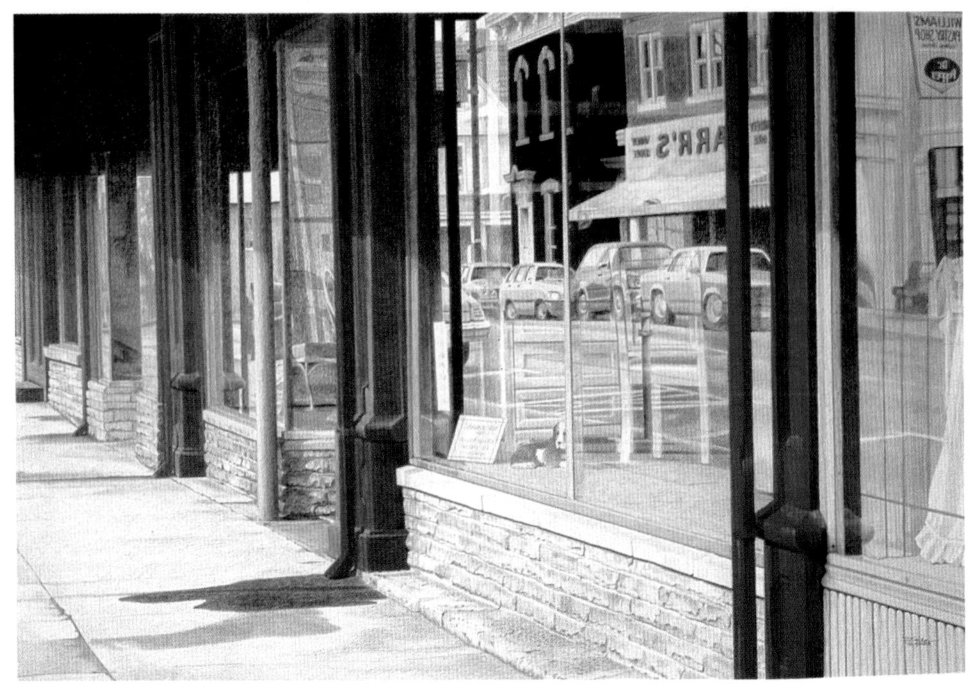

1

Janie Gildow

1 *Covington Morning*
15 x 22" (368 x 552 mm)
Crescent Cold Press #99 Illustration Board
Technique: Burnishing

2 *Sparklers*
15 x 12" (381 x 292 mm)
White Rising Stonehenge
Technique: Burnishing

Dava Dahlgran

3 *Piper Dreams*
25 x 20" (622 x 492 mm)
Canson Mi-Tientes Pastel Paper

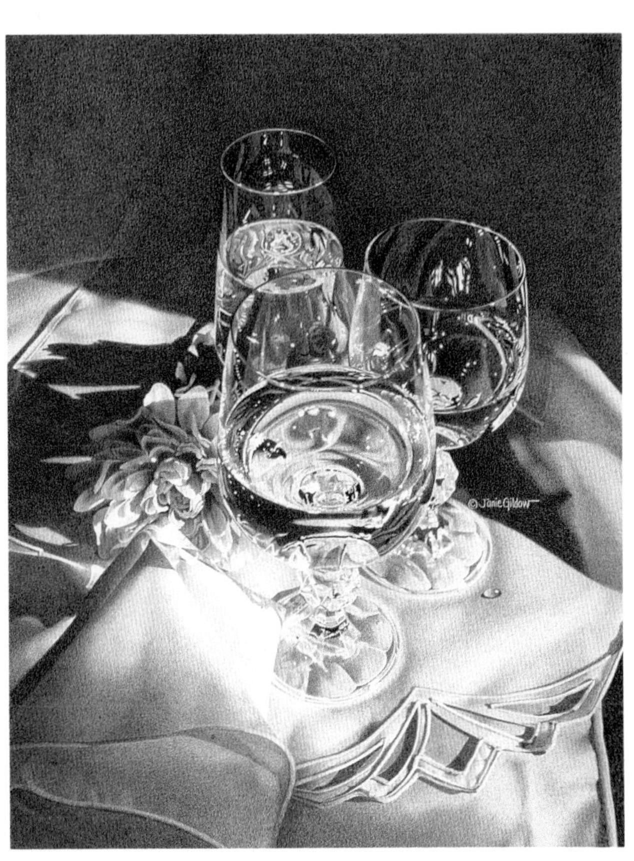

2

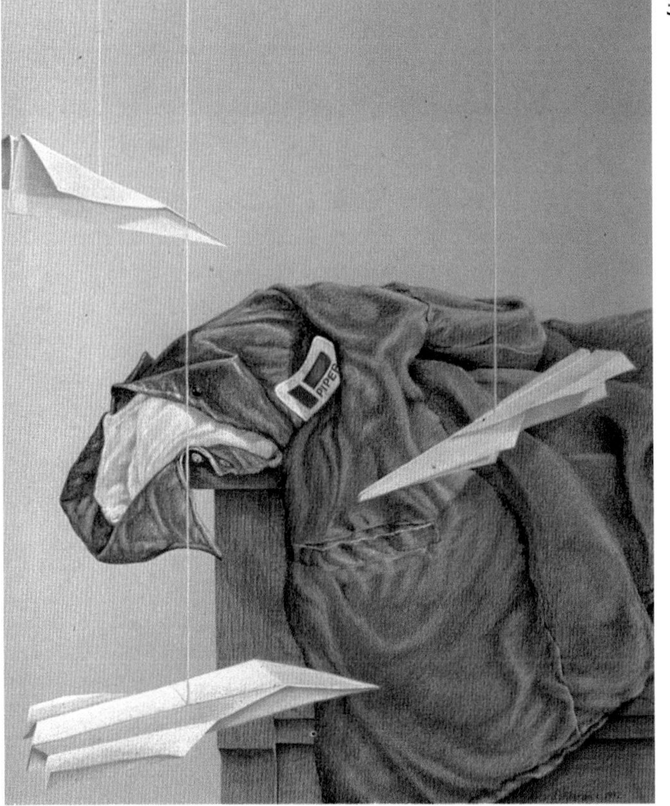

3

Jeanne Goodman

1 *The Symphony*
32 x 40" (813 x 1,016 mm)
Rives BFK Paper

2 *At The Bench*
27 x 20" (686 x 508 mm)
Rives BFK Paper
Technique: Colored Pencil and Art Sticks

1

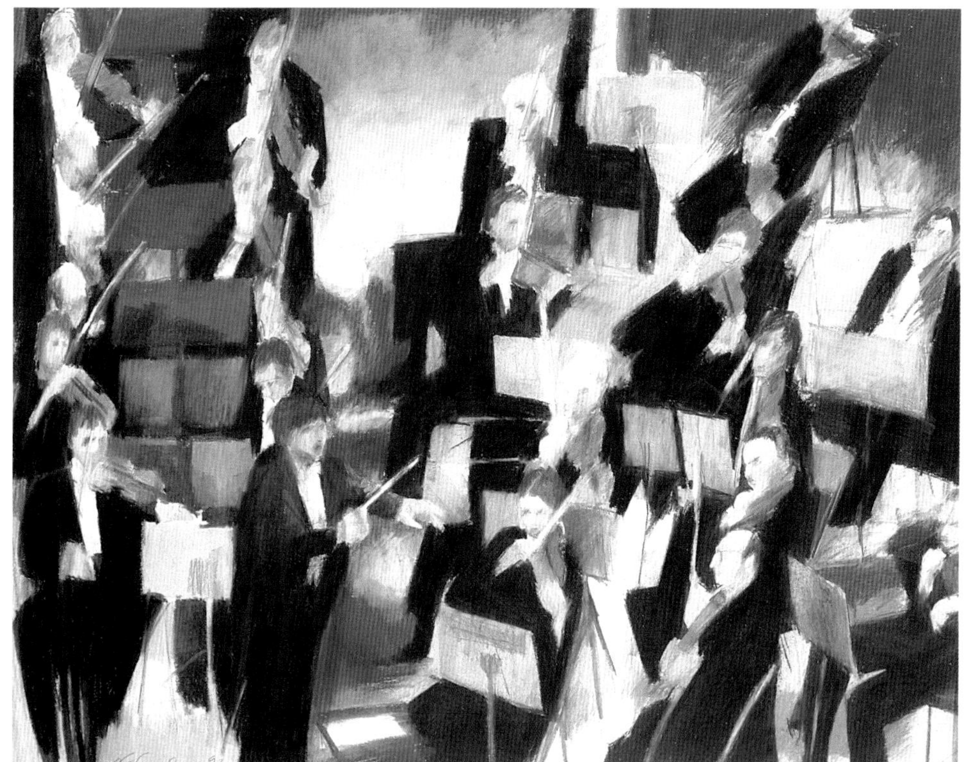

2

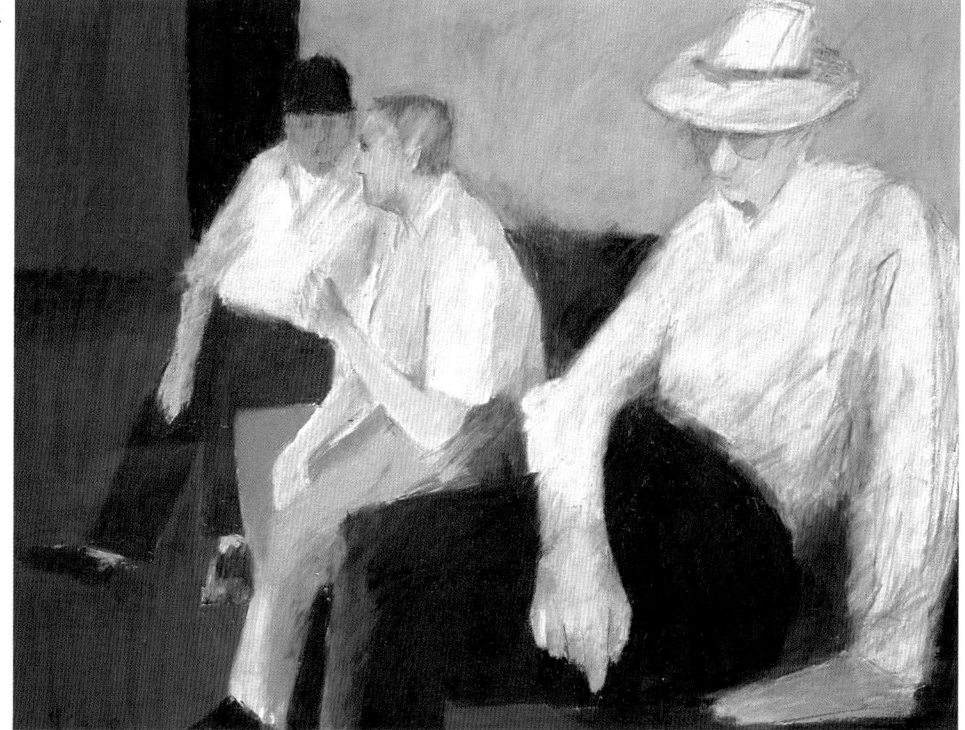

Susan Lane Gardner

1 *Quince and Red Pears*
13 x 22" (337 x 340)
2-ply Rising Museum Board

Merren Walker Frichtl

2 *19th Century Nocturne*
12 x 16" (305 x 406 mm)
100% Rag, 4-ply Museum Mat Boar
Technique: Colored Pencil over Gesso

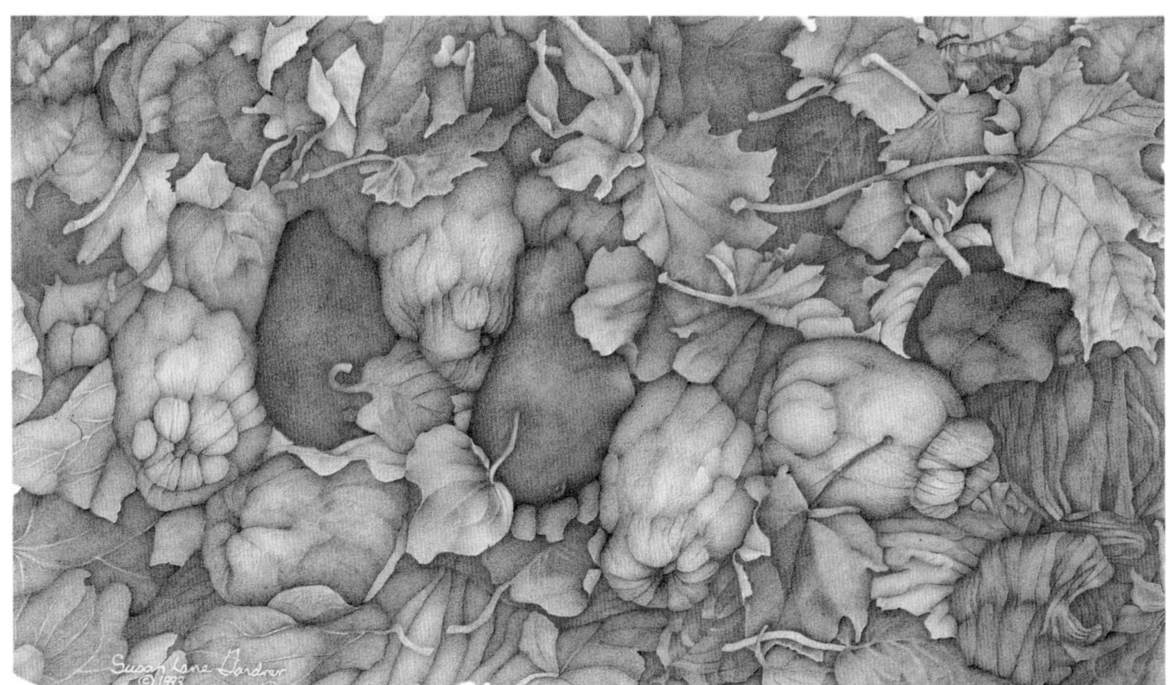

1

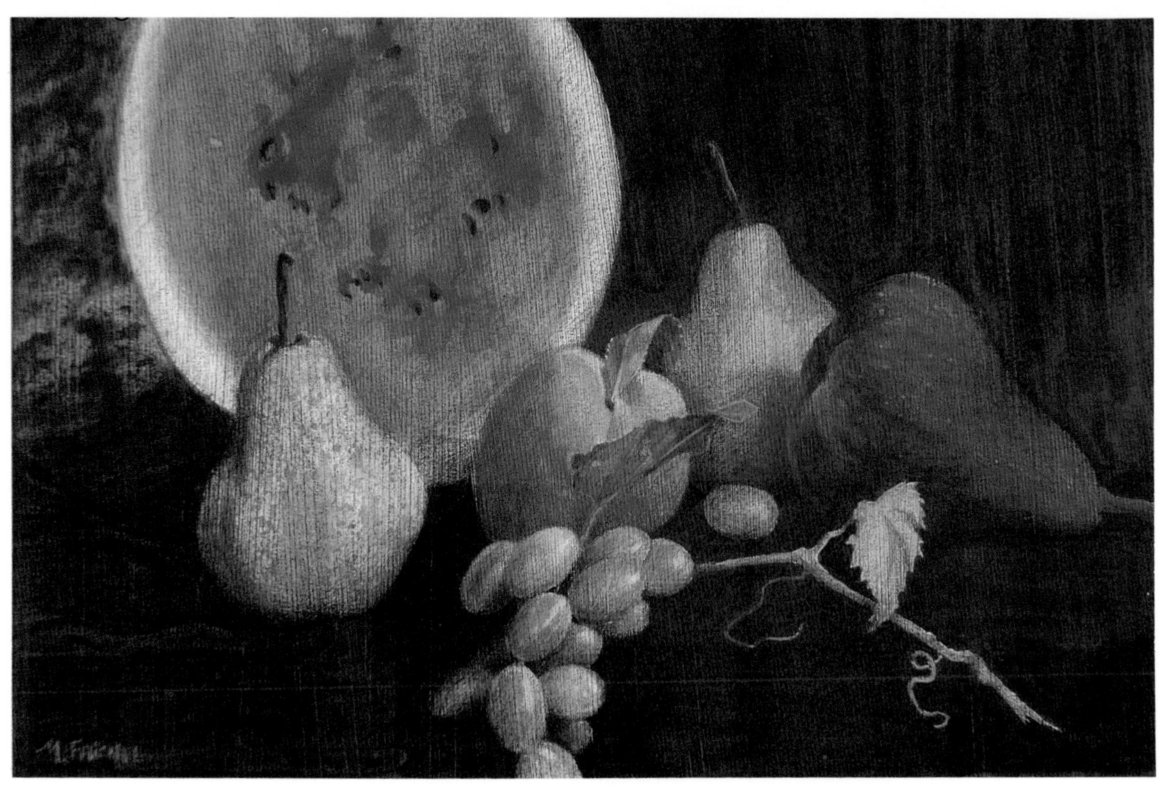

2

Nancy Blanchard

1 *Hubbard Squash*
22 x 30" (565 x 762 mm)
140 lb. Hot Press Fabriano
Technique: Burnishing

2 *Granny Smith w/Salt Crode*
22 x 30" (565 x 762 mm)
140 lb. Hot Press Fabriano
Technique: Burnishing

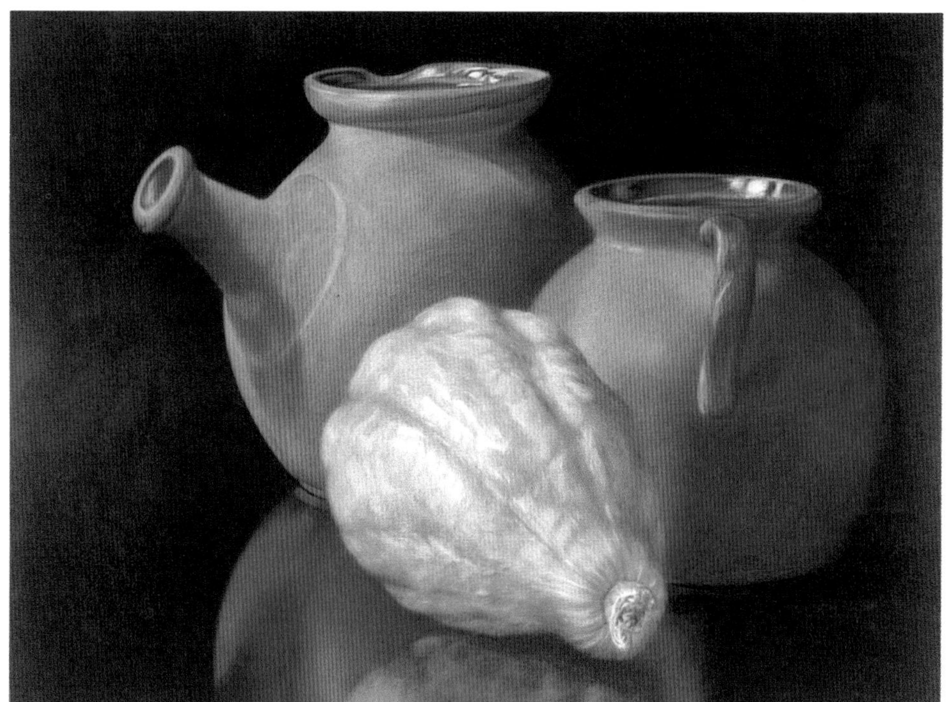

1

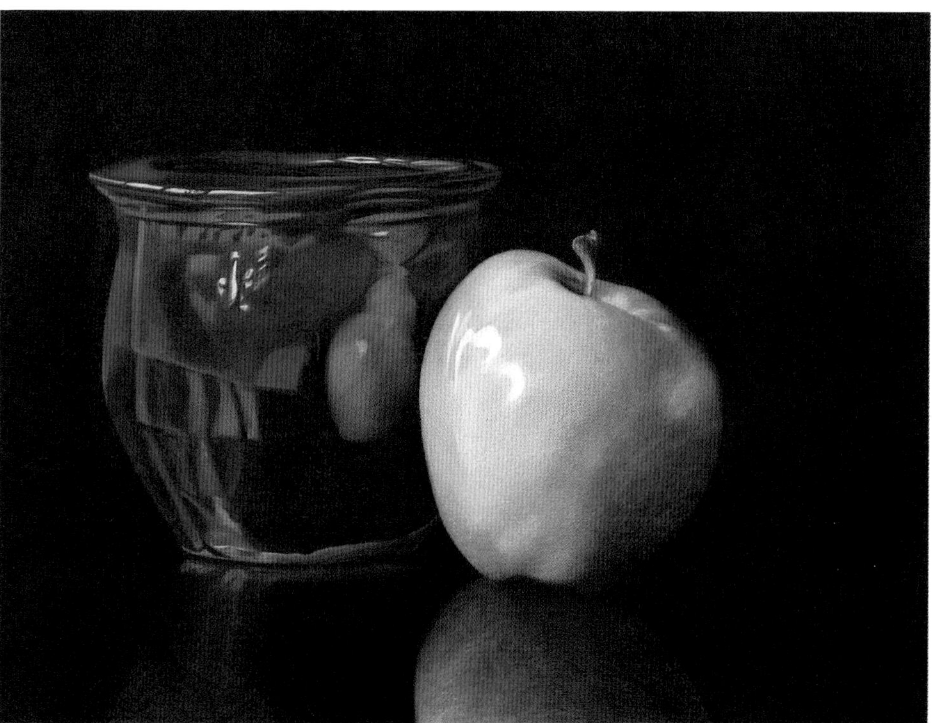

2

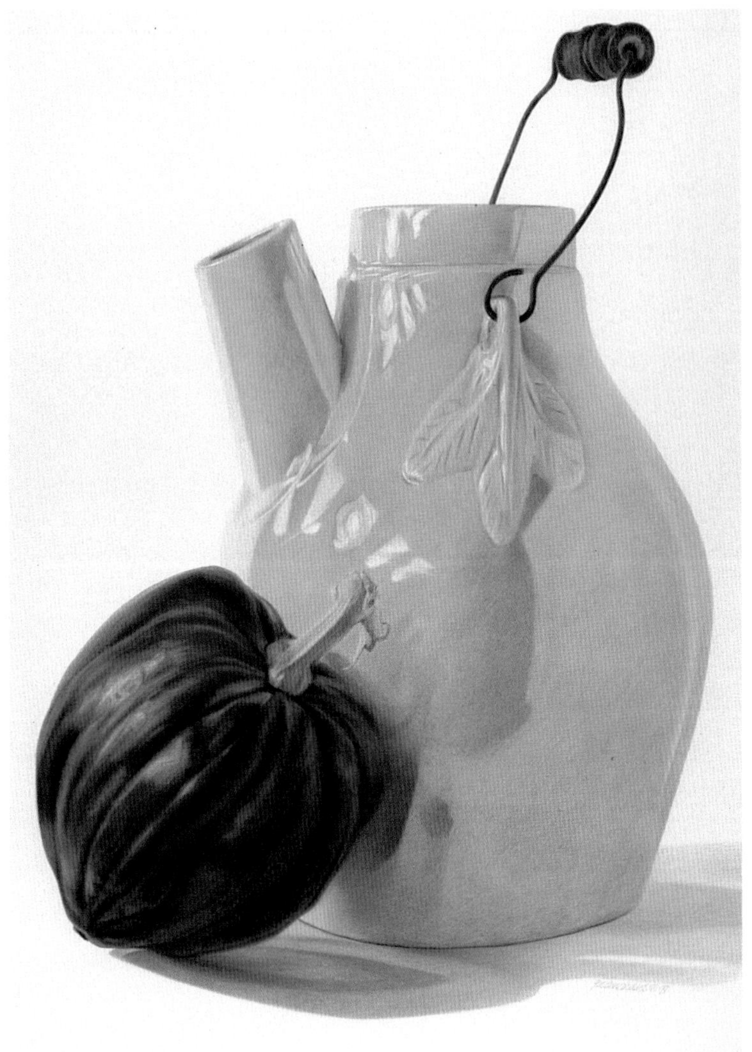

1

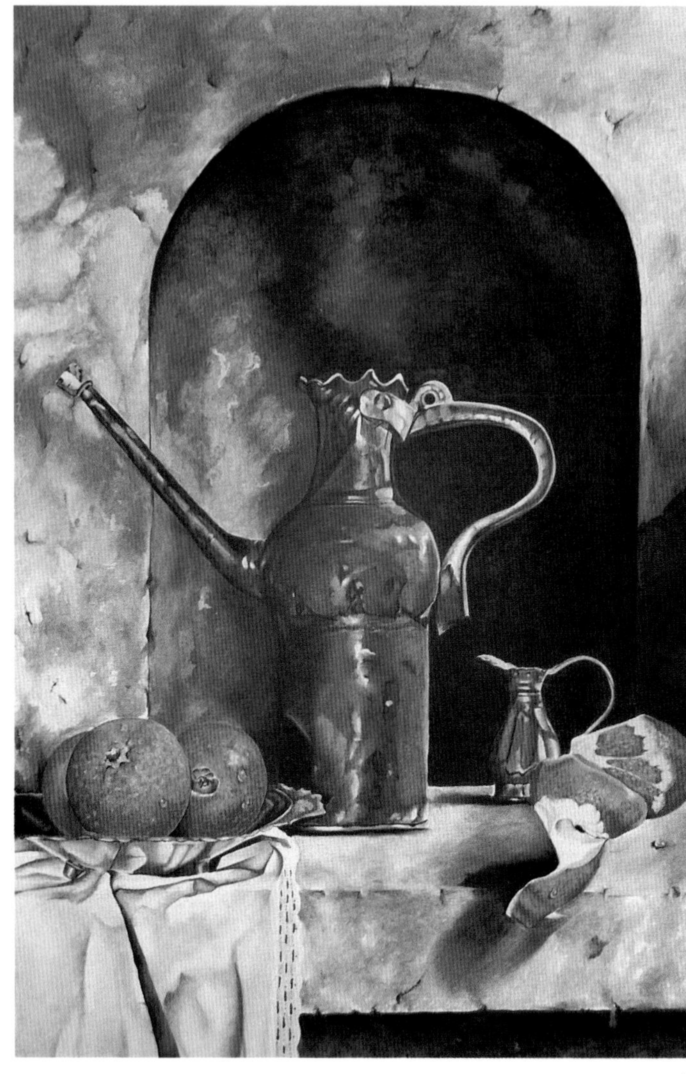

2

Nancy Blanchard

1 *The Batter Jar*
30 x 23" (762 x 572 mm)
140 lb. Hot Press Fabriano
Technique: Burnishing

Dian Donicht Vestin

2 *Orange Master*
28 x 24" (711 x 610 mm)
Strathmore 500 Illustration Board Plate Finish
Technique: Burnishing over color removed by electric eraser

Barbara Newton

1 *Nectarines*
9 x 12" (216 x 298 mm)
Rising Stonehenge Paper

2 *Elephant Garlic*
18 x 25" (445 x 635 mm)
Crescent Colored Mat Board

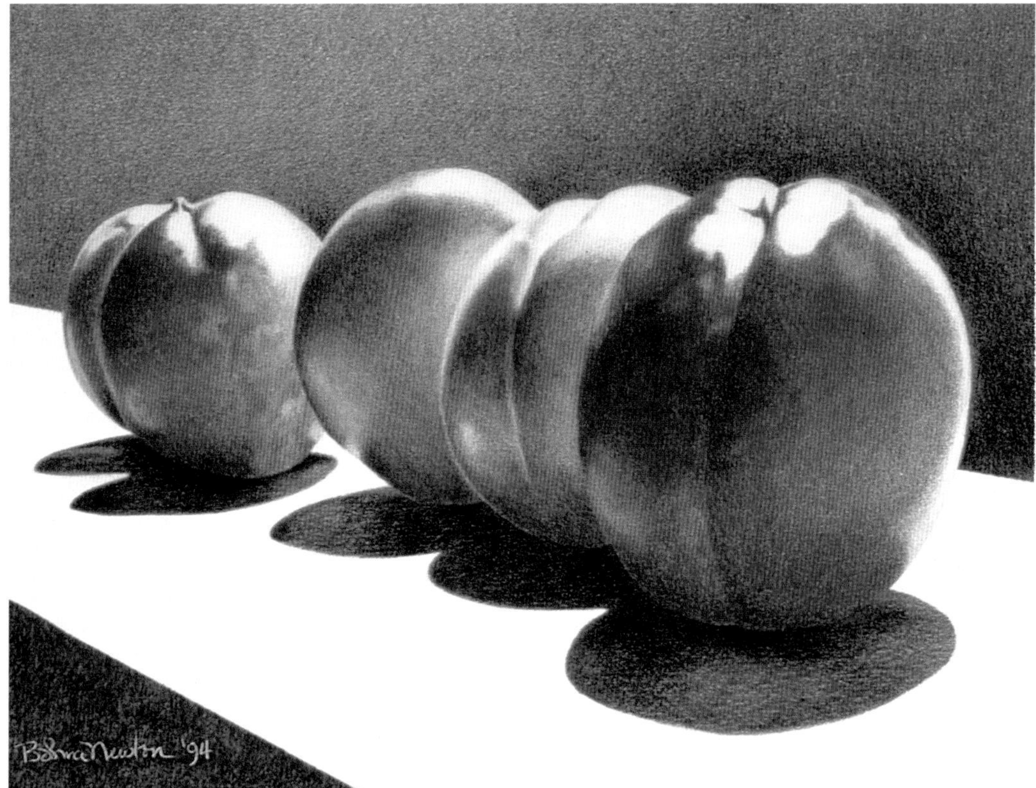

1

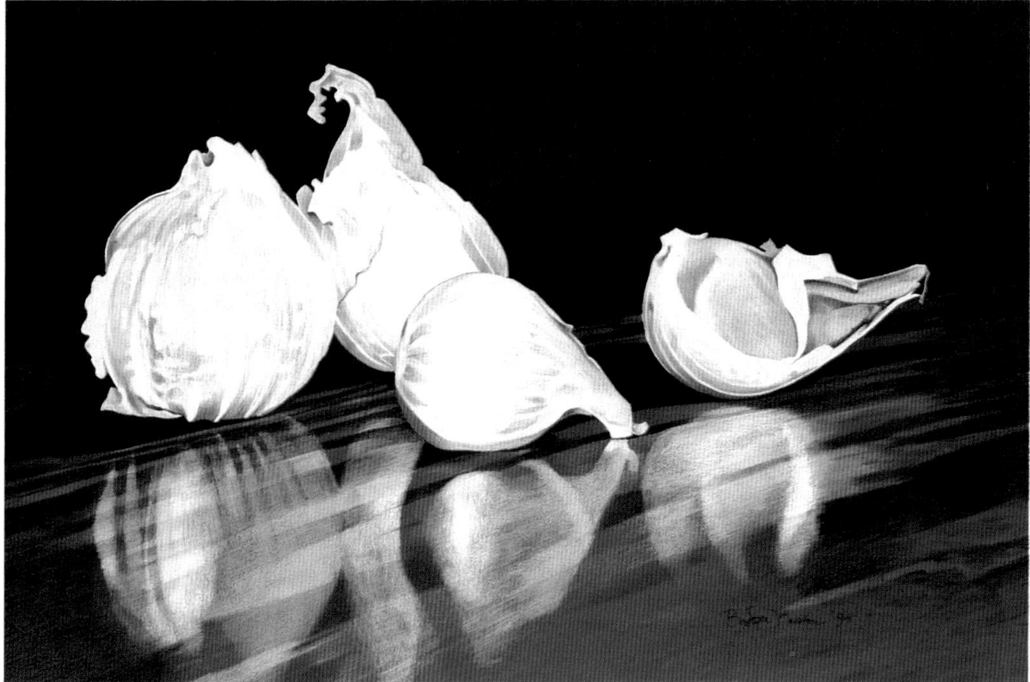
2

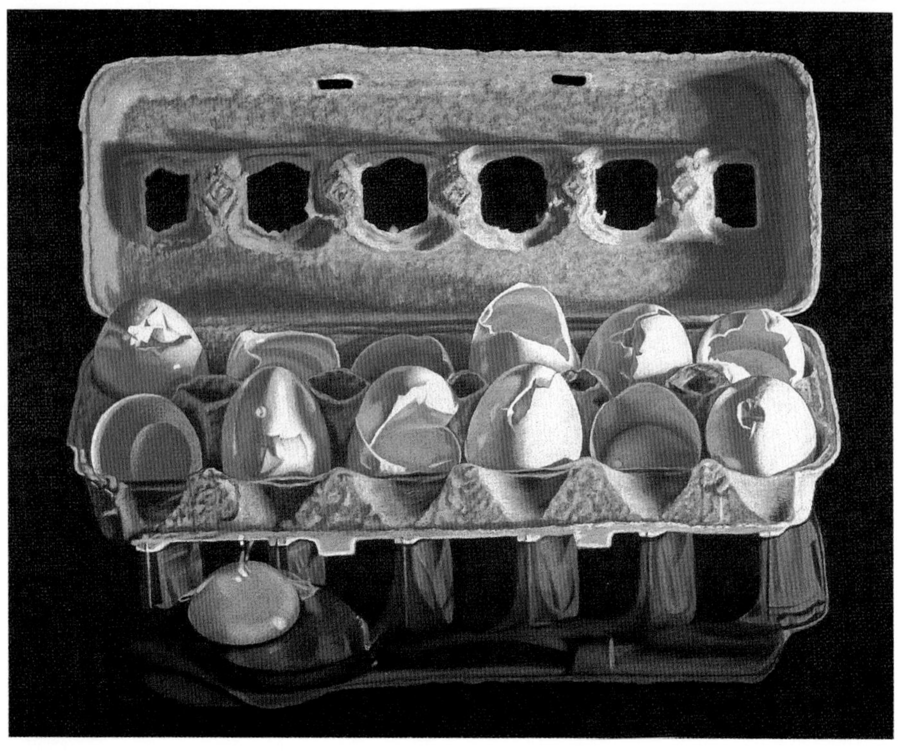

1

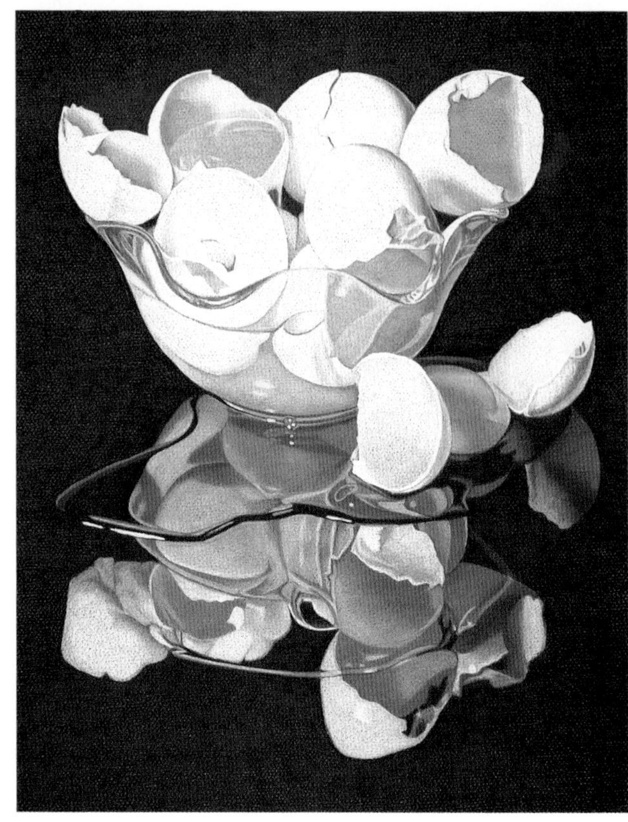

3

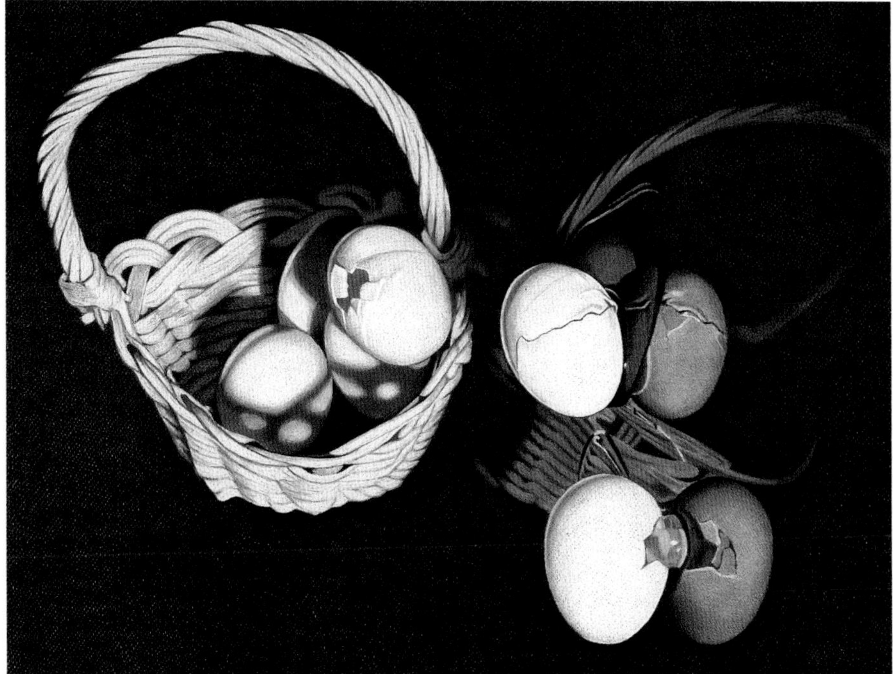

2

Ronni Wadler

1 *Eggs #5*
17 x 23"(432 x 584 mm)
Canson Mi-Tientes

2 *Eggs #6*
18 x 16" (457 x 406 mm)
Canson Mi-Tientes

3 *Eggs In A Basket*
24 x 18" (610 x 457 mm)
Canson Mi-Tientes

L. Maija Earl

1 *Master Chef*
19x 26" (470 x 648 mm)
White Bristol Board

2 *Welcome Rain*
19 x 26" (470 x 648 mm)
White Bristol Board

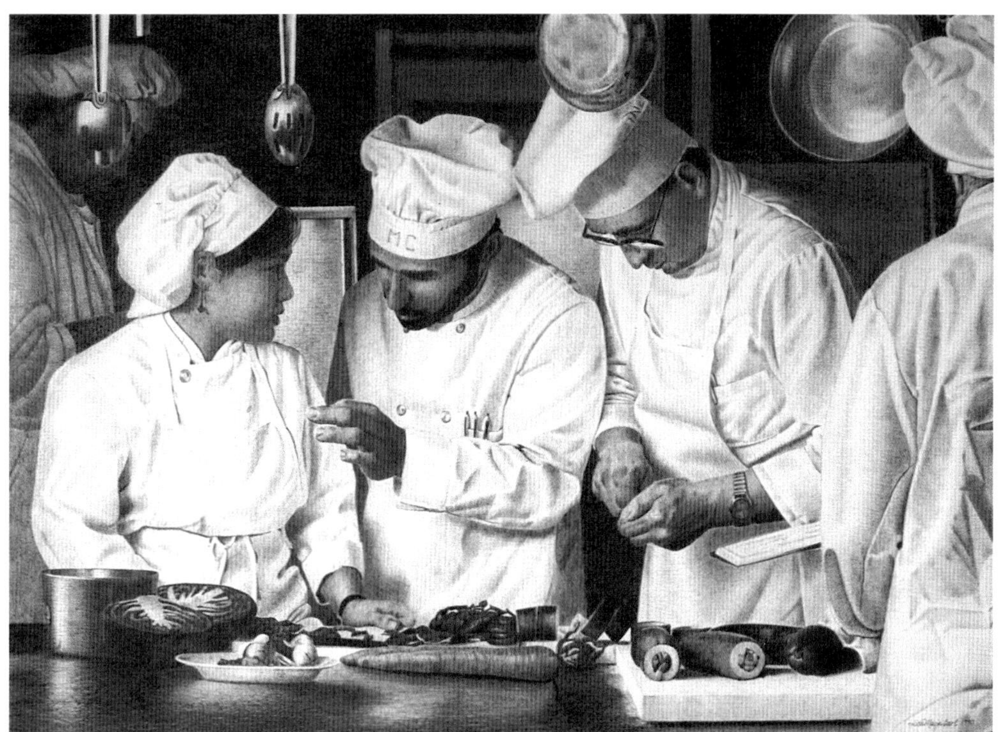

1

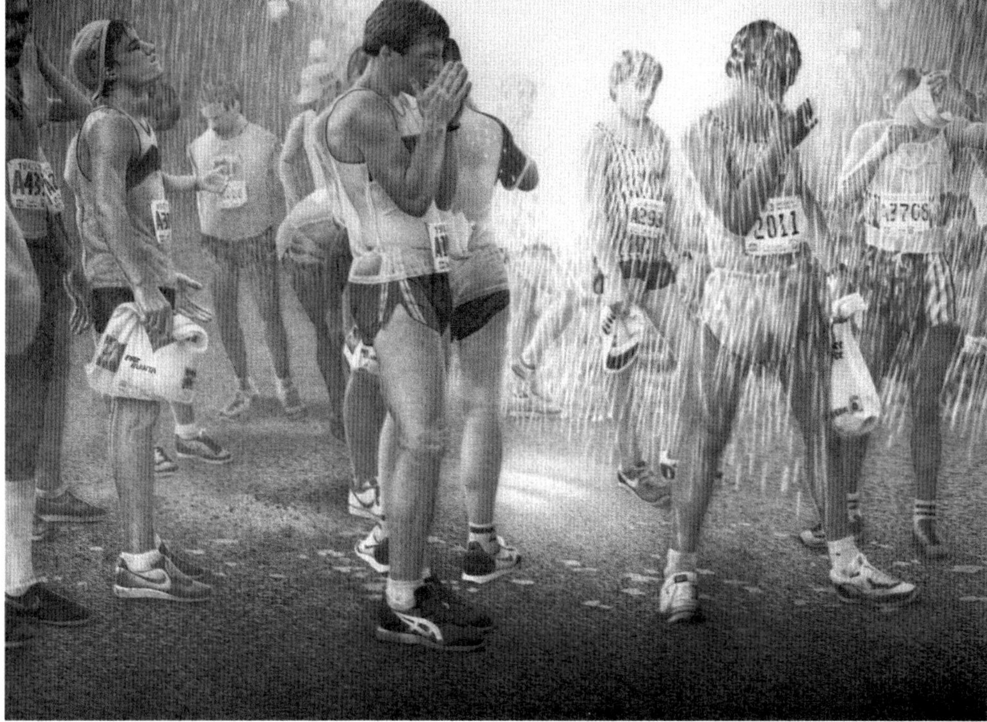

2

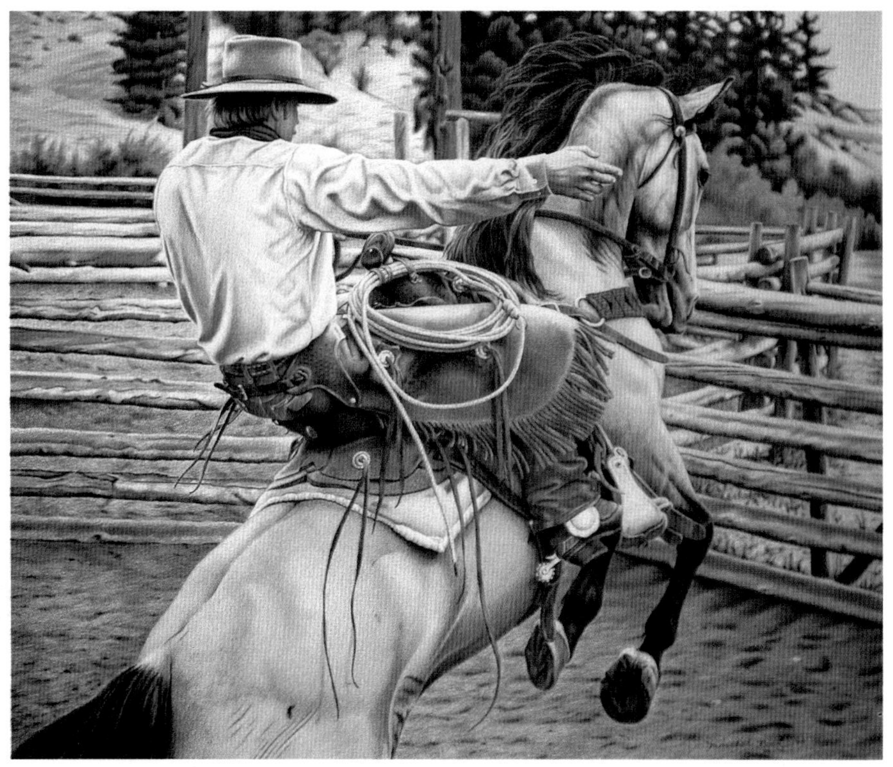

1

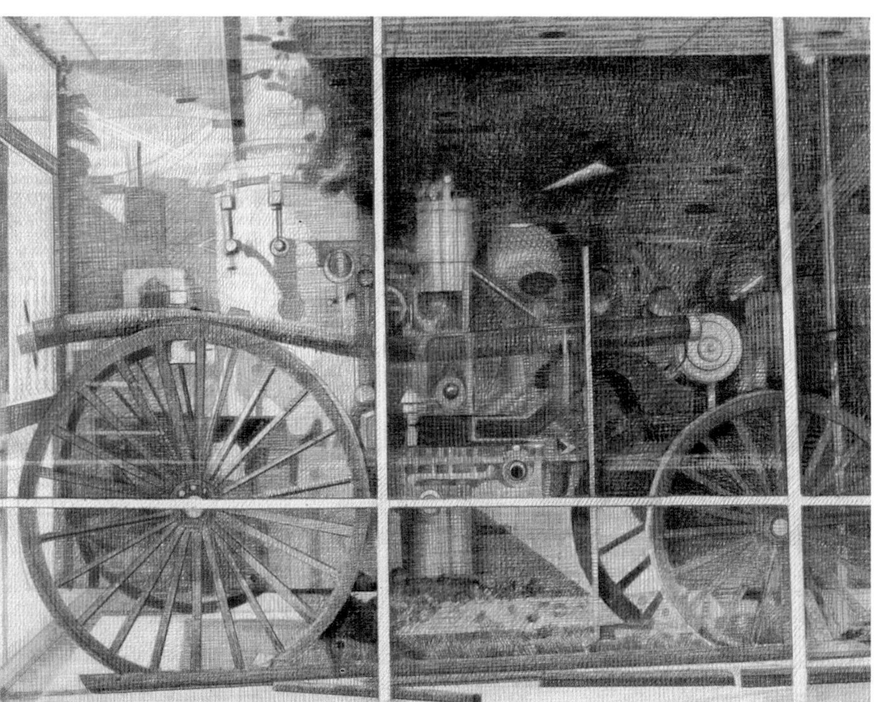

2

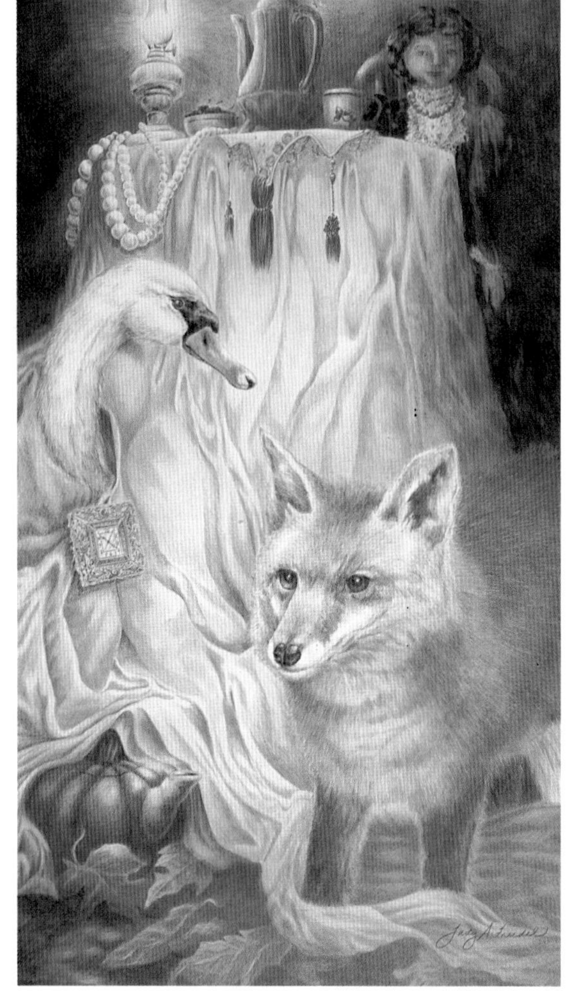

3

Marchel Reed

1 *School Days*
19 x 19" (482 x 482 mm)

Judy A. Freidel

2 *Invited Guests*
21 x 12" (533 x 305 mm)
Arches Hot Press 140 lb. Water Color Paper

Lee Sims

3 *Green Street Fire Engine*
11 x 15" (279 x 381 mm)
Strathmore Bristol Plate Finish

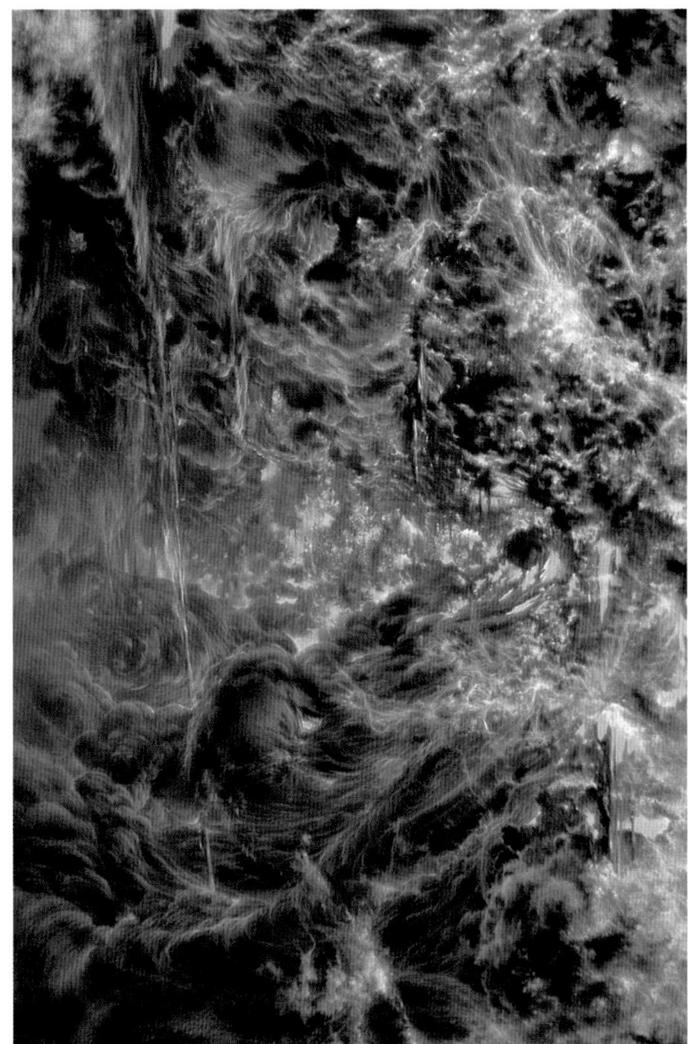

1

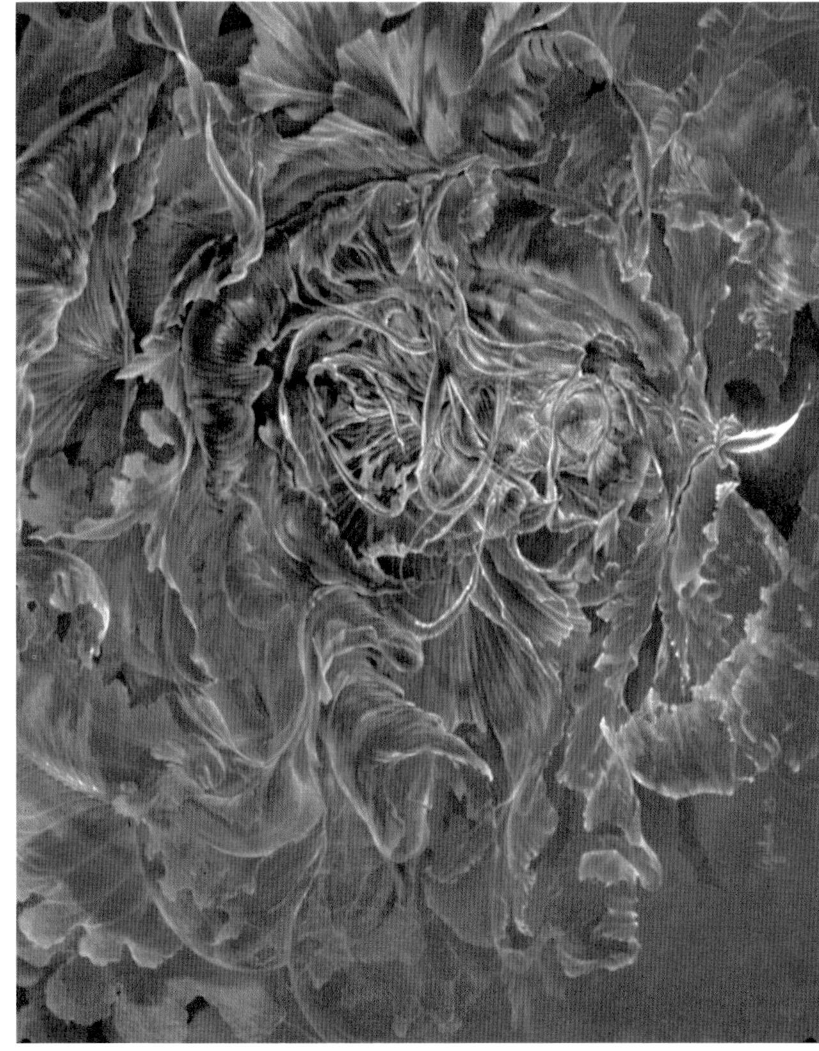

2

Charles Aquilina

1 *Untitled*
60 x 80" (1,524 x 2,032 mm)
Strathmore Board

2 *Mnajdra*
40 x 60" (1,016 x 1,524 mm)
Strathmore Board

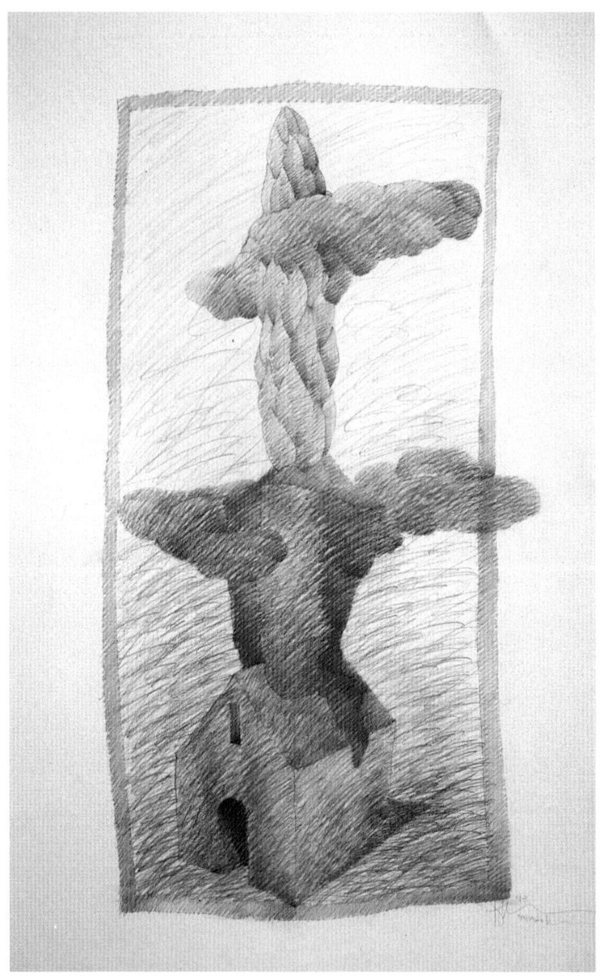

1

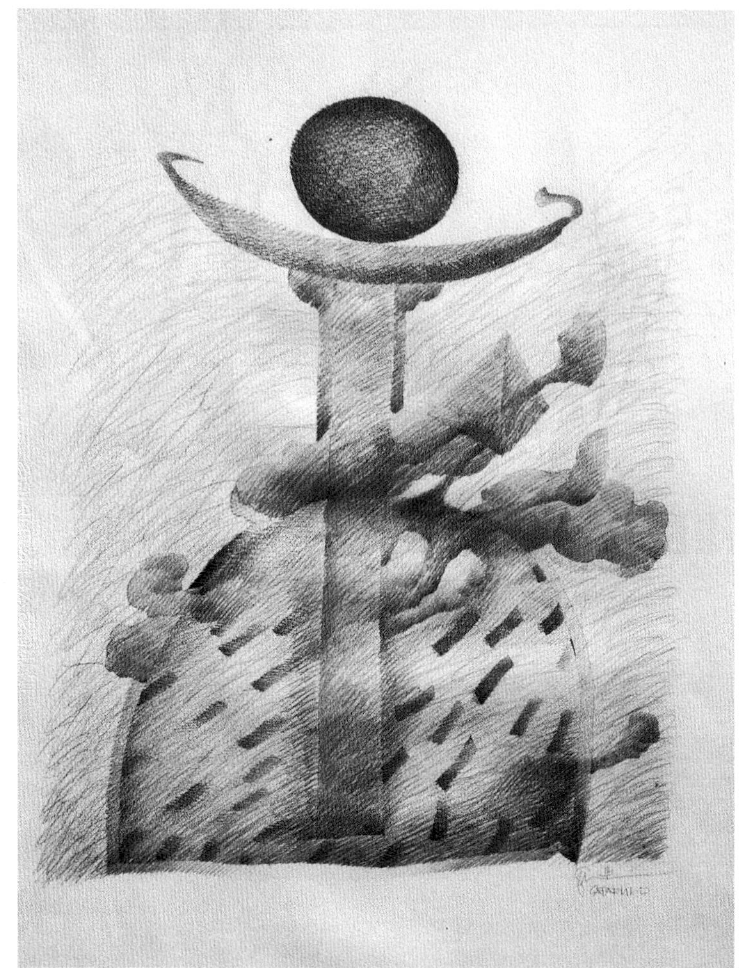

2

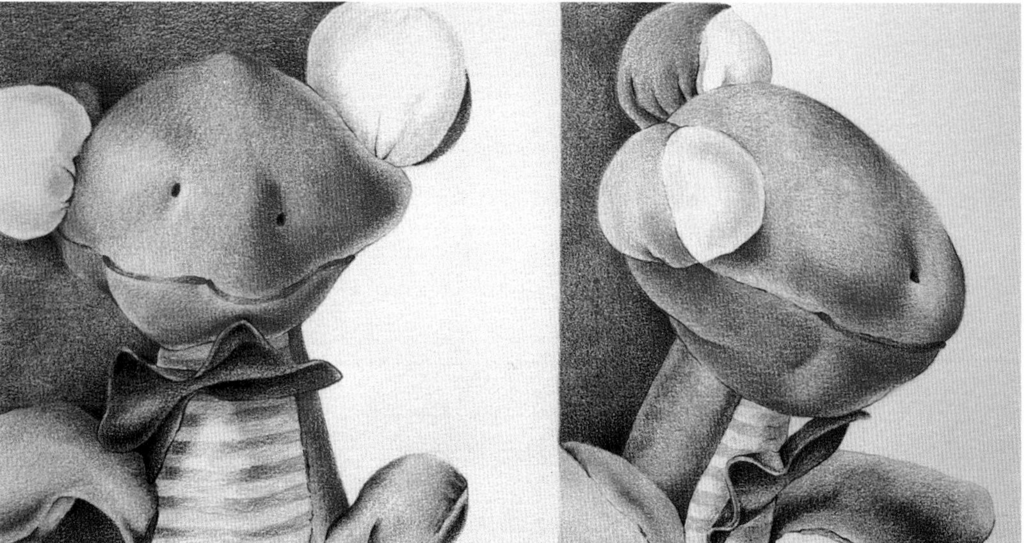

3

Ralph D. Caparulo

1 *Ascending Asparagus*
30 x 22" (762 x 559 mm)
100% Rag 4-ply Drawing Paper
Technique: Cross Hatching

2 *Amenite's Midnight Journey*
22 x 30" (559 x 762 mm)
100% Rag 4-ply Drawing Paper
Technique: Cross Hatching

Susan Field

3 *Mug Shot*
13 x 18" (330 x 4157 mm)
Rising Museum Board

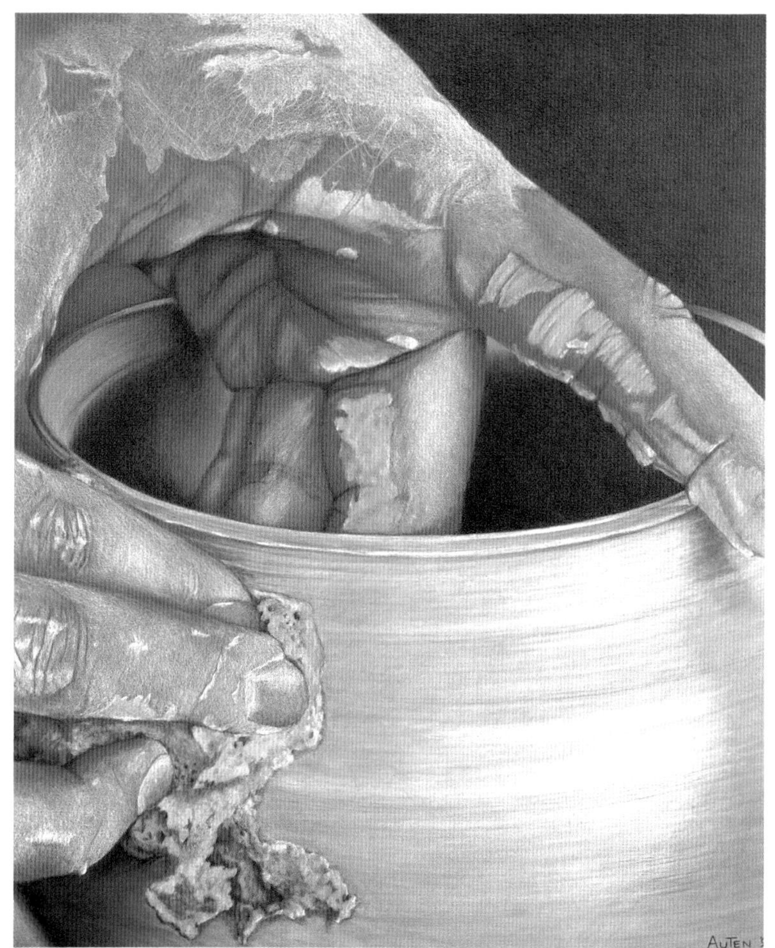

1

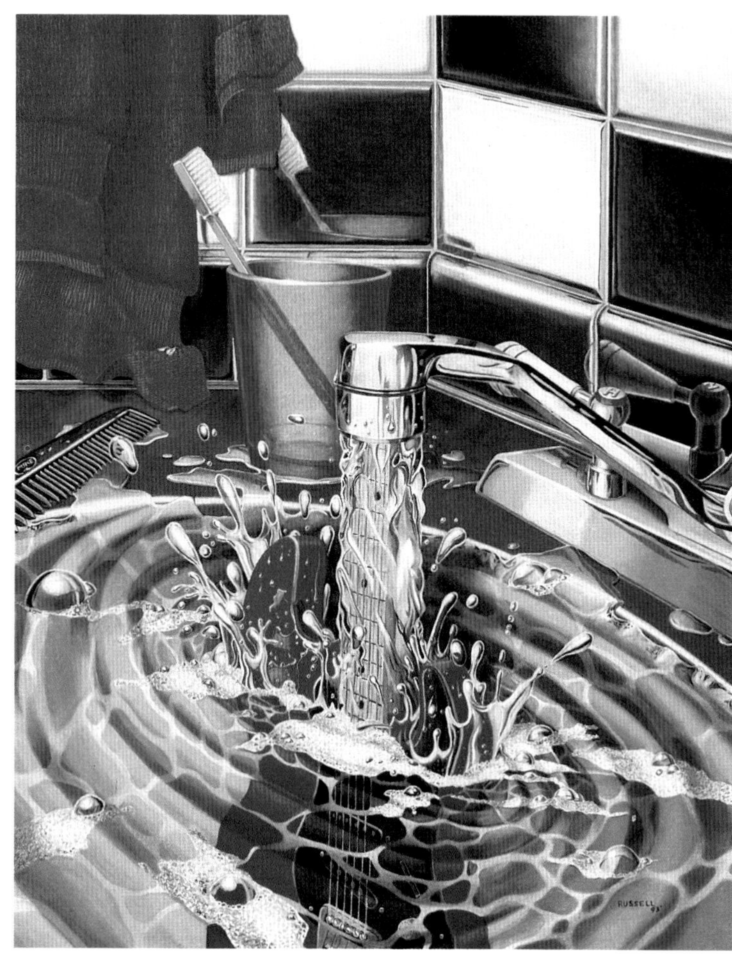

2

Bonnie Auten

1 *Hands of the Potter I*
21 x 18" (533 x 457 mm)

Mike Russell

2 *Bathroom Splash*
12 x 15" (304 x 380 mm)

Jane Shibata

3 *No Parking n L.A.*
10 x 26" (248 x 660 mm)
Strathmore Museum Board
Technique: Burnishing

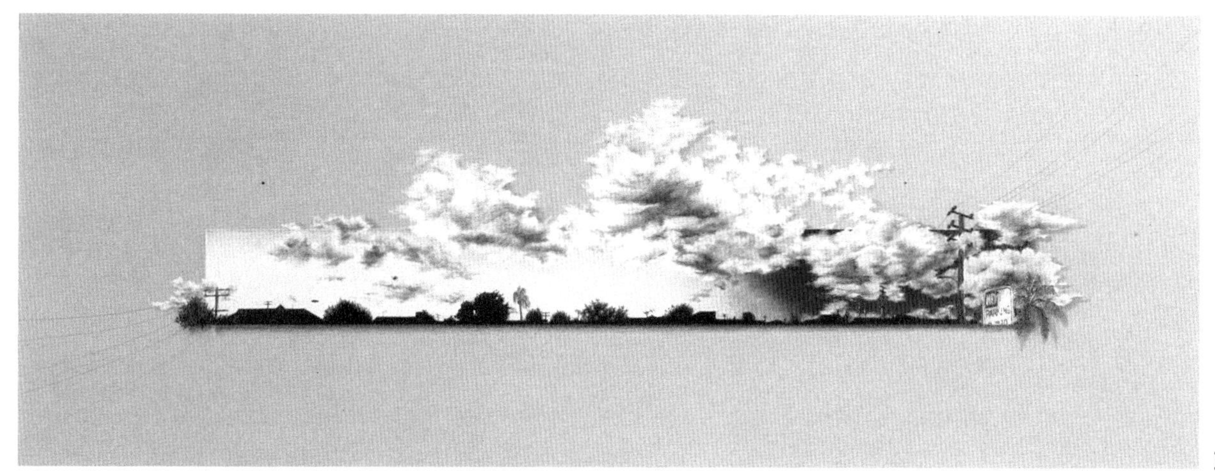
3

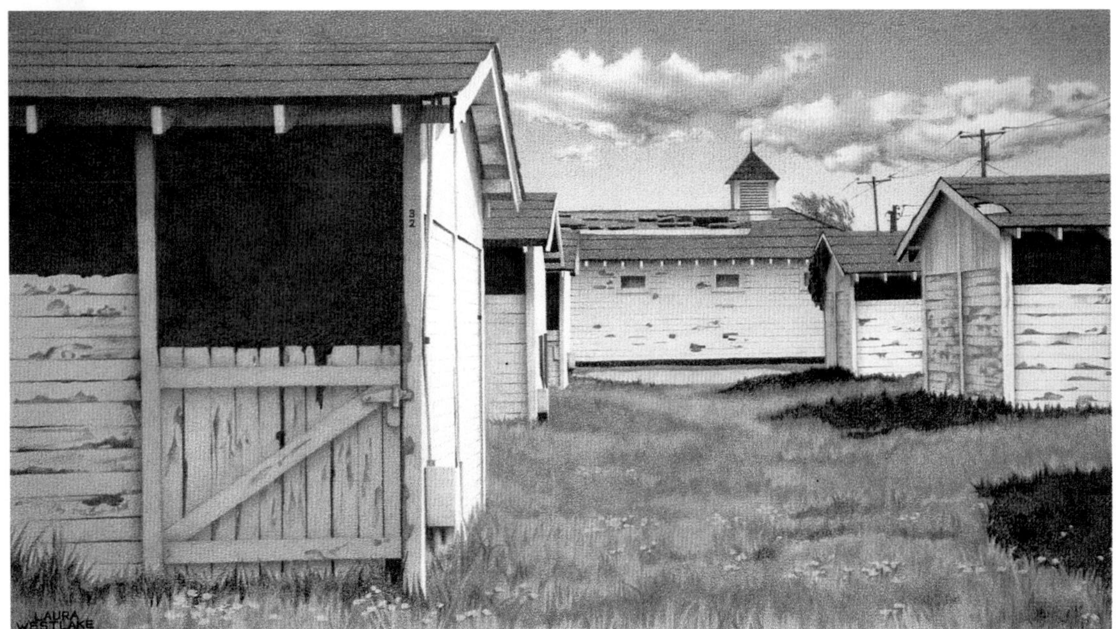

1

Laura Westlake

1 *Every Summer Day - 1993*
12 x 22" (292 x 559 mm)
Strathmore100% Rag Bristol Vellum Finish

2 *The Old Clammer's House - 1992*
17 x 22" (419 x 559 mm)
Strathmore 100% Rag Bristol Vellum Finish

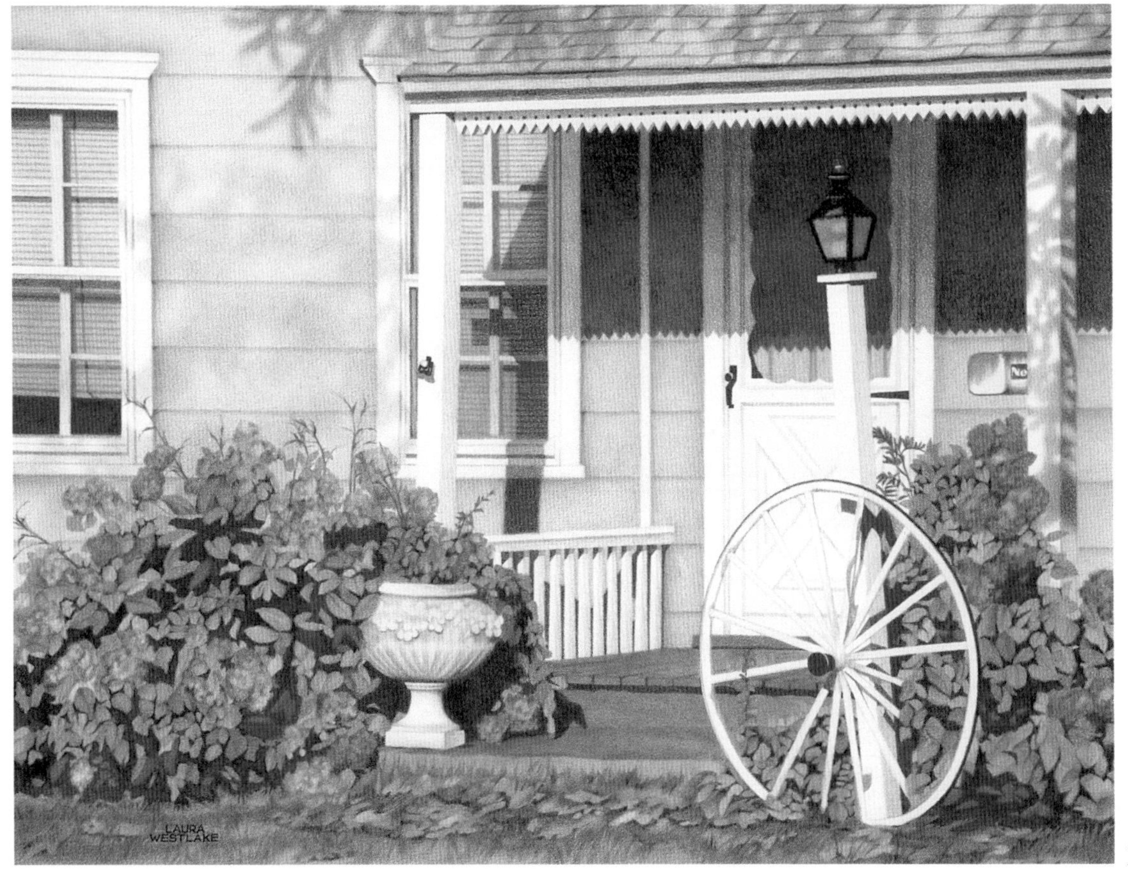

2

Judy McDonald

1 *Red Shoes*
31 x 24" (787 x 610 mm)
Acid Free Rising Stonehenge Paper

June R. Conway

2 *Dora Beth*
10 x 7" (254 x 178 mm)
Arches Print Making Paper

Bruce S. Garrabrandt

3 *Yesterday's Playmates*
8 x 10" (203 x 254)
Strathmore 100% Cotton 2-ply Paper

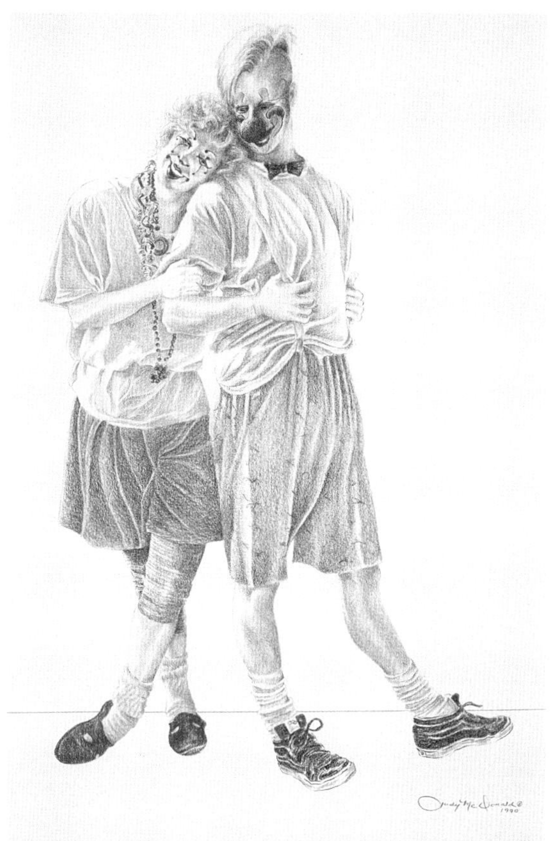

1

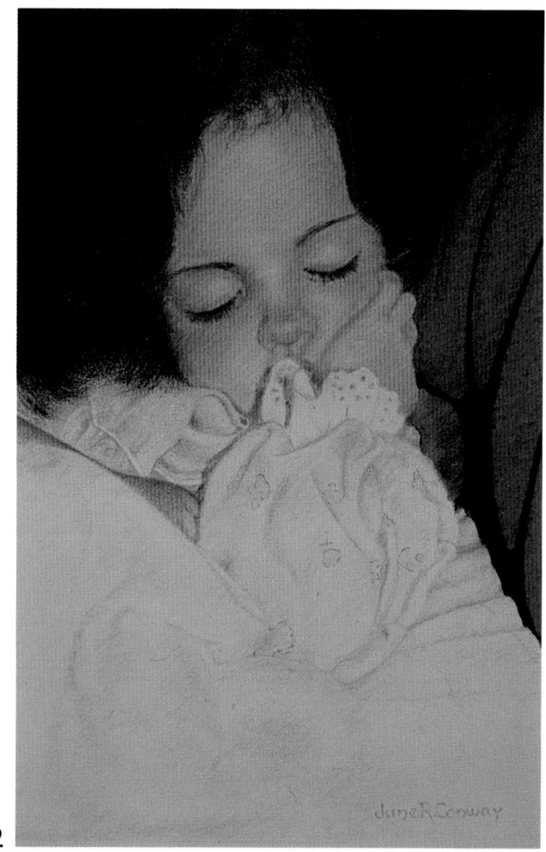

2

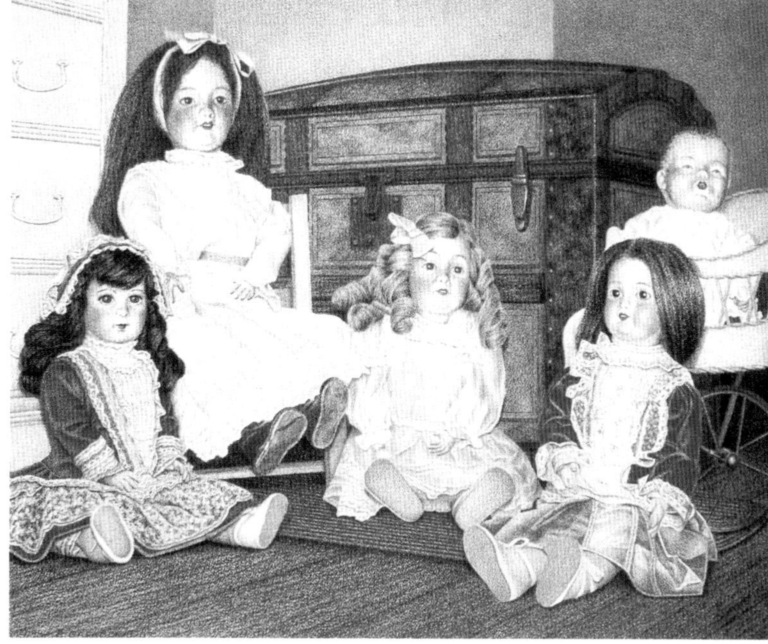

3

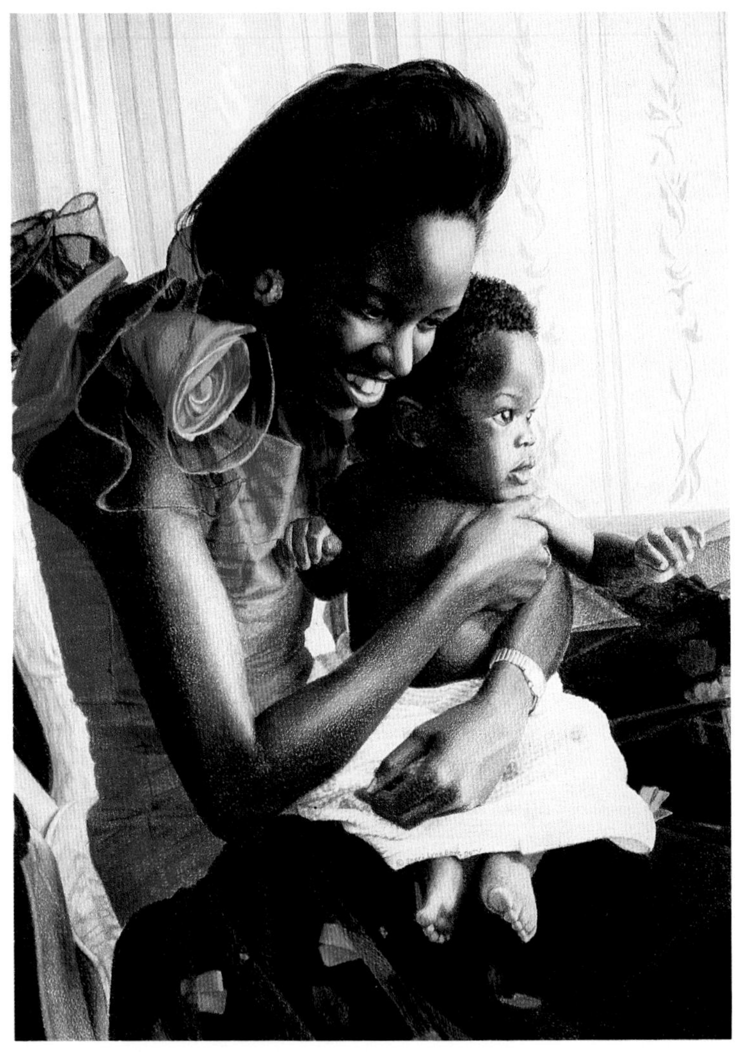

1

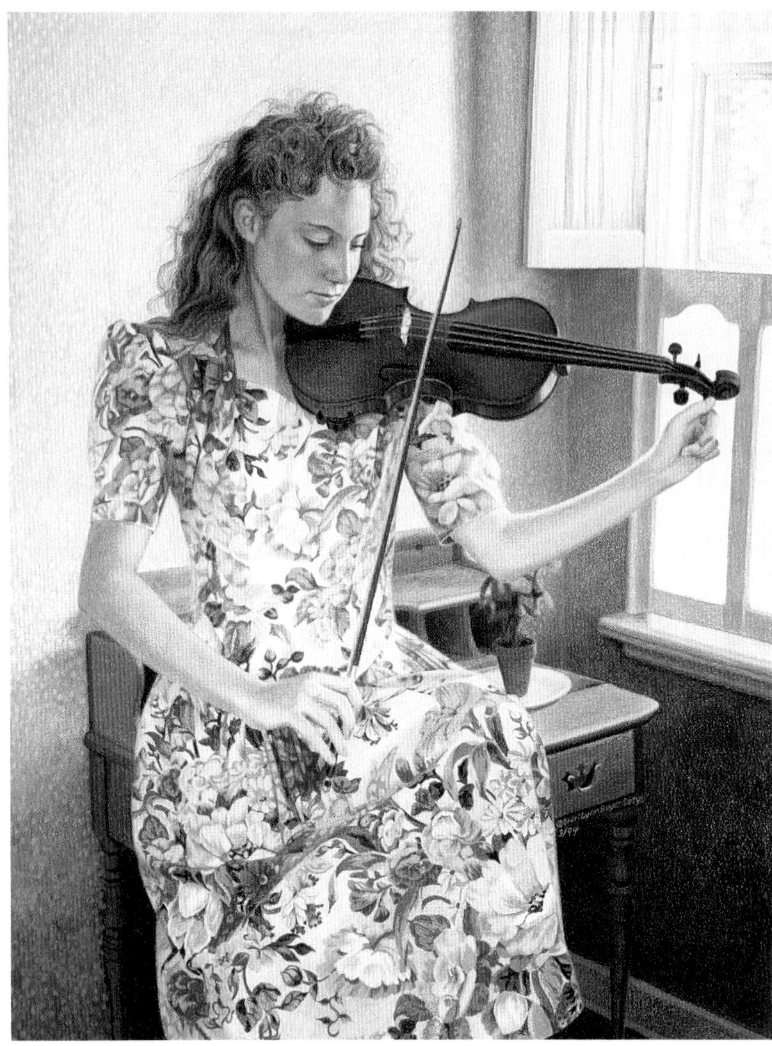

2

Sheri Lynn Boyer Doty

1 *Madonna of Zaire*
19 x 15" (483 x 368 mm)
100% Cotton Rag 4-ply Bristol, Medium Texture
Technique: Colored Pencil, Colorless Blender Burnishing

2 *The Tuning*
15 x 19" (368 x 483 mm)
100% Cotton Rag 4-ply Bristol, Medium Texture
Technique: Colored Pencil, Colorless Blender Burnishing

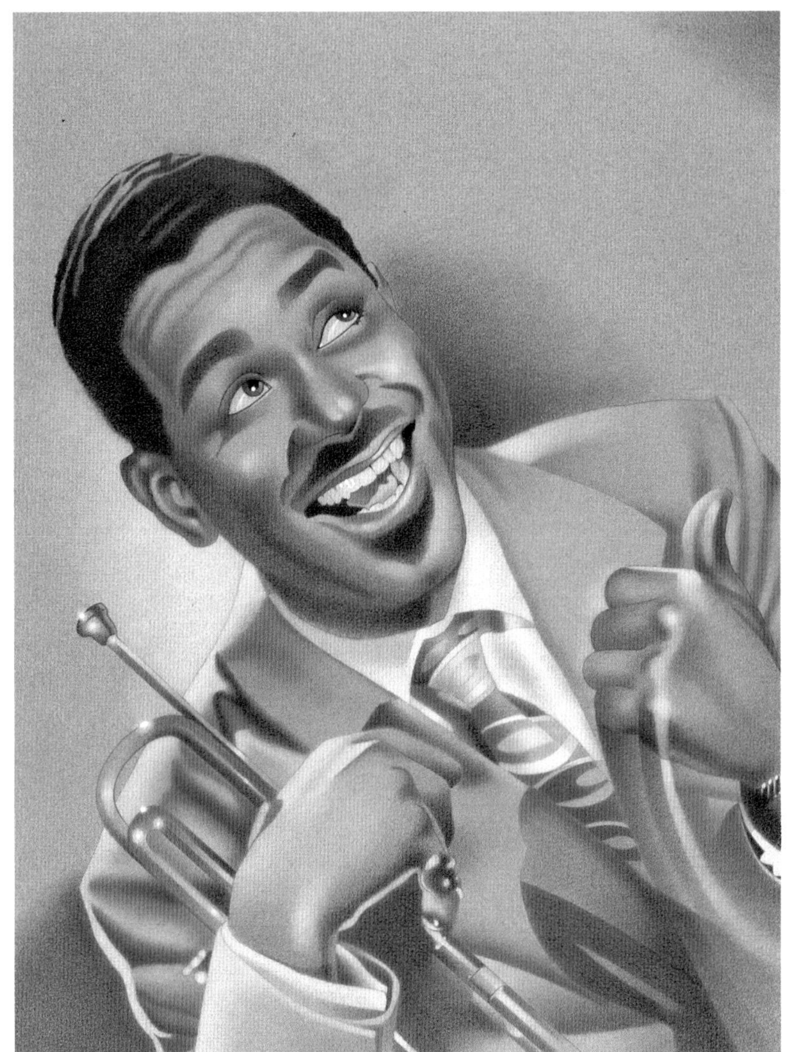

1

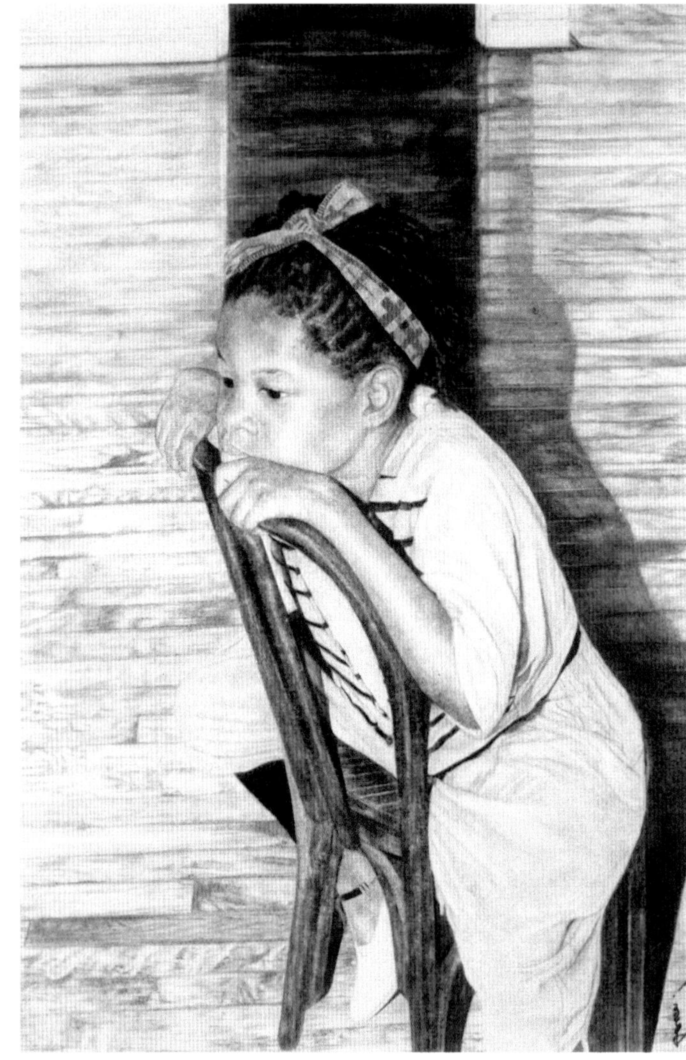

2

Randy McCafferty

1 *I'm Dizzy*
24 x 20" (610 x 508 mm)
Canson Pastel Paper

Dawn Rolland

2 *Nia*
14 x 11" (356 x 279 mm)
Hot Press Bainbridge Board

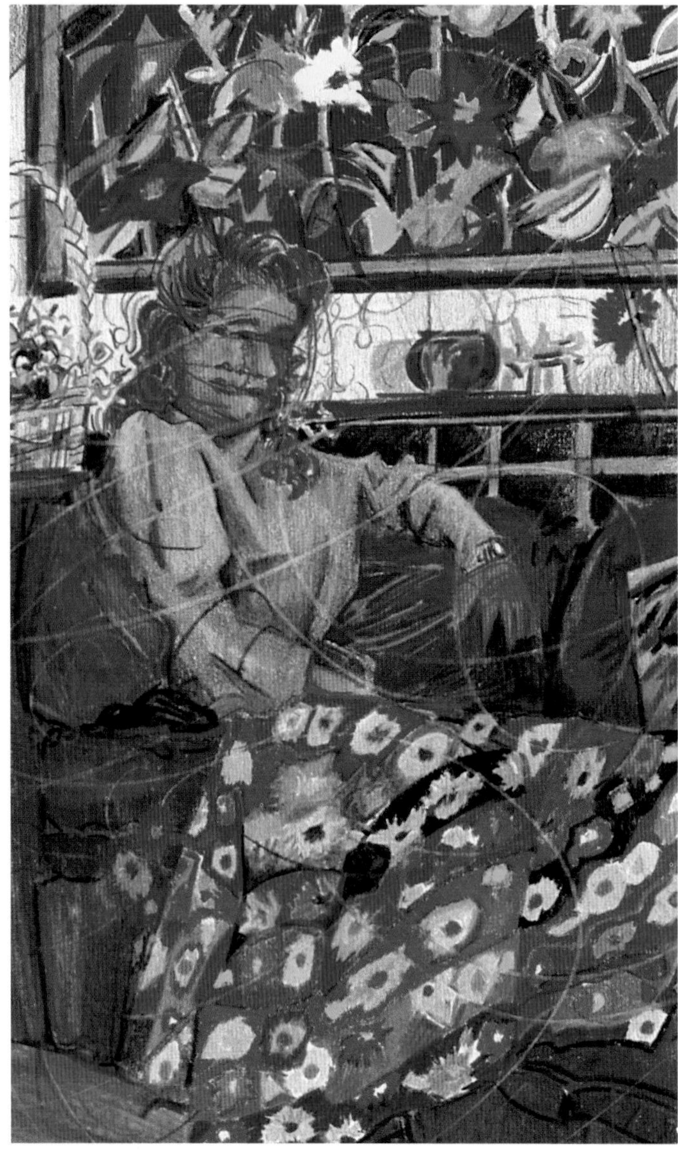

1

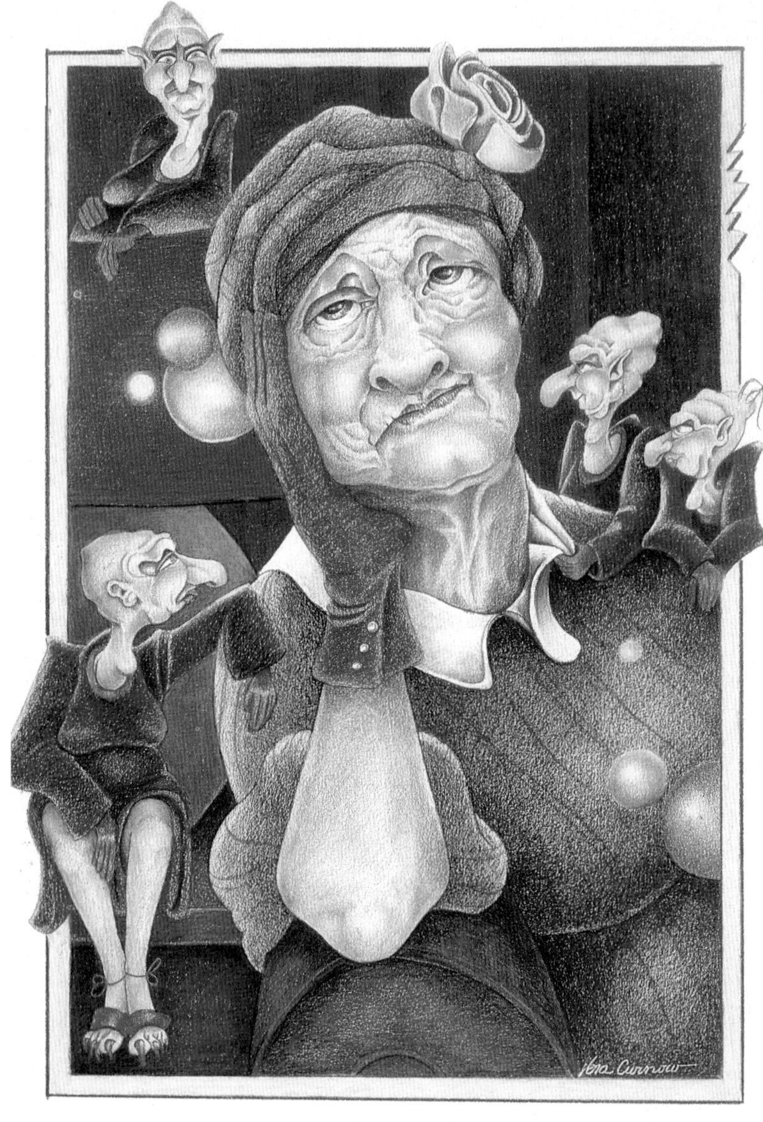

2

Judith Surowiec

1 *The Redhead*
9 x 6" (222 x 140 mm)
Acid Free Mat Board

Vera Curnow

2 *Dixie Feels A Little Remorse*
15 x 10" (381 x 254 mm)
100% Rag Cold Press Illustration Board
Technique: Burnishing, Impressed Line

Creative Palettes for Non-Traditional Effects

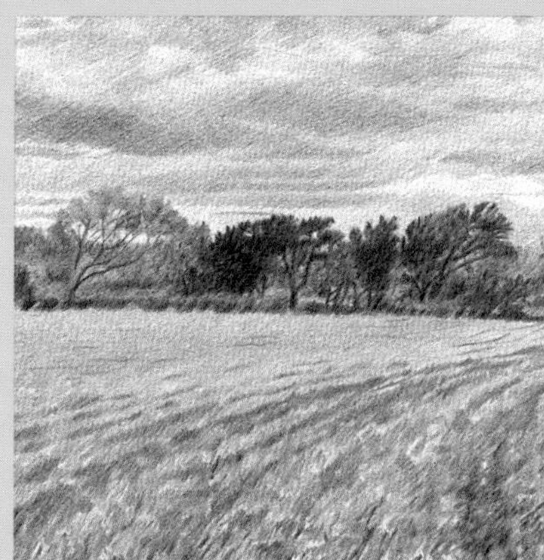

Three Art Sticks: No Limits

Mike Pease

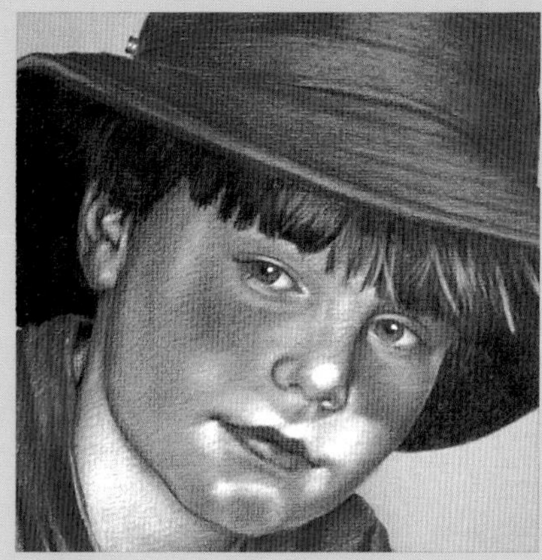

Face Value: Working In the Shadows

Bernard Poulin

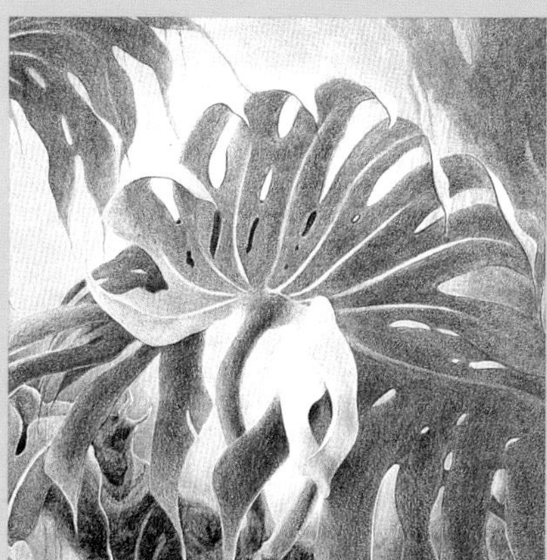

Eat Your Greens: Lush Flora

Dyanne Locati

The student looking at a landscape will paint green and blue. An artist will include the goldenrod and ultramarine that is also there. But a creative artist, seeing with the mind's eye, will *add* the fuchsia and turquoise that mother nature has forgotten.

Because of the very nature of this medium, the application of color to our work can never be an afterthought. We don't pick up a pencil after all; we choose a color. Add to this the fact that our painting surface is the palette. This is where colored pencil artists develop hue, value and saturation one stroke at a time. It's no wonder then, since colored pencil is less forgiving than most media, that many new artists use a literal approach to building colors – rarely venturing much beyond the subject's local color and mixing the same combinations until they are a familiar formula.

If you think a spin of the color wheel will produce nothing new, just consider the infinite variety of music in the world and the fact that all the musicians use the same twelve notes to create it. Visual artists must also work with the same colors. But we can make them distinctively our own by using them in a different order, in new proportions, and on another subject. Working with three colors or fifty, the artists in this section demonstrate that it's not the size of the palette that makes us creative. It is the artistic ability to interpret and explore the infinite combinations, and to have the conviction to express in colors what we see, think, and feel.

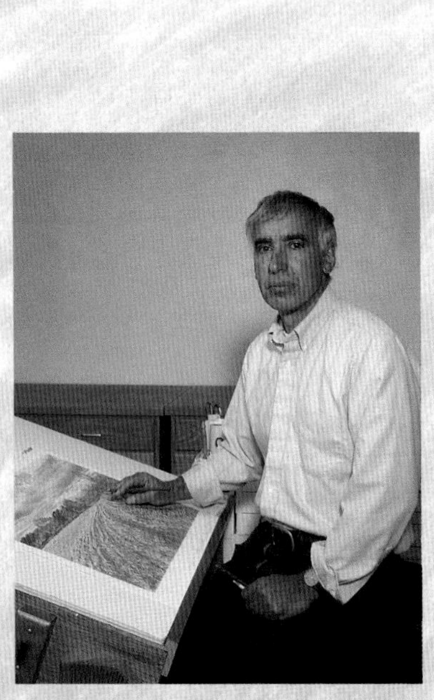

Mike Pease

San Francisco native Mike Pease studied architecture at the University of California-Berkeley and worked as an architect until 1980. He initially shunned art as a career, finding public school instruction "discouraging," despite the encouragement of his family, which boasted several artists. Mike's work in colored pencil, watercolor and other media has been widely exhibited; it has also been featured in several publications and in private and public collections throughout the United States and abroad. His colored pencil paintings and prints are represented by several galleries. Mike teaches workshops on freehand drawing and his own three-color process colored pencil technique.

CHAPTER 5

Three Art Sticks: No Limits

Mike Pease easily made the shift from practitioner and teacher of architecture to full-time, professional artist. While once he created physical harmony between man and nature, now he artistically balances the landscape's complexities on paper. Through the use of light and form, each of his scenic colored pencil paintings projects a different mood. Color plays a dominant role in the work, it is never an afterthought. Mike's color choices are always deliberate – and always the same. Although there is an overwhelming spectrum of colors available in today's pencils, he works with only three: blue, magenta, and yellow. The sequence seldom varies. What does vary is the myriad of options this limited palette can give. Printers use these three primary colors to process full color images. Just by laying the right amount of each color, one over the other, and letting the right amount of white paper show through, you can create virtually any palette. As layers are added and colors take form, Mike prefers to keep his pencil strokes visible. This gives a vibrancy to his work. Letting the contrasting and complementary color strokes read through also helps eliminate flat, muddy areas. The components of hue, value, and saturation are then optically blended and a color unity emerges. This is an extremely intimate approach to working with color. By controlling the gradations and proportions in this three-color procedure, you learn to interpret each color's relationship to the whole. In the process, you also become a better observer capable of seeing the color nuances in any subject.

GETTING STARTED

A non-yellowing, 2-ply white museum board is used as the surface. Its smooth finish lets you see the texture of the pencil stroke, not texture of the paper. Working with reference slides taken during field trips, Mike projects the image directly onto the drawing surface and transfers it with a blue pencil. MATERIALS: Soft wax-based colored pencils, Frisket Film for lifting color from the paper, mat knife to taper the wood casing and expose the full width of the pencil's lead. No spray fixatives are used when the work is completed.

PALETTE

True blue, magenta, yellow.

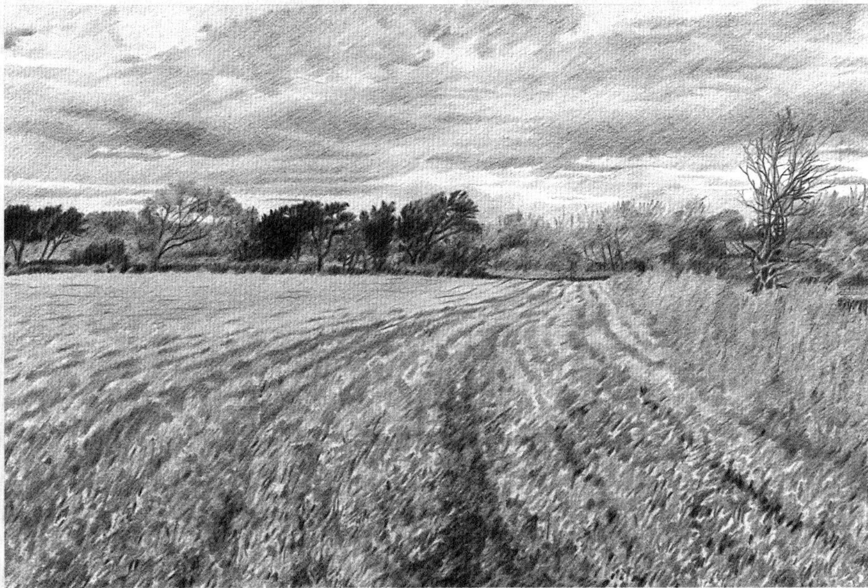

October Fields, Denmark
16 x 24" (406 x 610 mm)

1 Using the blue pencil, the subject is drawn directly over a projected slide image. Instead of outlining the shapes, each area is defined with firmly placed diagonal strokes. The lightest areas of the image are left white – this includes the highlights in the grass. Blue is applied with varying degrees of pressure to create lights and darks. Working with a blunt pencil lead, the strokes are intentionally kept visible. This first blue undercoat is aimed at capturing the blue components that will be part of the finished work. Mike is careful not to overwork this stage. Except for corrections, this and all subsequent colors are applied in one layer.

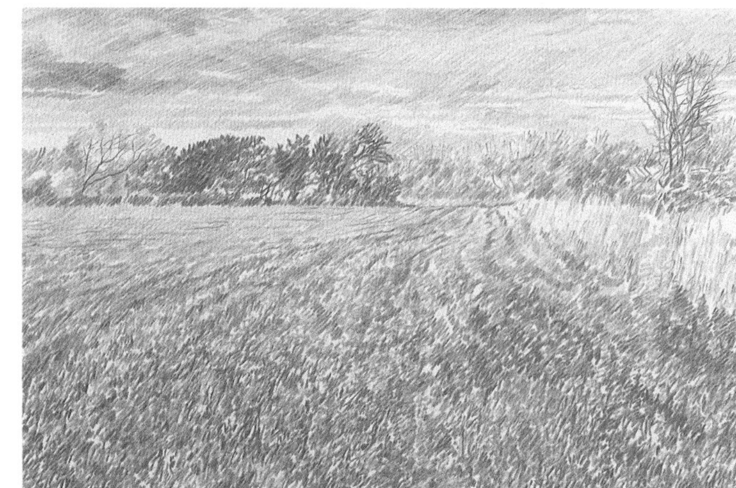

2 Adjustments are made to the blue layer to build stronger contrast and definition. The foreground furloughs are deepened to emphasize perspective. Shadowed areas are darkened. Tree trunks are added to the far left and the tree to the right is given form. In this stage, editing decisions are made and details are clarified; it is the most time-consuming part of the work.

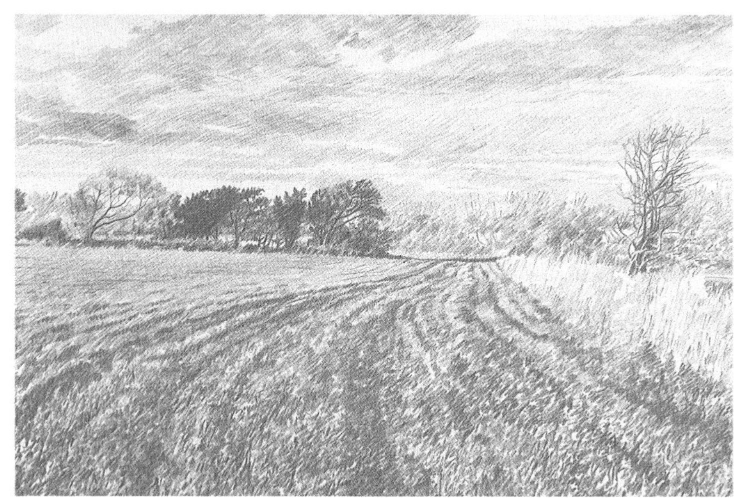

3 A layer of magenta is added to three areas – the first row of trees, the gnarled tree at the right, and the foreground field. (The right foreground was left undone for comparison.) With the blues and reds now combined, the final value structure is essentially determined. At this stage it's also easier to see what the final hues will be and to make adjustments: colors that lean toward blue will end up blue or green; reds will stay red or become orange; purples will become dark yellow, grays, or remain purple; whites will remain white or become yellow.

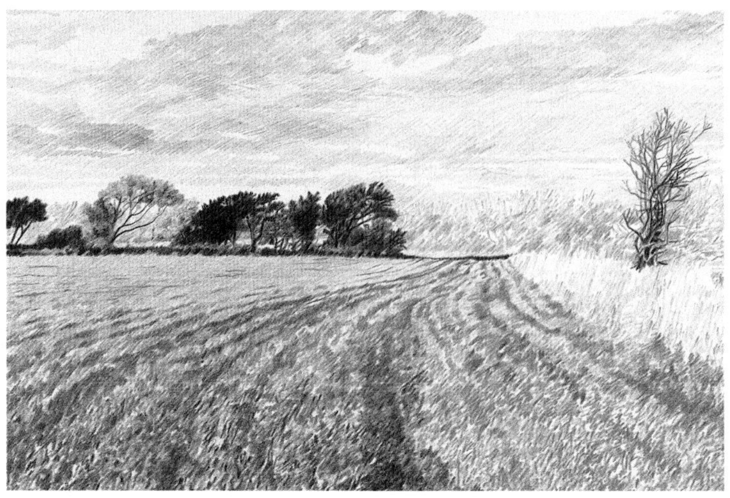

4 Except for the tall grasses on the right, all of the magenta is added. A layer of yellow is applied to the trees and grasses on the left – once again leaving the right side undone for comparison. Mike continues to make minor color corrections to keep the underlying blues and reds in balance.

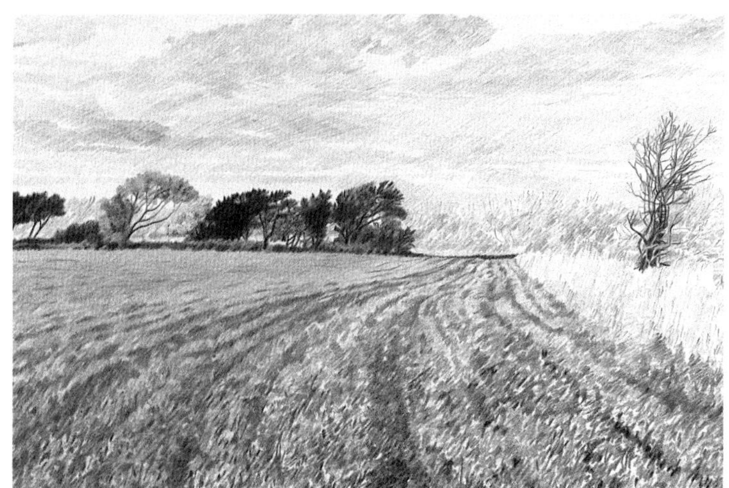

5 Here the yellow layer is completed. The blue is corrected in the sky and background. A row of tall grasses on the right shows three stages of completion for comparison: the extreme right is just a blue layer, the middle is blue with a layer of red added, and the last segment has all three color layers.

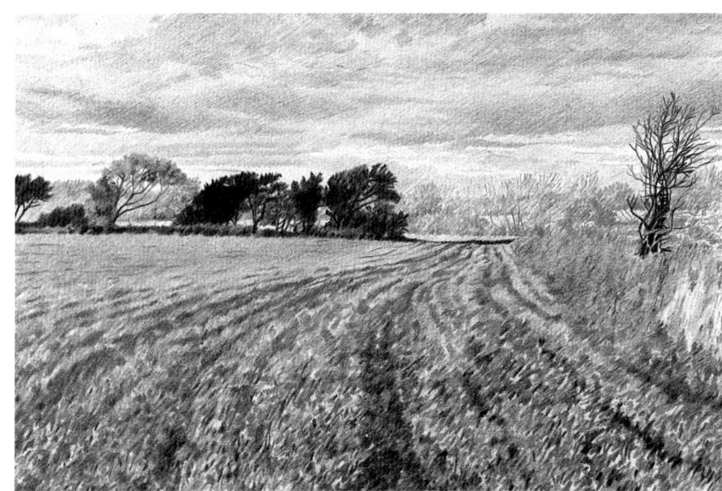

6 Mike finishes adding the colors to the incomplete areas and makes minor adjustments to areas completed earlier. After all the layers are in place, the yellows almost always need strengthening. Now finished, the jeweled tones in *October Fields, Denmark* are an excellent example of what can be accomplished with a limited palette of three colors.

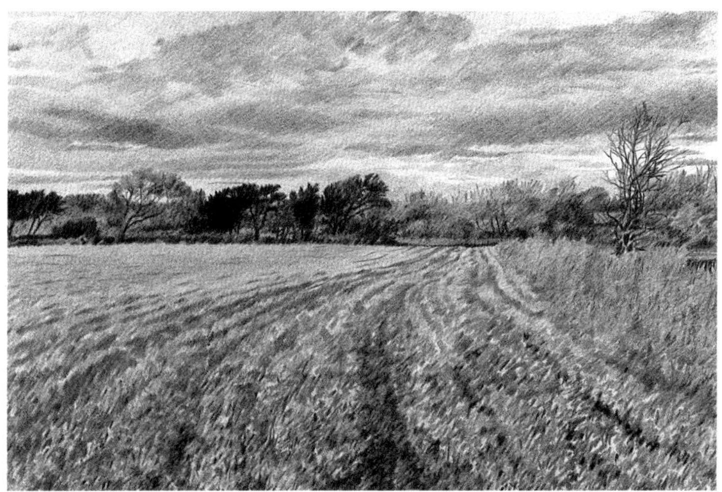

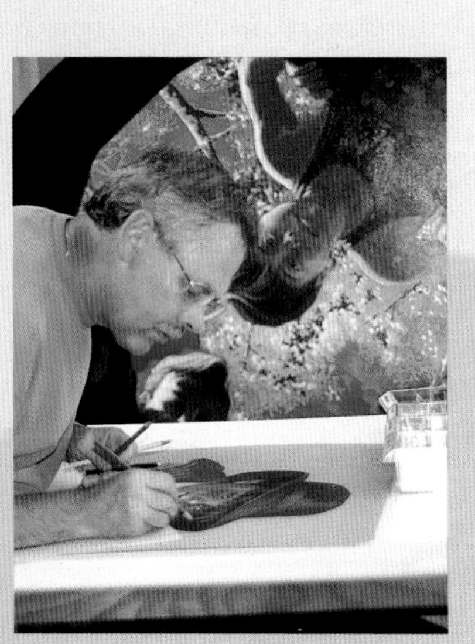

Bernard Poulin

Canadian Bernard Aime Poulin is best known as a portrait artist whose drawings and paintings are displayed in collections throughout the world. In recent years, he has gained a reputation for work in other media, most notably bronze sculpture, oil murals, and mixed media. Primarily a self-taught artist, Bernard shares his talent and knowledge through lectures, articles and workshops. He is the author of six colored pencil books, the most recent of which is *The Complete Book of Colored Pencil*. In 1980, the Hadassah-Wizo Organization of Canada honored Bernard by establishing two art scholarships in his name.

CHAPTER 6

Face Value: Working In the Shadows

Any competent draftsman can draw a smile. An accomplished artist, however, can portray happiness. While we need technical skills to duplicate a subject, it's the human qualities we bring to our work that help us interpret it. In looking at Bernard Poulin's colored pencil portraits, it's not the exact likeness of the model's features that first catches our eye. That comes later. What predominates is his ability to capture the subtle essence of a person. Attitudes and emotions – even when not blatantly expressed – are carefully unveiled. In Bernard's portrait of a young girl, the child's innate gentleness is made as obvious as her outward determination. These very human contradictions are revealed through a delicate balance of flow and tension. In "Chris Sporting My Tillie" Bernard first applies a monochromatic layer of color, called a grisaille, over the established shadow areas. This sets the mood. He then develops interest and variety through the use of contrasting values, strokes and colors. Heavy pressure is used in dark areas; areas with the strongest highlights are left untouched. Bold and visible strokes show fabric texture, while soft tonal gradations render facial features. Warm colors are applied to cool ones for added depth. By selectively omitting spots of color to let the paper show through, Bernard integrates subject and drawing surface for a more believable presentation. He also establishes a natural color flow by adding the same local color to both the shadowed and highlighted areas. Shadows are never flat or monochromatic. Bernard approaches these dark values as "a construction of colors rather than an application of a single color." Working from dark to light, he gradually builds richness and depth to give the shadows realistic dimension. Everything from the initial pose and paper surface to the final pencil stroke influences Bernard's direction. Beyond the technical skills used to render the image, we see a portrait that was executed with compassion, sensitivity and, most of all, respect for the subject.

GETTING STARTED

Working from a live model, and later from slides, Bernard sketches the subject with a sienna brown pencil onto jade-green tinted Strathmore charcoal paper. The smooth finish allows for soft color passages, but has enough "tooth" to hold the color. MATERIALS: Soft, wax-based pencils, art sticks (used in large dark areas), plastic eraser, electric and standard crank pencil sharpeners. Workable fixative is applied on the finished work.

PALETTE

HAT: indigo blue, ultramarine, violet blue. SHIRT: indigo blue, ultramarine. SKIN: indigo blue, light peach, tuscan red, yellowed orange, orange, violet, purple, lime, yellow ochre, blue violet, lilac, pumpkin. HAIR: sienna brown, indigo blue, tuscan red. EYES: indigo blue, tuscan red, slate gray, white.

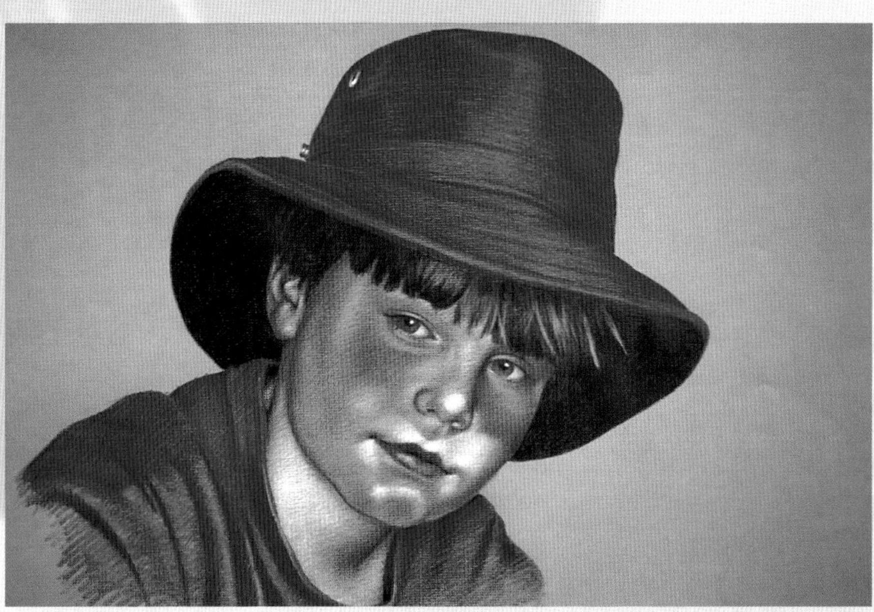

Chris Sporting My Tillie
16 x 20" (406 x 507 mm)

1 A line drawing of the subject, with outlines defining the light and shadow areas,is done with a sienna brown pencil. The mid- tone and dark values are established with indigo blue while the brightest highlights are left untouched. Varying pressure is used and diagonal hatch strokes are left visible. An indigo blue art stick saves time in densely coloring the darkest area of the hat. This monochromatic undercoat establishes the values and sets the mood of the painting. The brighest highlights are now covered with light peach.

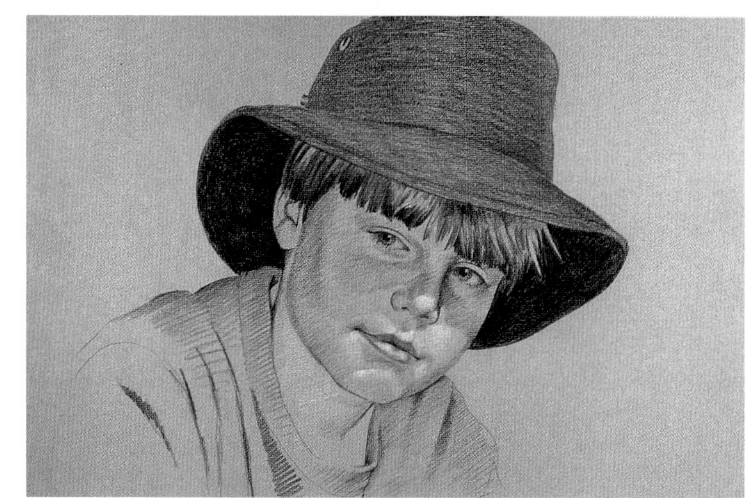

2 Flesh tones in the shadows are warmed with heavy to light applications of tuscan red. Yellow-orange lightly applied over all of the skin makes it glow and provides a natural color balance between the light and shaded areas. The shadow areas of the hat and hair are deepened with a heavy application of tuscan red.

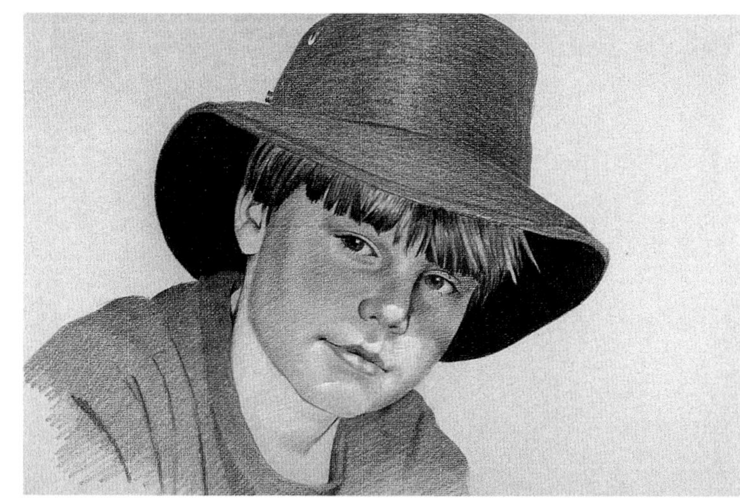

3 The shirt is saturated in ultramarine with heavy cross-hatching. In this vignette portrait, the strokes are gradually feathered at the edges as the color flows away from the center of interest. The outside of the hat is heavily covered with violet blue which is then blended with indigo blue to give it a dimensional roundness. The hair is a combination of sienna brown, indigo blue, and tuscan red layers. A light layer of orange is added to the shaded skin area, but not to the highlight areas or the eyes.

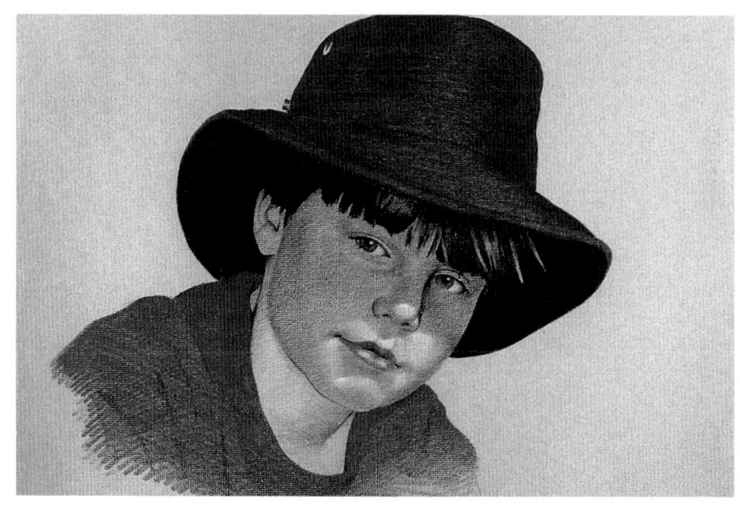

4 A non-traditional palette for skin tones models the face while keeping the shadow area bright and three-dimensional. Violet causes the darkest shadows to recede and makes them luminous. Orange heightens the cheeks, ear lobe, chin and eyelids, making them glow. Purple makes the shadow between ear and chin recede, and accents the lower eyelid folds, eyelashes, and the dark area between the left cheek and nose. Lime softens the left cheek; yellow ochre softens the highlights. Blue violet, lilac, and pumpkin are used for accents. Note the colors used in this stage alone.

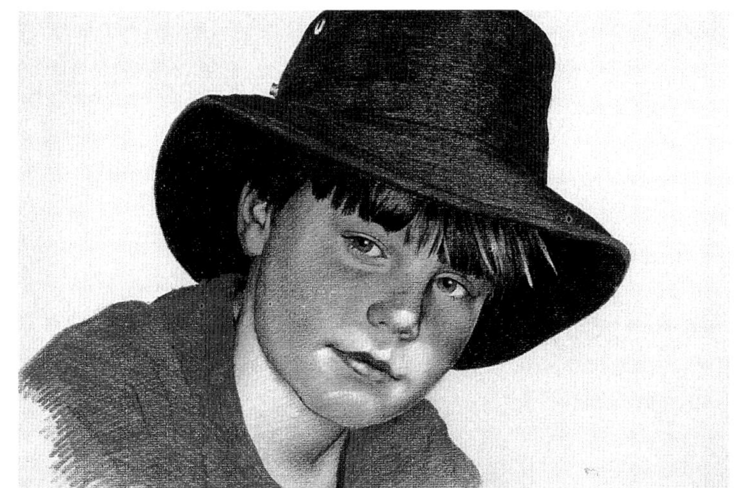

5 The deepest shadows of the shirt are redefined with indigo blue. The heavy pressure and the coarse, cross-hatched strokes give the fabric a thick, woven appearance – rather than the look of thin cotton. The shirt's texture is a nice juxtaposition to the smoothness of the face. Heavy applications of light blue highlights on the shirt direct the viewers gaze back to the subject's face. The highlights on the canvas hat, done in slate blue, make the dome of the hat recede from the brim and separate the brim from the darkness of the hair.

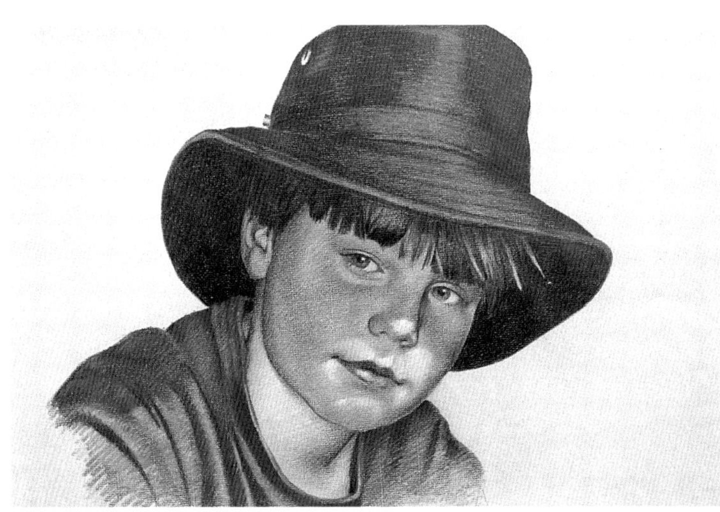

6 Blue is now added to the jawline, chin, and nose, to simulate the reflected blue tint of the shirt. Final adjustments are made to further define form and balance light. This painting is an exciting mix of warm, cool, and high key colors that energizes the flesh tones beyond mere beige. The delicately blended gradations eliminate any color clashes and harsh transitions. Bernard's painting of *Chris Sporting My Tillie* is finished with a white highlight that puts a sparkle in his subject's eyes.

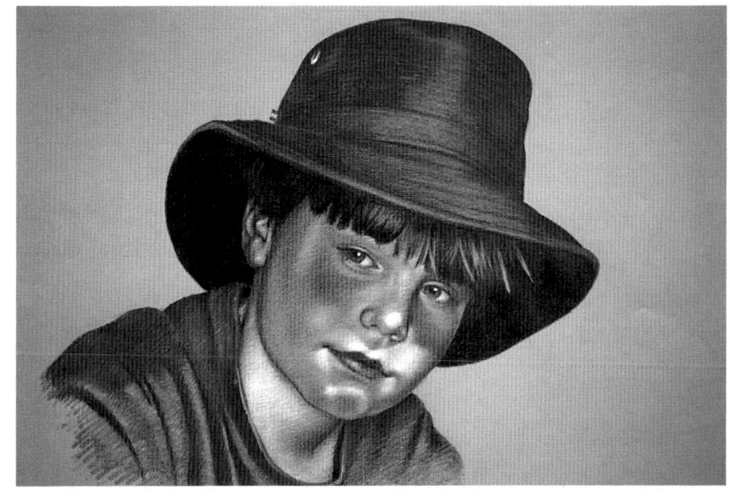

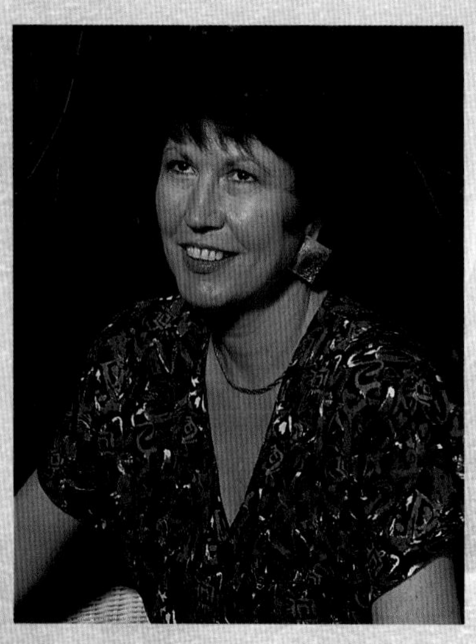

Dyanne Locati

Dyanne Locati finds the business side of art just as exciting and rewarding as the process of creating it. The owner of Locati Creative Art Center in Gladstone, Oregon, she is a professional artist and a workshop instructor who also juries and organizes exhibitions. Her work has appeared in juried exhibitions and gallery invitational shows. It is in public and private collections and is in three publications including The Best of Colored Pencil book. Dyanne is the Executive Vice President of the Colored Pencil Society of America serving on its governing board.

CHAPTER 7

Eat Your Greens: Lush Flora

Imagine this: no preliminary sketches, color studies or projected slides. Without even a preconceived composition, Dyanne Locati faces the blank, white paper and simply begins. Even the most experienced colored pencil artist might cringe at this approach. Dyanne, however, thrives on it."If I plan the complete drawing," she explains,"I feel my creativity is suppressed. That's also why I don't predetermine colors. The mind has a tendency to say, 'leaves are green.' That thought process can stifle the ability to explore color – making your work predictable."

While her approach is spontaneous, it is not random. Her first step is to establish the focal point. Working with organic shapes, she then carefully orchestrates their direction and rhythm to lead the viewer through the work. Abstract patterns, intentionally created by the negative shapes, are given as much importance as the subject. Color comes next. Delicious limes and fuchias bordered by goldenrod in a nest of cerulean blue. Crisp, clear, and unconventional. Dyanne avoids a muddy palette by not mixing warm and cool colors. Rather than layering her colors, she keeps their intensity by placing them next to each other. She also avoids monochromatic monotony by adding pure "hits" of unexpected color within a layer. To do this, she lifts patches of color with a kneaded eraser, then adds a contrasting hue. One leaf may consist of 21 different colors. Her strokes, while aggressive and deliberate – "get color on the paper!" – are done with a firm, not heavy, pressure. She applies the same aggressive stokes in both light and dark areas. This creates areas of light that are filled with substantial color; as opposed to areas of light defined by weak, thin, color strokes. There are no insipid colors in Dyanne's work. We are plunged into a great wash of exploding hues that are at once stimulating and soothing. There is no visual discord. Every hue is expertly woven as Dyanne's visionary nature combines abstraction with reality to create an illusion.

GETTING STARTED

Lightly drawing shapes with a number 2 graphite pencil, Dyanne works directly on four-ply Strathmore Museum Board. This surface takes color well and stands up to lifting and erasing. Dyanne has been known to create an entire painting using one leaf as a reference. MATERIALS: Soft, wax-based colored pencils, Pink Pearl and kneaded erasers, electric and hand-held sharpeners. The finished work is lightly sprayed with four coats of matte fixative.

PALETTE

Blush, light flesh, cream, lemon, jasmine, yellow, sand, goldenrod, salmon, orange, mineral orange, vermillion red, beige, rose beige, clay rose, henna, scarlett red, magenta, purple, dark purple, yellow bice, light yellow-green, light green, chartreuse, parrot green, aquamarine, peacock green, olive green, true green, grass green, dark green, non-photo blue, light cerulean blue, delft blue, true blue, peacock blue, electric blue, prussian blue, copenhagen blue, ultramarine, blue-violet, indigo blue, sienna brown, terra cotta, dark brown, burnt umber, dark umber.

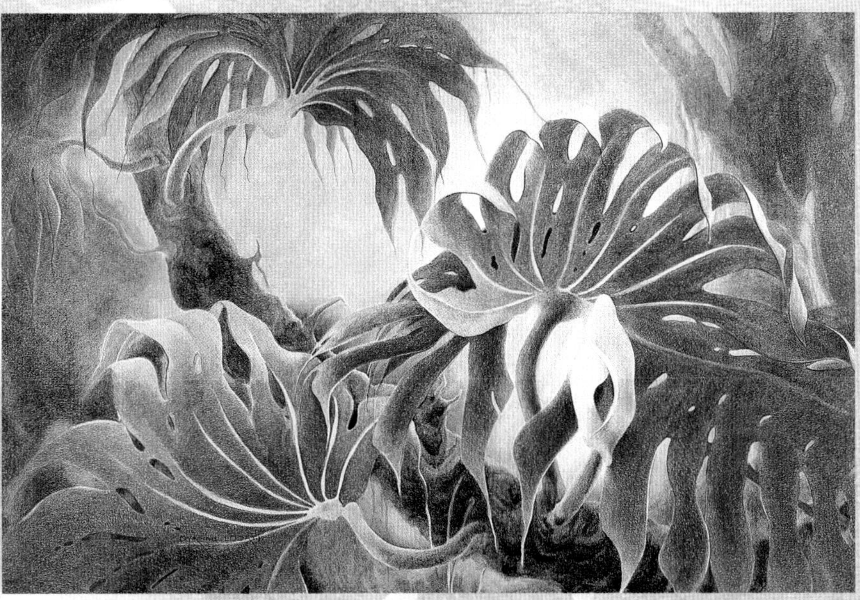

Dawn
22 x 34" (558 x 862 mm)

1 The painting is begun with only a general concept in mind ("foliage in morning light") and is done one section at a time. Before the composition is expanded, each area – subject and background – is sketched and completely colored. By imagining a horizon line, a focal point is established; from there a graphite outline of a blossom, leaf, stem, and trunk is drawn. As the work progessses, objects are drawn in a calculated direction. (What is this pointing to? Where is it going?) The background shapes are just as important as the shape of the subject.

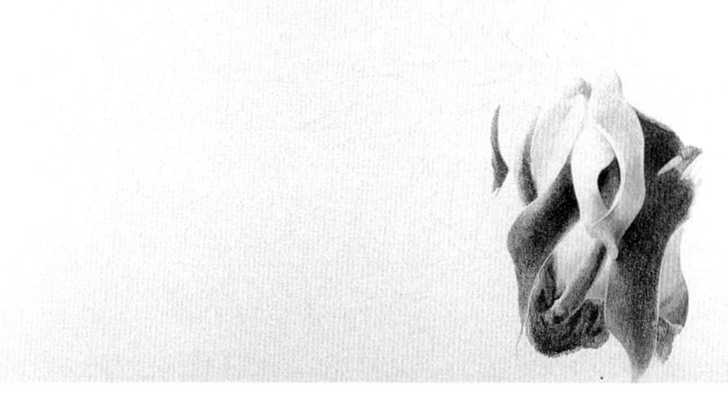

2 Referring to a color wheel, a dominant color and at least three accent colors are chosen. Colors are not applied in solid layers over each other. Instead, the first color is applied by cross hatching with an even pressure. Then, using a kneaded eraser, spots of color are lifted out and another color is blended into the area. This process continues as each color is applied and then lifted to allow "hits" of complementary color to show through. Notice how color balance and flow is created through the addition of red to both the left- and right-hand sides and in the trunk. These reds, when placed next to the blues and greens, keep their intensity and add excitment to the layout.

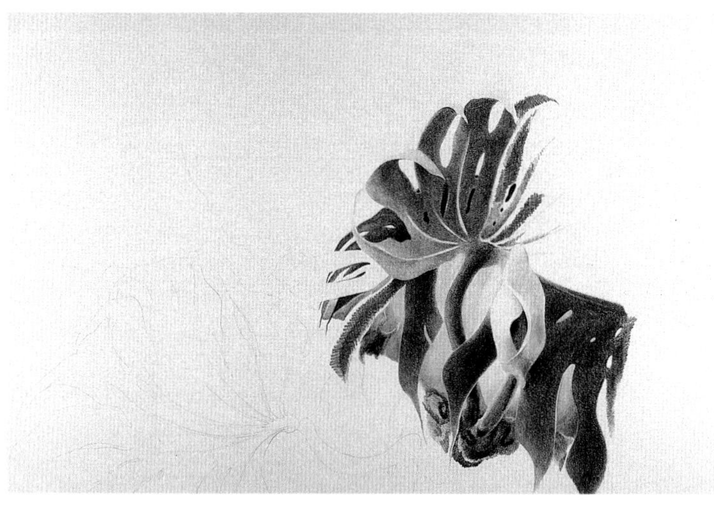

3 No single color is used for very long. When making color changes within an object, values are kept constant (lights together, darks together). Color transitions, as in the leaves and background, are a smooth flow from one hue into another. If the colors were changed too abruptly, the leaves would just look like a patchwork of different colors and wouldn't be believable. Hard edges used in the color changes of the trunk, however, create texture and form. Notice how the curved stem at the bottom center leads the viewer back into the work.

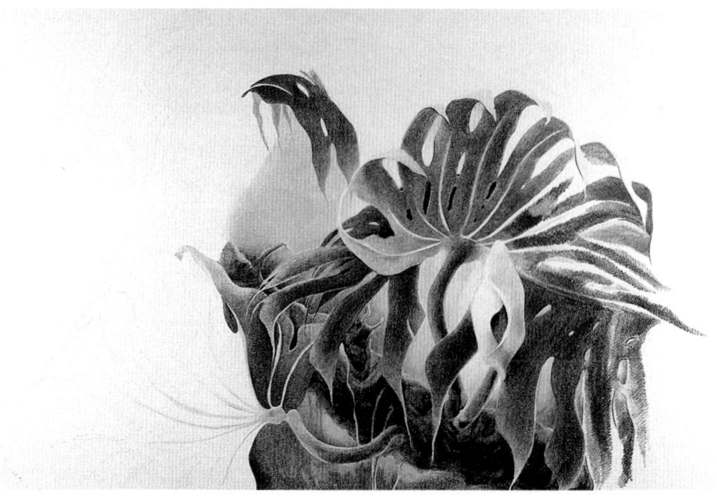

4 This detail shows how aggressive and blunt the stokes are. Contrary to their hurried appearance, they are deliberate and controlled. The pressure is firm but not heavy. Cross hatching allows various colors to show through and helps make a gradual color transition. Except in very dark areas, warm colors are not mixed with cool, but are placed next to them. This keeps the colors from becoming dull and muddy. For example, the transition from red to green on the same leaf is made by blending the red into hues of red-blue, then to blues, and finally to green.

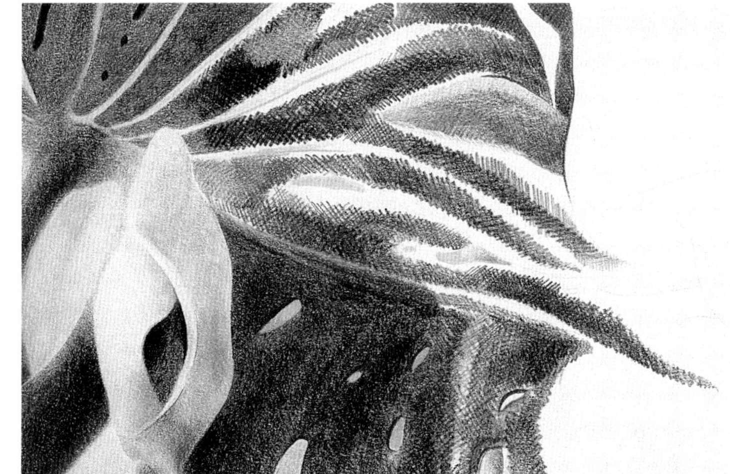

5 The cross-hatched strokes are applied in opposite directions until the finished layers become smooth and dense. Leaves are backlit as the "glow" of the light extends across the painting from the focal point. Note how the light filters through the top center leaf and how the leaf's downward curved shape directs you back to the focal point. The varying shapes and shades of the colors in the background give the environment space, movement and depth. By thinking "light next to dark" rather than "subject next to background," the open background area is integrated with the subject.

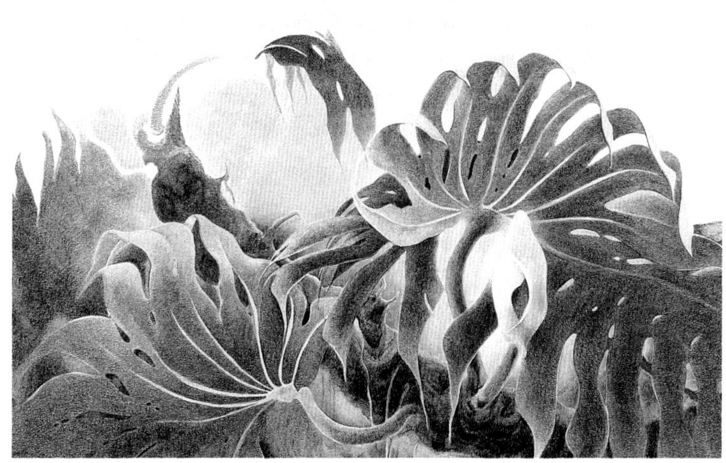

6 In finishing the painting, the goal is to keep the lightest light and the darkest dark around the focal point. The top corners are kept neutral while stronger colors are used towards the middle. Soft shapes in the top right corner counterpoise those in the bottom left. The exotic colors are blended, balanced, and repeated to make this mystical scene believable. The mood is hot and steamy. Dyanne creates further drama in *Dawn* by placing us on the dark side of the jungle to look toward the light.

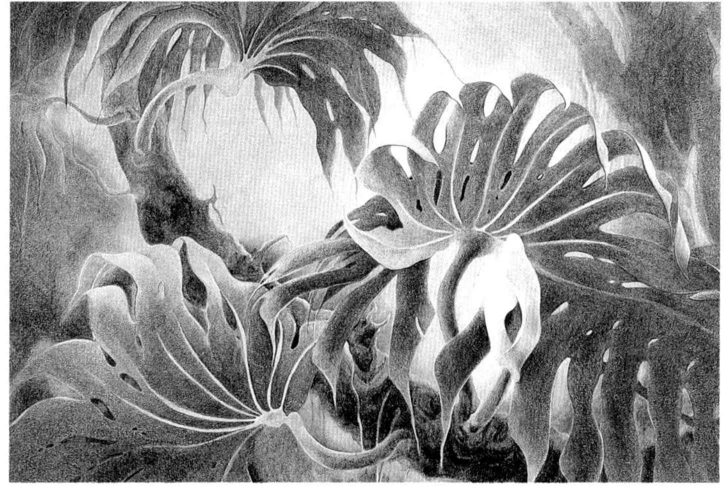

Dyanne Locati

1 *Tropical Foliage*
17 x 23" (431 x 584 mm)
Rising Museum Paper

2 *A Forest of Palms*
32 x 40" (813 x 1,016 mm)
Rising Museum paper

3 *Tassels*
20 x 18" (508 x 445 mm)
Rising Museum Paper

4 *Designing Kale Cabbage*
15 x 13" (584 x 330 mm)
Rising Museum Paper

5 *Designing Cabbage*
27 x 17" (686 x 432 mm)
Rising Museum Paper

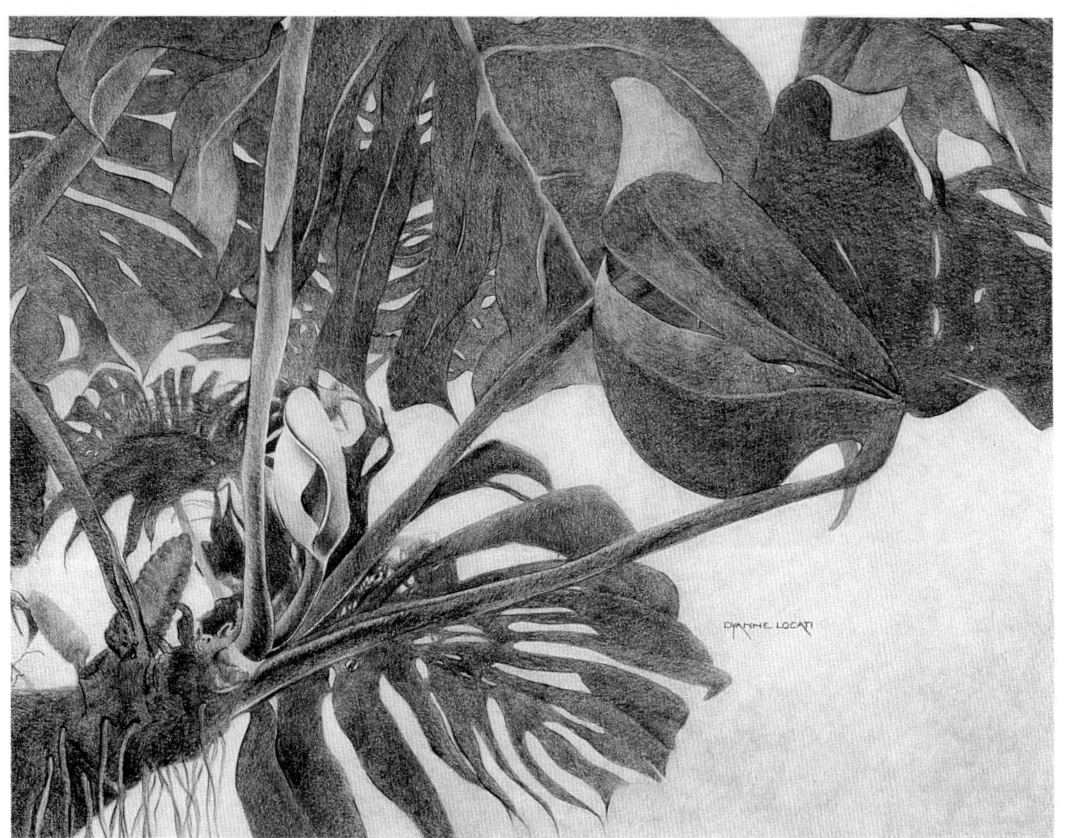

1

2

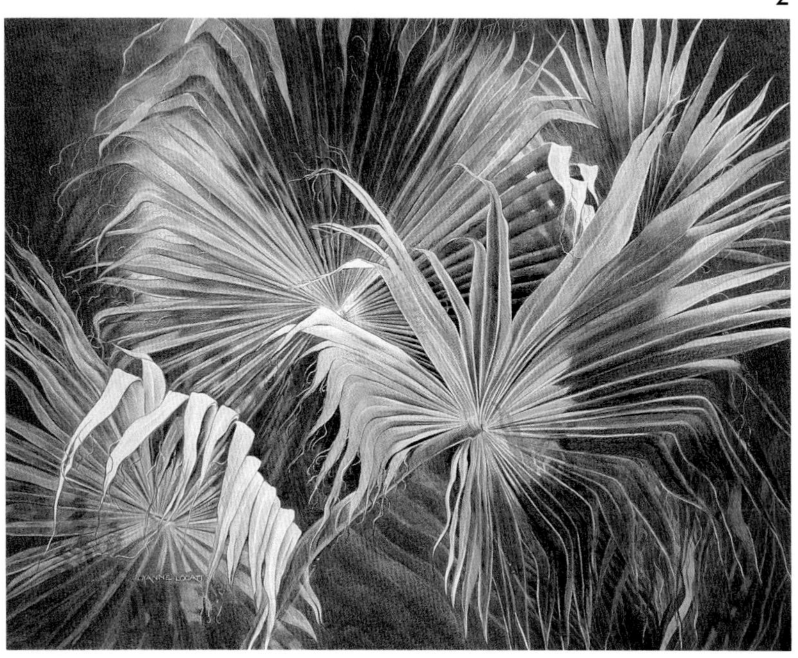

3

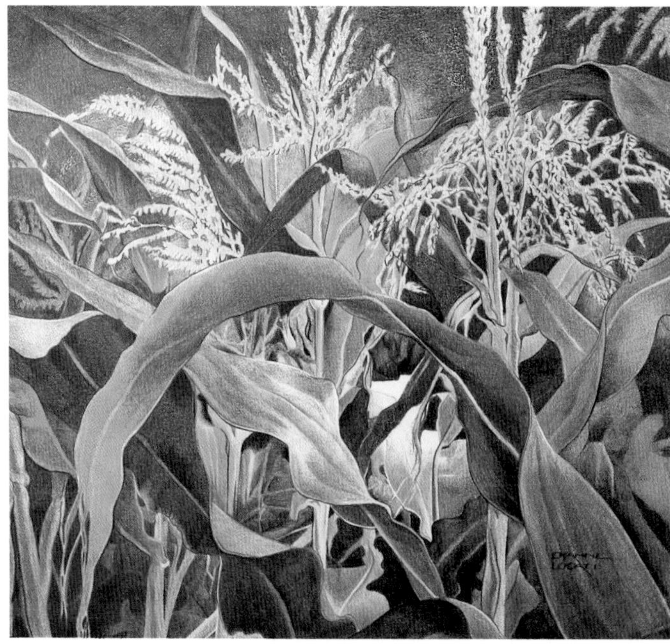

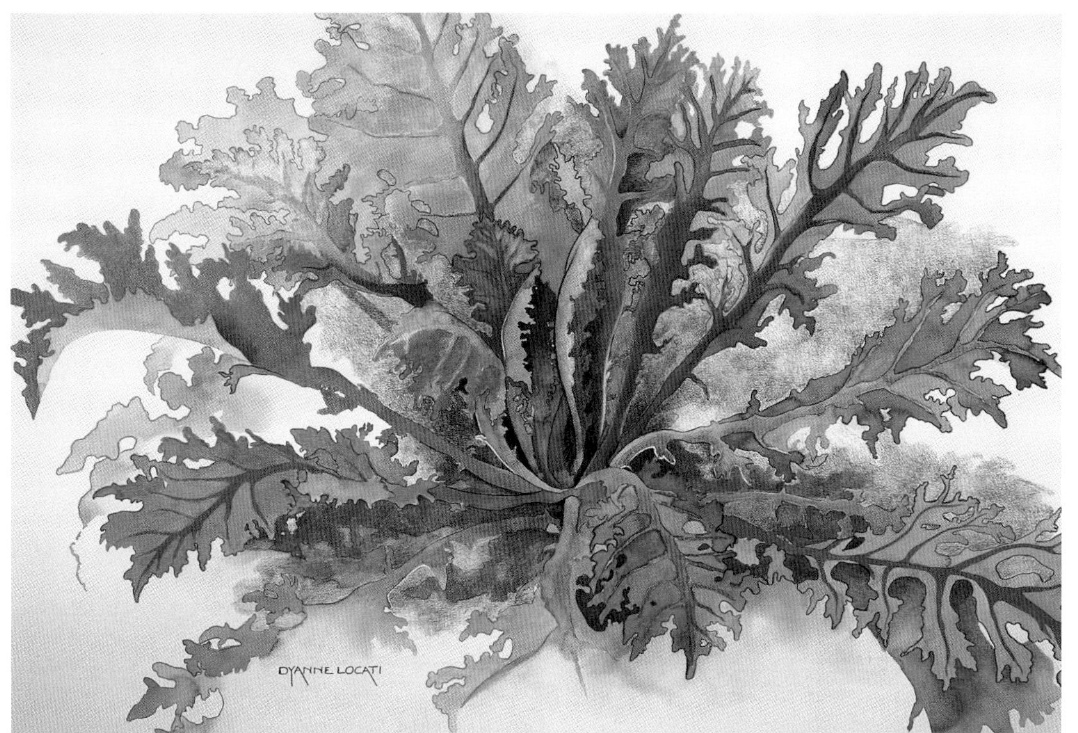

4

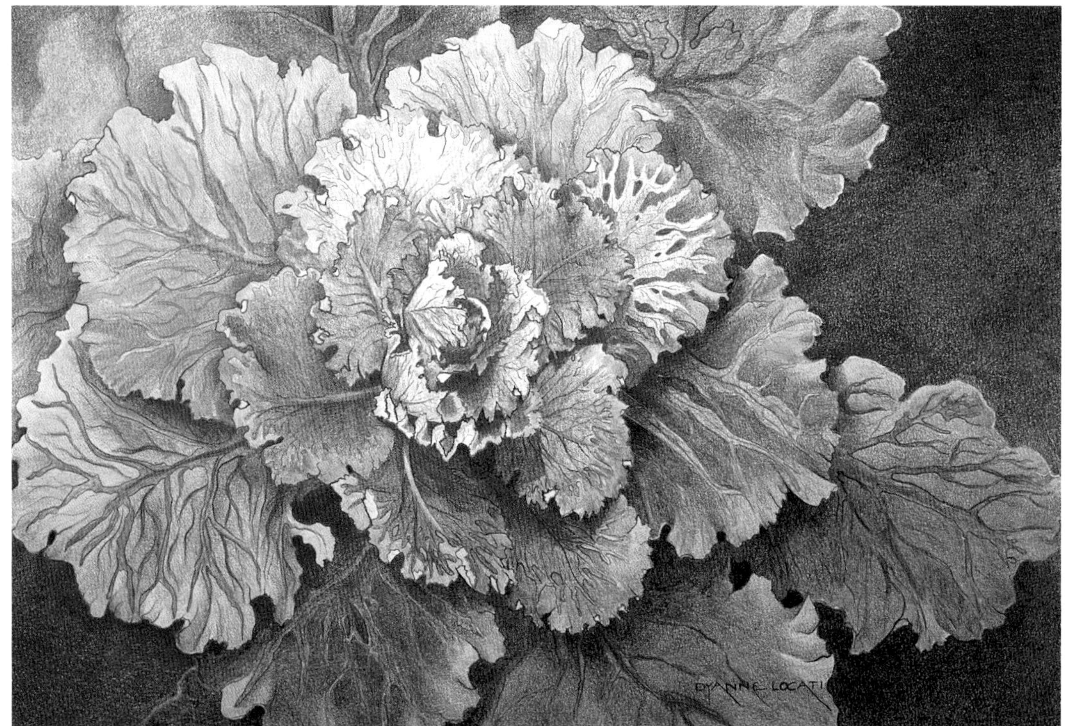

5

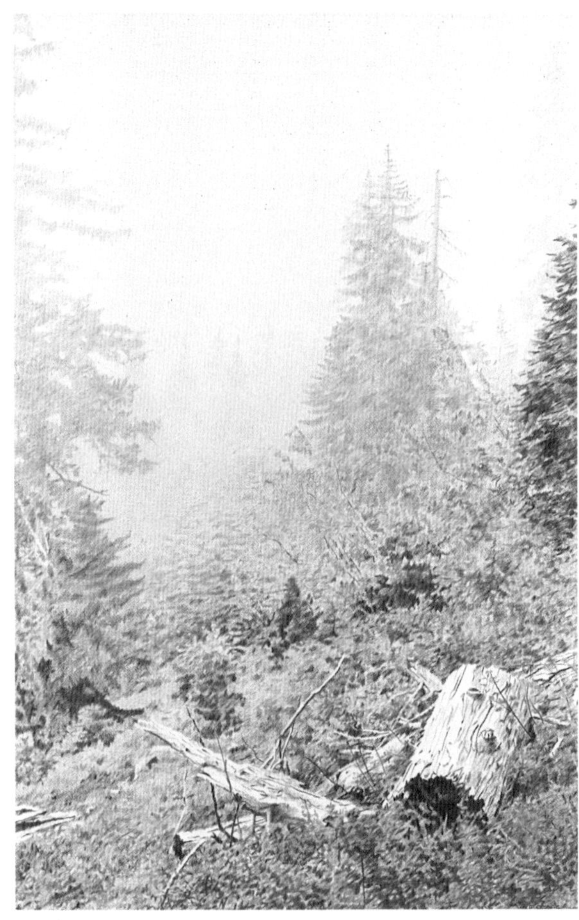

1

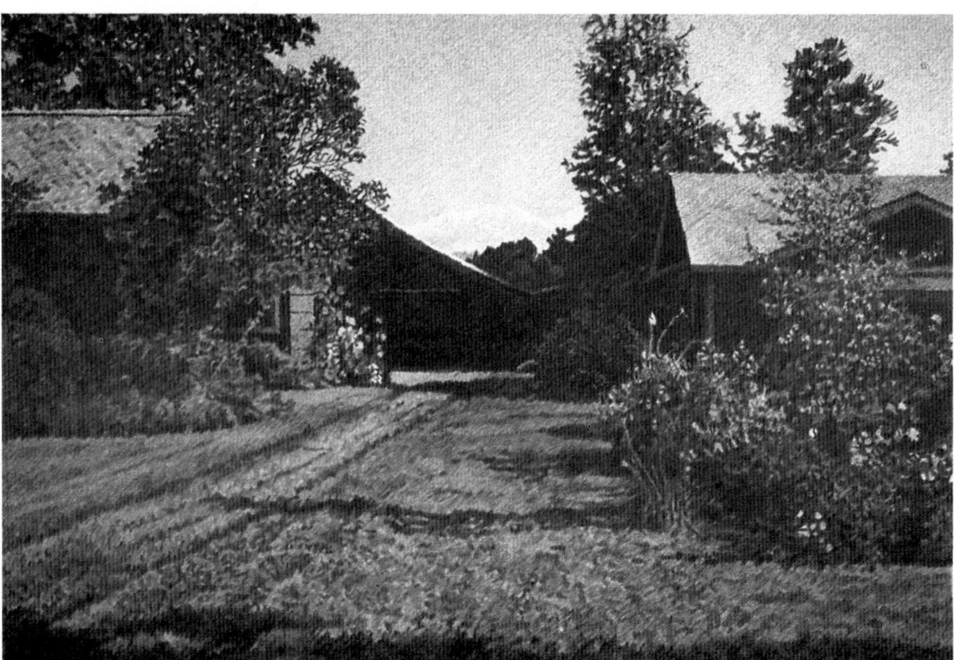

2

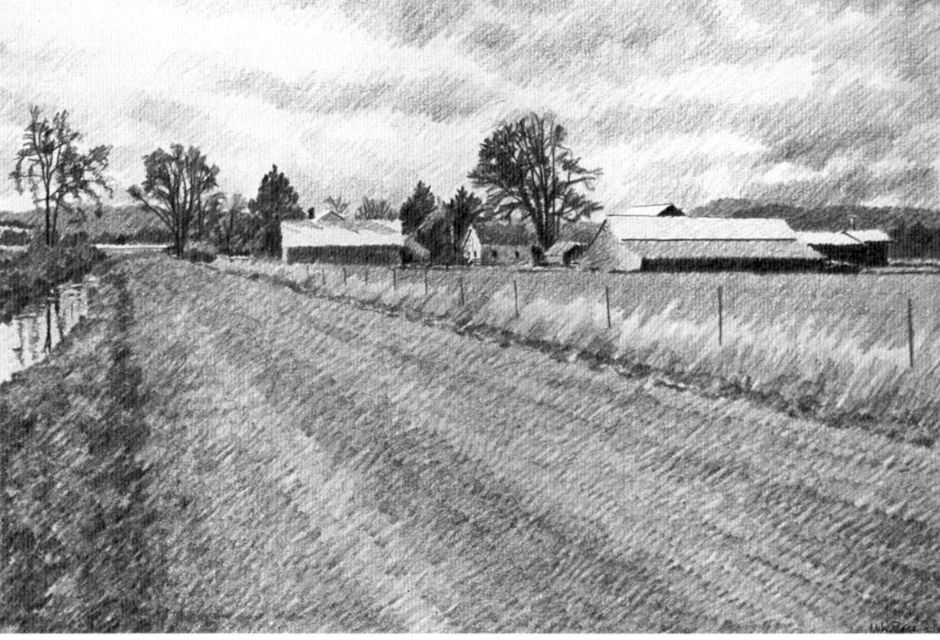

3

Mike Pease

1 *Morning Light*
36 x 24" (912 x 608 mm)
2-ply Museum Board
Technique: 3-Color Process

2 *Seavey Loop Farm*
24 x 36" (608 x 912 mm)
2-ply Museum Board
Technique: 3-Color Process

3 *Oregon Farm*
18 x 27" (456 x 684 mm)
2-ply Museum Board
Technique: 3-Color Process

4 *Fall Creek*
24 x 36" (608 x 912 mm)
2-ply Museum Board
Technique: 3-Color Process

5 *Forest Floor*
24 x 36" (608 x 912 mm)
2-ply Museum Board
Technique: 3-Color Process

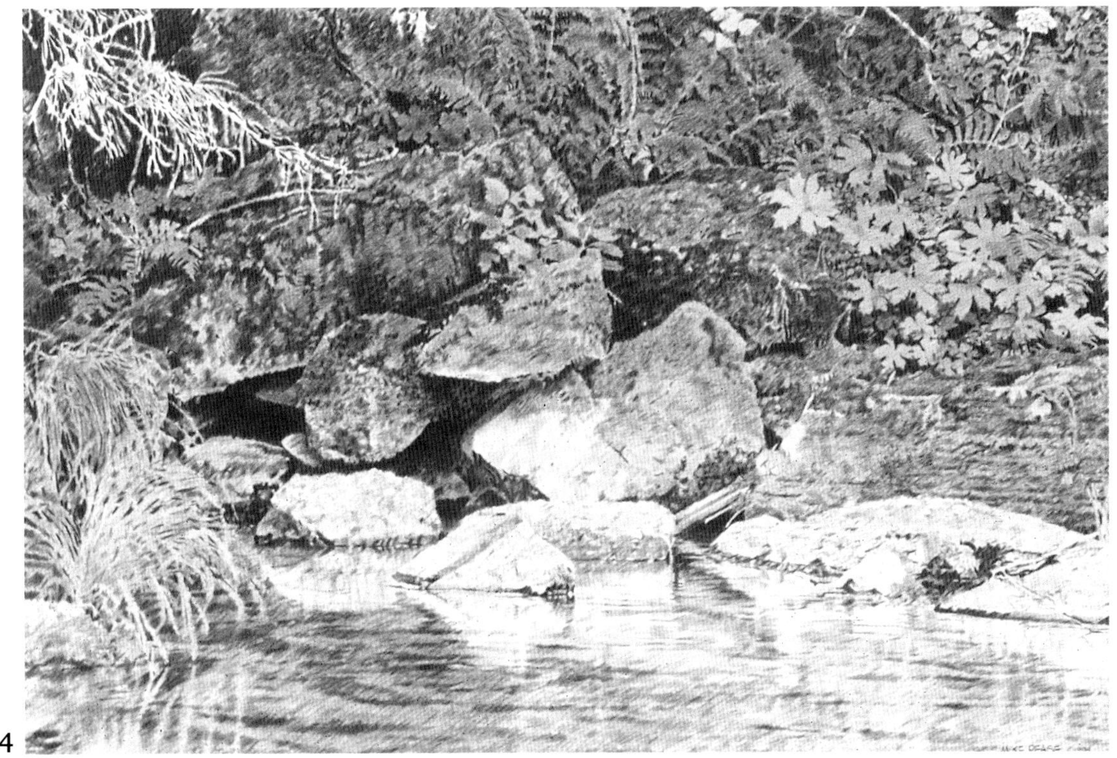

4

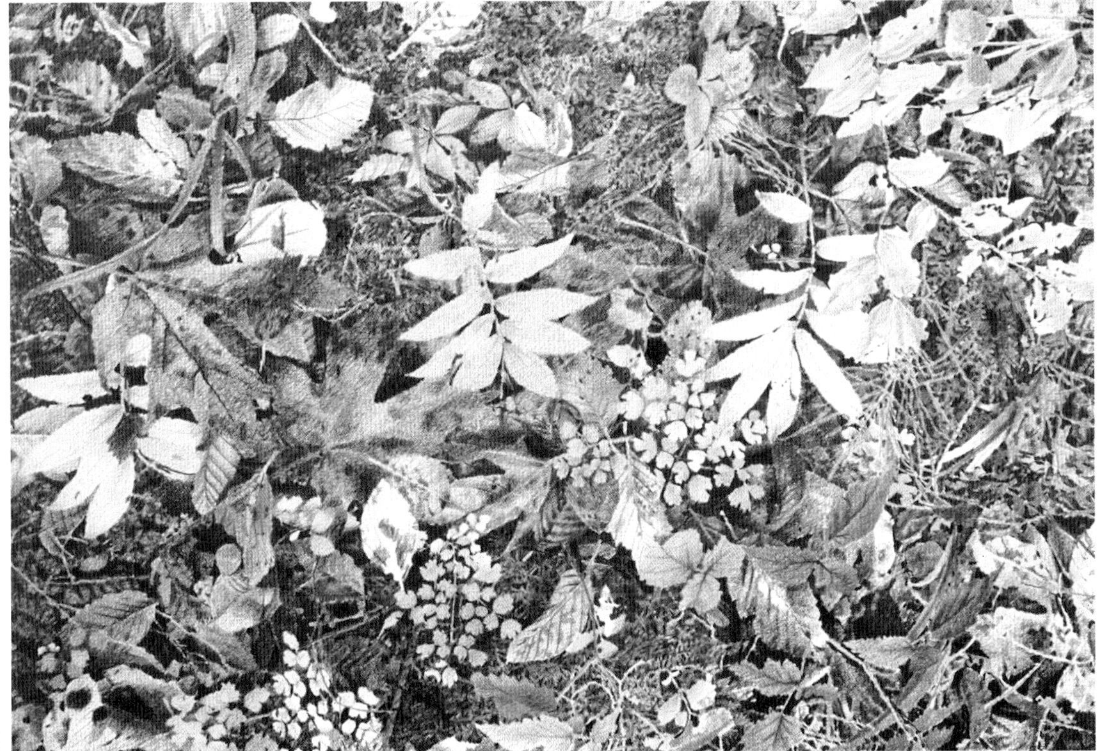

5

Mike Pease

1 *Farmyard*
26 x 26" (659 x 659 mm)
2-ply Museum Board
Technique: 3-Color Process

Bernard Aime Poulin

2 *Catherine, Joanna & Jonathan*
24 x 30" (610 x 762 mm)

3 *Sam*
24 x 20" (610 x 508 mm)

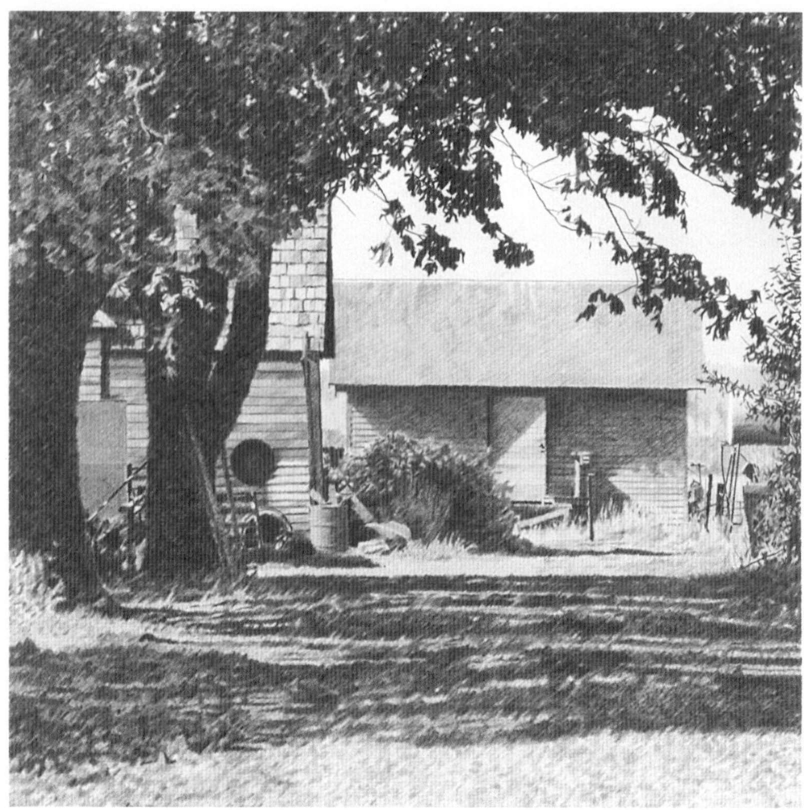

1

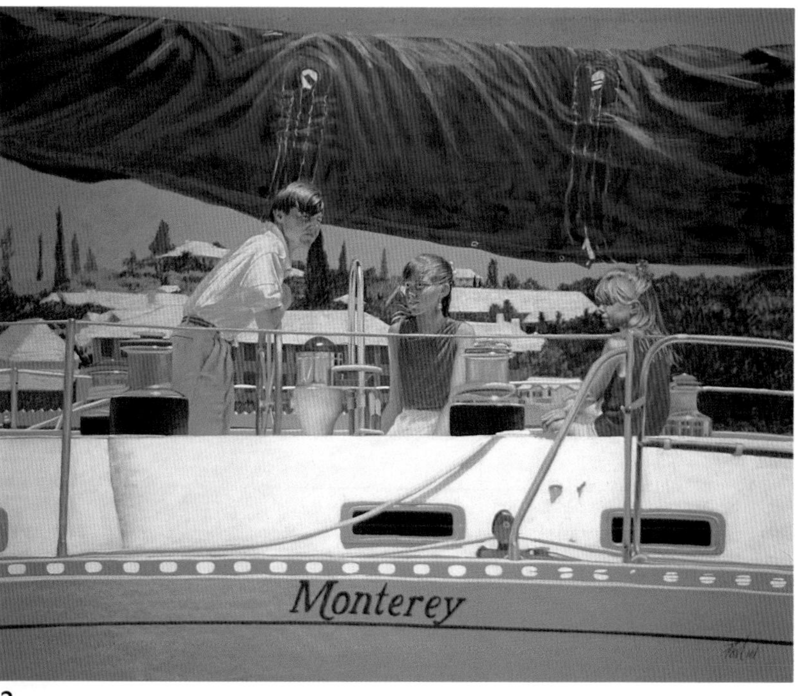

2

3

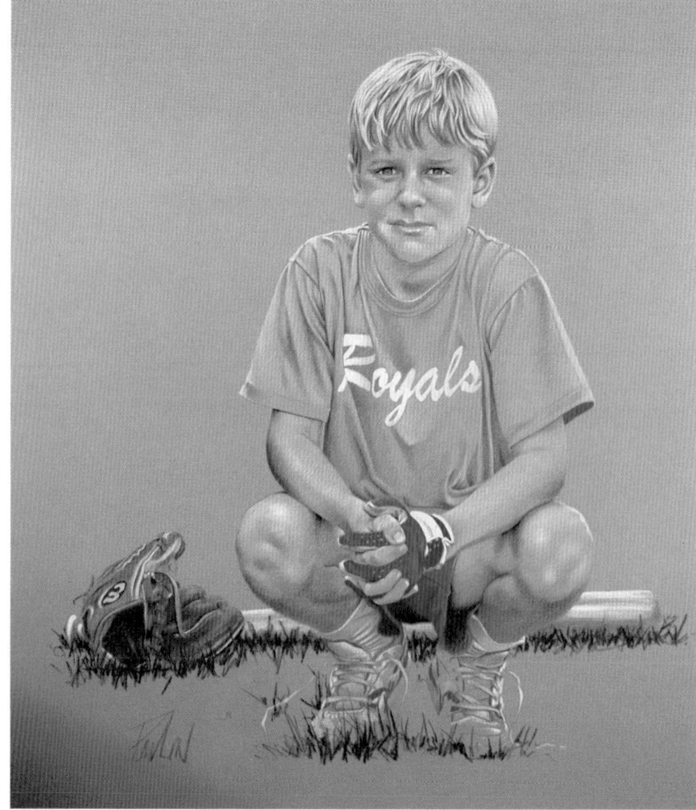

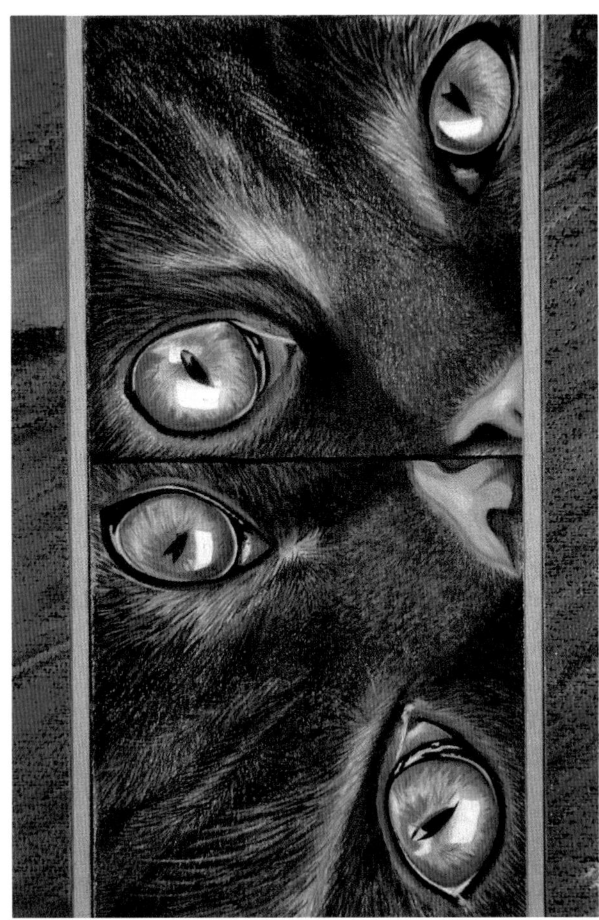

1

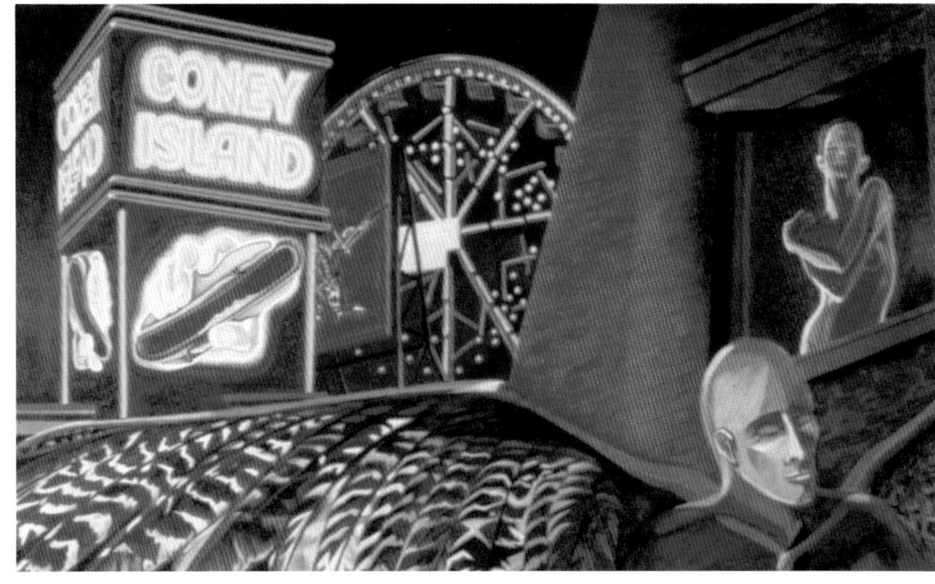

2

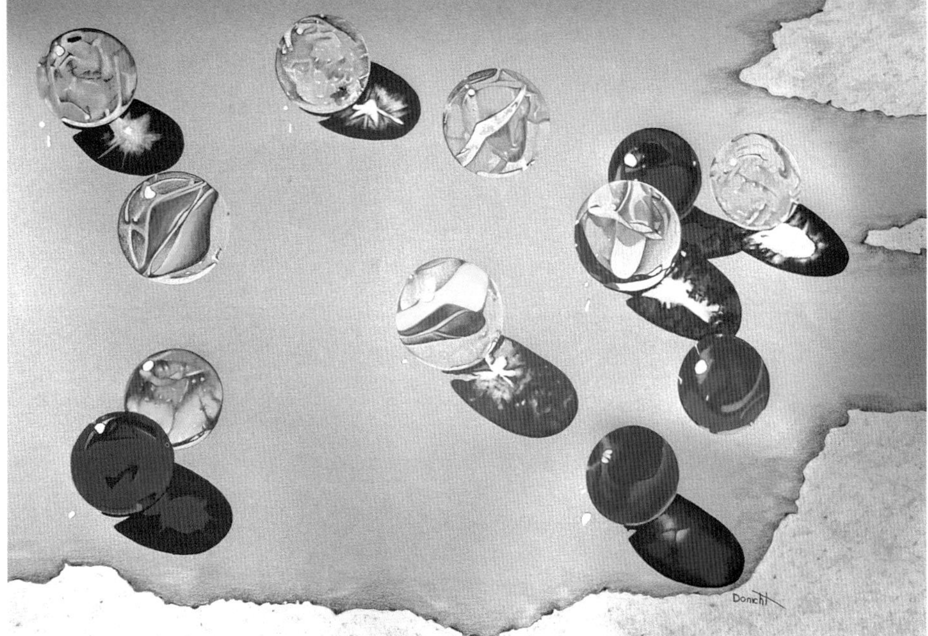

3

Robert S. Hunter

1 *Cats Eye Citadel*
8 x 4" (203 x 102 mm)
Stathmore Bristol Board 2-ply Regular Finish
Technique: Burnishing, Sgraffito

2 *Coney Island Dawn*
20 x 30" (508 x 762 mm)
Strathmore Bristol Board 2-ply Regular Finish

Dian Donicht Vestin

3 *Lift Off!*
24 x 29" (610 x 737 mm)
Canson Mi-Tientes Smooth Diniah
Technique: Burnishing

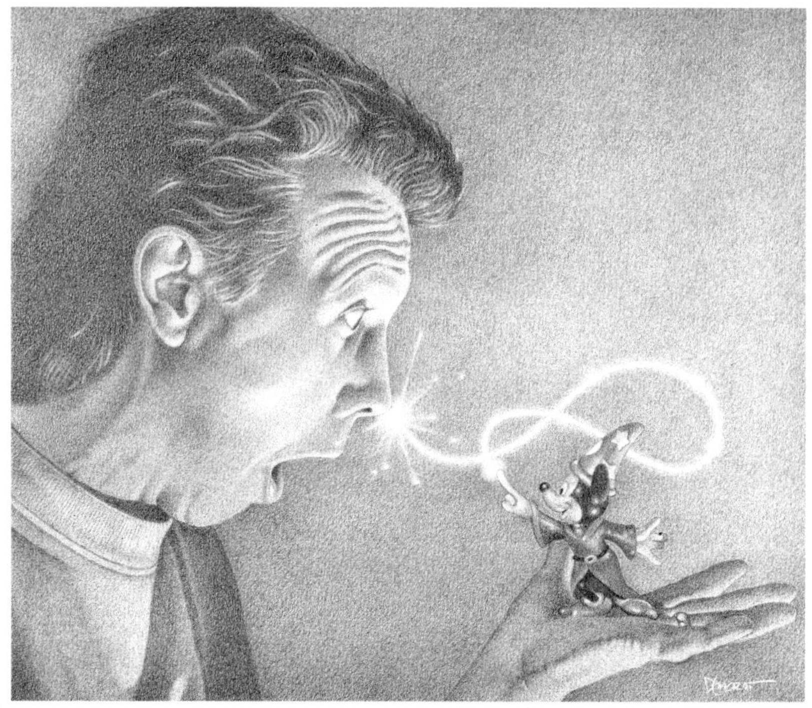

1

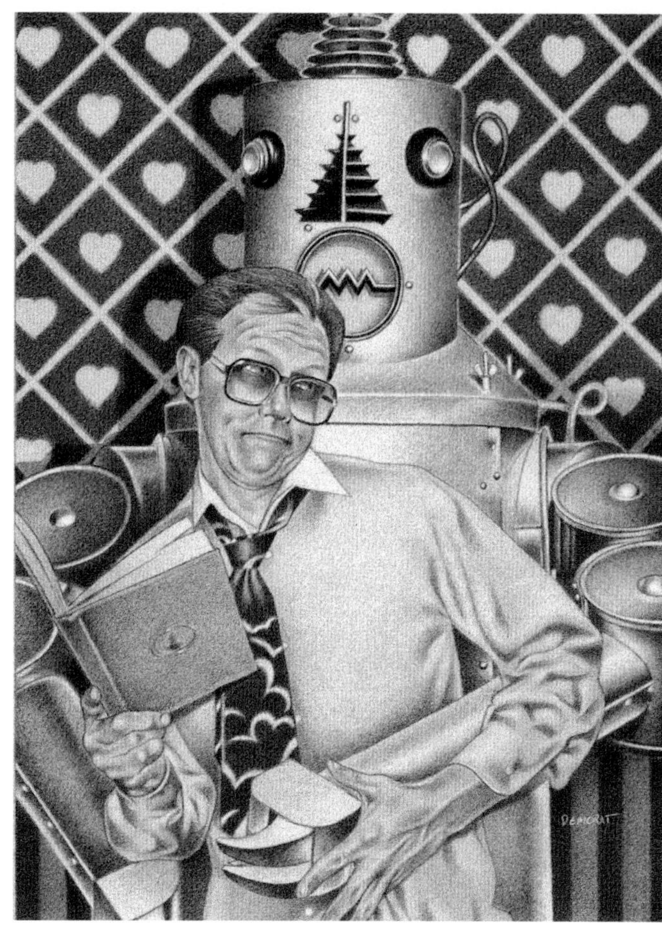

3

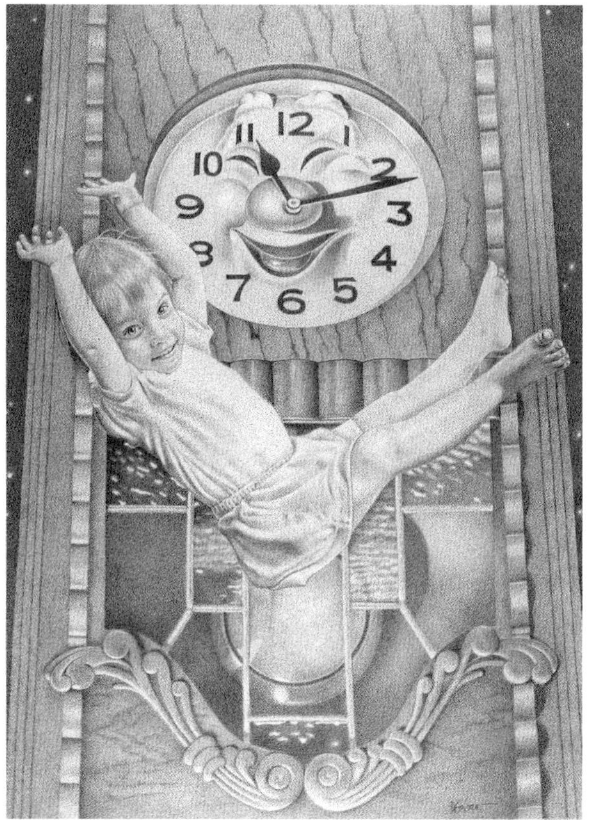

2

Chuck Demorat

1 *D.W. and The Mouse*
11 x 14" (279 x 356 mm)
Canson Paper

2 *Fred 'N' Wilma*
14 x 11" (356 x 279 mm)
Canson Paper

3 *Time Passing*
20 x 15" (508 x 381 mm)
Canson Paper

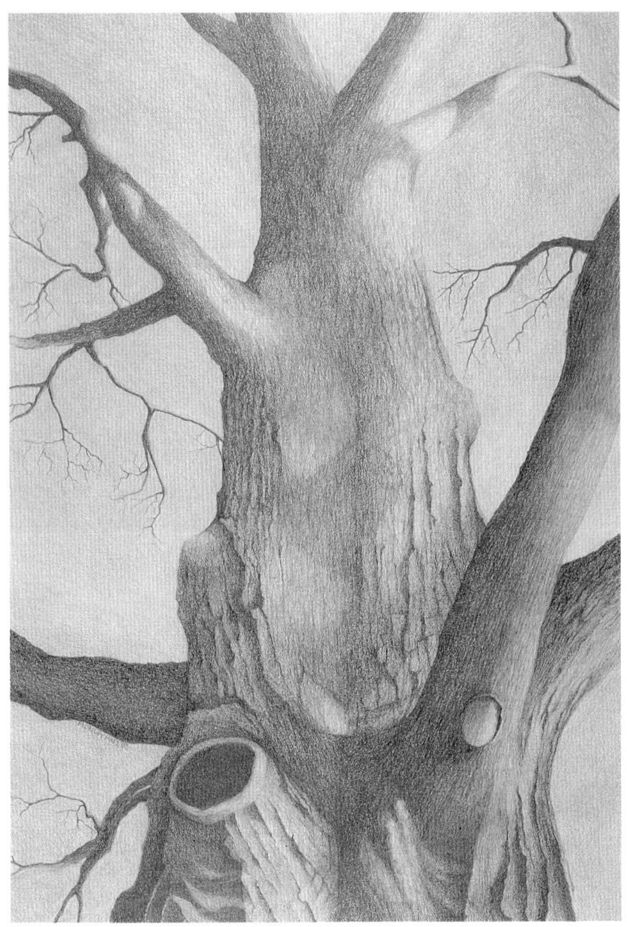

1

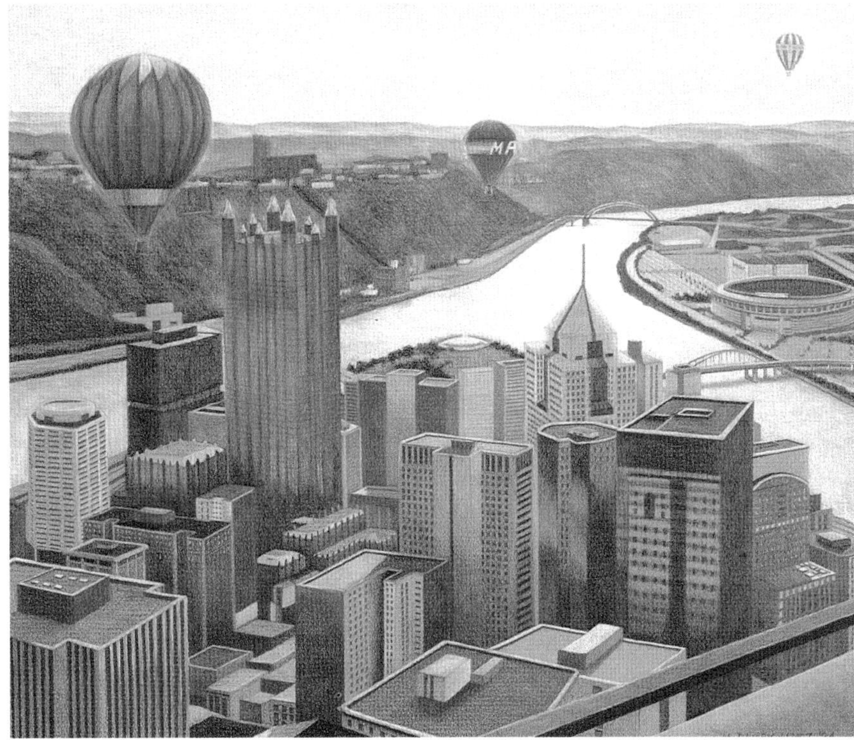

2

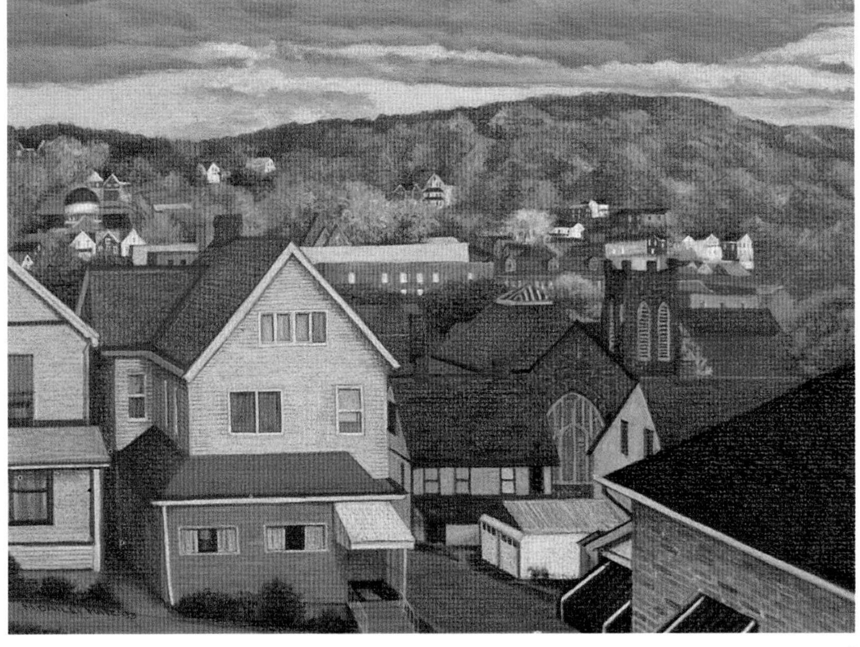

3

Marguerite Dailey Matz

1 *The Hackberry Tree*
30 x 20" (762 x 508 mm)
Illustration Board

2 *Take It From The Top*
22 x 28" (559 x 711 mm)
Crescent Mat Board

3 *From My Parent's Back Porch*
9 x 12" (229 x 305 mm)
Strathmore Charcoal Paper

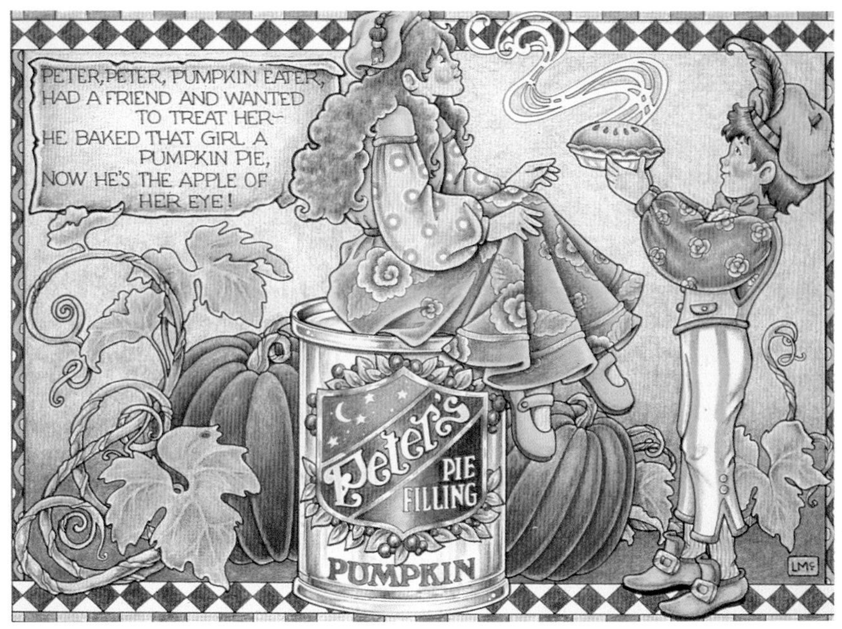

1

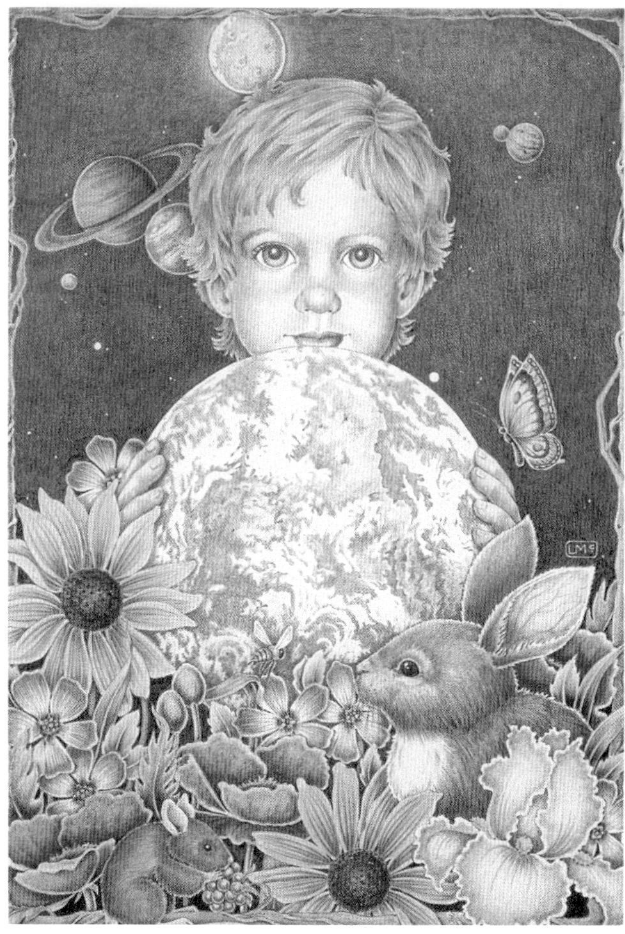

2

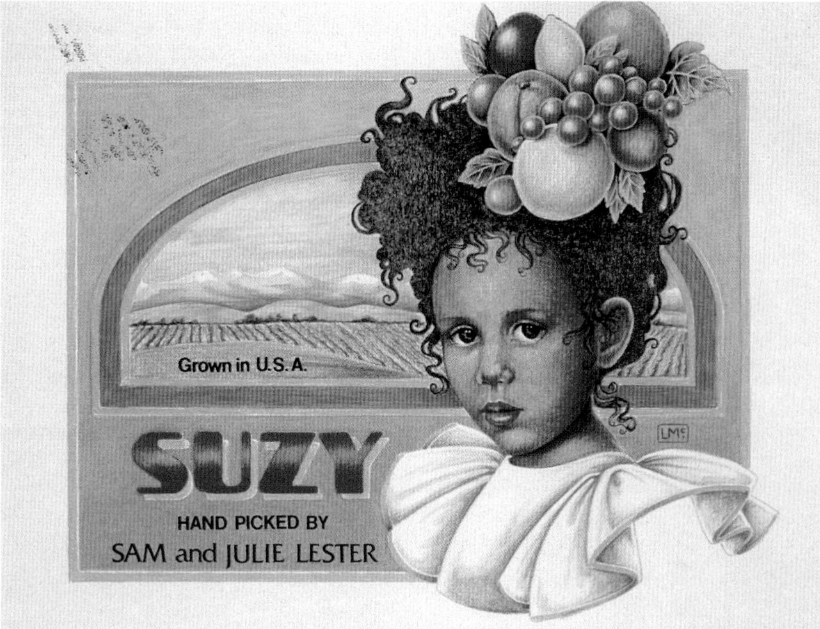

3

Lynn McClain

1 *Pumpkin Eaters*
7 x 10" (184 x 257 mm)
2-ply Vellum Finish Bristol Board
Technique: Burnishing

2 *Forrest's World*
13 x 9" (337 x 235 mm)
2-ply Vellum Finish Bristol Board
Technique: Burnishing

3 *Suzy*
8 x 9" (203 x 229 mm)
2-ply Vellum Finish Bristol Board
Technique: Colored Pencil, Press Type

Thomas M. Thayer Jr.

1 *5th and Main*
16 x 20" (406 x 508 mm)
Black Crescent Mat Board Smooth Surface

2 *Yakima Docking in Edmonds*
20 x 22" (508 x 559 mm)
Black Crescent Mat Board Smooth Surface

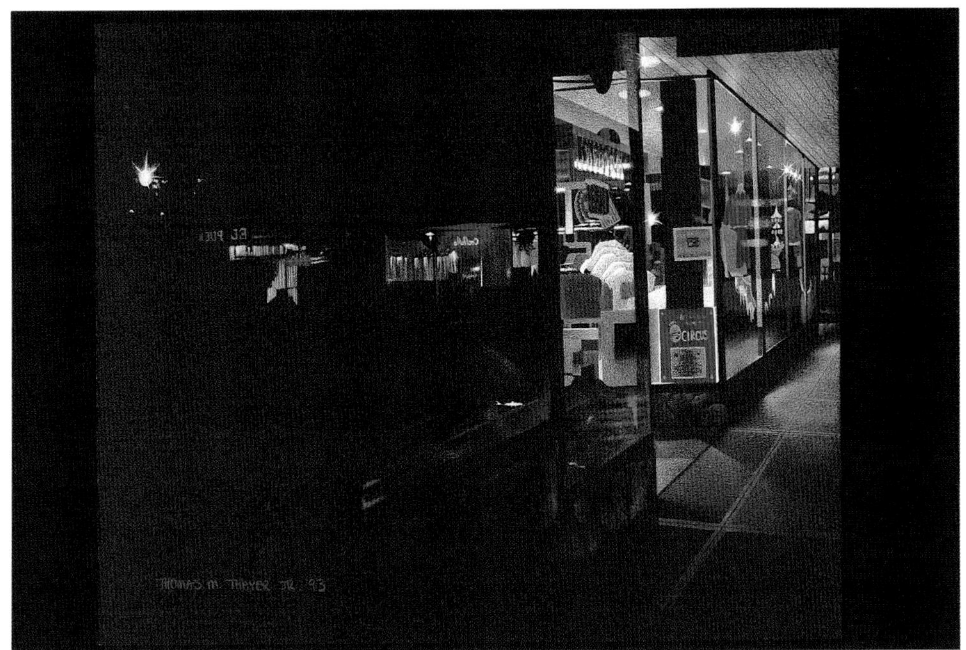

1

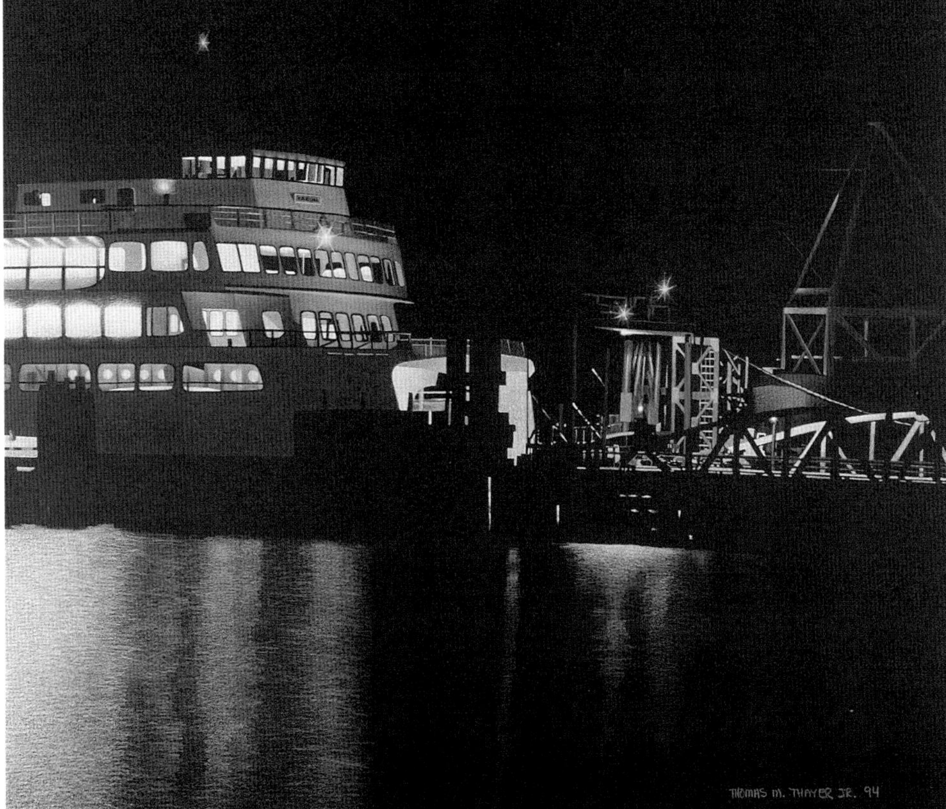

2

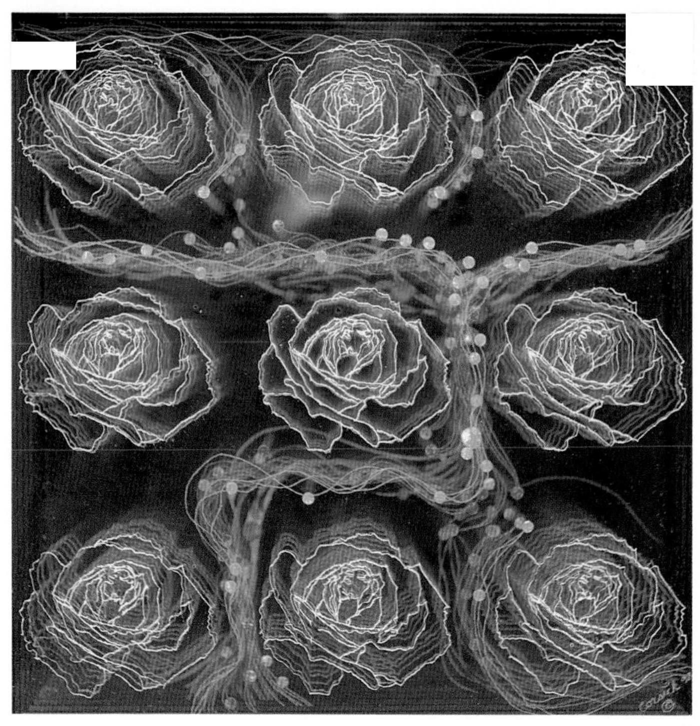

1

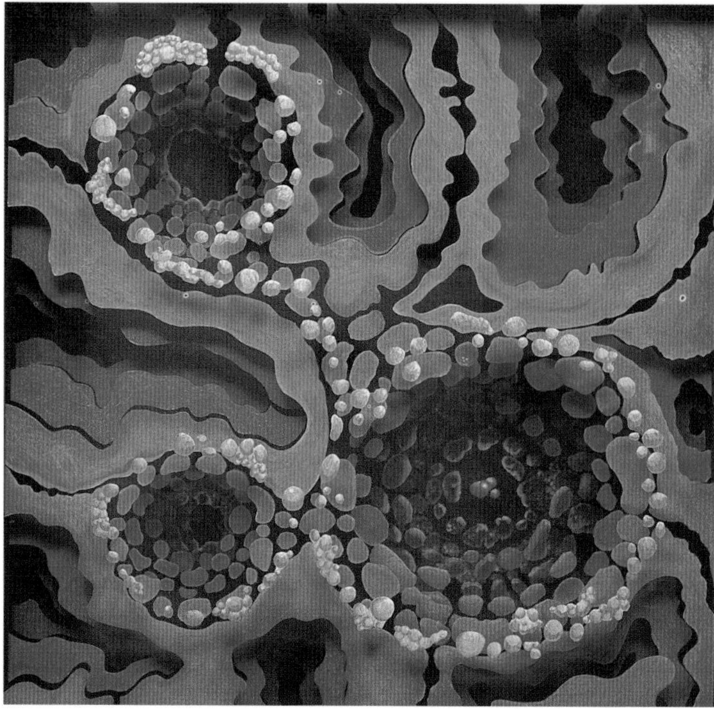

2

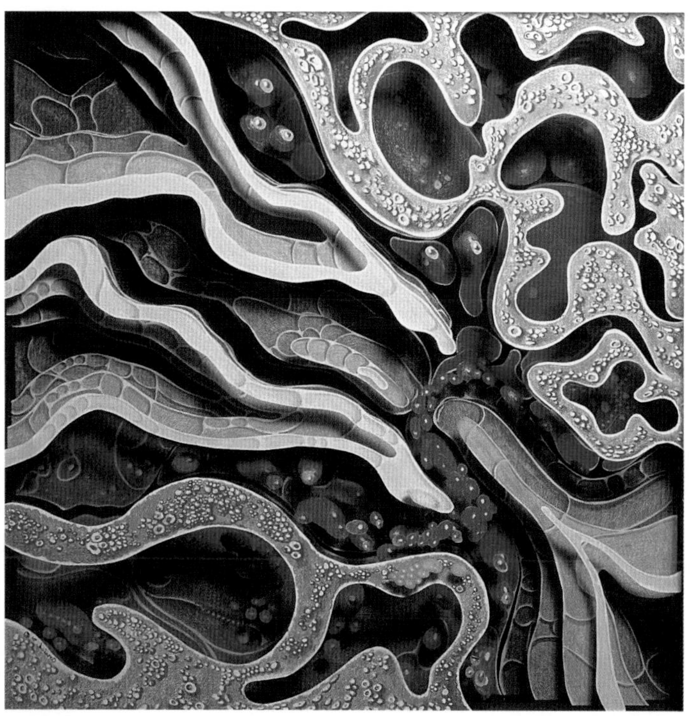

3

Bill Corsick

1 *Rose Fugue*
17 x 17 x 6" (432 x 432 x 140 mm)
Strathmore 400
Technique: Colored Pencil applied into etched lines in six sheets of Plexiglas installed 1/2" apart in wooden box

2 *Orange Jazz*
25 x 25 x 6" (635 x 635 x 140 mm)
Strathmore 400
Technique: Colored Pencil applied into etched lines in six sheets of Plexiglas installed 1/2" apart in wooden box

3 *Inter Connectivity*
25 x 25 x 6" (635 x 635 x 140 mm)
Strathmore 400
Technique: Colored Pencil applied into etched lines in six sheets of Plexiglas installed 1/2" apart in wooden box

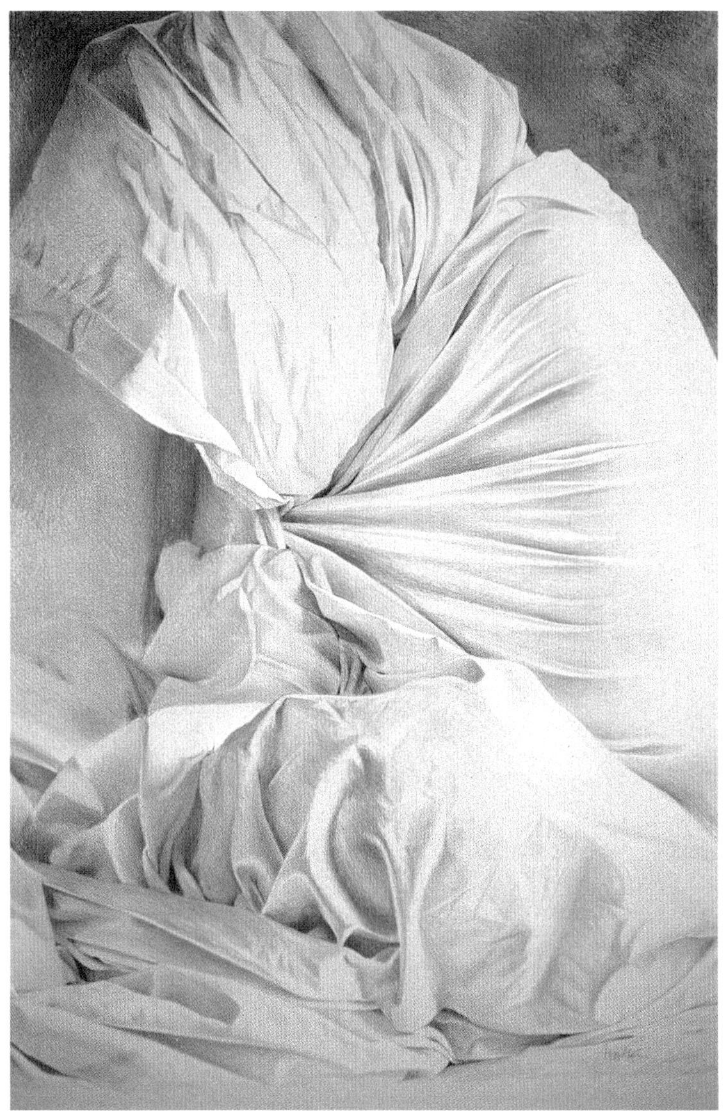

1

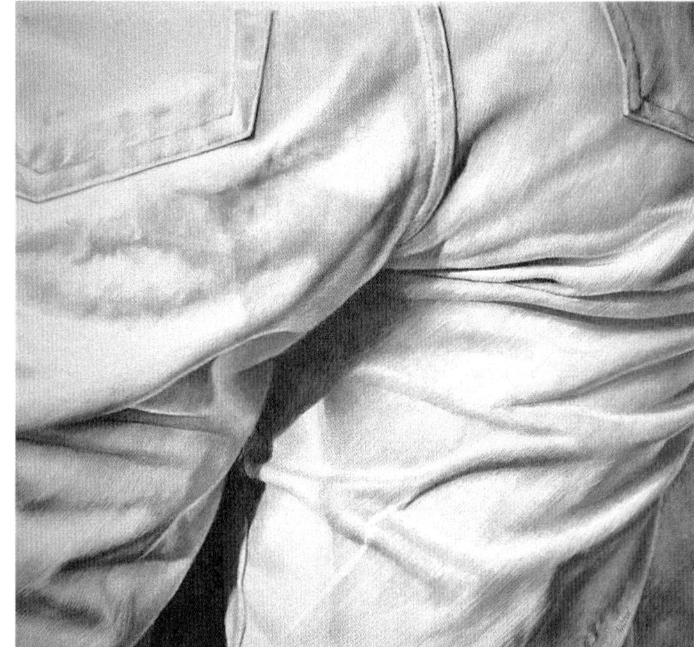

2

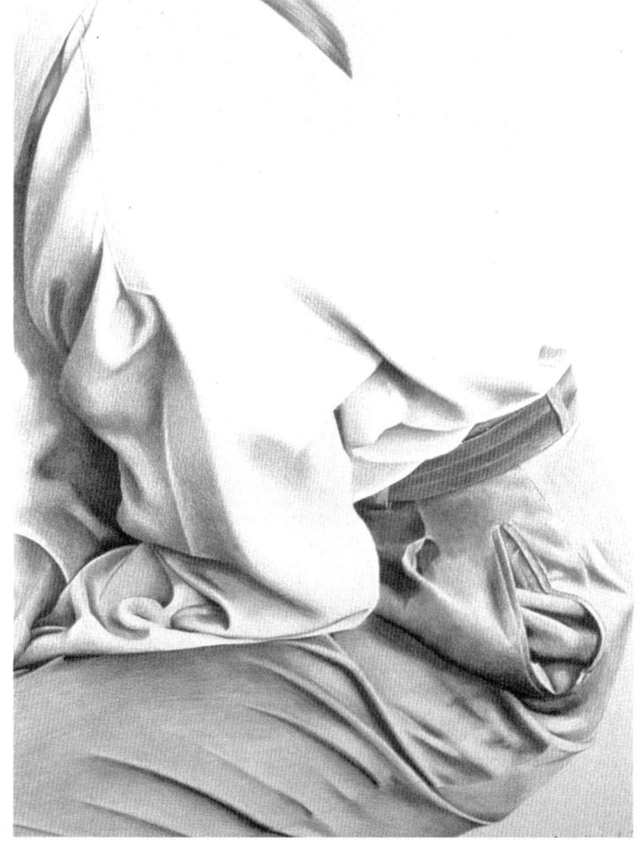

3

Susan Avishai

1 *Wrapped Self*
27 x 18" (673 x 457 mm)
Grey BFK Rives 100% Rag Paper

2 *Contraposto II*
22 x 23" (559 x 584 mm)
Grey BFK Rives 100% Rag Paper

3 *Crouching Woman*
25 x 20" (622 x 495 mm)
Grey BFK Rives 100% Rag Paper

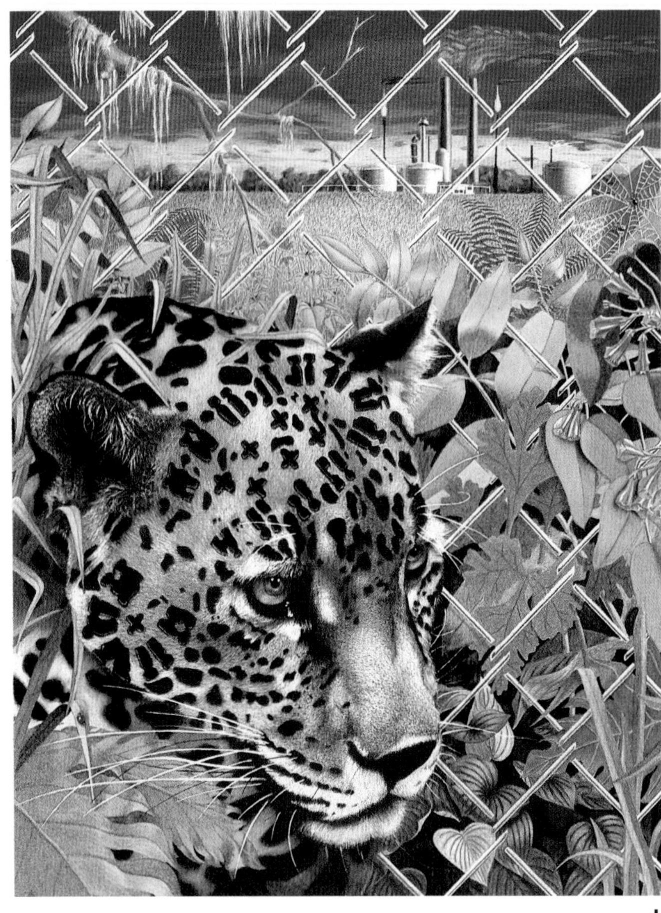

1

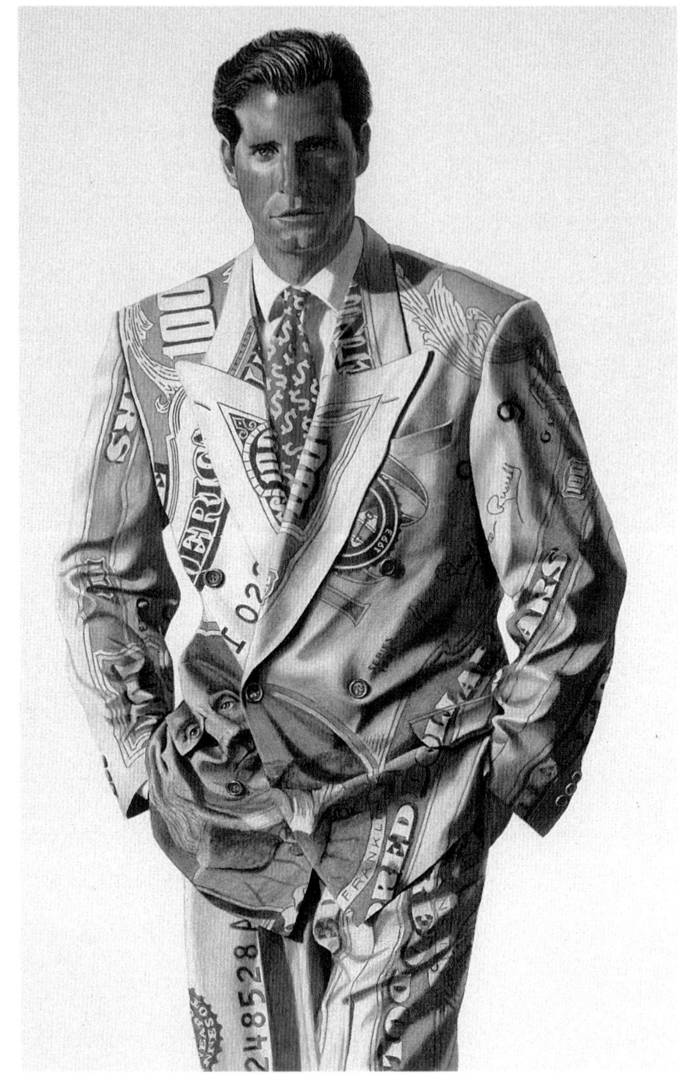

2

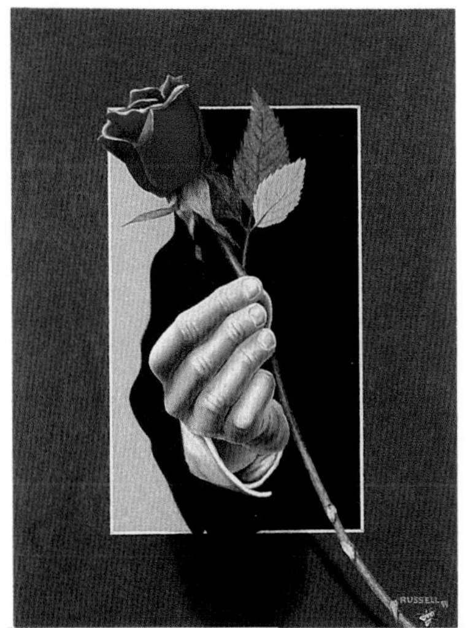

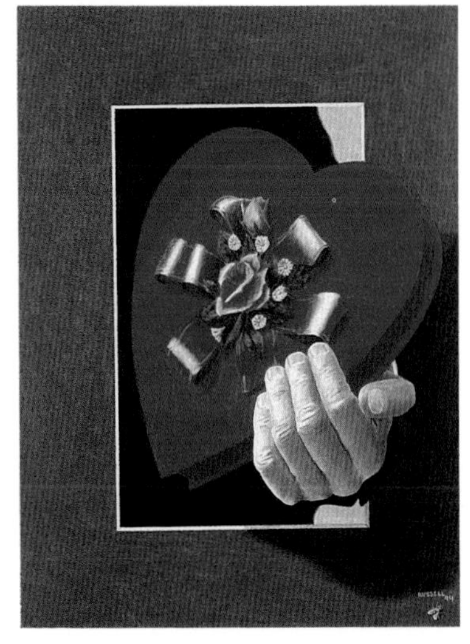

3

Mike Russell

1 *Endangering Species*
20 x 16" (508 x 406 mm)
Crescent Board

2 *Dressed for Success*
16 x 10" (406 x 254 mm)
Crescent Board

3 *For You*
12 x 9" (305 x 229 mm)
Crescent Board

Kenneth L. Zonker

1 *Red Reflections*
14 x 21" (356 x 533 mm)
Crescent Illustration Board Cold Press #110
Technique: Burnishing

2 *Morning Light*
14 x 21" (356 x 533 mm)
Crescent Illustration Board Cold Press #110
Technique: Burnishing

3 *Objects in Waiting*
21 x 14" (533 x 356 mm)
Crescent Illustration Board Cold Press #110
Technique: Burnishing

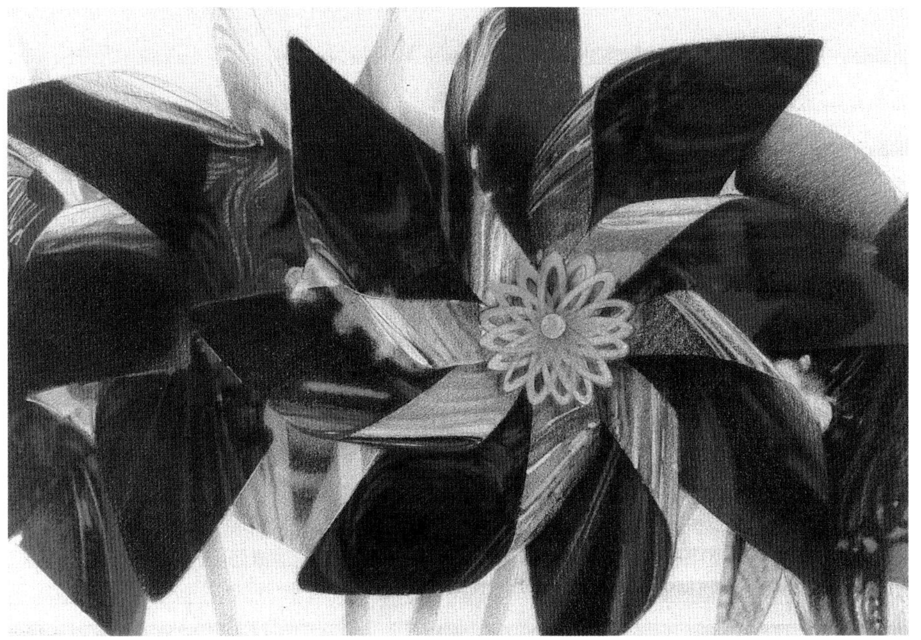

1

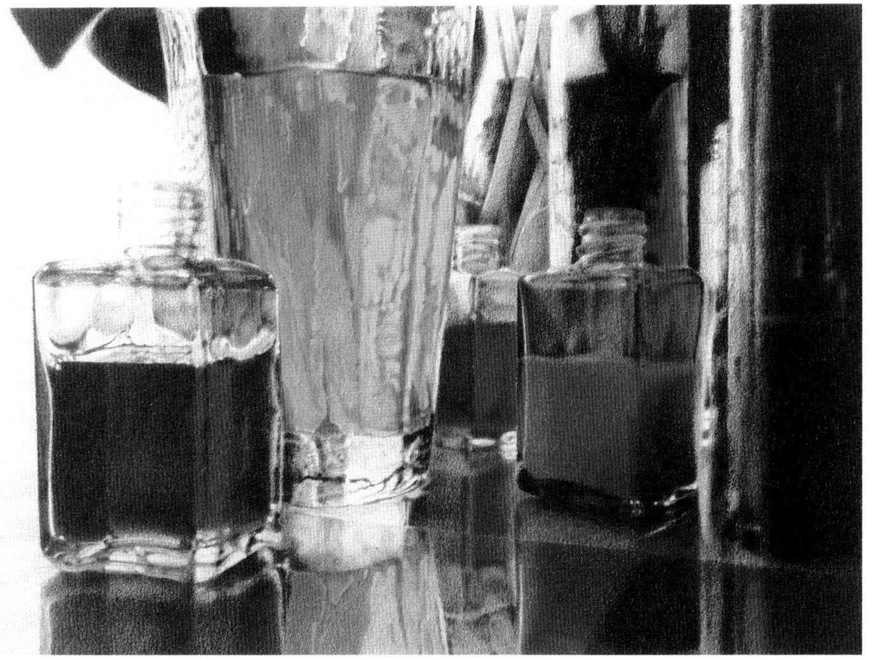

2

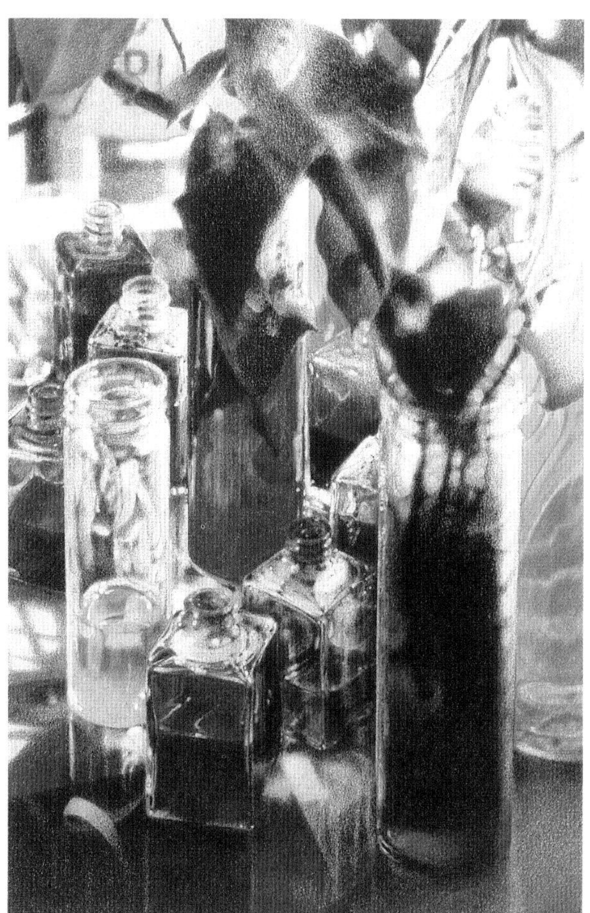

3

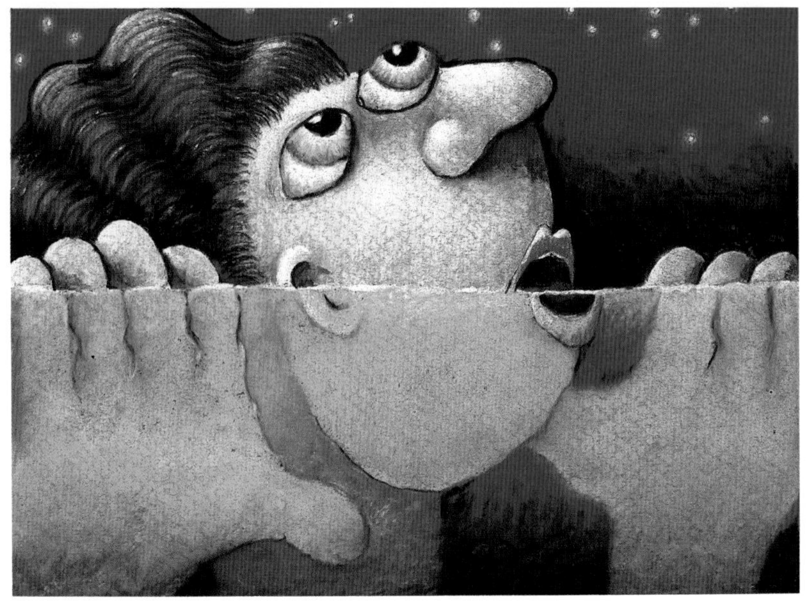

1

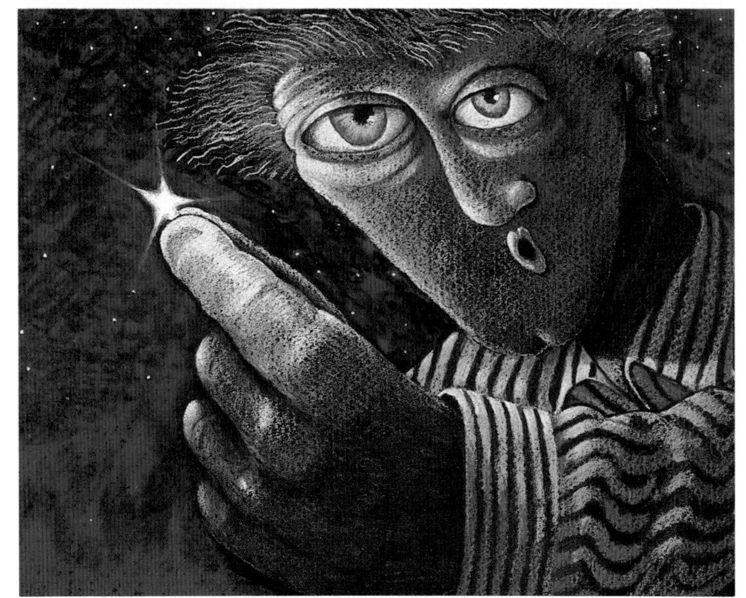

2

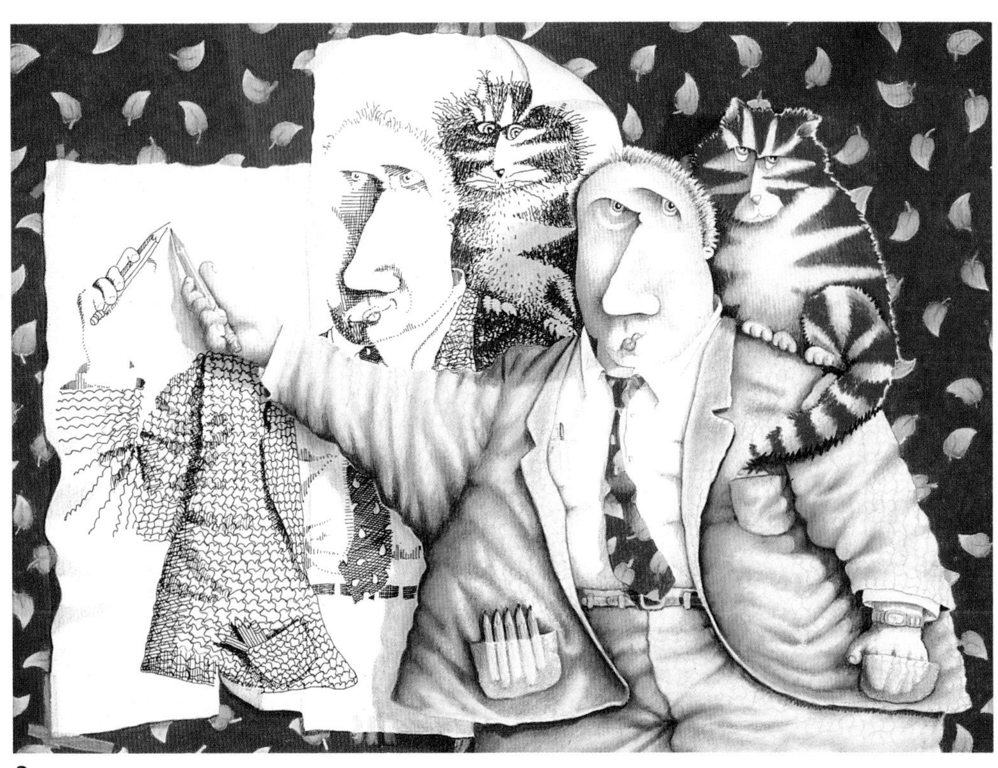

3

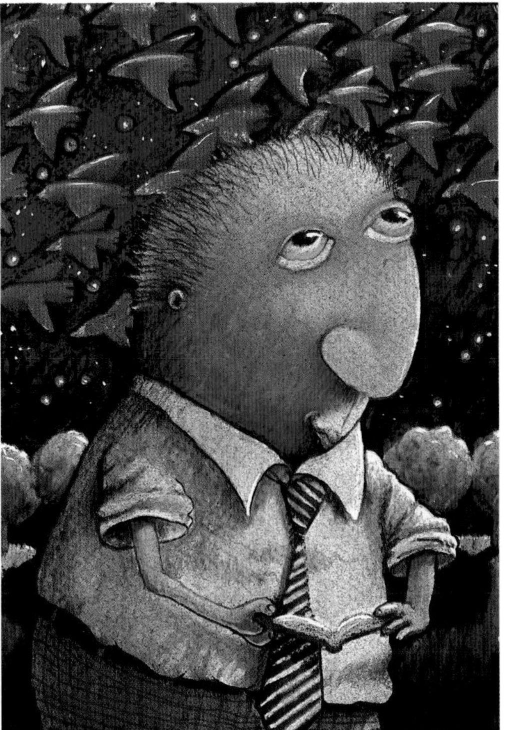

4

Facing Page
Don Sullivan

1 *Lake Nite Swim*
5 x 7" (127 x 178 mm)
Canson Paper

2 *Fallen Star Found*
12 x 8" (305 x 203 mm)
Canson Paper

3 *History of Illustration*
21 x 14" (533 x 356 mm)
Stonehenge Paper

4 *Phlamingos*
5 x 7" (127 x 178 mm)
Canson Paper

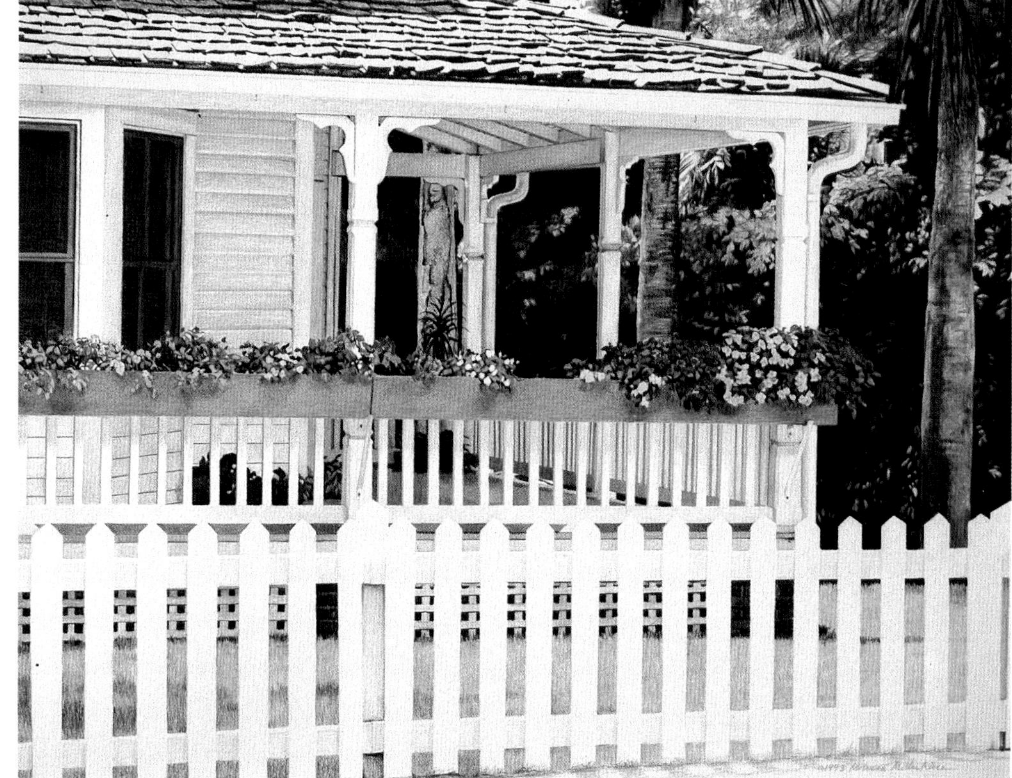

1

This Page
Melissa Miller Nece

1 *Green and White*
22 x 28" (559 x 711 mm)
Letramax 2200 Cold Press Illustration

2 *Night Neon I (Twilight Zone)*
20 x 32" (508 x 813 mm)
Black Illustration Board

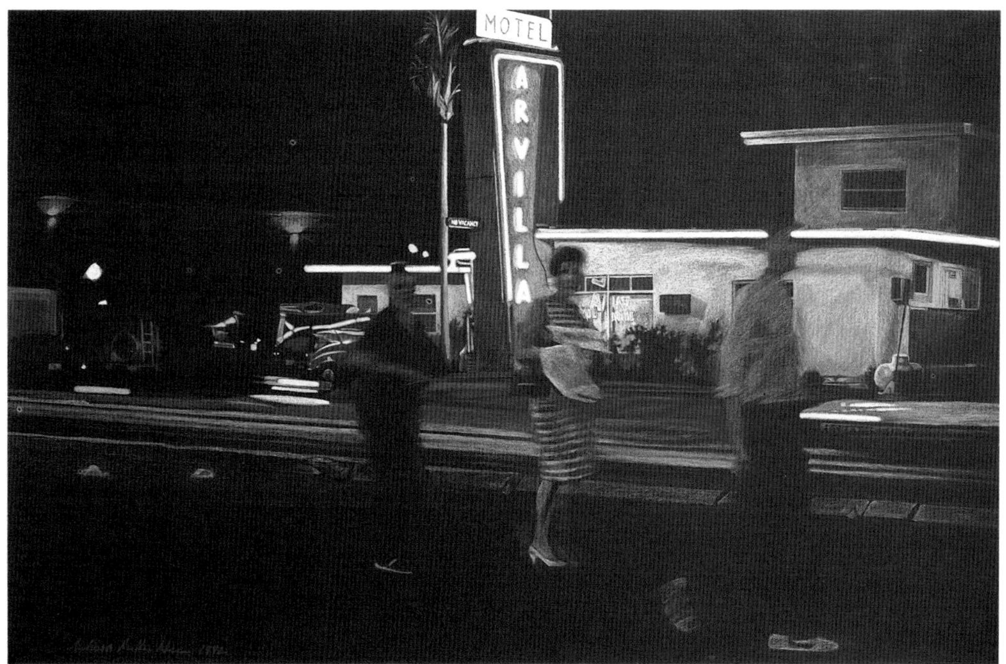

2

Jan Rimerman

1 *Treasures of Tutankhamun's Tomb*
41 x 31" (1,041 x 787 mm)
100% Rag Board, 8-ply
Vellum Finish

Marjorie Post

2 *Sun Storm*
42 x 27" (1,067 x 686 mm)
4-ply Rising Museum Board

3 *Trio*
19 x 38" (482 x 965 mm)
Crescent Rag Board

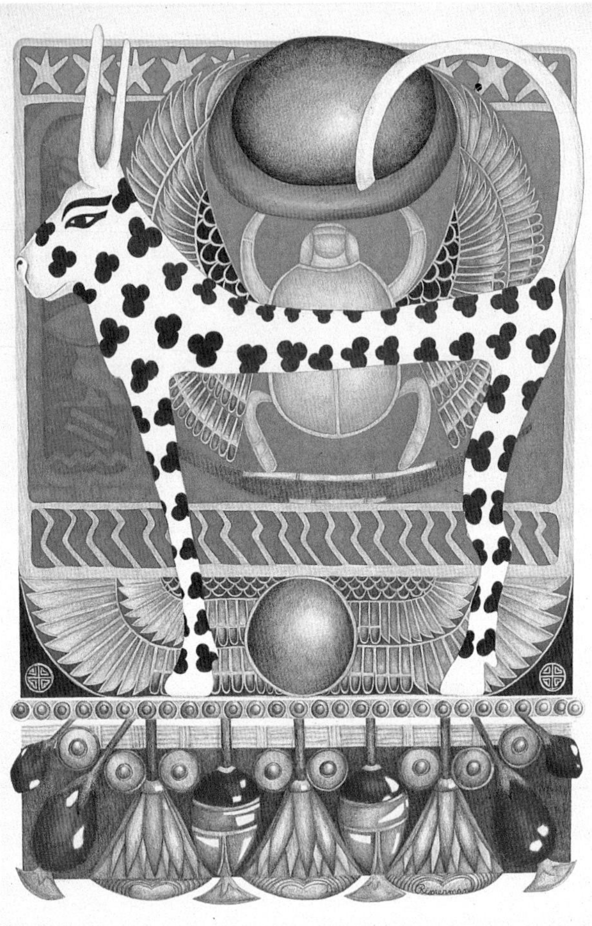

1

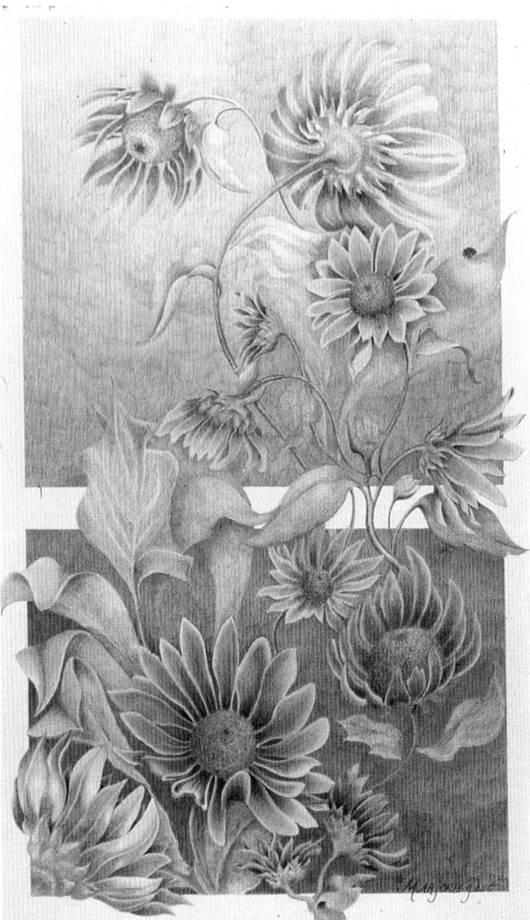

2

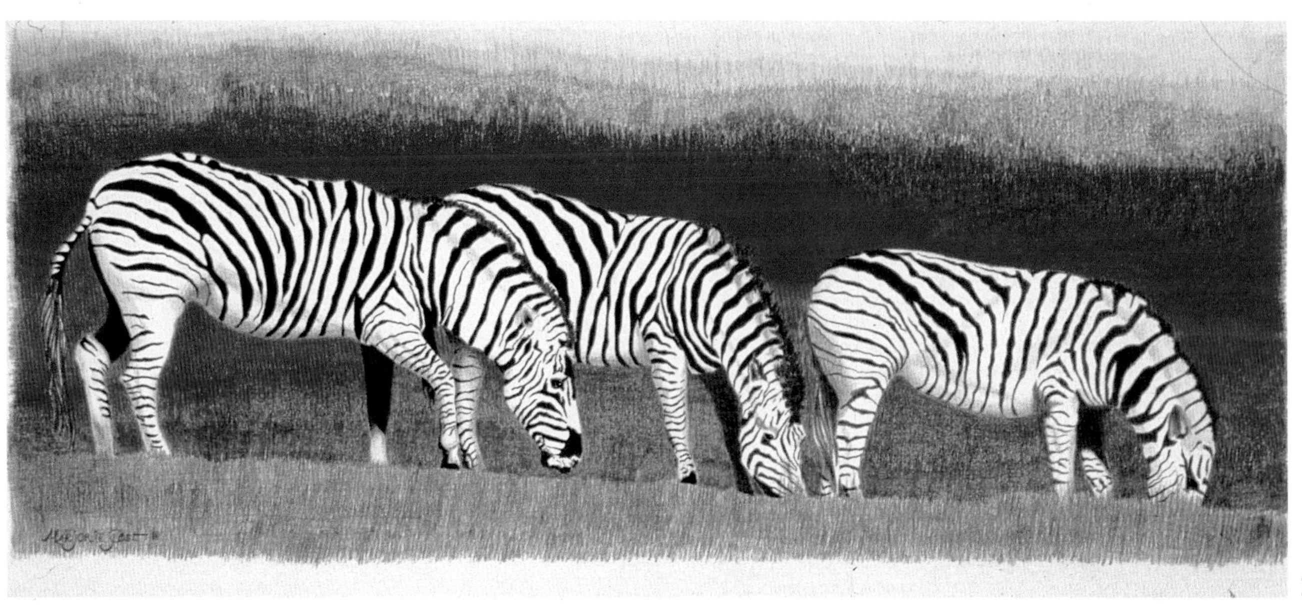

3

1

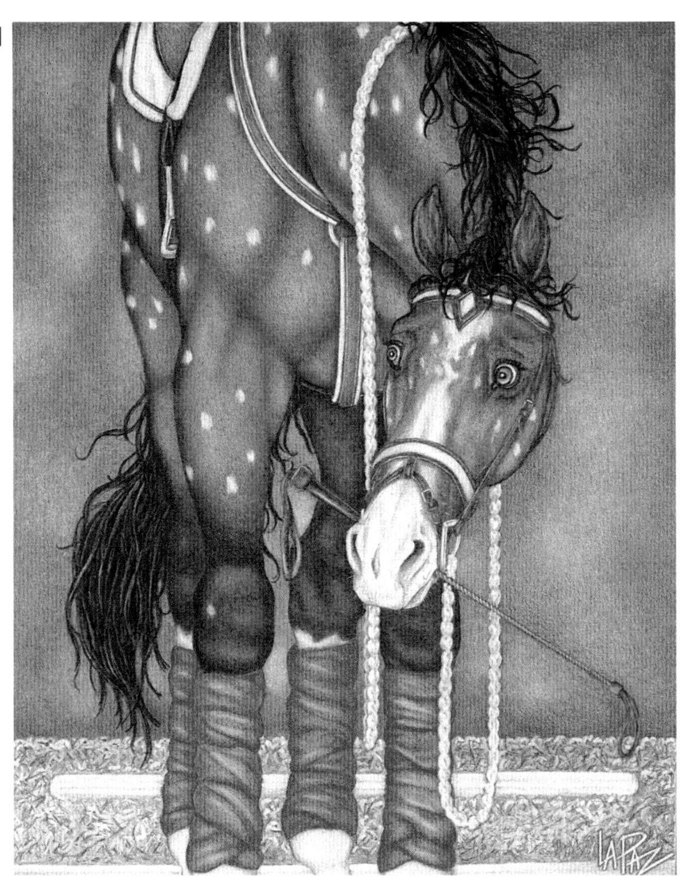

2

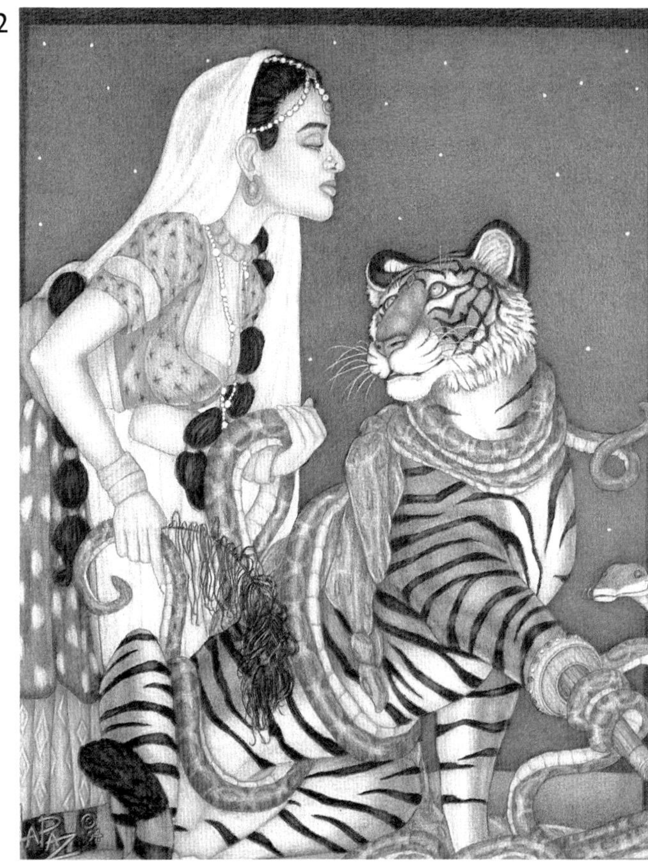

Viktoria La Paz

1 *Fifine Loses Her Rider*
15 x 12" (381 x 305 mm)
Crescent Hot Press 215 Illustration Board
Technique: Colored Pencil, Watercolor

2 *Tiger Is Teased*
19 x 15" (483 x 381 mm)
Crescent Hot Press 201 Illustration Board

Susan Y. West

3 *Precious Paisley*
12 x 16" (292 x 394 mm)
Rives Smooth

3

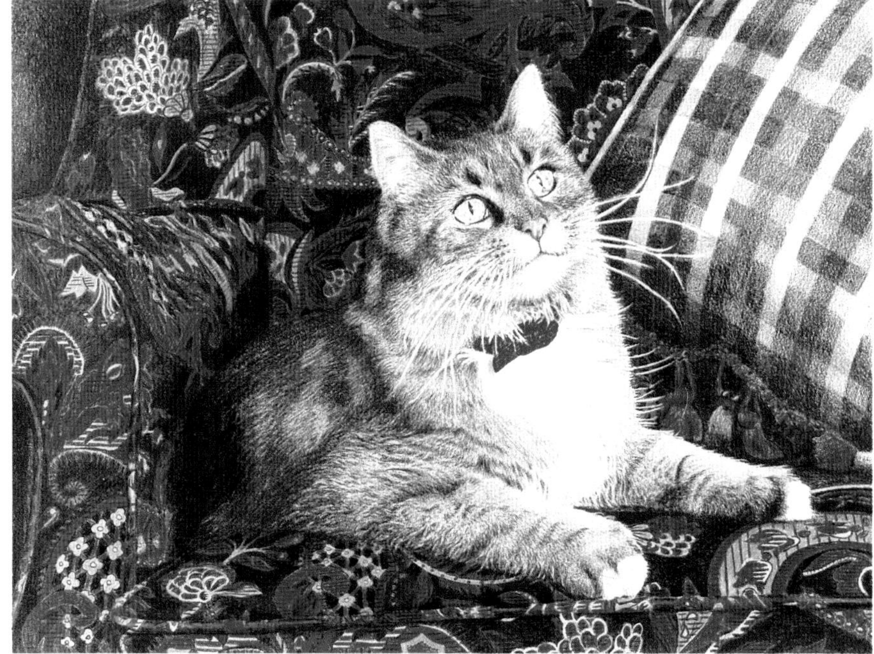

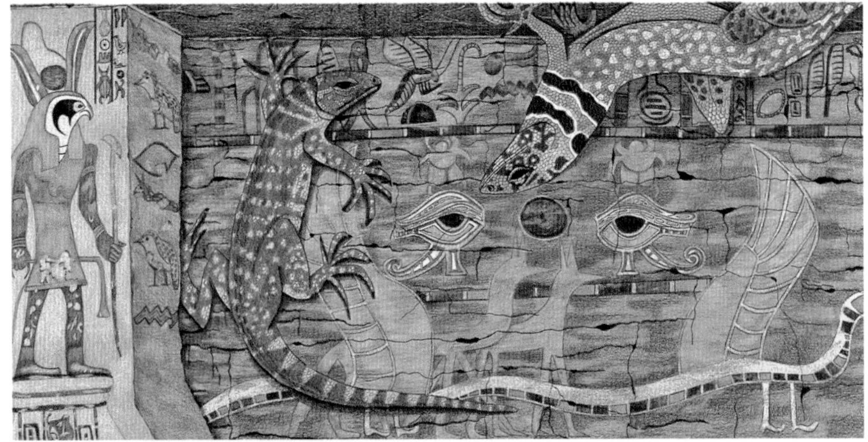

1

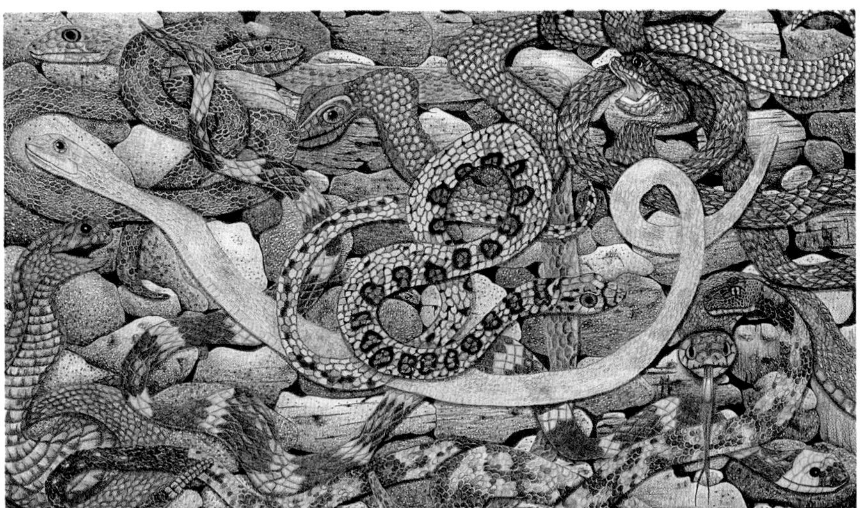

2

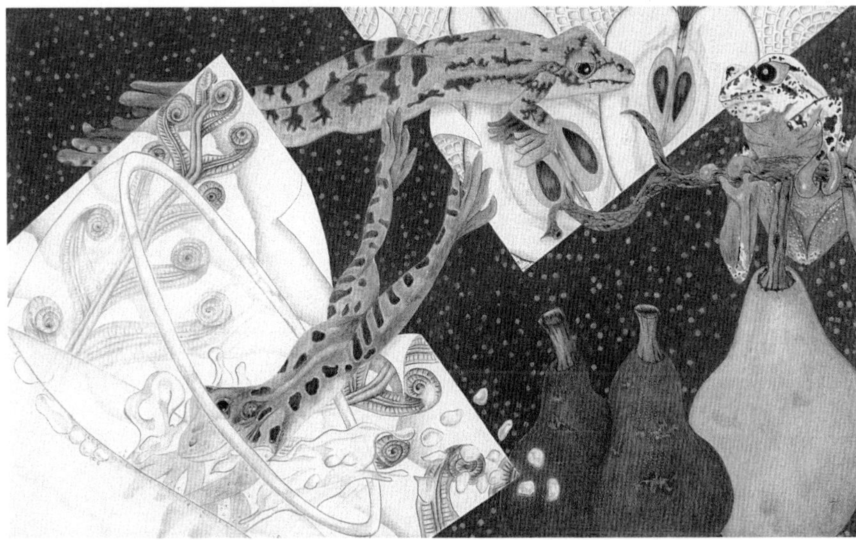

3

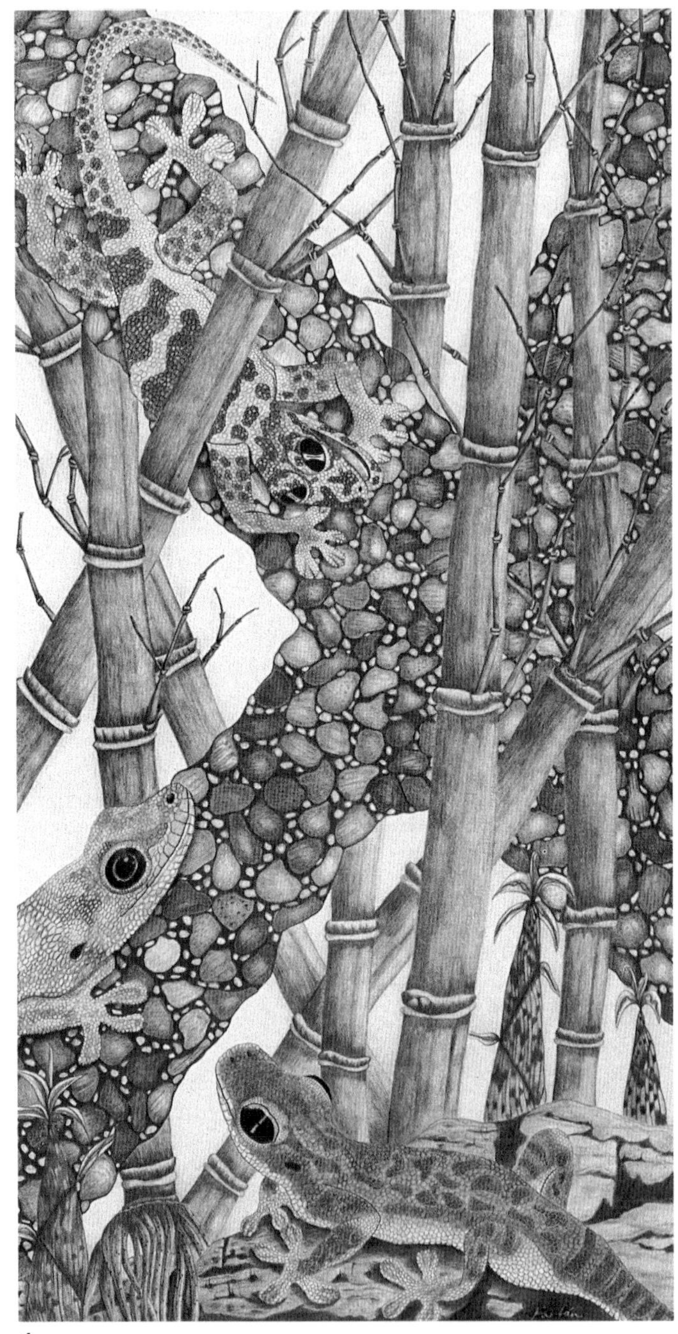

4

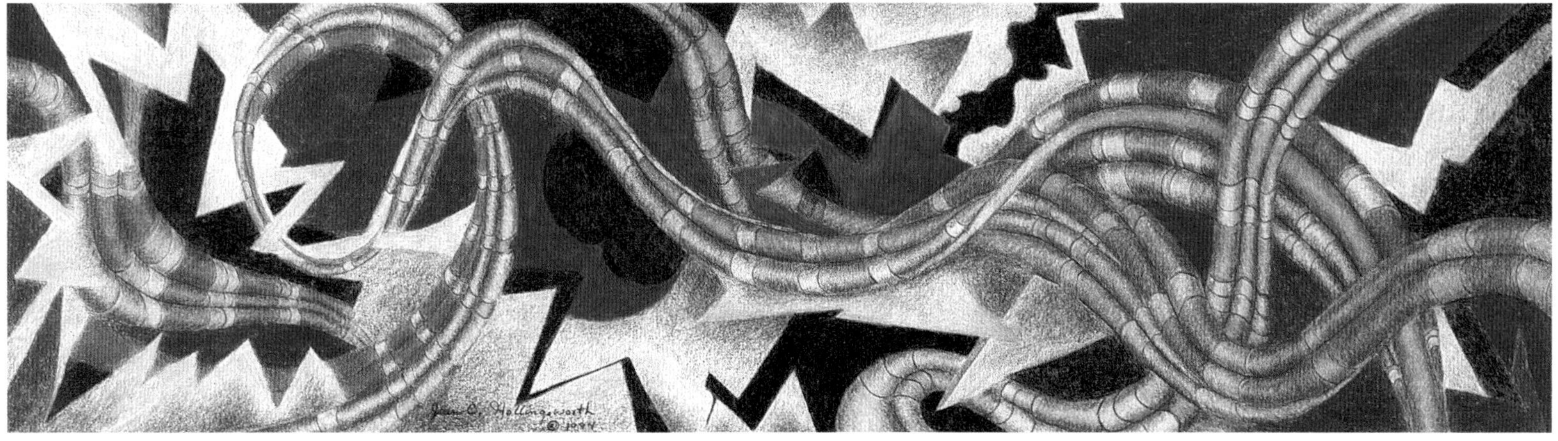

1

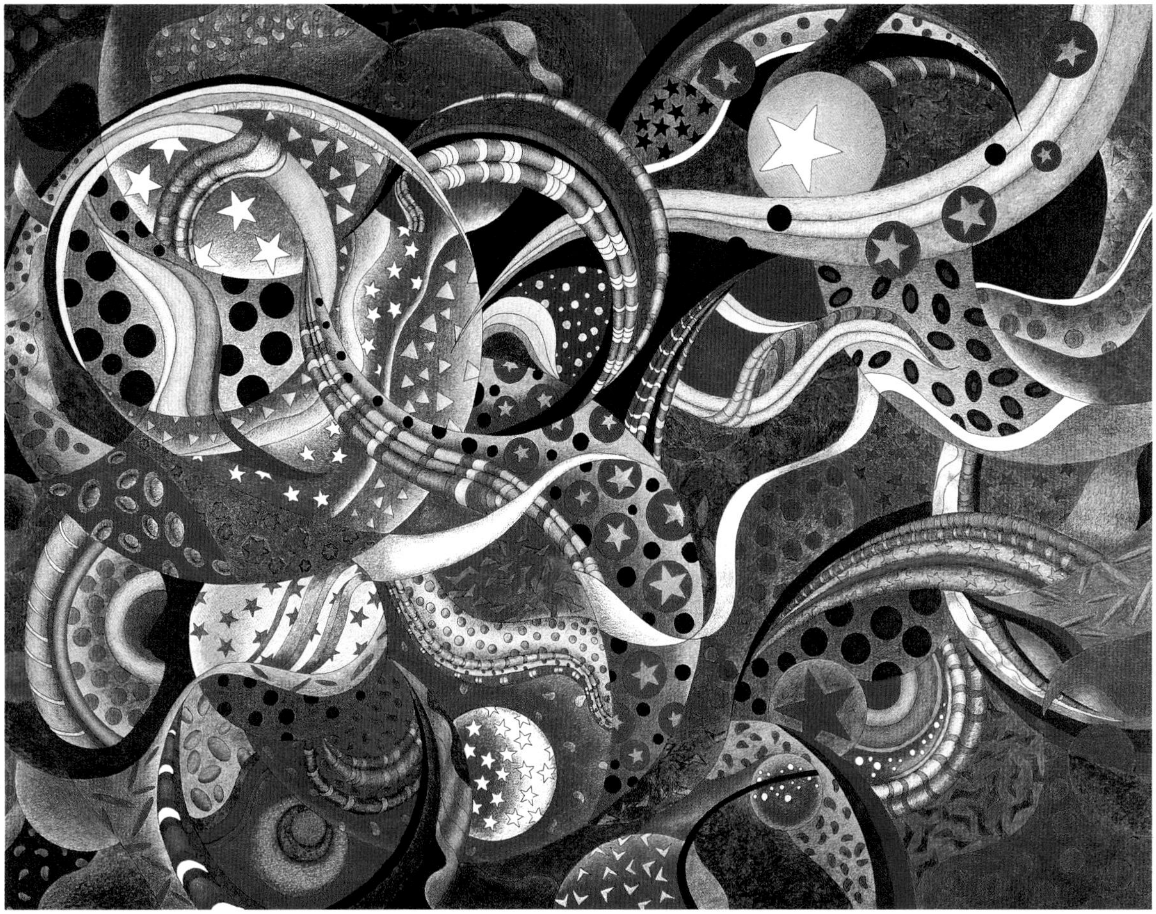

2

Facing Page

Rhonda Farfan

1 *At The Eyes of Horus*
 14 x 29" (356 x 737 mm)
 Crescent 2-ply Museum Board

2 *Mr. Line On The Rocks*
 15 x 27" (381 x 692 mm)
 Crescent 2-ply Museum Board

3 *Leap of Faith*
 17 x 29" (432 x 740 mm)
 Crescent 2-ply Museum Board

4 *Crossroads*
 29 x 15" (740 x 381 mm)
 Crescent 2-ply Museum Board

This Page

Joan C. Hollingsworth

1 *Untitled*
 6 x 22" (152 x 559 mm)
 3-ply Museum Board
 Technique: Burnishing

2 *Heaven of Stars*
 28 x 36" (711 x 914 mm)
 3-ply Museum Board
 Technique: Colored Pencil, Black Ink Burnishing

Mark Frazer

1 *(Big Green Pea) Series*
11 x 17" (279 x 432 mm)
Acid Free Copy Paper

2 *(Big Green Pea) Series*
11 x 17" (279 x 432 mm)
Acid Free Copy Paper

Timothy A. Smith

3 *Mick Jagger*
14 x 11" (349 x 267 mm)
Canson Mi Tientes Paper

4 *Jim's Fall*
16 x 13" (406 x 330 mm)
Canson Mi Tientes Paper

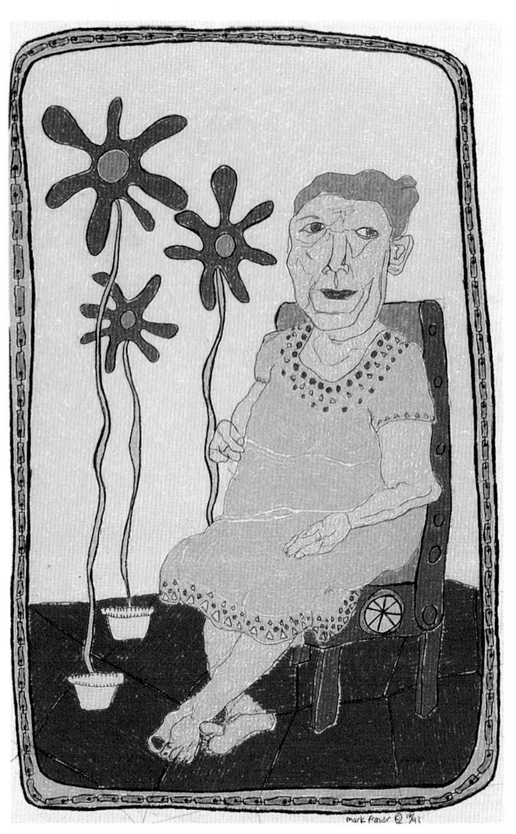

1

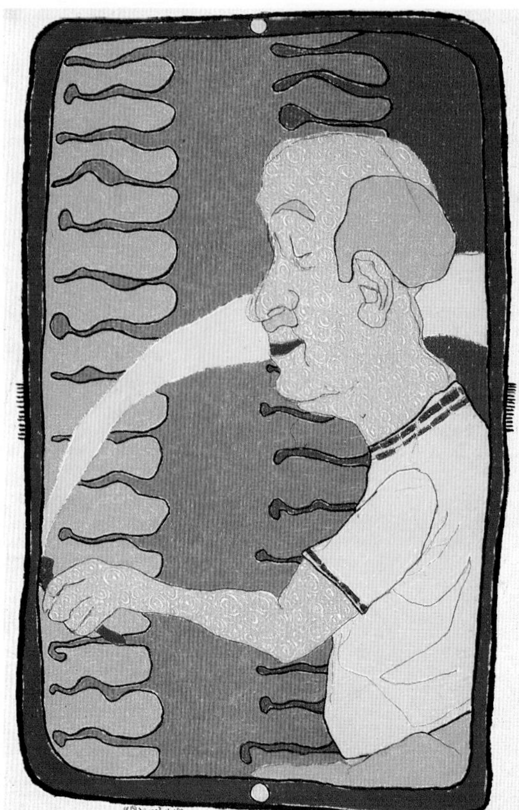

2

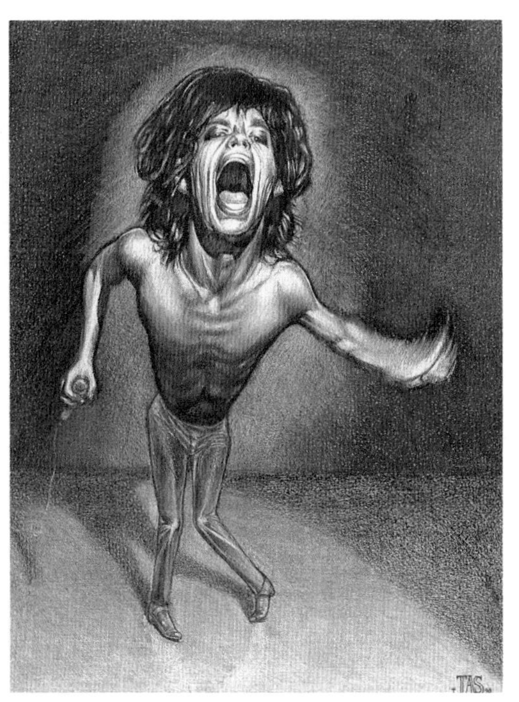

3

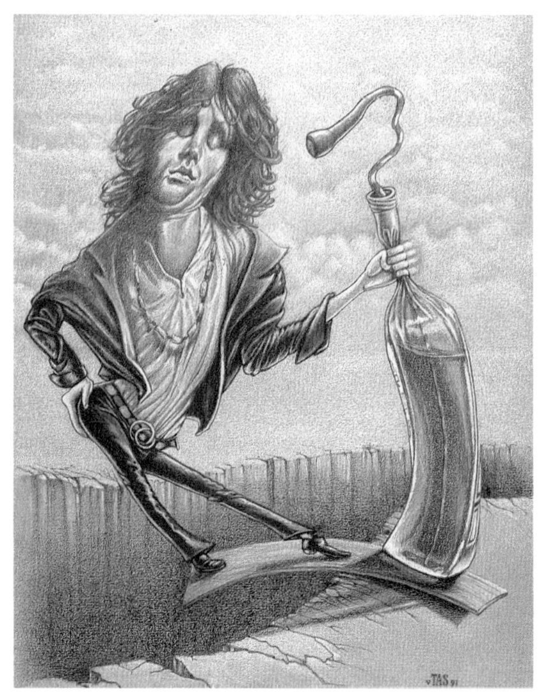

4

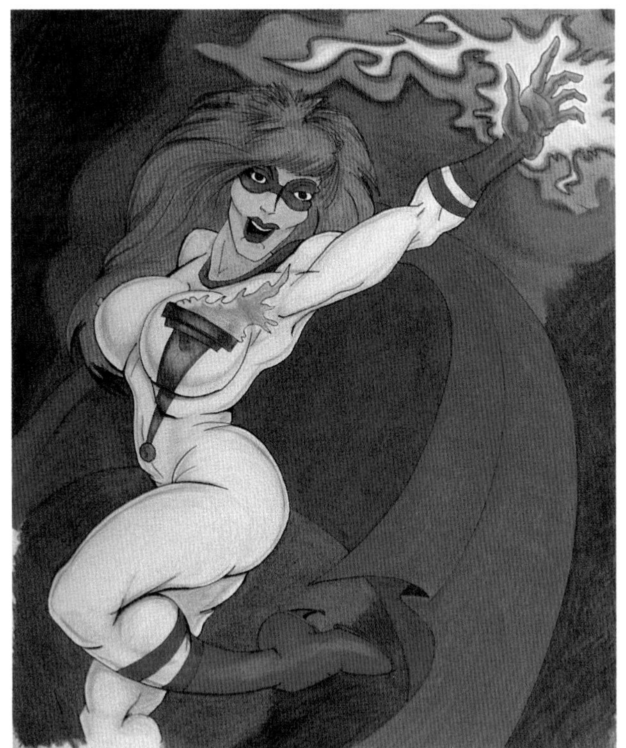
1

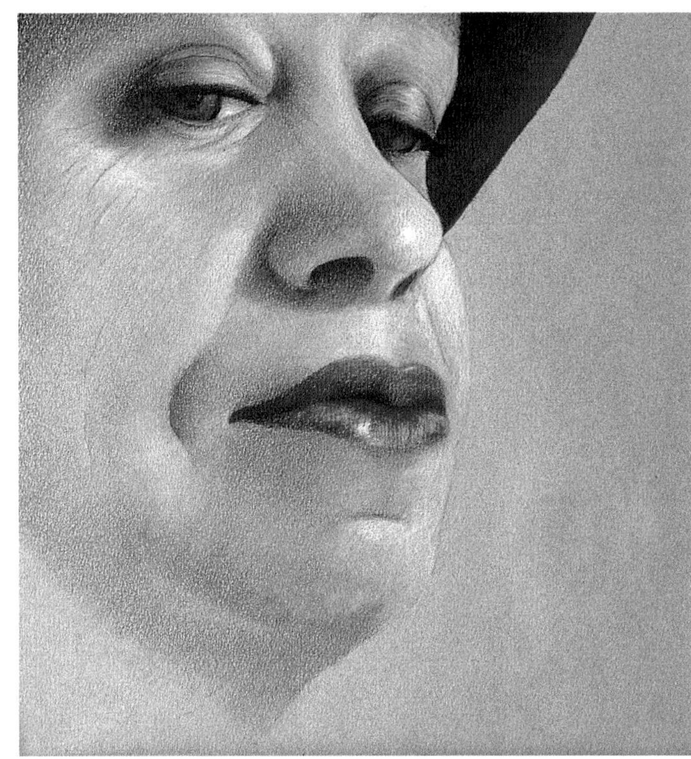
2

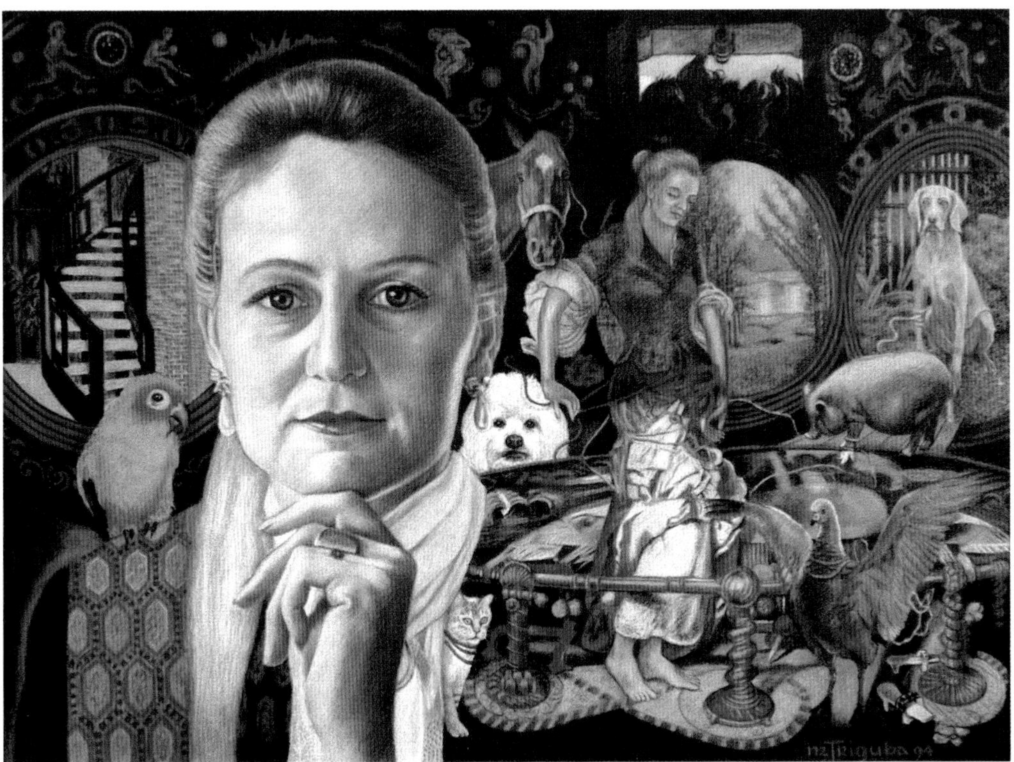

3

Brian Bednarek

1 *Torchy*
17 x 14" (432 x 356 mm)
2-ply Bristol Medium
Technique: Colored Pencil, India Ink

Margot Van Horn

2 *Marlene*
11 x 10" (279 x 254 mm)
Grey Canson Paper

Marvin Triguba

3 *Dream Weaver*
18 x 24" (457 x 610 mm)
Canson Paper
Technique: Burnishing

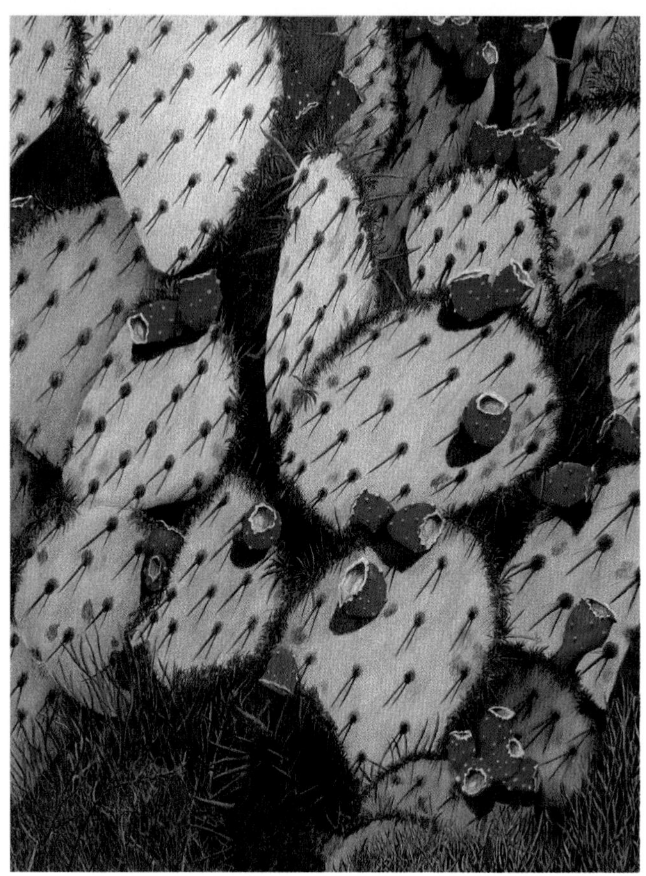

1

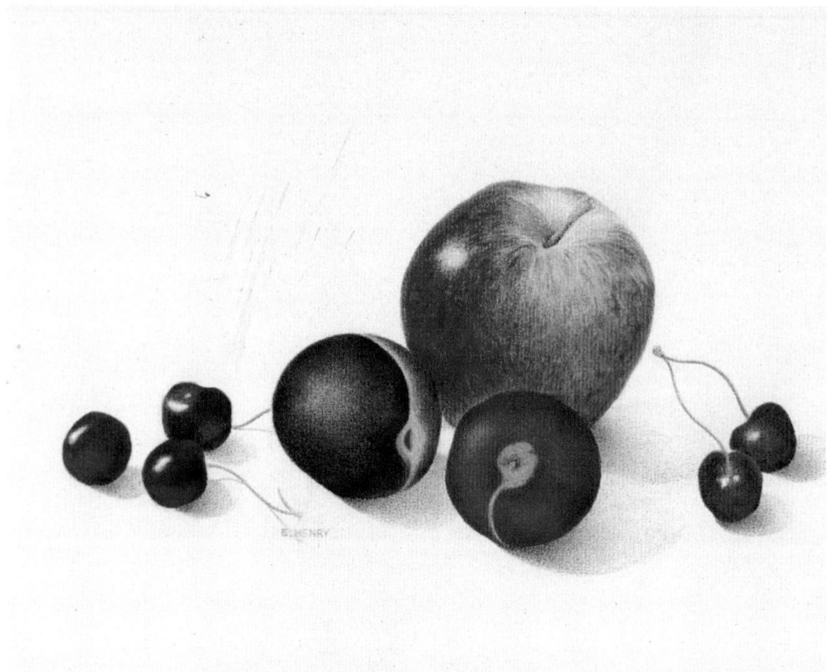

2

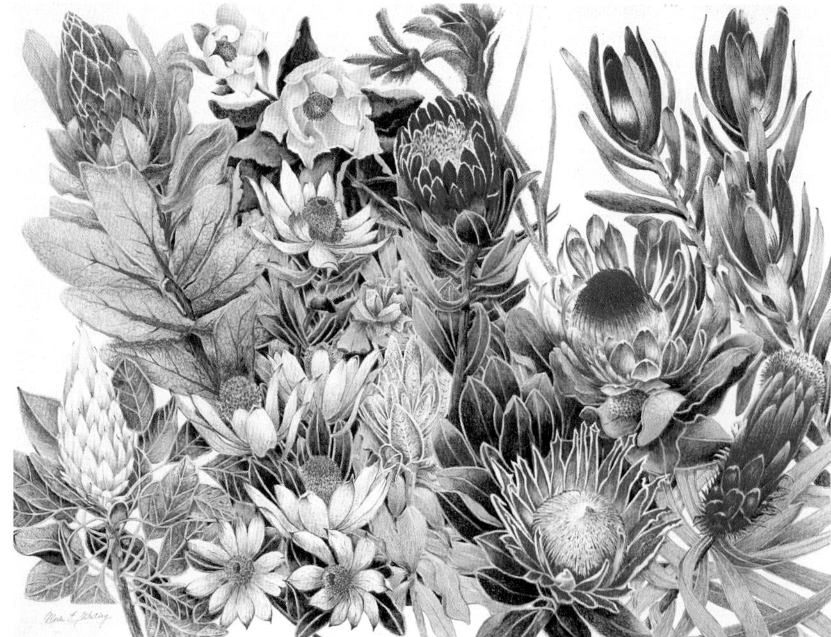

3

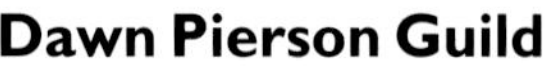

Dawn Pierson Guild

1 *Prickly Pear Cactus*
16 x 13" (406 x 330 mm)
Smooth Bristol Paper
Technique: Burnishing

Edna L. Henry

2 *Fruit*
7 x 10" (178 x 254 mm)
2-ply Rising Museum Board

Merle E. Whitley

3 *Protea # 1*
22 x 28" (559 x 711 mm)
Strathmore Plate Finish Board

Shelly M. Stewart

1 *Meadowlights*
11 x 20" (279 x 508 mm)
Strathmore Plate Bristol

2 *Sol's Harvest*
13 x 17" (318 x 432 mm)
Strathmore Plate Bristol

Brenda Woggon

3 *Spring Light*
30 x 22" (762 x 559 mm)
D'Arches Cold Press Watercolor Paper

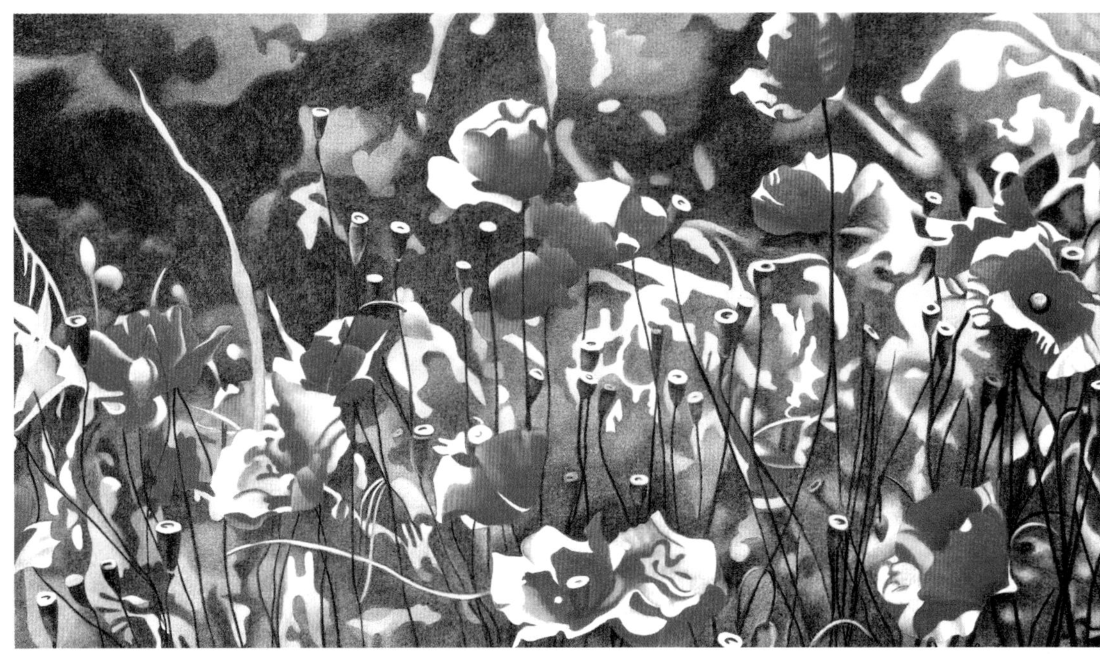

1

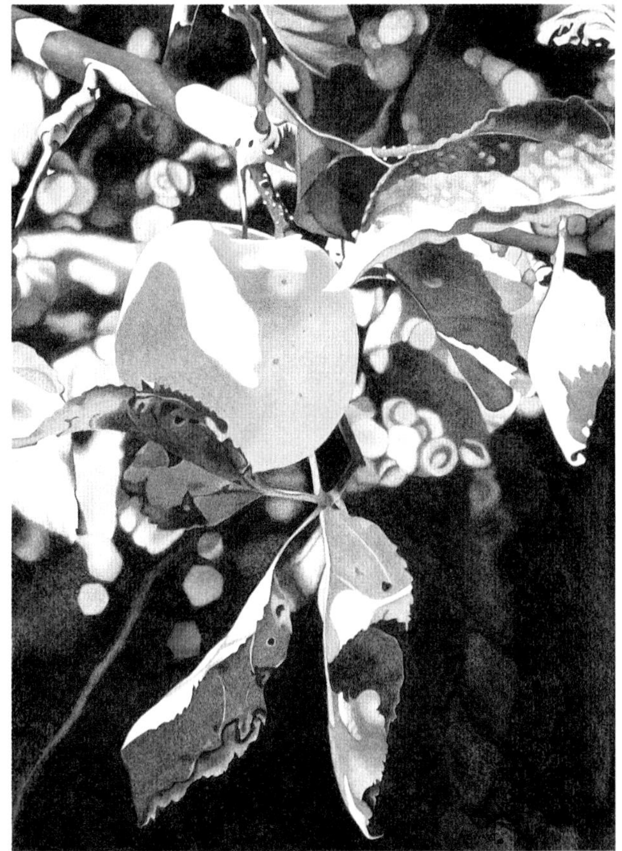

2

3

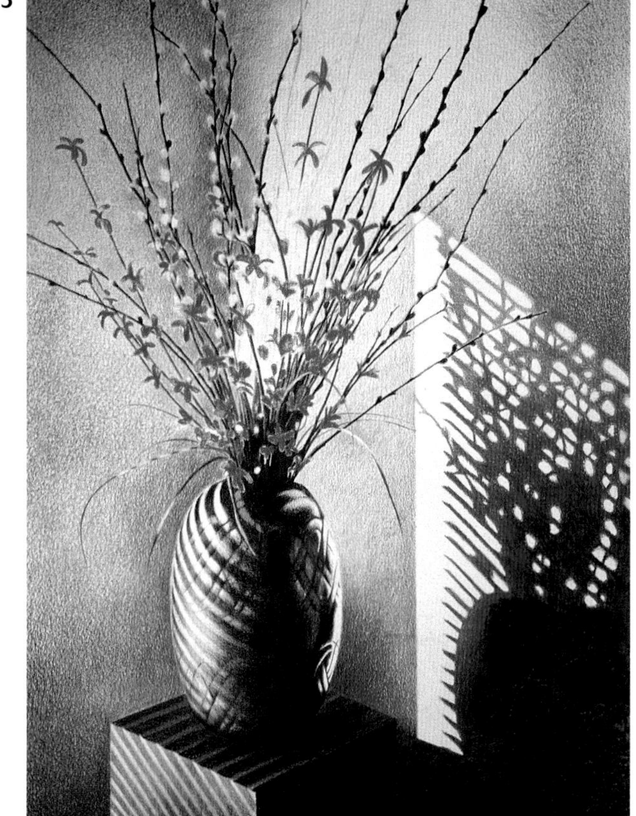

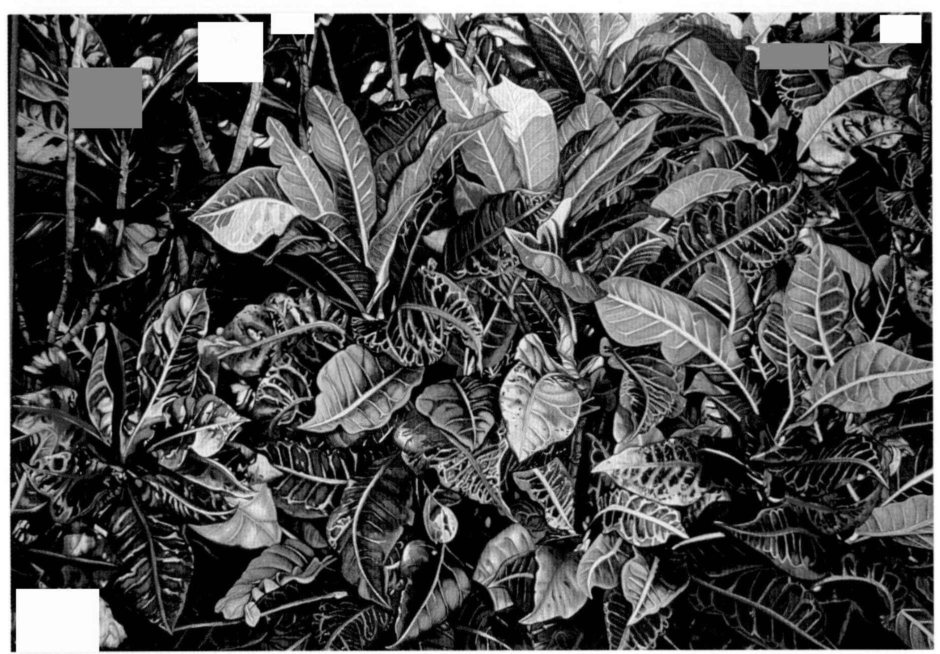

1

Mary Pohlmann

1 *Croton*
30 x 44" (762 x 1,118 mm)
Somerset Satin Board
Technique: Burnishing

Carlynne Hershberger

2 *Windblown*
12 x 9" (305 x 229 mm)
Ivy Canson Pastel Paper

Charles Aquilina

3 *Rubicon*
40 x 30" (1,016 x 762 mm)
Colored Strathmore Board

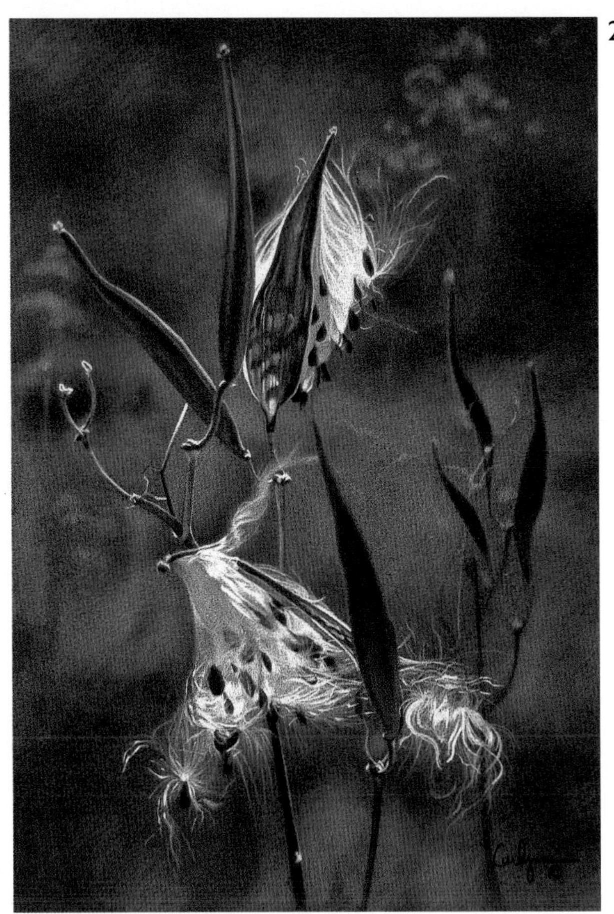

2

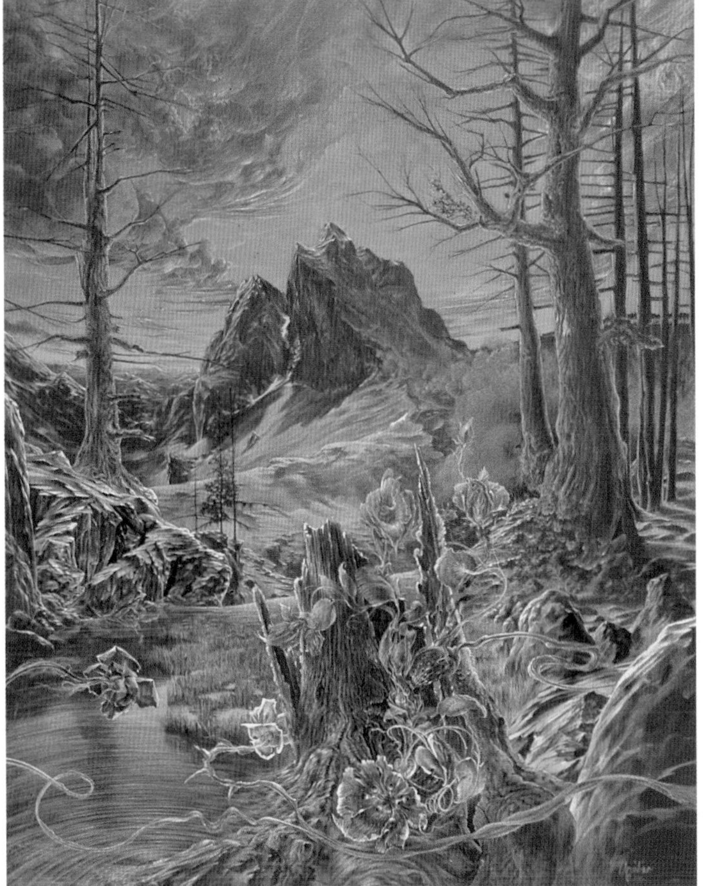

3

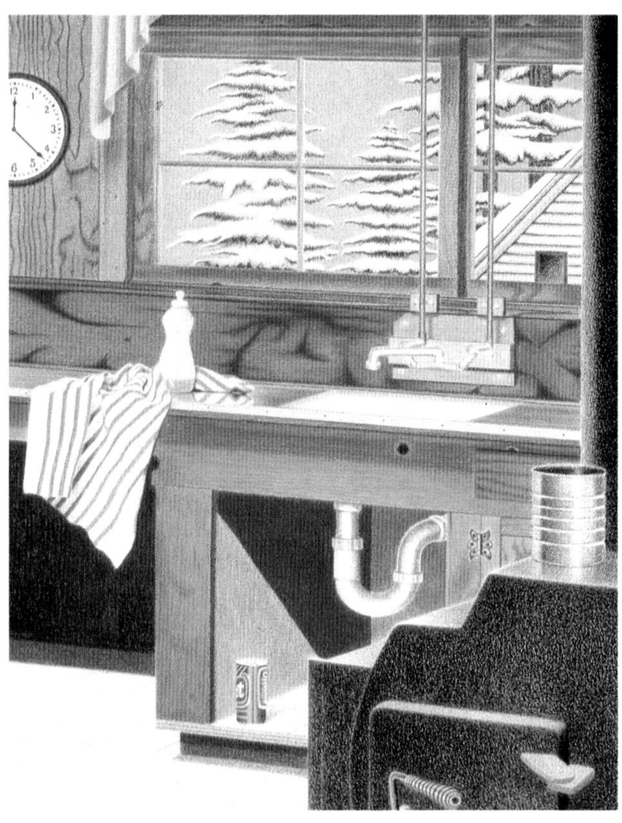

1

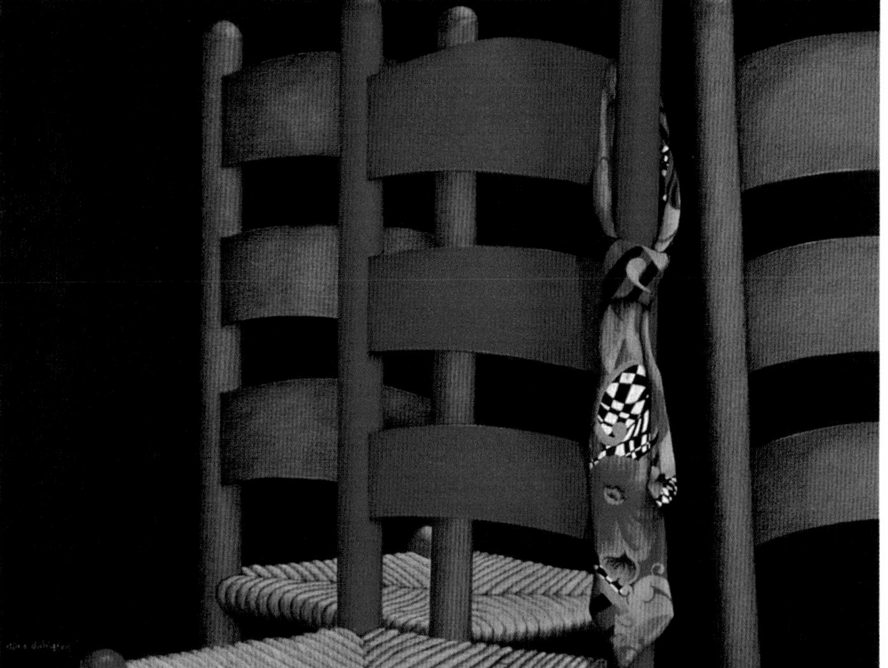

2

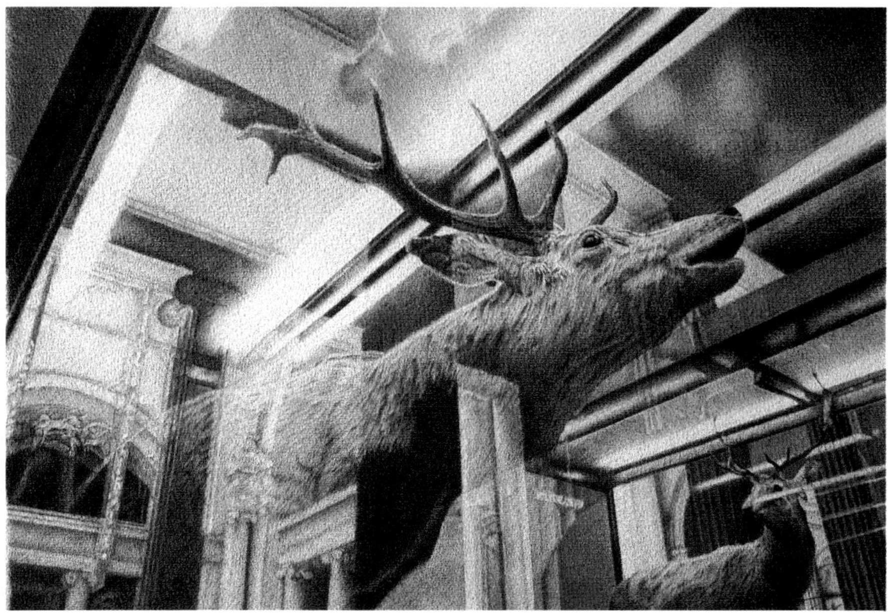

3

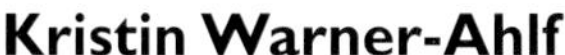

Kristin Warner-Ahlf

1 *A View From The "Jay"*
11 x 9" (279 x 216 mm)
3-Ply Strathmore 500 Bristol, Regular Surface

Dava Dahlgran

2 *Passive Cacophony*
20 x 25" (495 x 635 mm)
Strathmore Pastel/Charcoal Paper-Board

Gilbert Rocha

3 *Reflections of a Red Deer*
9 x 12" (216 x 311 mm)
Fabriano 140 lb. Cold Press
Technique: Watercolor Paper

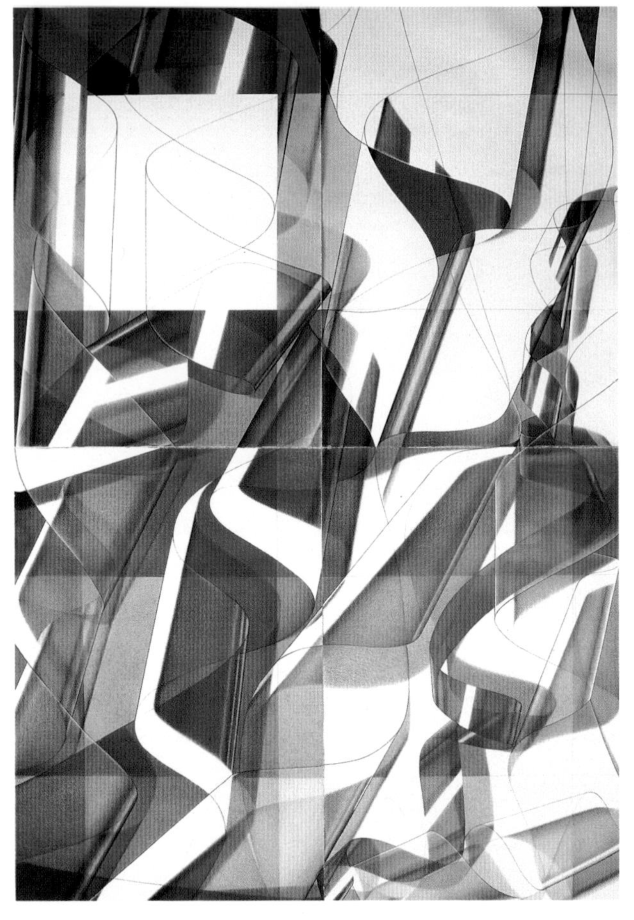
1

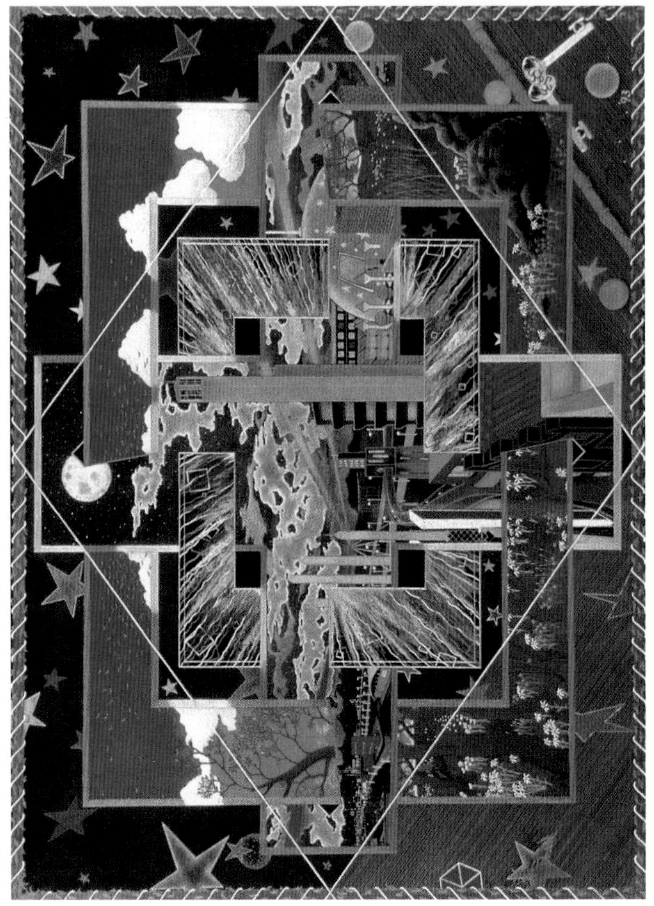
2

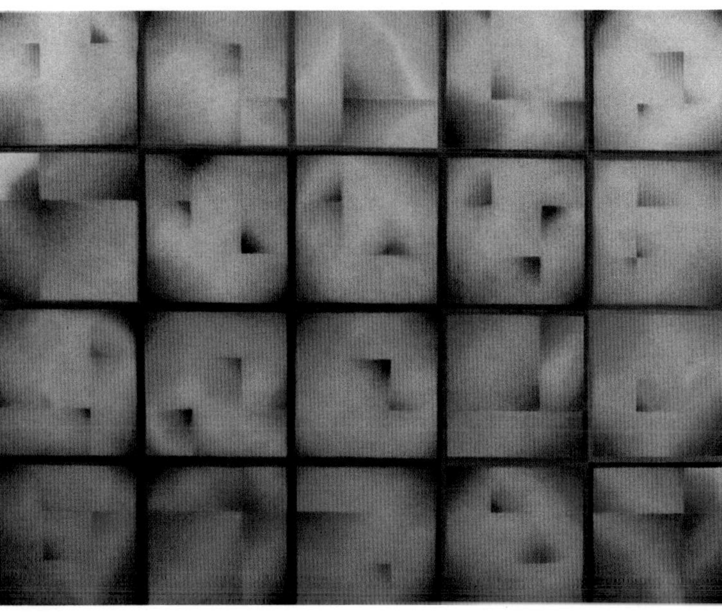
3

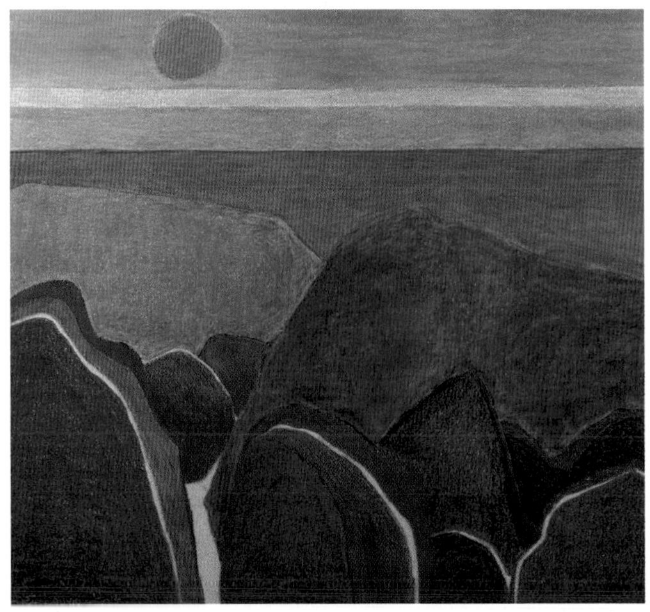
4

Facing Page

Lula Mae Blocton

1 *SRPO*
30 x 41" (762 x 1,041 mm)
100% Rag Paper

Jerry L. Baker

2 *Untitled*
19 x 14" (489 x 362 mm)
Letramax Super Black

Steph Lanyon

3 *The Color of Money*
16 x 20" (394 x 495 mm)
Bristol Board

Janet Louvau Holt

4 *Setting Sun*
14 x 16" (349 x 406 mm)
2-ply Rising Museum Board
Technique: Burnishing

This Page

Lee Sims

1 *Magic Lantern*
8 x 12" (197 x 305 mm)
Canson Mi Tientes Colored Paper

Linda C. Vanden Bosch

2 *On a Summer's Afternoon*
20 x 30" (508 x 762 mm)
Hot Press Illustration Board
Media: Colored Pencil, Black Marker
Technique: Burnishing

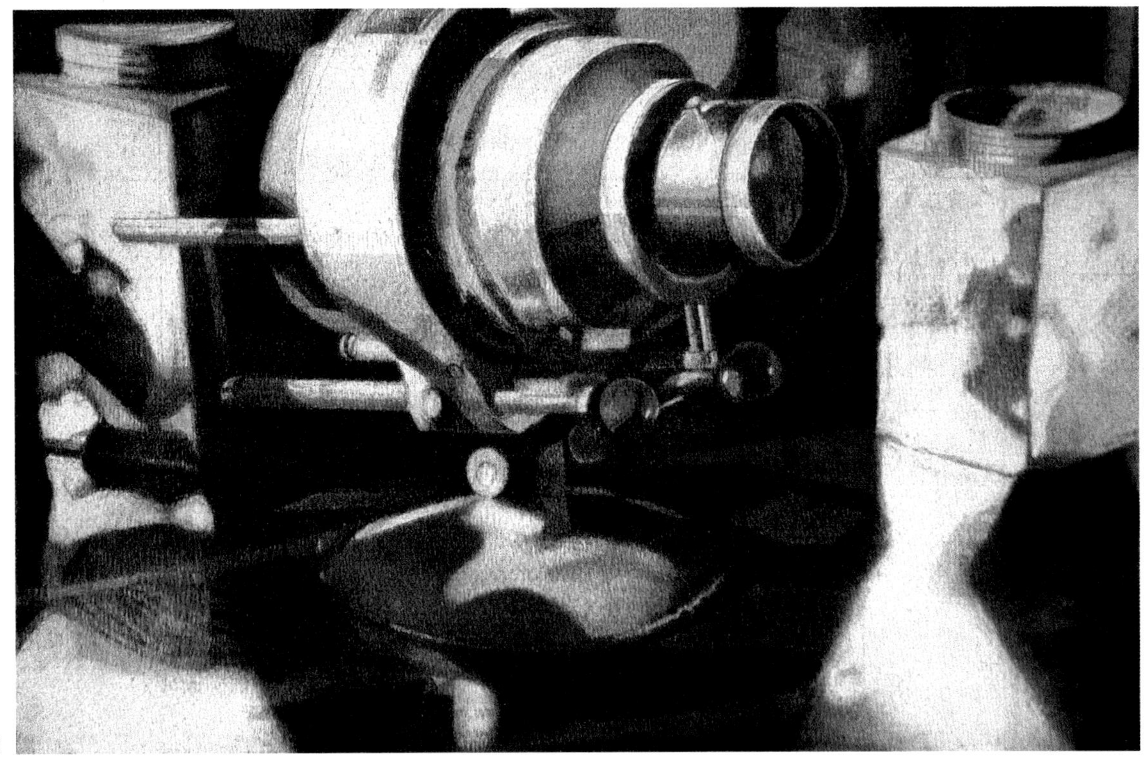

1

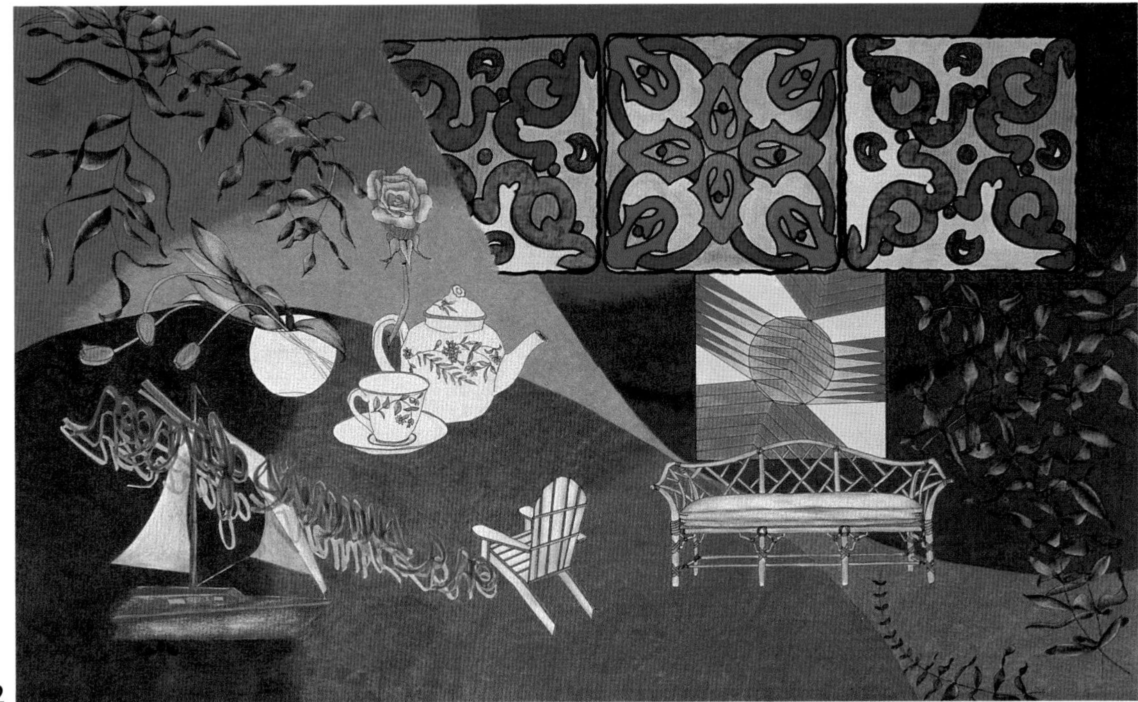

2

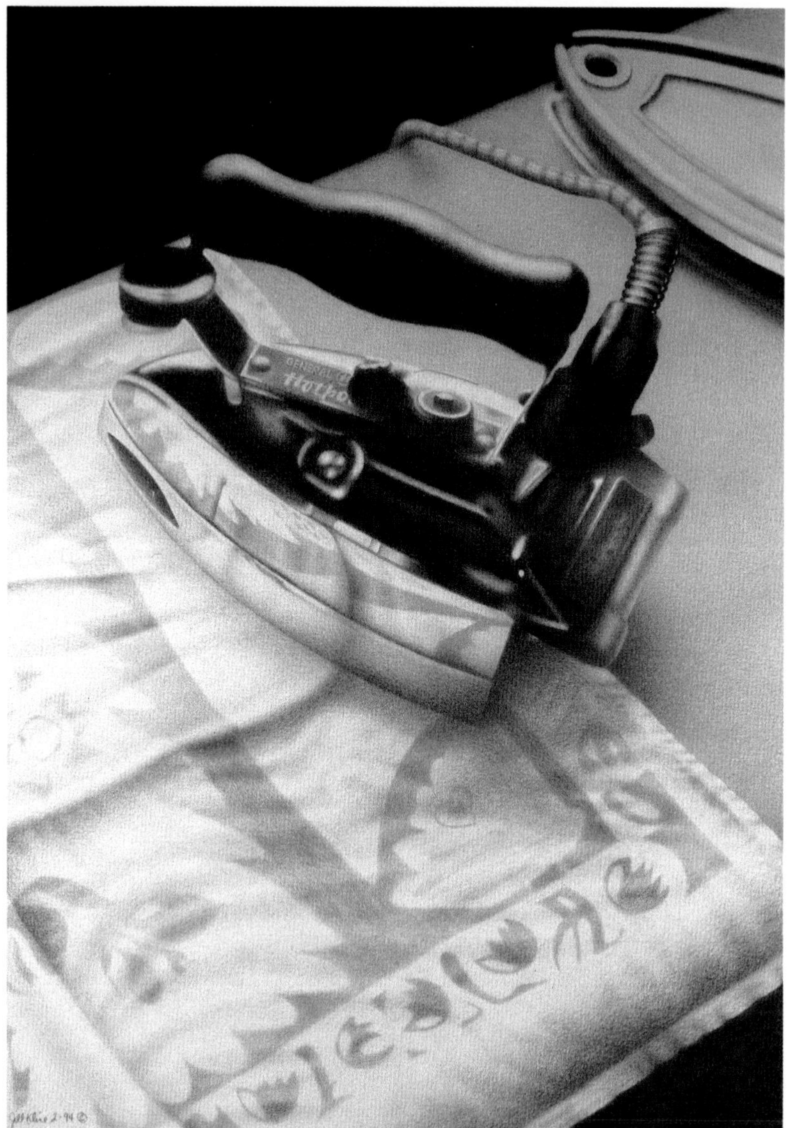

1

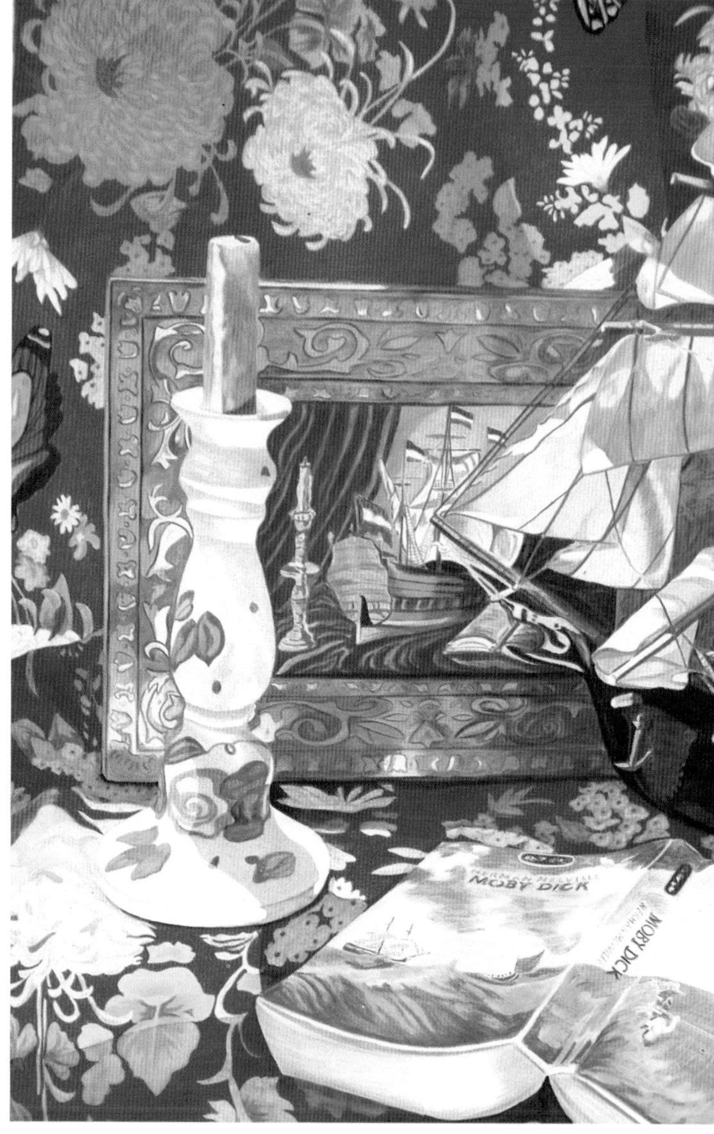

2

Jill Kline

1 *Frayed*
20 x 15" (495 x 38 mm)
3-ply Bristol Board

Valerie Rhatigan

2 *The Sewing Box*
37 x 27" (940 x 686 mm)
140 lb. Hot Pressed Arches Paper

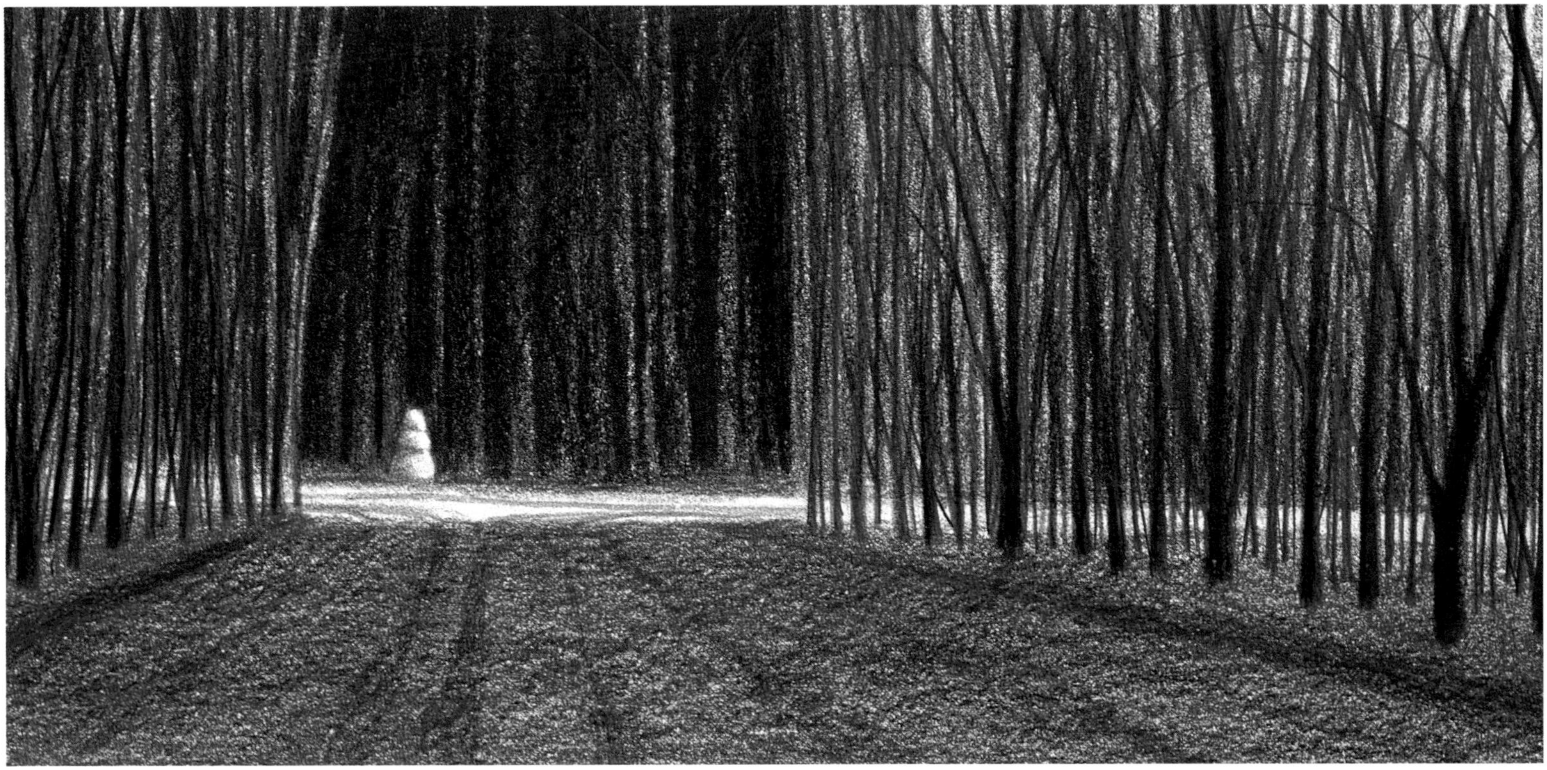

1

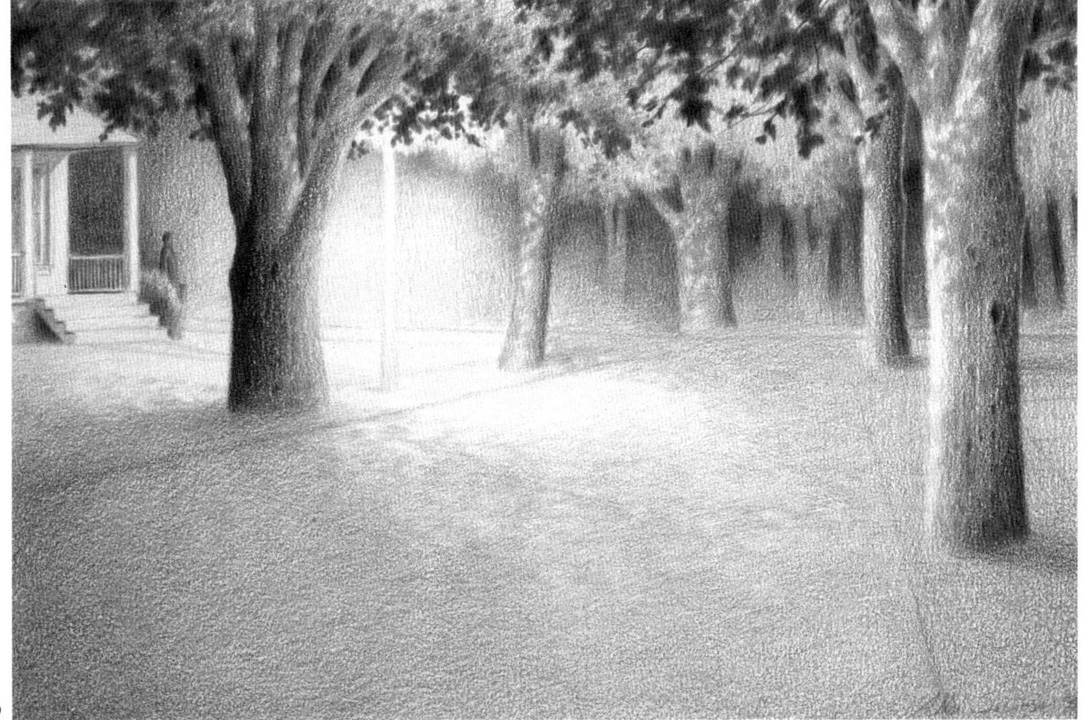

2

Allan Servoss

1 *Street of Mystery*
12 x 15" (305 x 381 mm)
Canson Paper
Technique: Tonal Application

2 *One Night in January*
12 x 20" (305 x 508 mm)
Canson Paper
Technique: Tonal Application

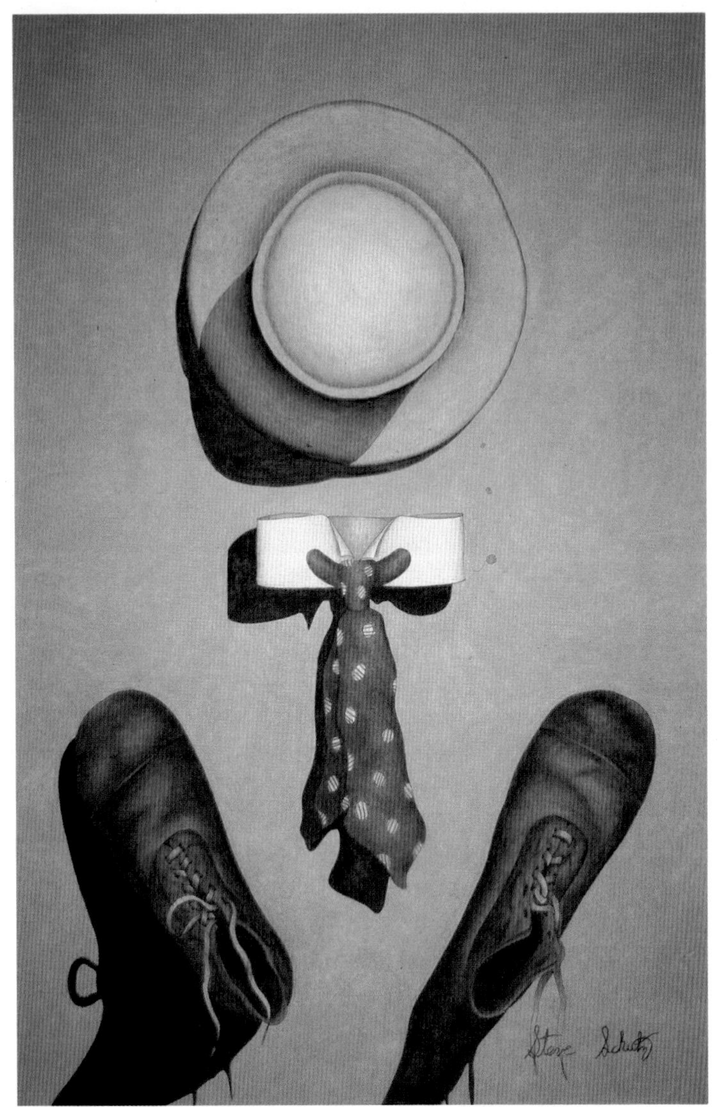

1

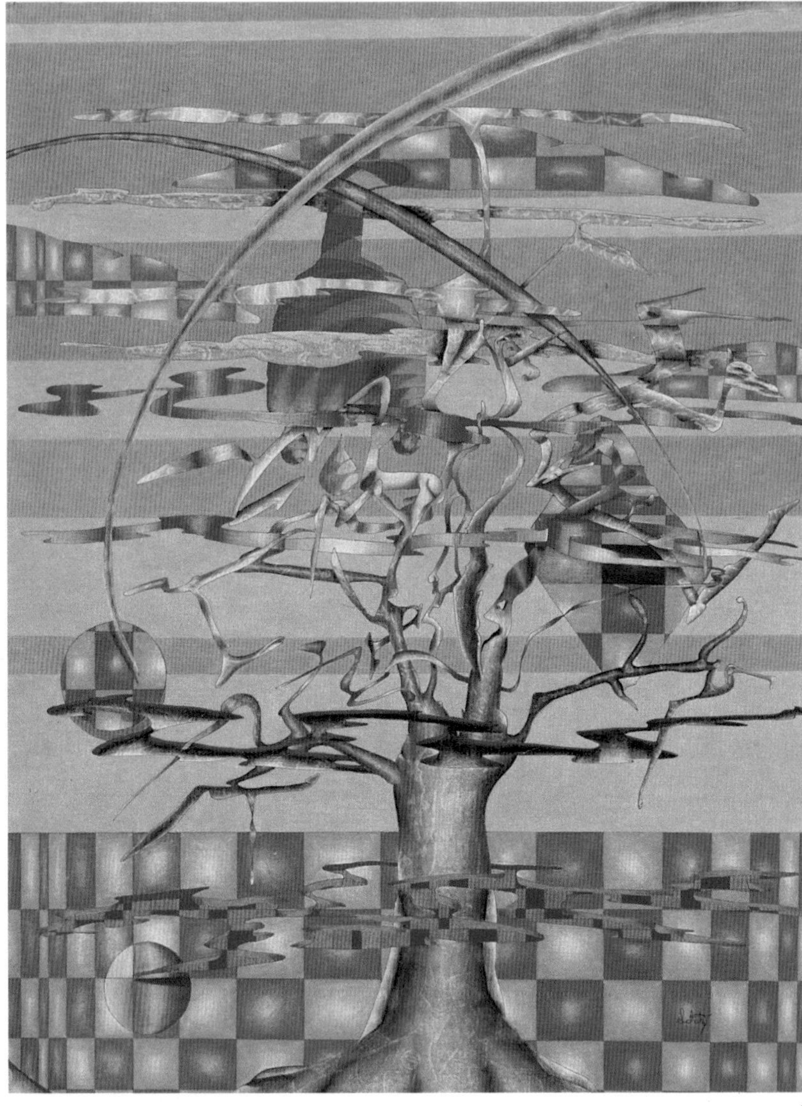

2

Steve Schultz

1 *Buster's Memory*
24 x 18" (610 x 457 mm)
Standard Crescent Board
Technique: Burnishing

2 *Tree # I*
22 x 28" (559 x 711 mm)
Standard White Craft Paper
Technique: Burnishing

June Noon Bensinger

1 *All These Distances*
26 x 35" (659 x 887 mm)

Linda Wesner

2 *Interlude III*
18 x 24" (457 x 610 mm)
Strathmore 500 Series

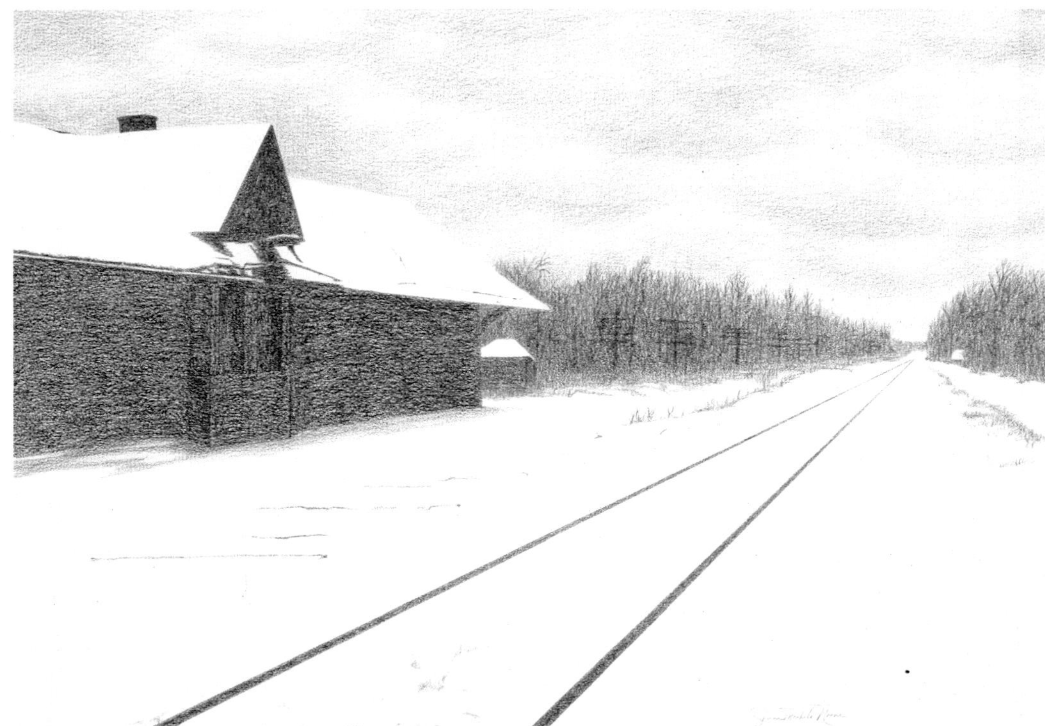

1

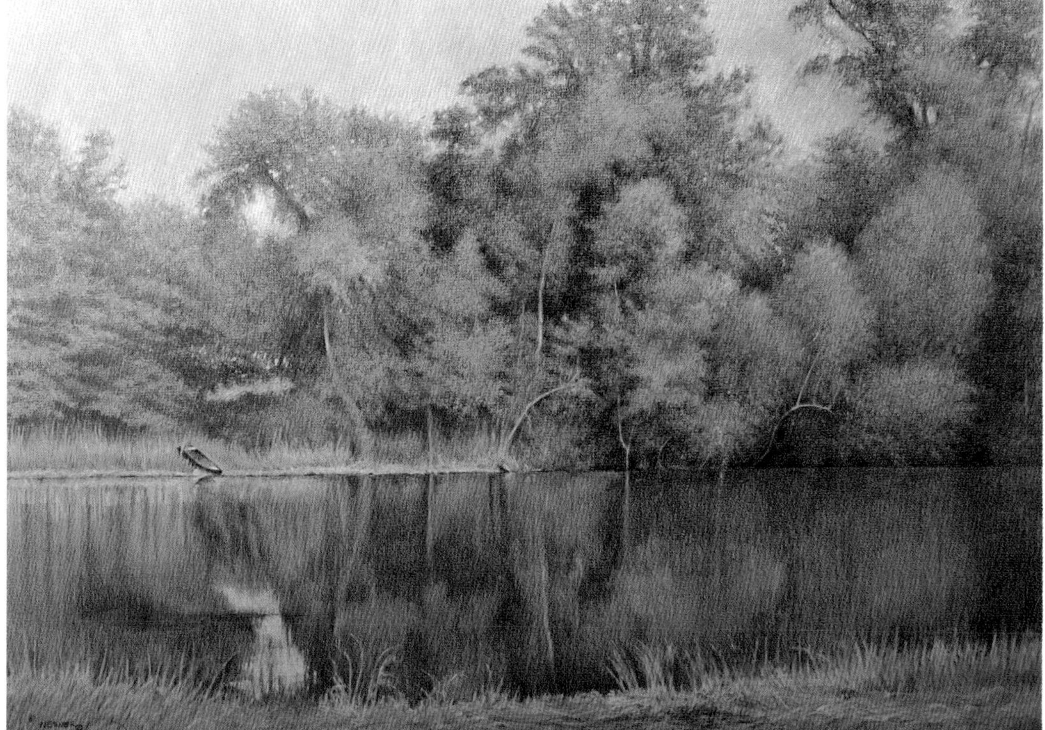

2

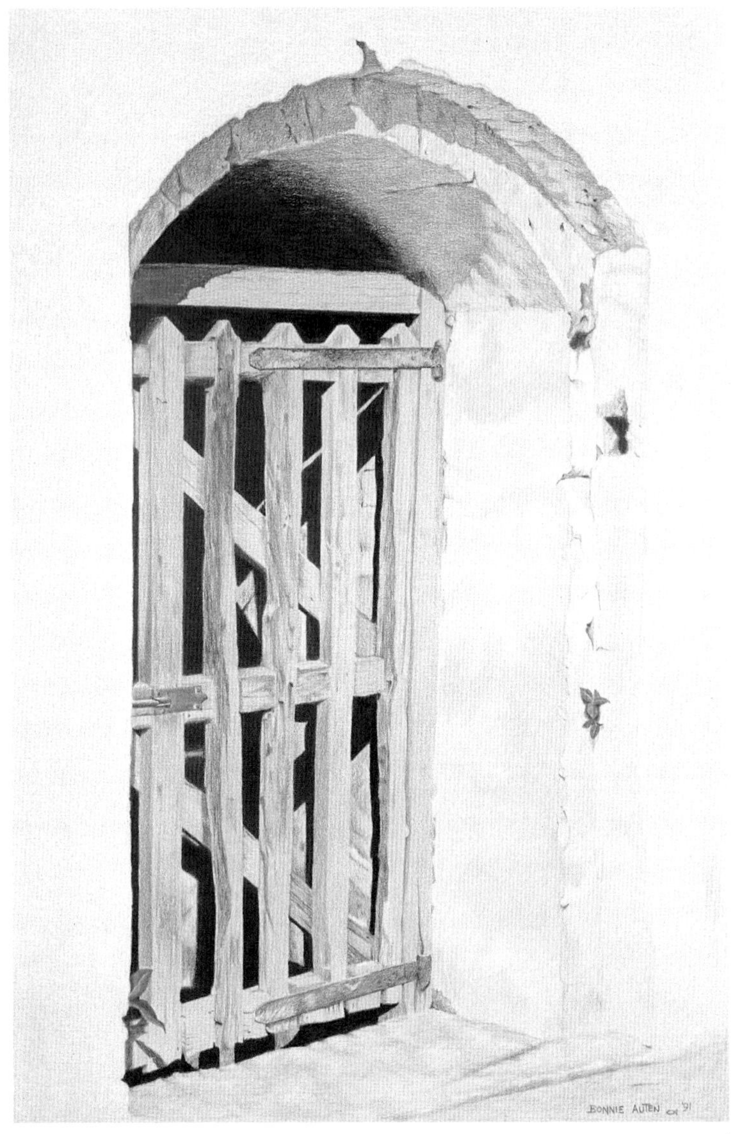

1

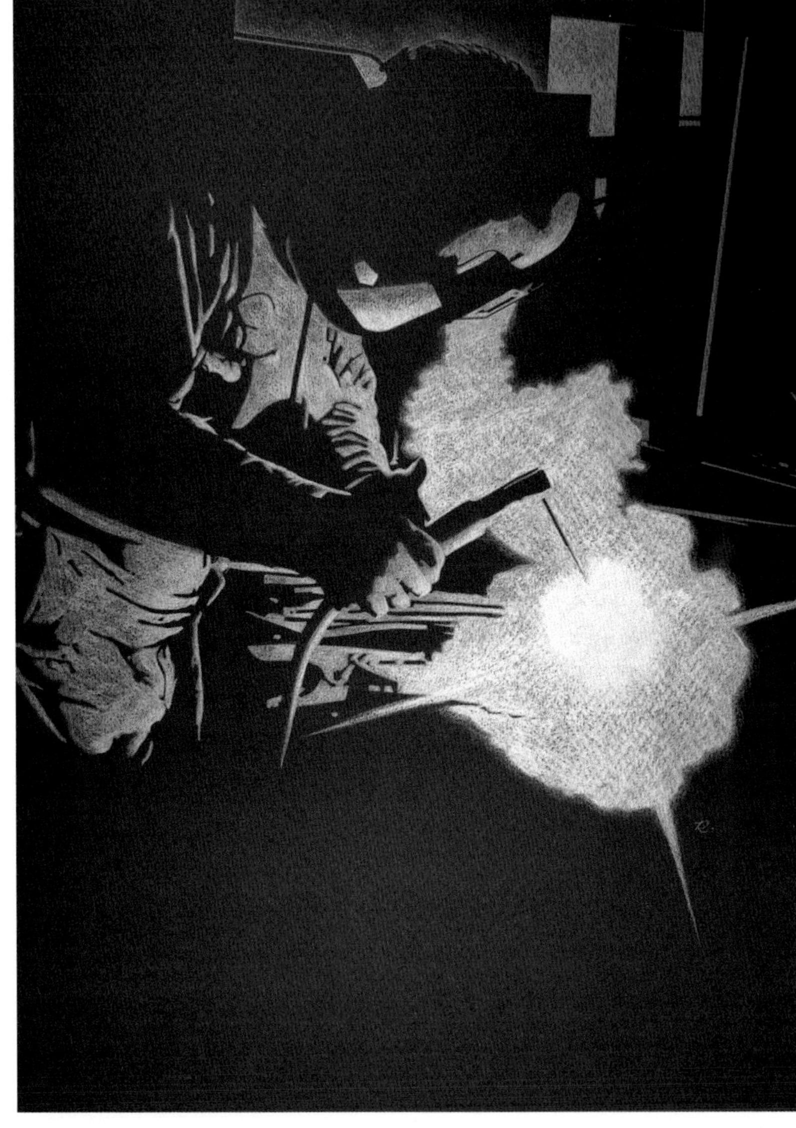

2

Bonnie Auten

1 *Gate*
25 x 17" (635 x 432 mm)
Colored Mat Board
Media: Colored Pencil, Blender Pen

Ken Raney

2 *Welder*
15 x 12" (381 x 305 mm)
Black Mat Board

Creative Mixes for Style and Speed

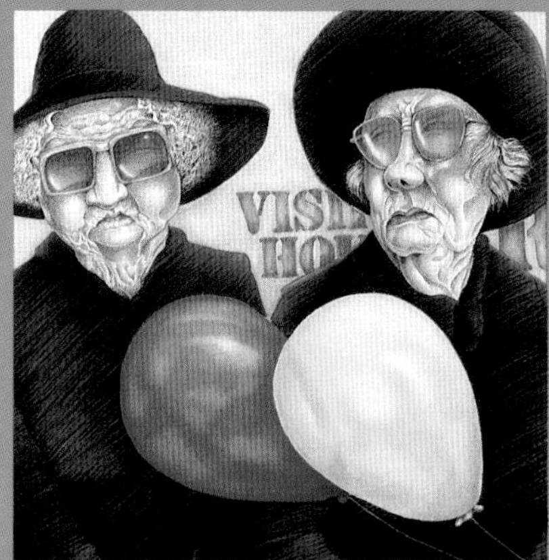

Colored Pencil and Turpentine
Vera Curnow

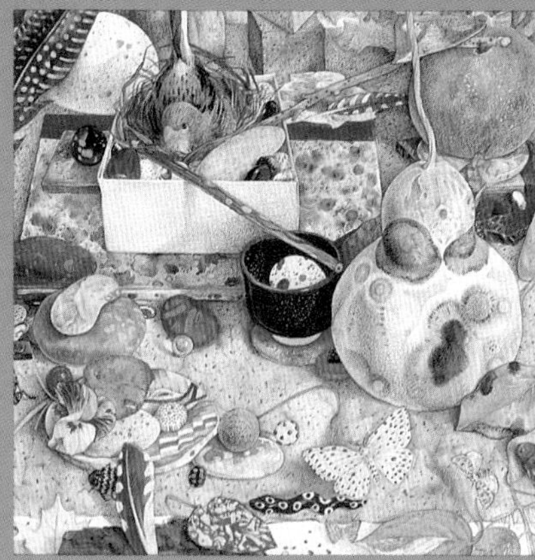

Colored Pencil and Watercolor
Karen Klein

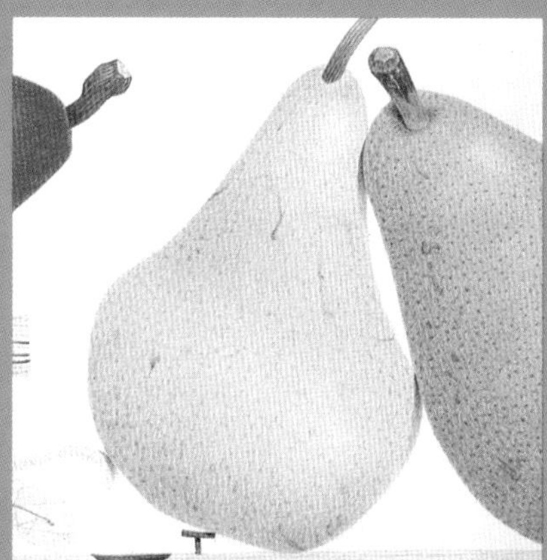

Colored Pencil and Graphite
Richard Muller

Creativity is often paired with words like "new" and "original." However, if we believe that "there is nothing new under the sun," then maybe being creative is simply a matter of doing the same things in innovative ways. Being creative demands change. For this to happen, we have to open the doors to possibility.

The paintings and drawings in this book attest to the versatility of colored pencil. Those who work with this medium certainly know the capabilities it has in its purest form. As artists, however, we should also explore the possibilities of colored pencil in various applications and combinations. Not just for the sake of change. This is not about working with new materials or a change of style or technique. This is about discovery and potential in our art and in ourselves.

The first step is to venture outside the "comfort zone." By mixing colored pencil with solvents or other media, artists can explore colored pencil's full potential and bring a fresh approach to their work. On the practical side, mixing media can wake up a palette with new color options, produce unique textures, and expand technical capabilities. It may even save time – letting you work in a larger format or achieve the same effects with half the effort. The artists in this section, and the gallery of work that follows, are inspirations to explore creative colored pencil combinations.

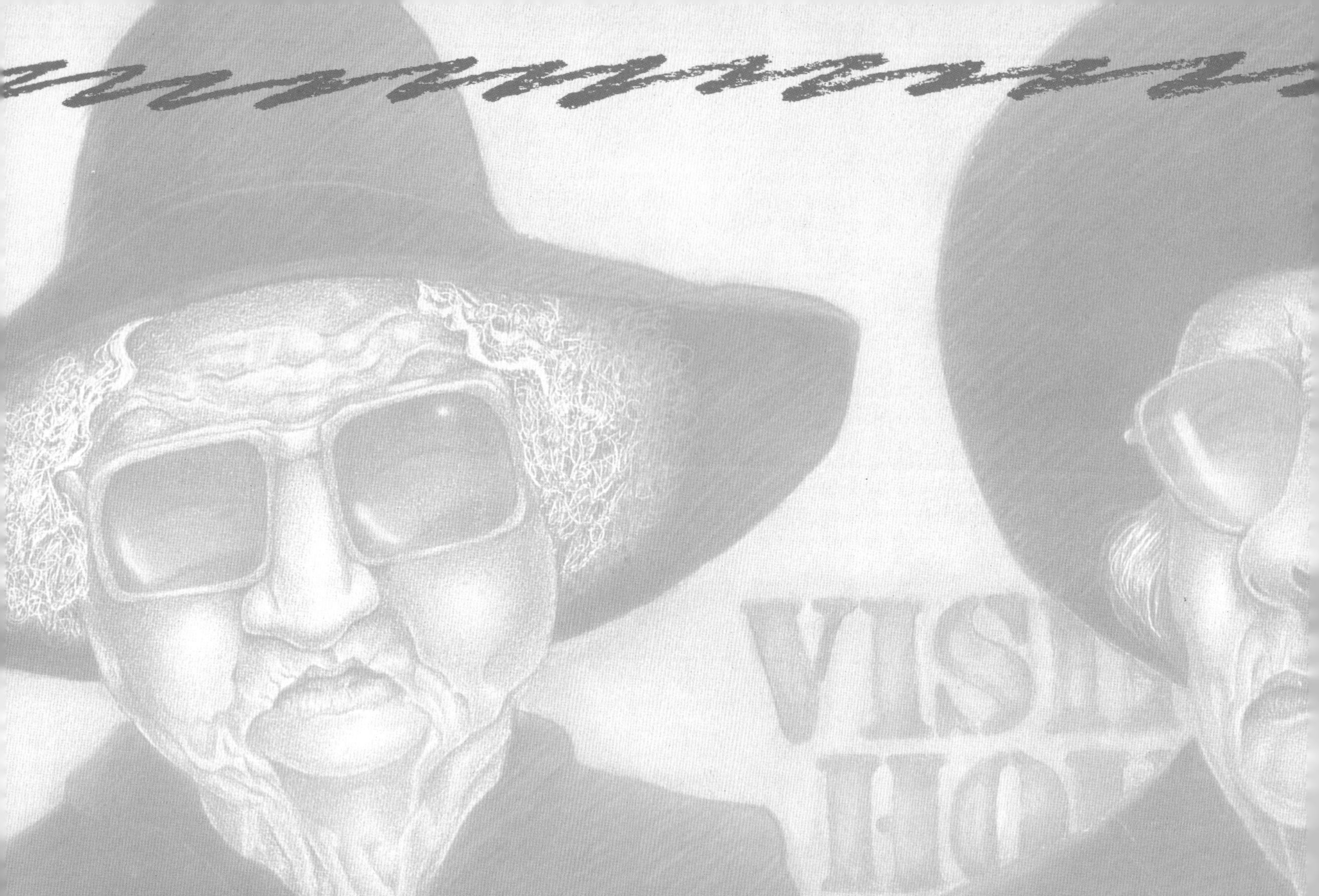

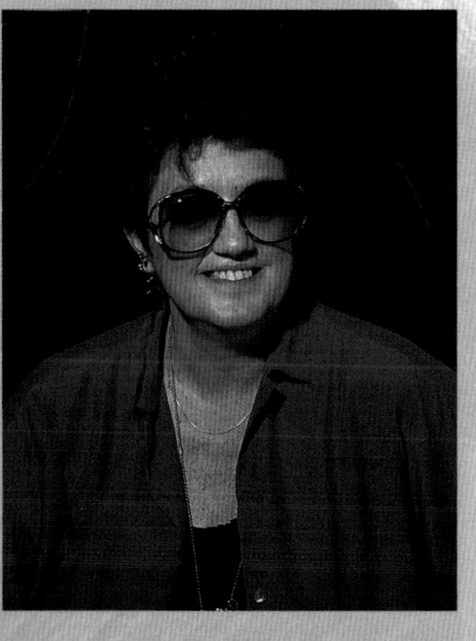

Vera Curnow

After 22 years in the corporate world, Vera Curnow escaped to the right side of her brain to visually create the images that lurk there. Her colored pencil paintings have been in national juried competitions and have captured many awards, most notably the top award for graphics from New York City's prestigious Salmagundi Club.

Vera's whimsical paintings of chronologically mature people have been published in *The Artist's Magazine* and in four books internationally, including *The Encyclopedia of Colored Pencil Techniques*. Her artwork is part of private and public collections, including that of the Fort Howard Foundation. She serves as an exhibition juror, lecturer, and workshop instructor.

In 1990, Vera founded the Colored Pencil Society of America. The Society now has over 1,200 members with District Chapters around the United States.

CHAPTER 8

Colored Pencil and Turpentine

It's okay to laugh. If you're looking for elegance or tranquility to lull your sensibilities, you won't find it in my paintings. Structured as visual narratives, rather than decorative art, I prefer to exaggerate my literal perceptions to express a more personal vision. The chronologically mature people I create are a result of these skewed observations. While I may borrow an intriguing jowl, furrowed forehead, or righteous posture from a photograph or friend, my subjects are mostly a composite taken from the soprano section of a church choir and the image in my mirror.

Mixing colored pencil pigment with a solvent (such as mineral spirits, paint thinner, turpentine or a turp substitute) is still experimental for me. The possibilities are fascinating. And challenging. This fluid technique defies the usual control and precision associated with wax-based colored pencils. Solvent dissolves the lead's binder so the pigment can be moved with a stiff brush, cotton swab, blending stump, or soft fabric. You can lightly tint the paper's surface or densely cover it. Results depend on the amount of pigment laid down, the quantity of solvent used, the pressure applied in dispersing the mixture and the size of the area. It is a good practice to make swatch tests since solvent can change a color's intensity and can sometimes alter the hue itself. Adding a solvent also turns the waxy shine of the color layers to a matte finish – no more wax bloom. Even the texture of the paper appears smoother. Using heavy pressure to apply the solvent melts and spreads the pencil's wax content to fill and level the paper's grain. The dispersed pigment can be left as is, mixed with more pigment and solvent, or used as a ground for dry pencil work. Small, intricate details are easier to create on this surface than they are over the slick concentration of wax that occurs in traditional layering.

The unpredictable nature of this method allows me to combine technical skills with creative spontaneity. It is refreshing to haphazardly apply color in large sweeps knowing that not every stroke has to be relevant. This method also saves an incredible amount of time. I can replace the stark glare of a large white ground with total color saturation in just minutes.

GETTING STARTED

The initial drawing is transferred with graphite paper to Crescent #110 cold press illustration board. Soft or thin surfaces don't hold up to the pressure of this smearing technique. Liquid frisket shreds some surfaces, so test it first. **MATERIALS:** Thin, hard-lead and soft wax-based pencils, color art sticks, plastic and kneaded erasers, liquid frisket, turpentine substitute, cut-up white cotton T-shirt, cotton swabs, #2 short, stiff-bristled paintbrush, electric pencil sharpener. Crystal clear fixative is applied to the finished art.

PALETTE

Cream, jasmine, sand, peach, yellow, yellow ochre, sunburst yellow, deco orange, neon orange, spanish orange, pumpkin, mineral orange, golden rod, sienna brown, terra cotta, burnt ochre, blush, pink, rose, lavender, raspberry, grape, hot pink, mulberry, magenta, process red, carmine, scarlet red, scarlet lake, tuscan red, violet, imperial violet, purple, non-photo blue, true blue, indigo, aquamarine, aqua, parrot green, light chartreuse, white, black.

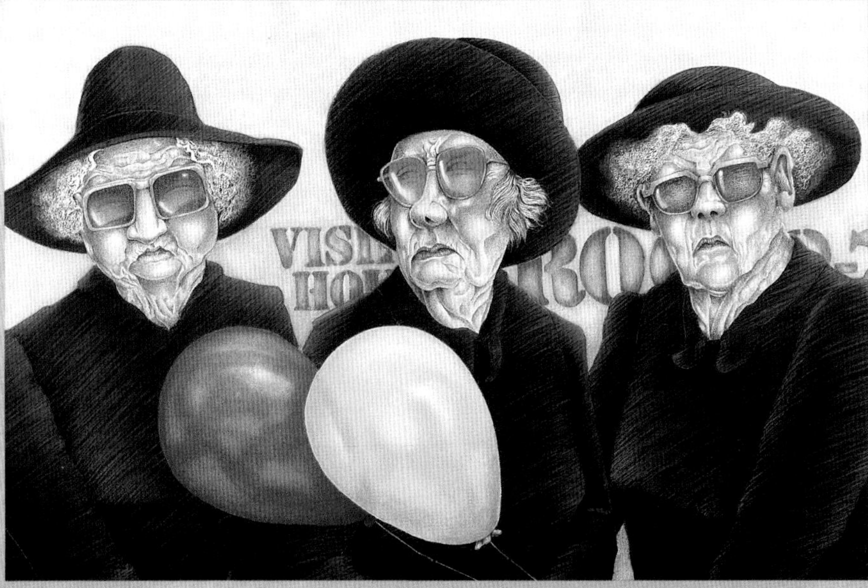

St. Ignatius Sunshine Committee
28 x 40" (709 x 1,014 mm)

1 The composition is separated into its major elements: background, clothing, faces, letters, balloons. The order in which these sections are worked determines where the liquid frisket is applied. For example, because the background is done first, the frisket must be placed inside the shapes that border it. Following the graphite lines, each section is masked off with frisket and a stiff flat brush. Small, tight areas are completely covered; large sections are only outlined. Using heavy pressure, strokes are applied to the background with art sticks. The direction of the strokes isn't important. Their only purpose is to get pigment on the paper.

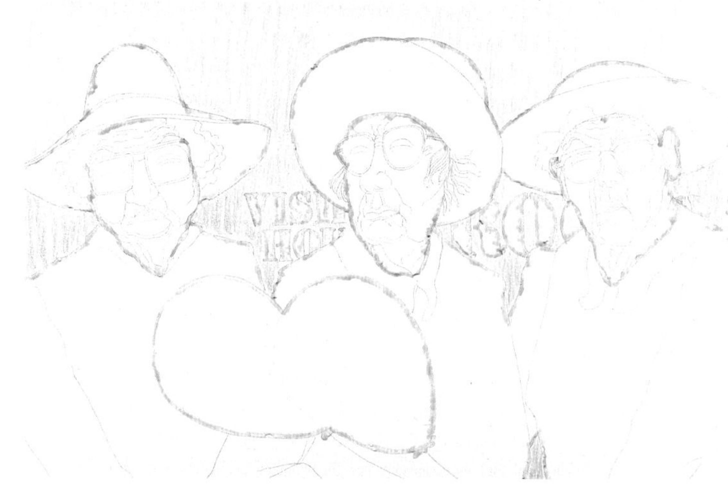

2 The pigment in the background area is dissolved, spread and blended with a cotton rag wrapped around two fingers and dipped in solvent. While this method is trial and error, it's also forgiving. More color is added. A dry tissue or more solvent removes excess pigment. Light colors are applied to dark, and darker colors are used to subdue bright ones. All this is done while the solvent mixture is still wet. The frisket is now removed from the clothing. Using art sticks and colored pencils, a separate color is firmly and densely applied to each coat. Note how the solvent used in the shoulder area changes the texture and color from that of the dry areas.

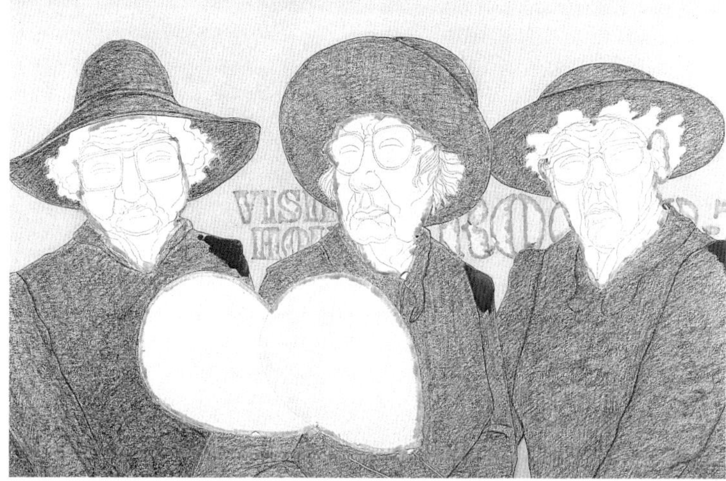

3 Black art stick is loosely applied to the shade areas of each coat. The black strokes and base coat are blended and spread using a clean solvent-dipped cloth — being careful not to smear outside the edges. It may help to lightly impress the outside lines using a blunt tip (e.g., a dried up ballpoint pen). This creates a well that helps keep the liquefied color inside the lines. A cotton swab or a small, stiff-bristled brush dipped in solvent works well to spread color in tight areas. It's best to use small quantities of solvent at a time, since too much solvent dissipates the pigment and leaves very little color.

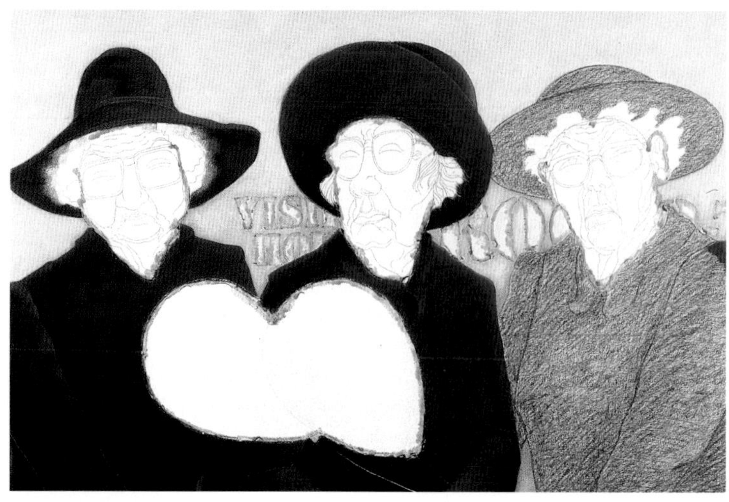

4 More base color and black are added until the clothing color is dark and dense. To add weight and bulk, light and medium values are established with loose diagonal pencil strokes in colors ranging from dark to screaming neon. These dry strokes are left visible to add texture and movement to this dark expanse of color. The wet surface of the solvent mixture has an oily residue that blends and subdues these strokes as they are made. As many as 15 layers are applied. Fewer layers are needed on a dry surface, but the effect of working dry on dry creates an effect that is somewhat different. Working dry on wet holds up to lots of abuse. The remaining frisket is now removed.

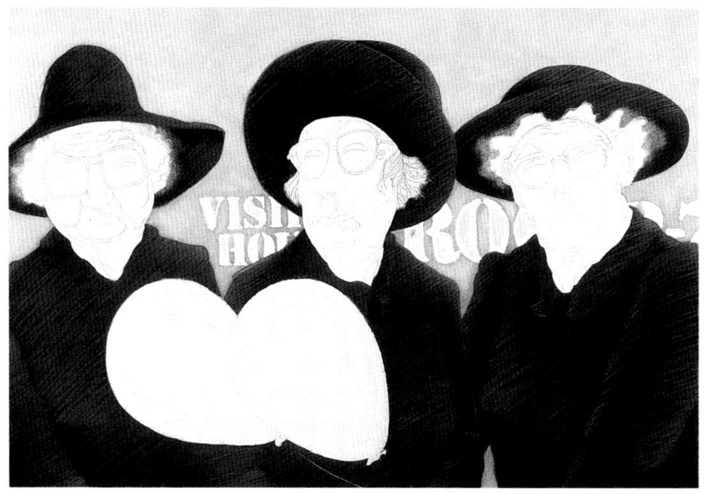

5 To capture their transparency, less pigment is applied to the balloons. They are then completed using the same colored pencil and solvent procedure. Clean cloths must be used for each color. Highlight areas are easily lifted with a kneaded eraser and blended with solvent. The letters are layered with pencil and blended with solvent on a cotton swab. Thin, hard-lead colored pencils are used to clean the edges. The value pattern in the faces is established with carmine red pencil. Color is applied to the eyeglasses leaving the lightest highlights paper white.

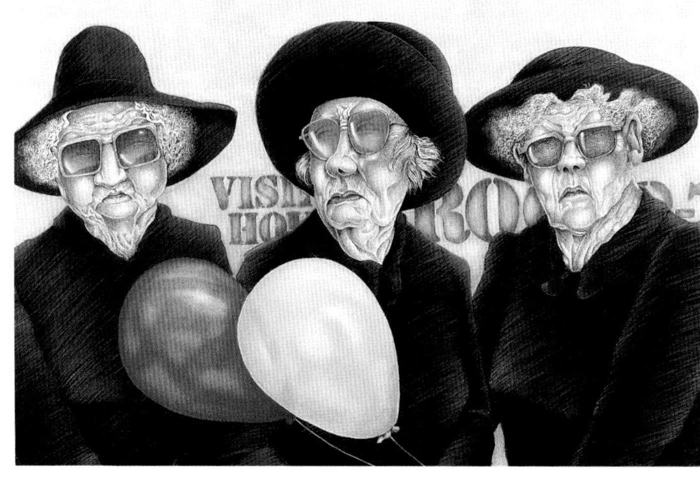

6 The faces are completed with the traditional layering technique. Allowing the grainy texture of the surface to show through contrasts well with the smooth denseness of the other areas. The eyeglasses are also completed with tonal layering and then lightly burnished. To retain white strands in the hair, impressed lines are drawn and color is applied over them – color was lifted to create the thin, frazzled ends. *St. Ignatius Sunshine Committee* shows how solvent can add a new look to painting with colored pencils.

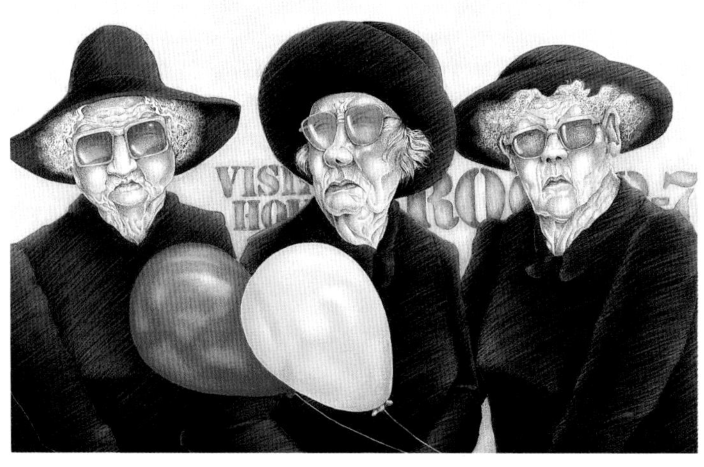

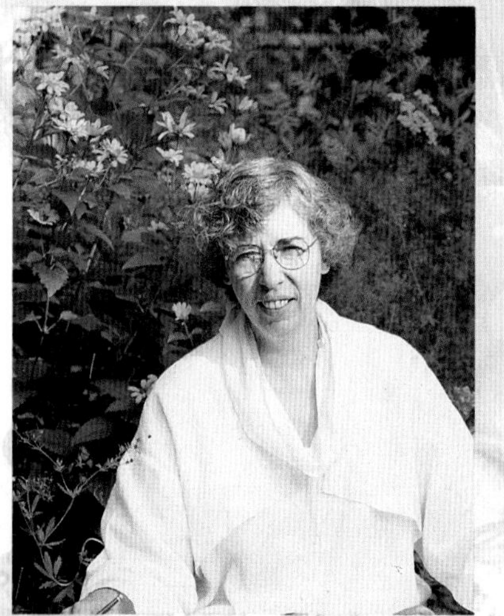

Karen Ann Klein

Originally a black-and-white printmaker, artist Karen Ann Klein worked in watercolors for ten years until, "they became too predictable." She now works in mixed media, combining colored pencil with watercolor. Her work has been exhibited in galleries and shows throught the Midwest and is part of both private and public collections, including those of the University of Michigan and the Hunt Institute at Carnegie-Mellon. Karen has taught oil painting, watercolor, and colored pencil workshops. Her work has been published in several publications, including *The Complete Colored Pencil Book*. Karen and her husband own the Arnold Klein Gallery in Birmingham, Michigan.

CHAPTER 9

Colored Pencil and Watercolor

Fruit, flowers, rocks and stems. Nothing rare or exotic. Simple ordinary objects of a common variety are the subjects of Karen Ann Klein's still life paintings. Placed in the context of her work, however, these everyday items become symbolic milestones in a personal journey. What may appear to be a nonchalant composition of incidental objects is actually a careful disposition of shapes and color. Karen visually connects these separate entities like a patchwork quilt to make a larger statement. Spatial relationships are delicately balanced. Compositional "weight" is evenly distributed. The painting's tempo is orchestrated item by item, with each object dependent on the other. To eliminate any element would disrupt the pictorial harmony. Once the overall impact is absorbed, Karen adeptly invites the viewer into the work. Repetitive shapes direct us down a path she deliberately creates. Open spaces are left for us to linger and rest. Larger objects reveal intricate patterns and color nuances within their structure. Karen keeps our interest by combining the dichotomies of colored pencil and watercolor. The precision and control obtained from one is coupled with the looseness and unpredictability of the other. Free-flowing washes complement tight renderings and hard edges. Translucent colors are juxtaposed with dense layers. Each medium plays a prominent role and works to enhance the other. Colored pencils subdue the pockets of activity created by the watercolors. Watercolors alter the texture and impact of the colored pencils — light pencil colors against dark watercolor backgrounds take on a luminous quality. Using the light-on-dark effect, Karen creates a rectangular backdrop to emphasize organic shapes and rich colors. This inner frame provides a structural unity that gives the separate components one voice. Each item has been carefully chosen and reverently placed. Visually traveling through Karen's painting, we realize this is not a casual accumulation of unrelated objects but rather a very private collection.

GETTING STARTED

Karen composes as she goes and doesn't hesitate to add, delete or change directions entirely while the work is in progress. Using the actual objects, she draws directly on Strathmore three-ply medium finish Bristol paper. MATERIALS: Hard and soft, wax-based colored pencils, Pink Pearl, Mars plastic and kneaded erasers, electric pencil sharpener, transparent watercolors, gouache, sable brushes. The finished work is sprayed with workable fixative.

PALETTE

Soft Wax-Based Colored Pencils: Lavender, parma violet, hot pink, white, deco aqua, non-photo blue, french grey, black, aqua, turquoise, sea green, gray, violet, tuscan red, purple, violet red, french green, process red, green, real green, light yellow, peacock green, yellow ochre, terra cotta, light peach, indigo blue, burnt carmine, orange, dark brown, kingfisher blue, brown, raw umber, olive, grass green,hot orange, seinna brown, carmine red, crimson lake, grayed lavender, metallic maroon, light aqua, scarlet lake, marine green, vermillion, chocolate, burnt ochre, aquamarine, pink, cream, chartreuse, blue violet, tan. Thin Hard-Lead Colored Pencils: White, sea green, rose, grass green, dark gray, blue violet, true green, indigo blue.

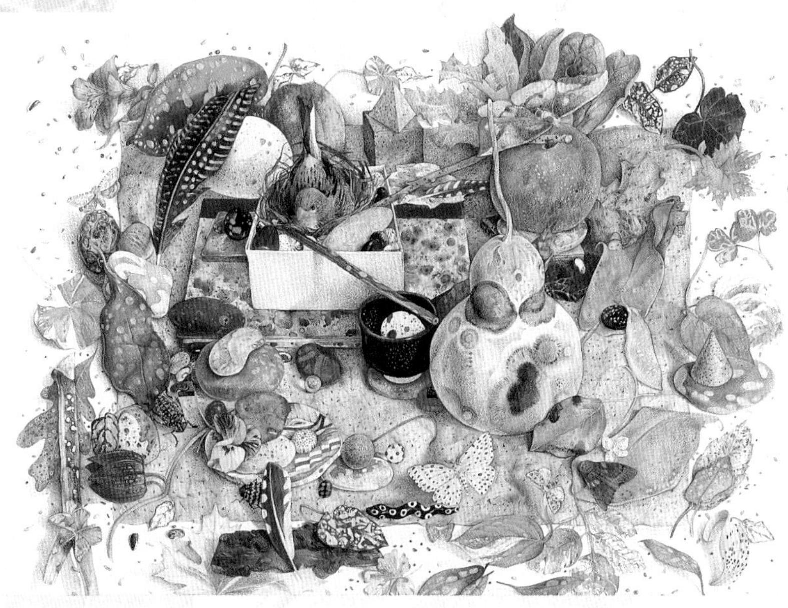

Spotted
18 x 24" (456 x 608 mm)

1 A still life of speckled objects is begun with only some of the items on hand. Graphite outlines of the available items are drawn, and a flat wash is applied to the main objects. Room is left in the layout to add objects as the work progresses. An object's size, shape, and color will dictate its placement. The image is built in small patches of color which are eventually brought together, and a color scheme evolves. An essential element, not yet visible, is the placement of a rectangular border that will unify the separate objects into a cohesive composition and will provide a backdrop to make them believable.

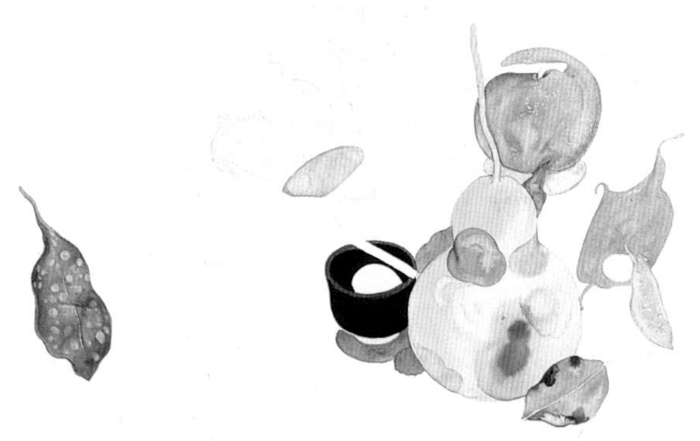

2 Unlike the time-consuming process of pencil-layering dense color, watercolor blocks in solid colors quickly. This eliminates the wax build up that occurs with heavy layering and provides a "gritty," rather than slick, surface for detailed pencil work. In this painting, watercolor is used primarily as a flat undercoat (in light or dark tones) for colored pencil. For example, the spots on the leaf to the left are created with colored pencil over an even wash. The mottled patterns on the gourd and the leaf in front of it, however, are created with watercolor. Colored pencil will be added to them for further definition.

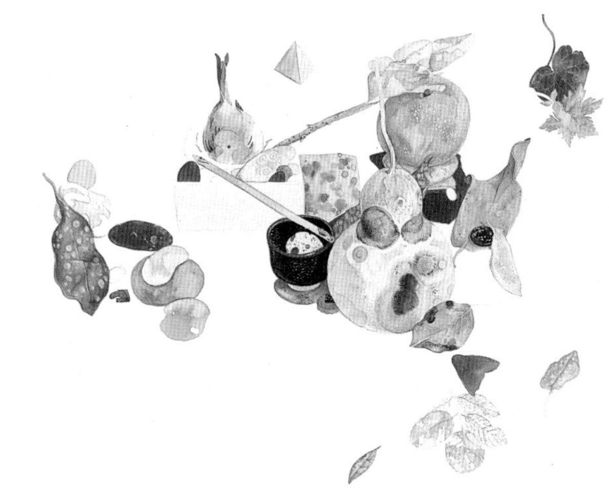

3 Color applications are made from one medium to the other. The dark rock on the corner of the book begins with a black watercolor wash while the markings are heavily burnished layers of lavender, violet, and hot pink. The modelling (using white, aqua, non-photo blue, french gray and black pencil) is done with light pressure so that the black wash shows through. The general pattern on the kidney-shaped rock is established by dropping a big water spot into the gray wash. Once the watercolor is dry, details are added with colored pencil.

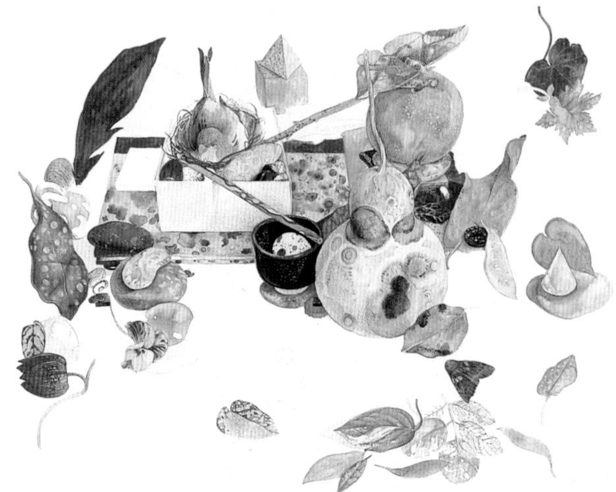

4 So far the subjects have been kept "floating" with white space behind them left open for new additions. In this step, the background is just being introduced. Cast shadows are added in soft gradations of colored pencil to settle the objects. The cool lavenders, grays, violets, and blues of the shadows are a nice contrast to the warm tan objects. Notice how the green leaves circle the focal point to create a visual flow and how dark objects are strategically placed to keep the "weight" balanced.

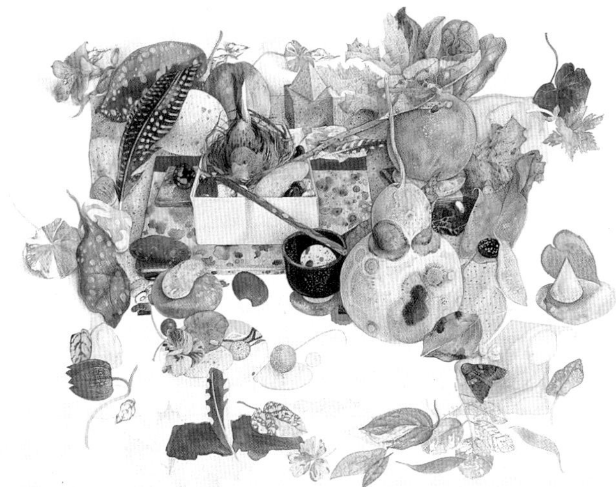

5 Eight new items (moths, butterflies, and beetles) are added. Each is begun with a wash and finished with colored pencil details. The black parts of the two beetles (lower left) are painted around the colored pencil spots to keep the markings luminous. The entire background, which also creates a border, is laid in with a combination wash of brown and a peach mixture. Waterspots create activity and keep the surface from becoming a flat plane of solid color. The flecks and lumps are a combination of black, brown, gray and terra cotta pencils. Thin, hard-lead pencils are used to create fine details and crisp edges.

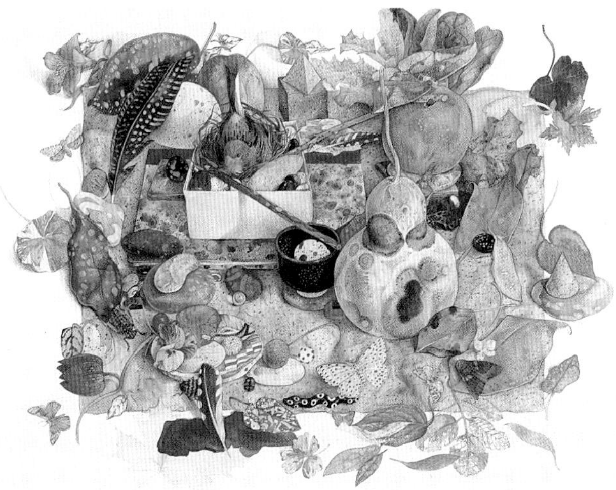

6 More new objects are balanced into the composition. Cast shadows are placed either to anchor objects to the surface or to give them "flight" – notice the two moths in the foreground. Details are further defined, and colors are adjusted – burnishing with white mutes loud patterns or brightens dull areas. While this painting includes an extensive palette, it was applied sparingly. Karen's active painting, appropriately named "Spotted," shows how colored pencil and watercolor can work together to create textures, patterns, and color harmony.

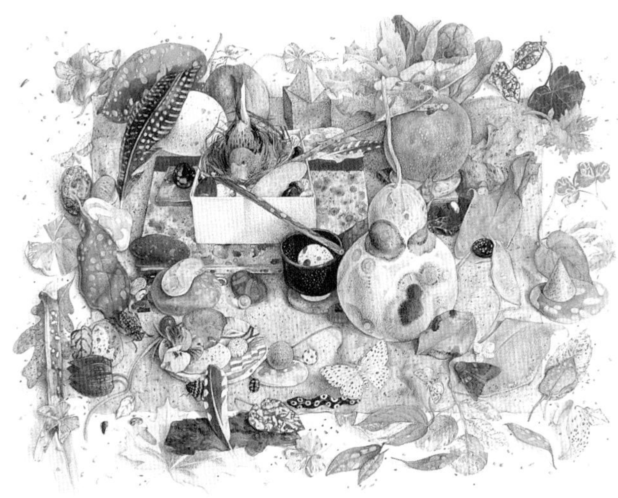

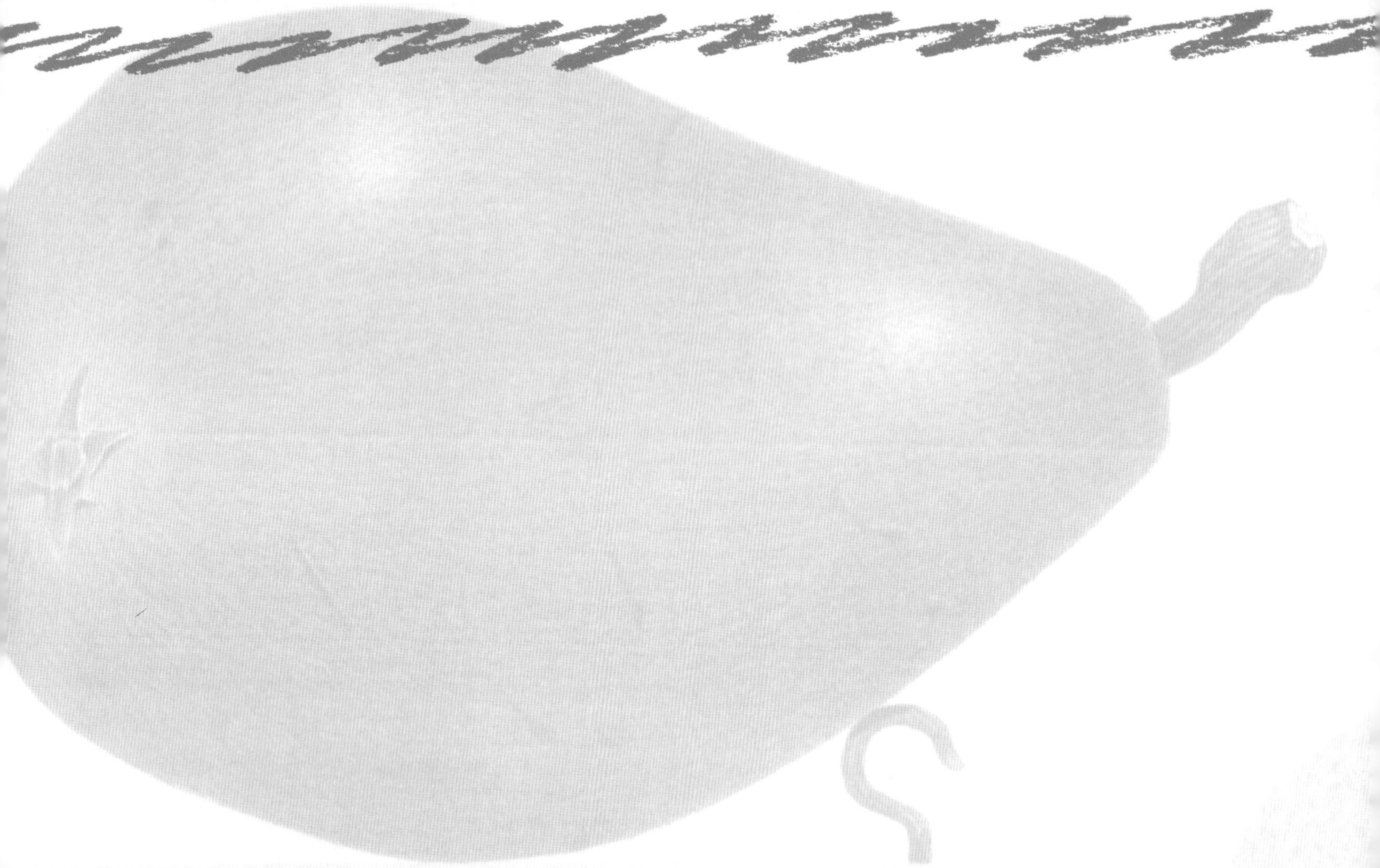

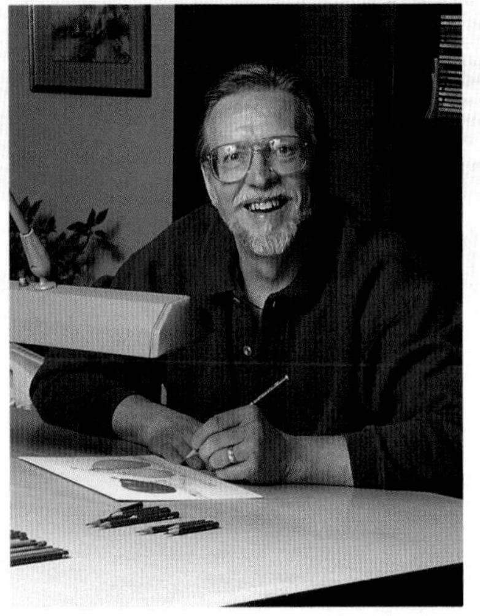

Richard Mueller

After more than 19 years as a full-time artist, Richard Mueller has made a name that extends beyond his home in Baileys Harbor, Wisconsin. He has won more than 200 awards, shown his work in national drawing exhibitions, and has captured the attention of private and public collectors in the United States, Europe, Australia and the Orient. Richard had taught workshops throughout the Midwest and is the owner of the Richard Mueller Gallery in Sister Bay, Wisconsin.

CHAPTER 10

Colored Pencil and Graphite

Without seeing the finished art, the very thought of this technique can be unsettling. You've just spent hour upon hour applying layer upon layer of colored pencil. The values are established. The subject has form. The colors are vibrant. The work is done. Right? Not according to Richard Mueller. For him, the next step is the most important. With every element seemingly in place, he adds just one more layer. A layer of graphite. Over everything. From the lightest highlights to the deepest shadows. Contrary to creating a muddy mass of color, "the graphite gives the work verve; it makes the colors sing." Richard's unique method has resulted in a formula of sorts. It begins with his choice of materials. He only uses the thin, hard-lead colored pencils. These make sharper lines and leave less color than the soft leads. His drawing surface is always slick and smooth with no "tooth" or grain. This allows him, and not the paper's surface, to create textures and values. And, unless the subject's local color is blue, he always begins with a minimum of three layers of yellow. Always. This yellow undercoat serves as a base for all additional colors and gives the work its "glow." All subsequent layers are applied in a succession of progressively darker colors within that spectrum (i.e., light green would be followed by grass green, olive green. etc.) By working with sharp leads and a light-to-medium pressure (never heavy), Richard controls the value scale necessary to model the forms. He never cross-hatches. Using linear, parallel strokes, he lets the subject dictate whether they should be applied vertically or horizontally. After the final color application, which may follow as many as 24 layers, he adds a single layer of graphite. It is the graphite that adds texture, awakens paler shades, subdues brighter ones, and makes the edges clean. All that's left to do is enjoy Richard's humor. Is that an eggplant with an attitude? An arrogant apple? Exhausted pears? Richard takes the usually inert fruit out of its stuffy, still-life format to give it posture and personality. Delightful.

GETTING STARTED

Richard carefully selects his models by fondling the fruit in the produce department. He draws his design directly onto Crescent #202 Hot Press (smooth) Illustration Board with a 2H graphite pencil. MATERIALS: Thin, hard-lead colored pencils, graphite pencils 2H, H, F, HB, B. 2B, kneaded eraser, standard hand-crank pencil sharpener, three coats of workable fixative is lightly sprayed on the finished art.

PALETTE: Lemon yellow, canary yellow, golden brown, flesh, terra cotta, sienna brown, scarlet red, carmine red, tuscan red, light green, grass green, olive green.

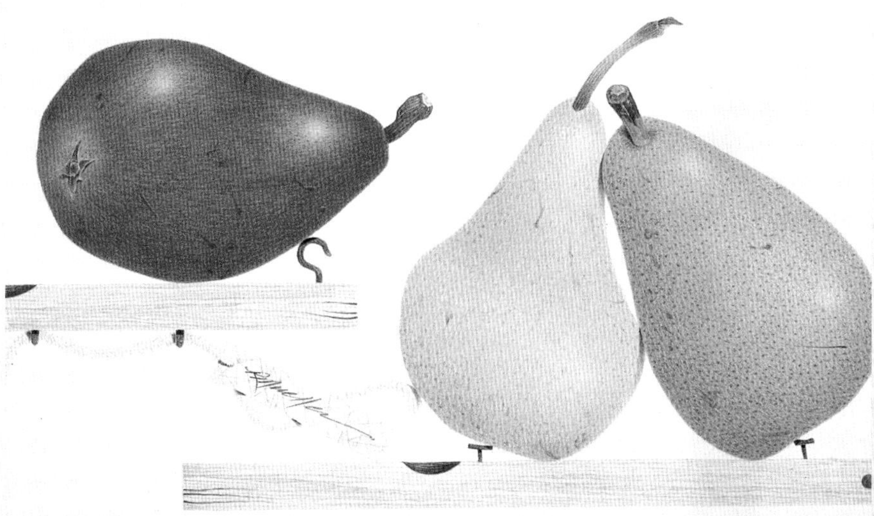

Resting At the Stop & Go
8 x 12" (203 x 304 mm)

1 A light outline drawing of the main components is made. Other items or details may be added to the composition as the work progresses. Using a thin, hard-lead lemon yellow pencil, the pears, including their stems, are layered with a very sharp pencil point. Light pressure is used to make parallel, linear strokes that are slightly curved to correspond with the subject's shape. Areas where the highlights will be are left untouched for now. These hard-lead pencils leave less color than the thicker, soft leads. They are also more difficult to lift or erase.

2 The graphite lines are gently lifted with a kneaded eraser. A layer of canary yellow is applied to all the pears. The pear on the left is layered with flesh and scarlet red pencils. Golden brown is applied to the center pear, and light green is added to the one on the right. Each color is softly blended into the highlight areas. Forms and value changes are beginning to emerge.

3 The color layers of the green pear are completed in this step. A minimum of three, and often as many as six, layers of the following colors are applied: lemon yellow, canary yellow, light green, grass green, and olive green. Colors are applied in alternating layers (yellow, green, yellow, green) rather than consecutive ones. This makes the colors luminous and keeps them balanced until the desired tone is reached. Golden brown and terra cotta are used on the stems and to create surface bruises. Dots of olive green mottle the skin.

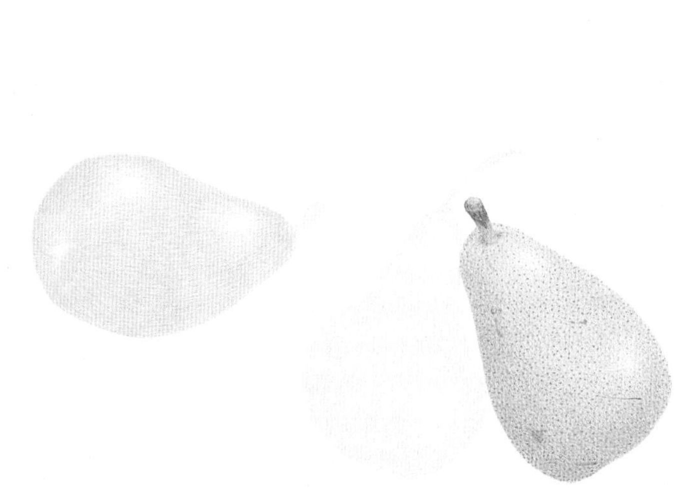

4 Using the same directional strokes, the following colors are alternately applied in several layers to the center pear: lemon yellow, canary yellow, flesh, golden brown, and sienna brown. This combination gives the skin an amber glow. The pear on the left is layered with scarlet red, carmine red, and tuscan red. Because of the slick, smooth finish on the illustration board Richard uses, the many applications of color can leave small beads of wax sitting on the surface. These are carefully lifted with an art knife and a kneaded eraser.

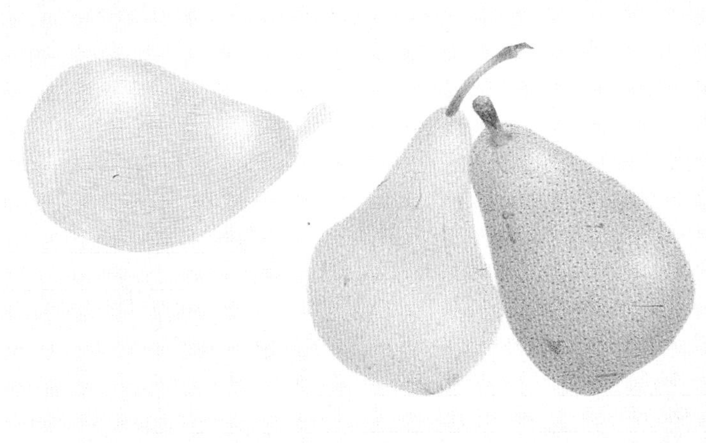

5 Nails are drawn at the base of the leaning pears for added interest and "support." All the remaining objects are layered in the following colors: lemon yellow, canary yellow, golden brown, flesh, terra cotta, sienna brown and olive green. The entire composition is now color complete and ready for the graphite.

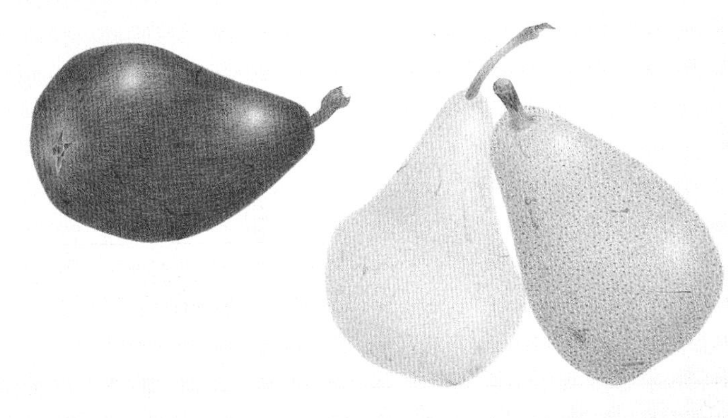

6 Just as in layering color, the graphite layer is applied following the contour of the subject with linear, parallel strokes. Only the sharp tip of the pencil is used – no shading is done with the side of the lead. And, just as in applying color, the value changes of the graphite are made by working from light to dark. Lightest areas receive graphite grades 2H and H, medium value areas receive a range of F and HB, and dark areas are covered with the B and 2B grades. Only one layer of graphite is applied and seldom is a grade harder than 2H or softer than 2B used. The last design element to be added in *Resting At The Stop & Go* is Richard's signature which is, of course, the final touch of graphite.

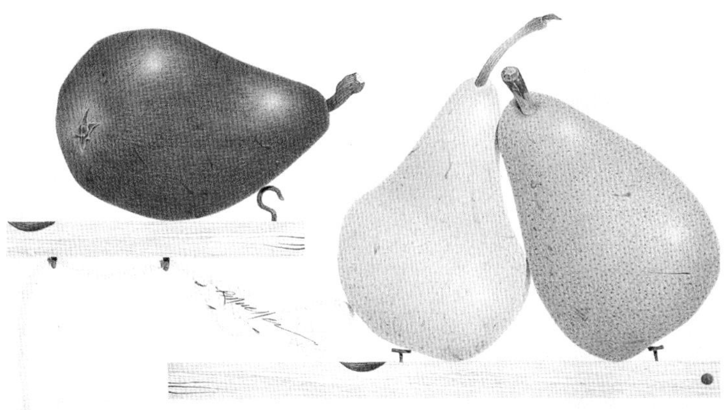

Vera Curnow

1 *Lillian Views Her Critics with Humor*
15 x 24" (381 x 610 mm)
100% Rag Cold Press Illustration Board
Media: Colored Pencil,Turpentine
Technique: Burnishing, Impressed Line

2 *Mid-Life Power Surge*
40 x 30" (1,016 x 762 mm)
100% Rag Cold Press Illustration Board
Media: Colored Pencil Collage with Found Objects and Turpentine, Bleach, Gloss Medium

Richard Muller

3 *Orchids*
14 x 10" (355 x 254 mm)
Media: Colored Pencil, Graphite

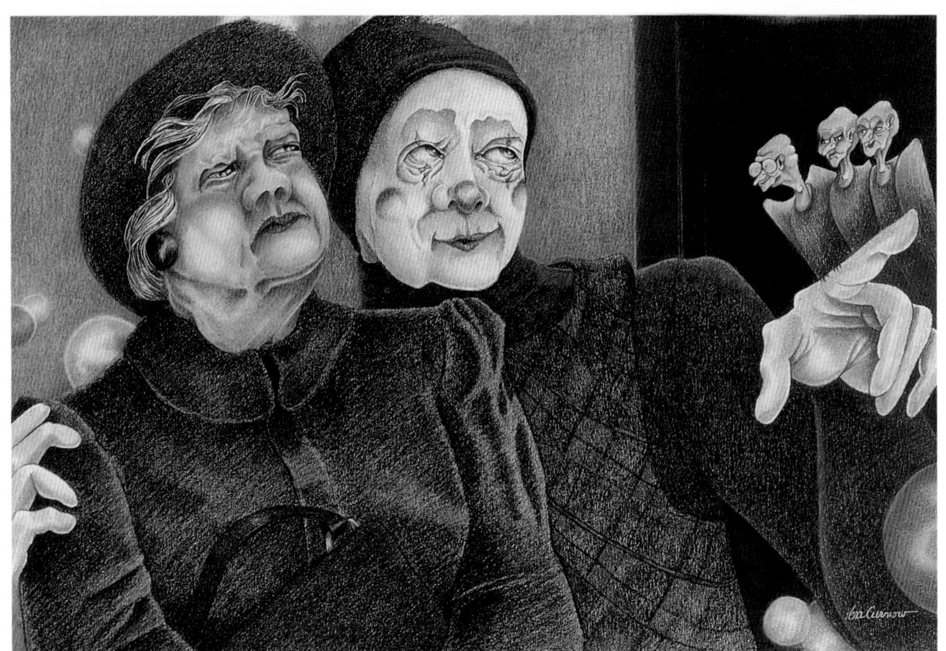

1

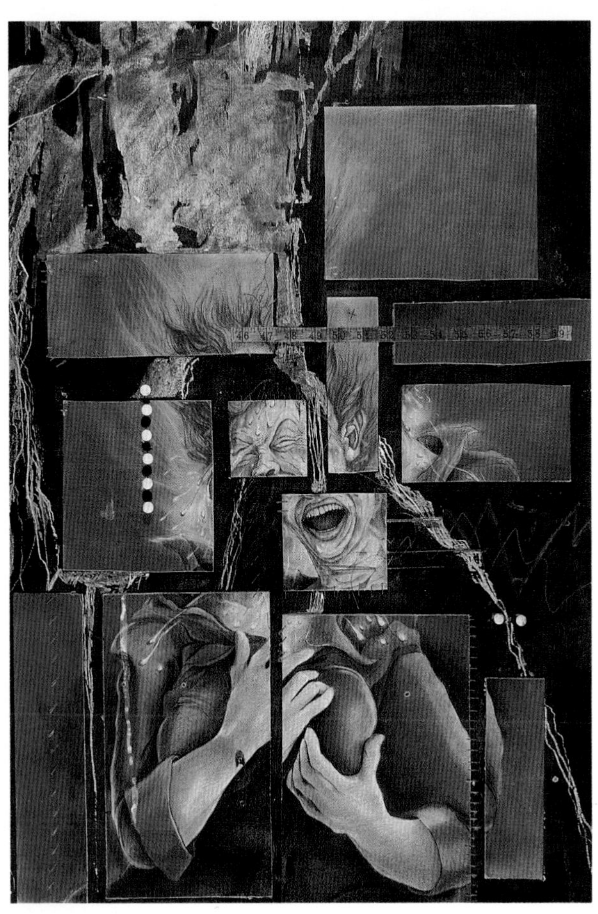

2

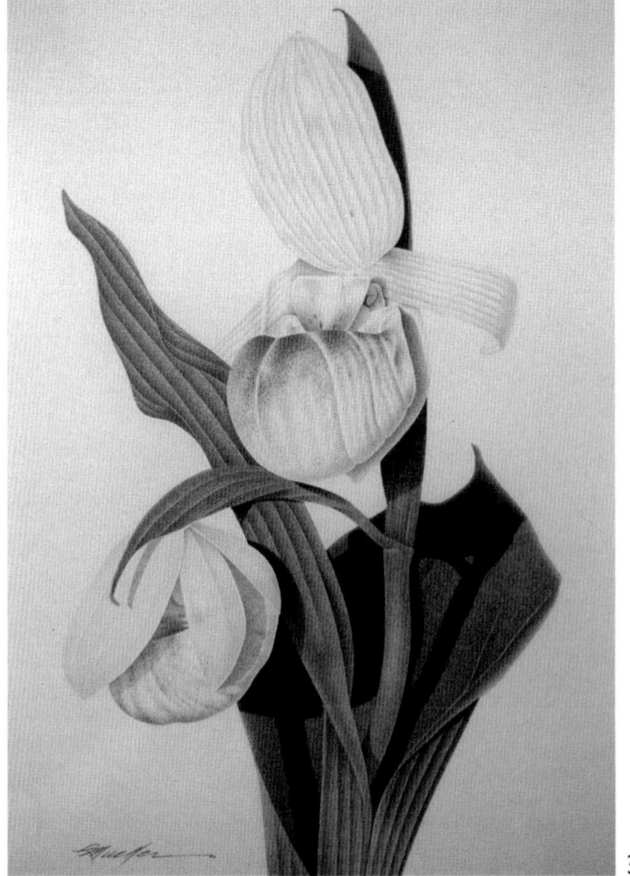

3

Richard Muller

1 *Just Egging Each Other On*
8 x 12" (203 x 304 mm)
Media: Colored Pencil, Graphite

2 *Shadowdance*
12 x 16" (304 x 405 mm)
Media: Colored Pencil, Graphite

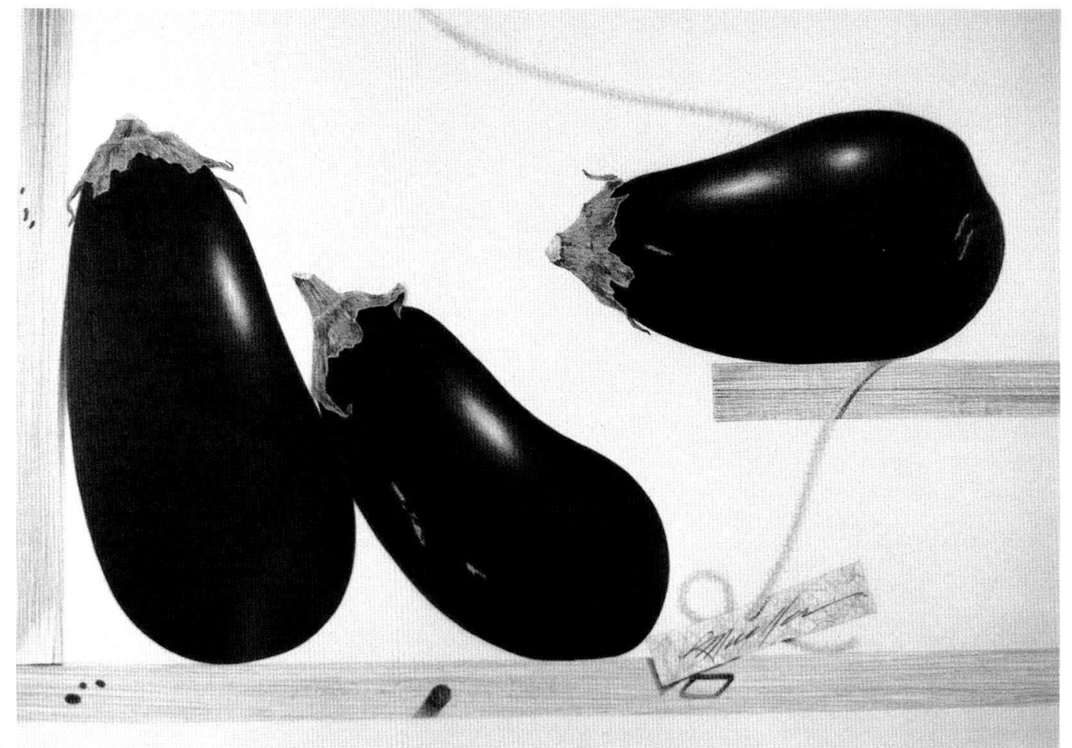

1

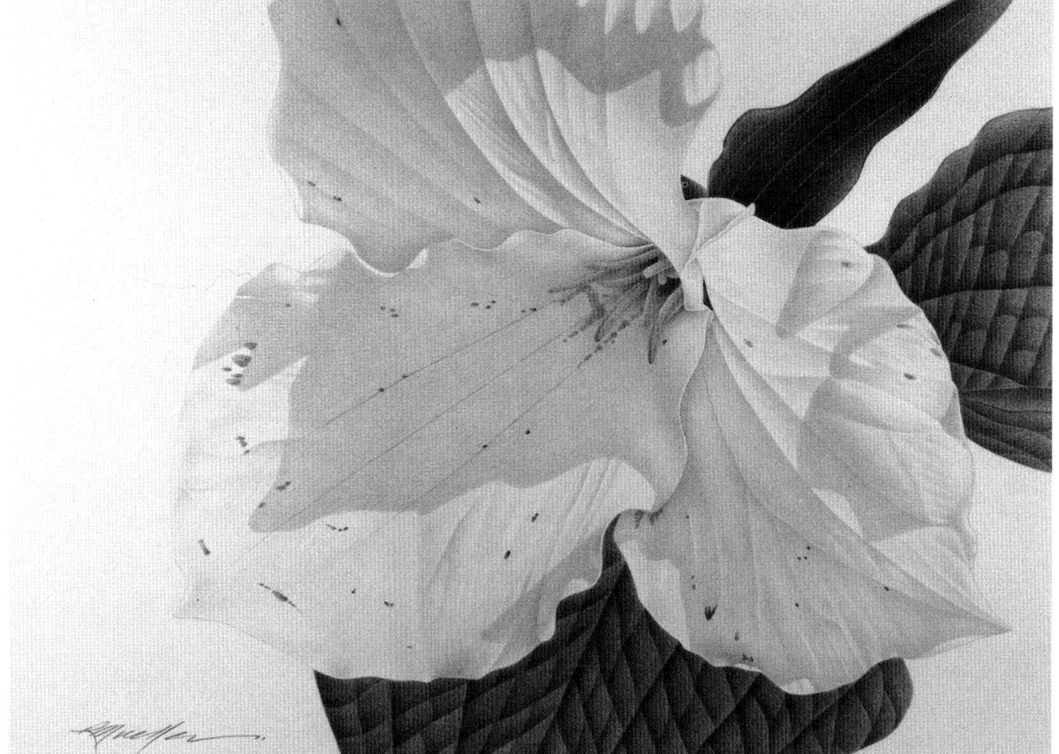

2

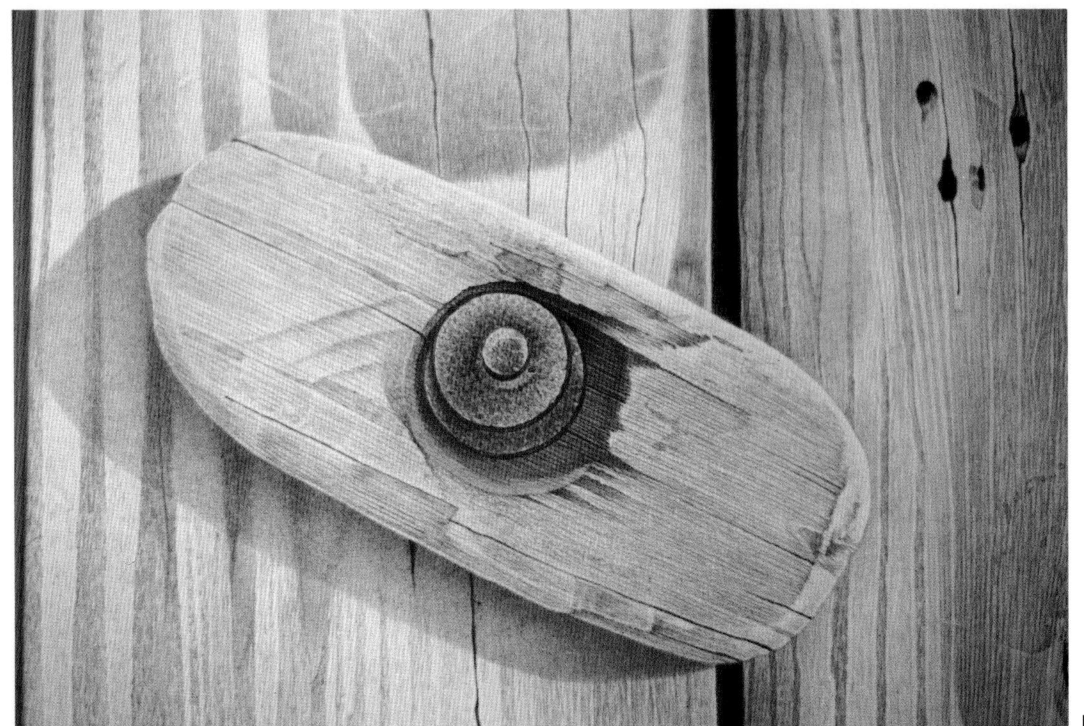

1

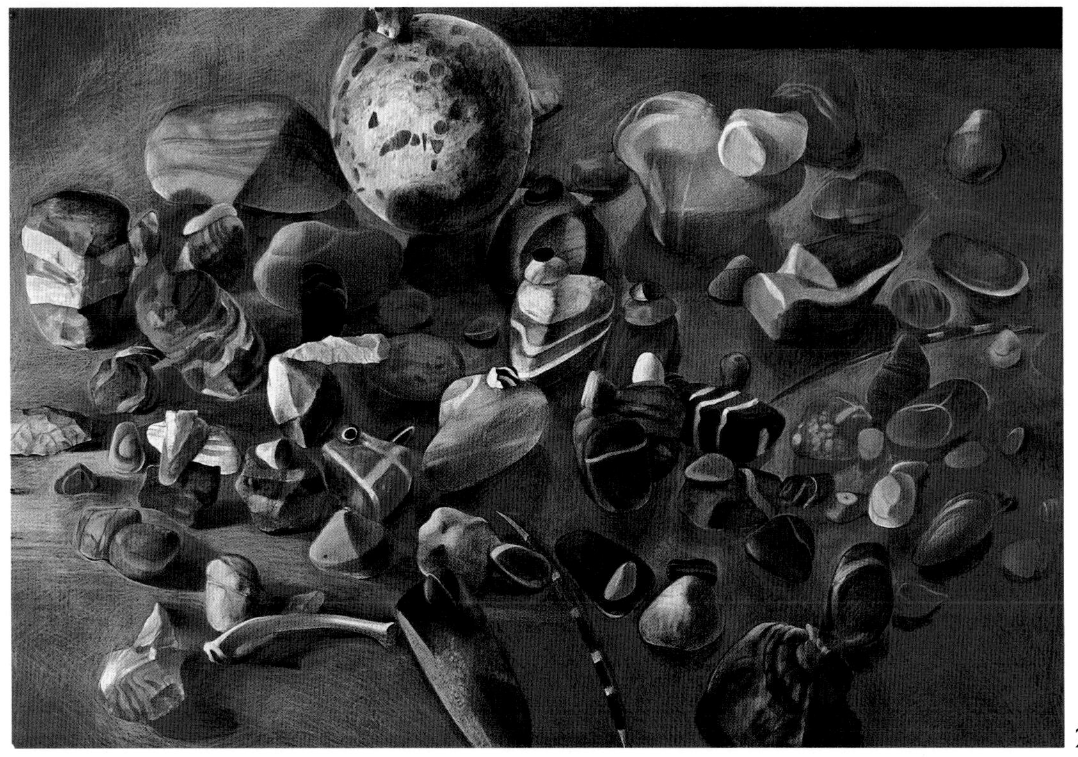

2

Richard Muller

1 *The Raft*
6 x 8" (152 x 203 mm)
Media: Colored Pencil, Graphite

Karen Ann Klein

2 *Ringed Rocks*
30 x 40" (760 x 1014mm)
Media: Colored Pencil, Watercolor

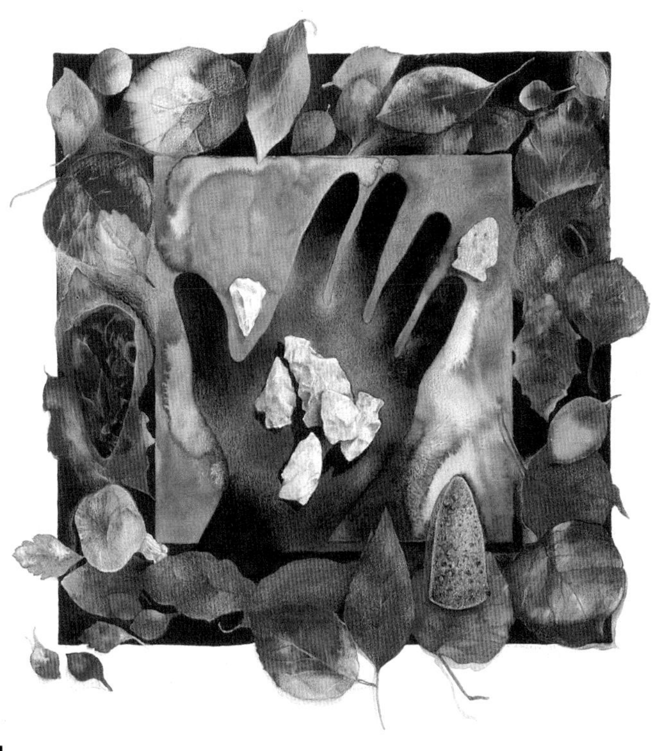

1

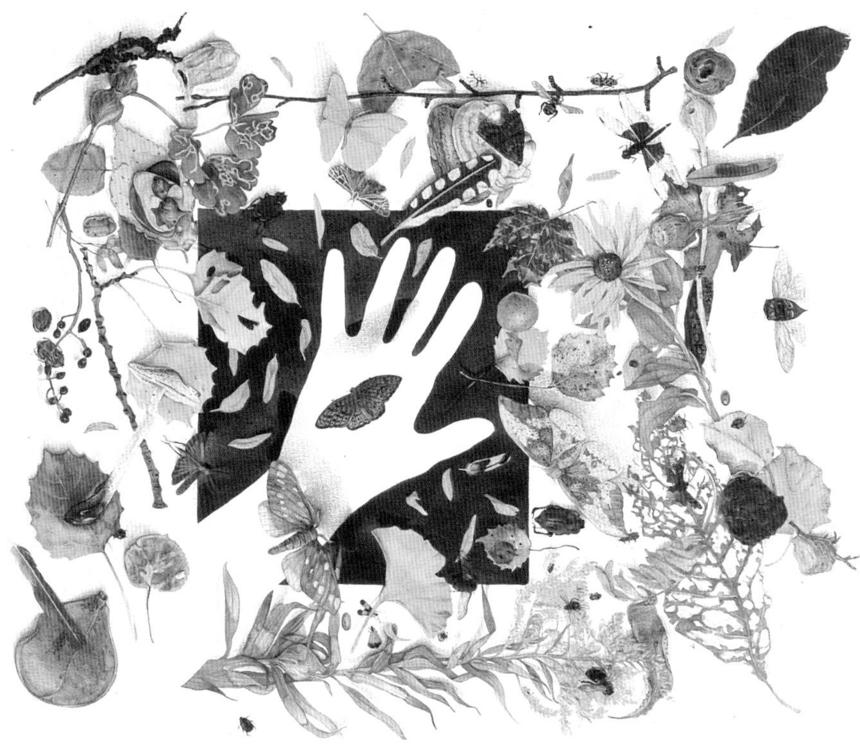

2

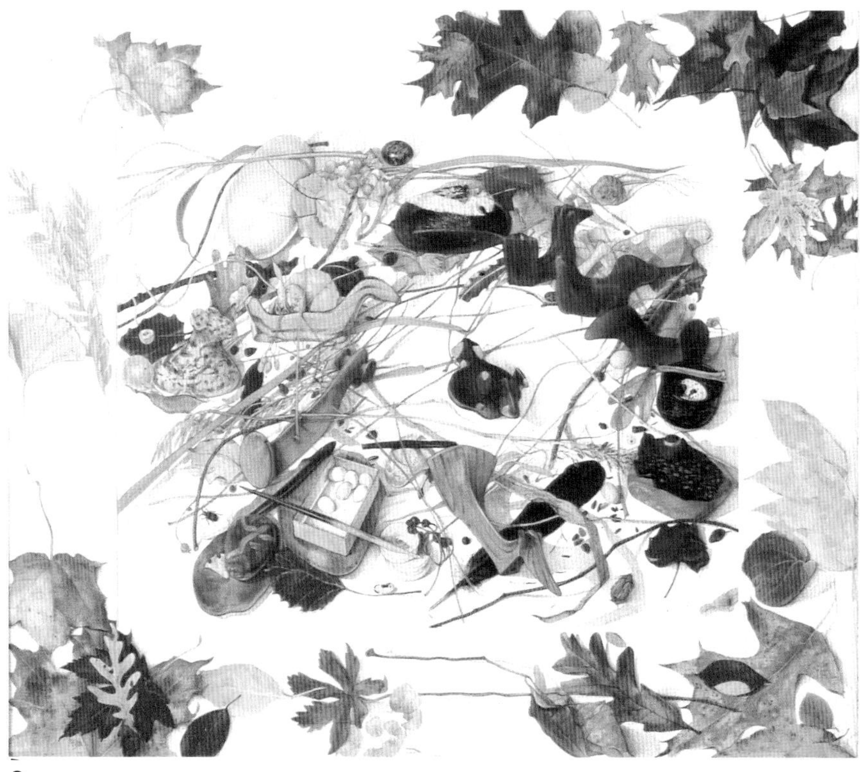

3

Karen Ann Klein

1 *David's Hand # 1*
16 x 16" (413 x 394 mm)
Media: Colored Pencil, Watercolor

2 *The Entomologist*
27 x 21" (686 x 552 mm)
Media: Colored Pencil, Watercolor

3 *Birdstones*
29 x 35" (737 x 876 mm)
Media: Colored Pencil, Acrylic

Karen Ann Klein

1 *Dark Fruit*
16 x 22" (413 x 546 mm)
Media: Colored Pencil, Watercolor

2 *The Entomologist*
13 x 22" (337 x 552 mm)
Media: Colored Pencil, Watercolor

Pat Barron

3 *The Fat Lady Sings*
20 x 14" (508 x 357 mm)
Arches Cover Black with Rives Light Weight
Media: Colored Pencil, Relief Print Collage

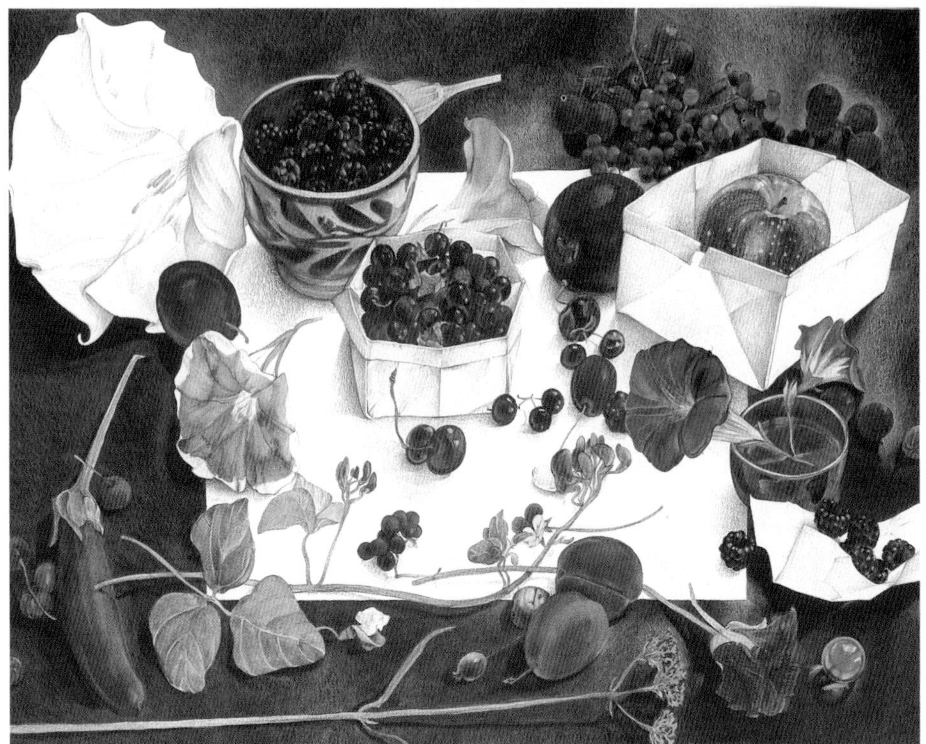

1

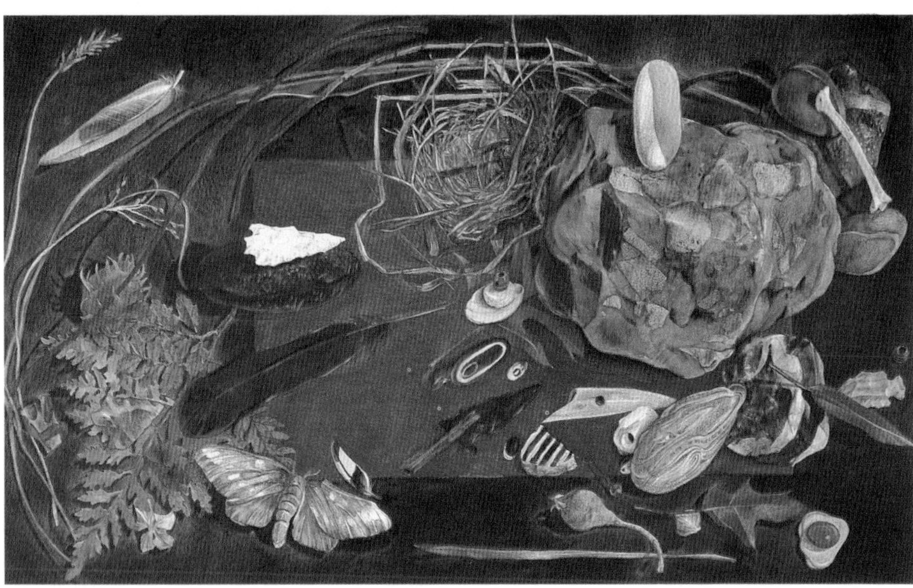

2

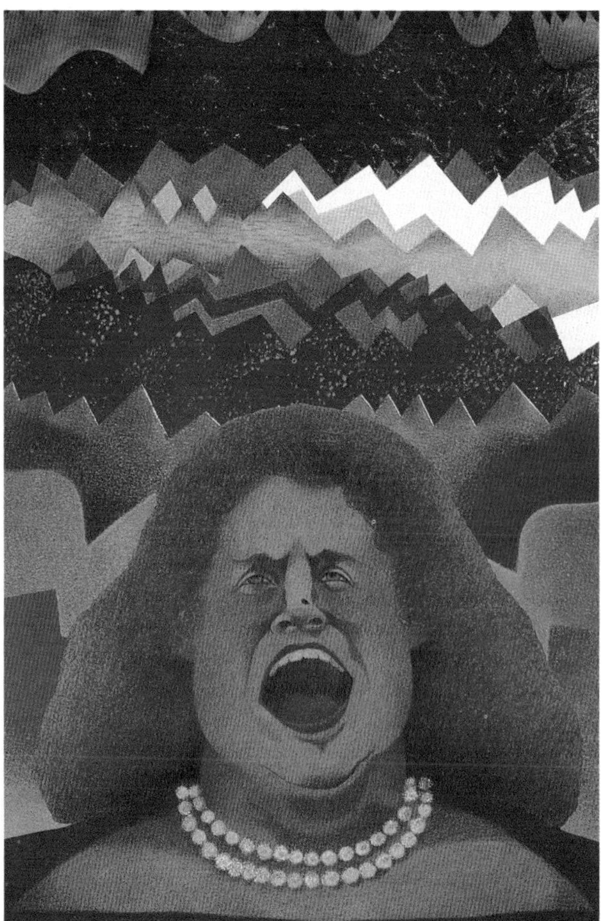

3

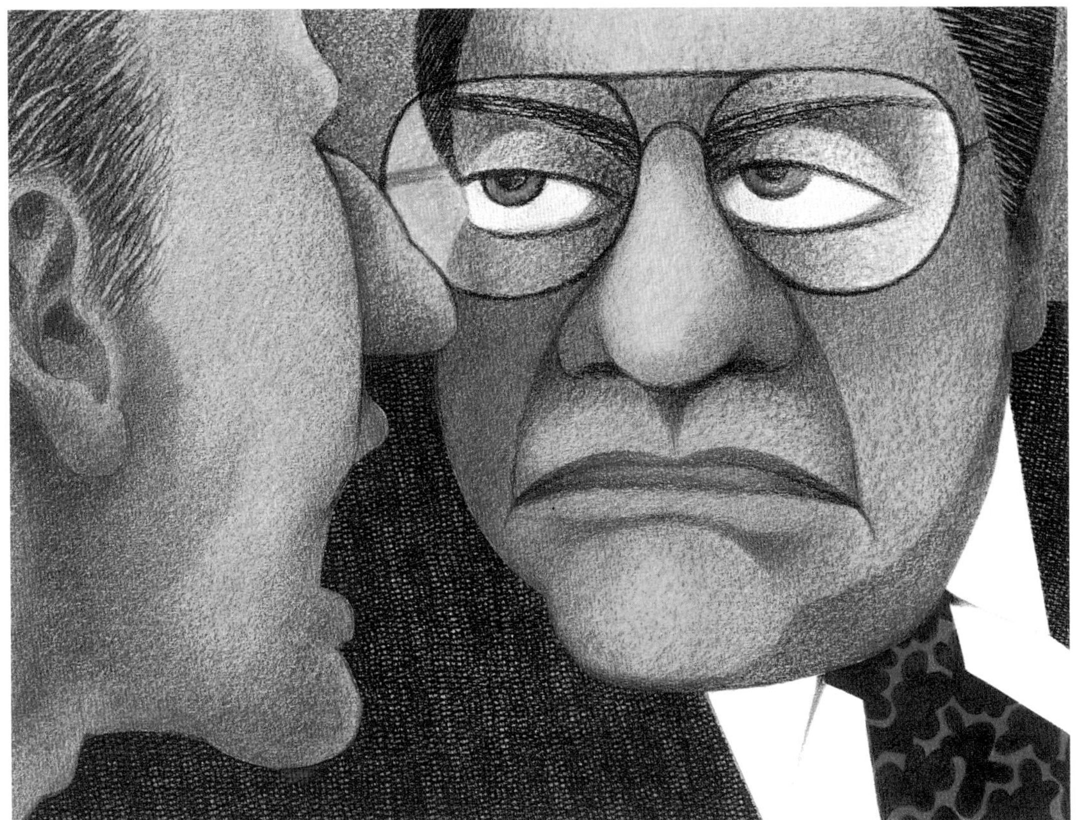

1

Pat Barron

1 *Voices From the Halls of Power*
14 x 16" (356 x 406 mm)
Arches Cover Black with Rives Light Weight
Media: Colored Pencil, Relief, and Monotype Collage

2 *Argument*
23 x 35" (584 x 889 mm)
Arches Cover Black with Rives Light Weight
Media: Colored Pencil, Relief Print Collage

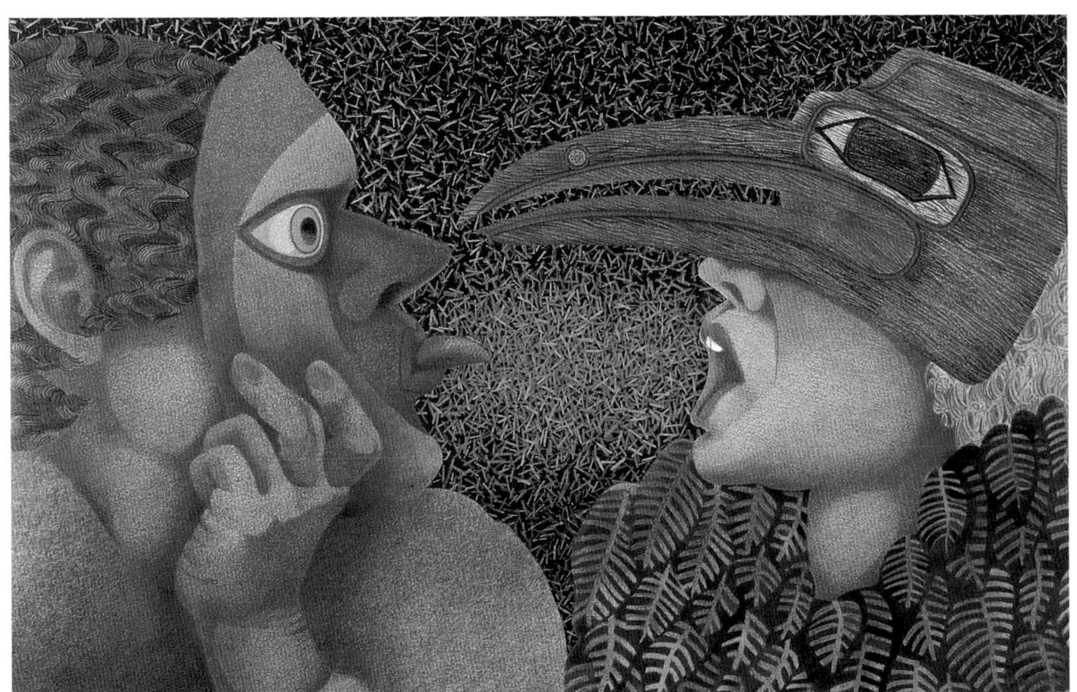

2

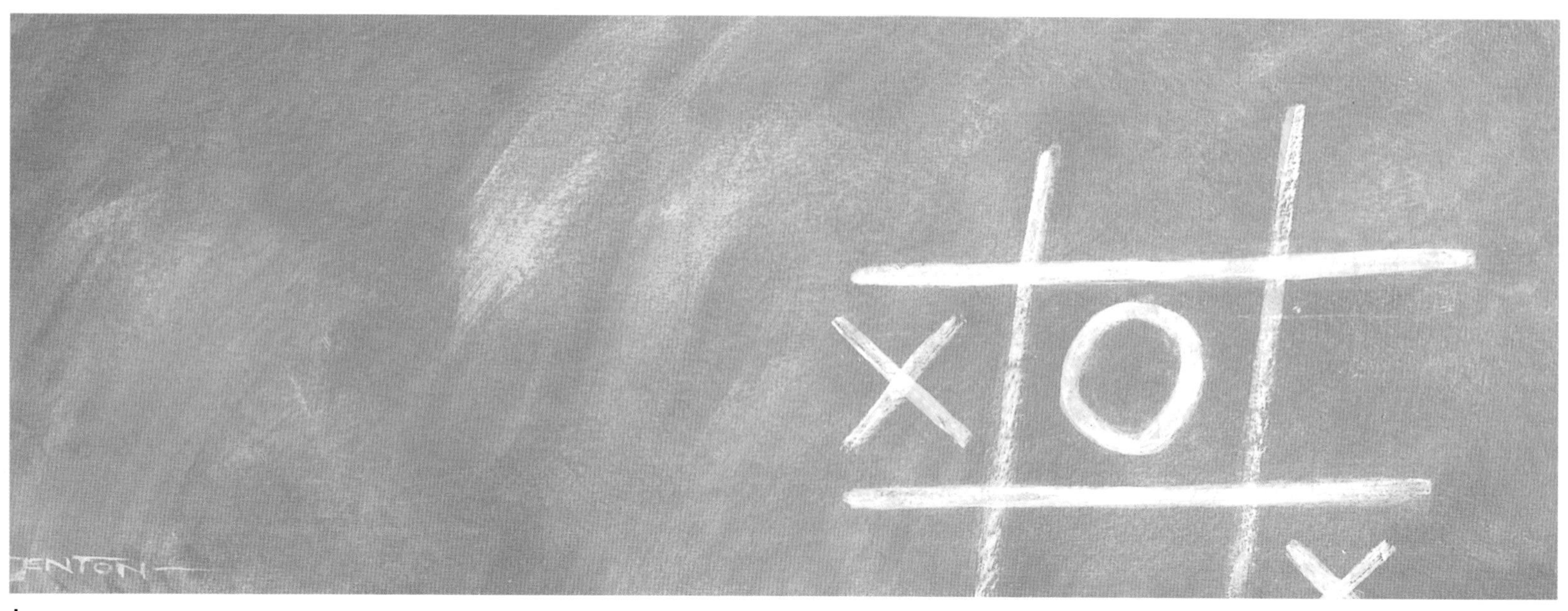

1

2

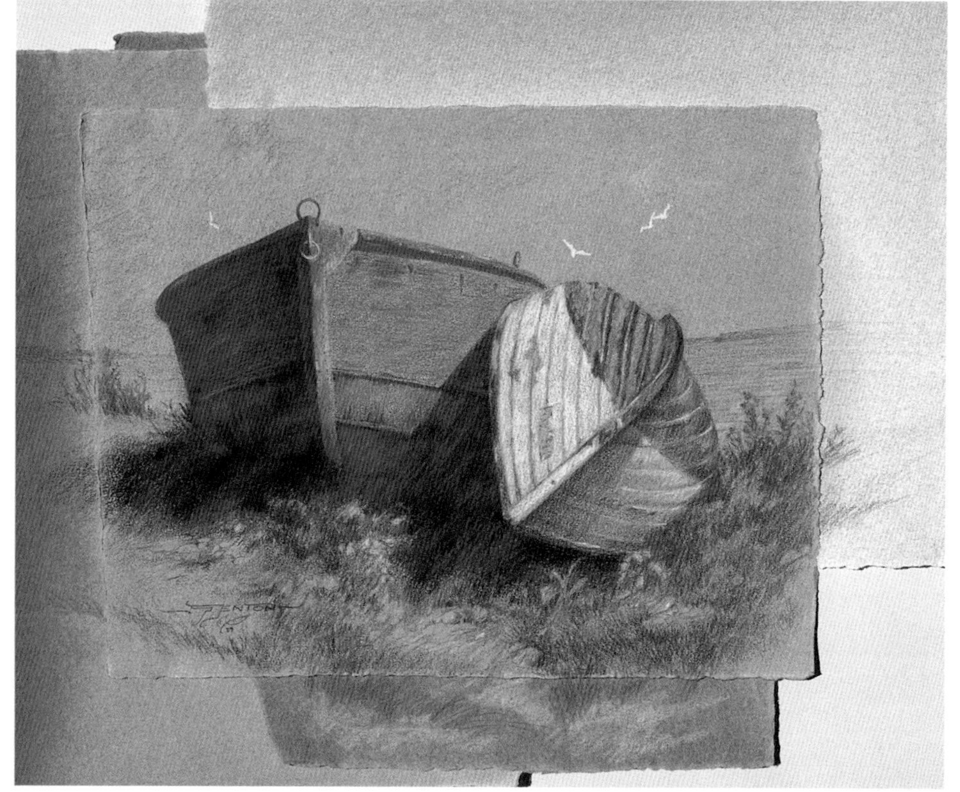

3

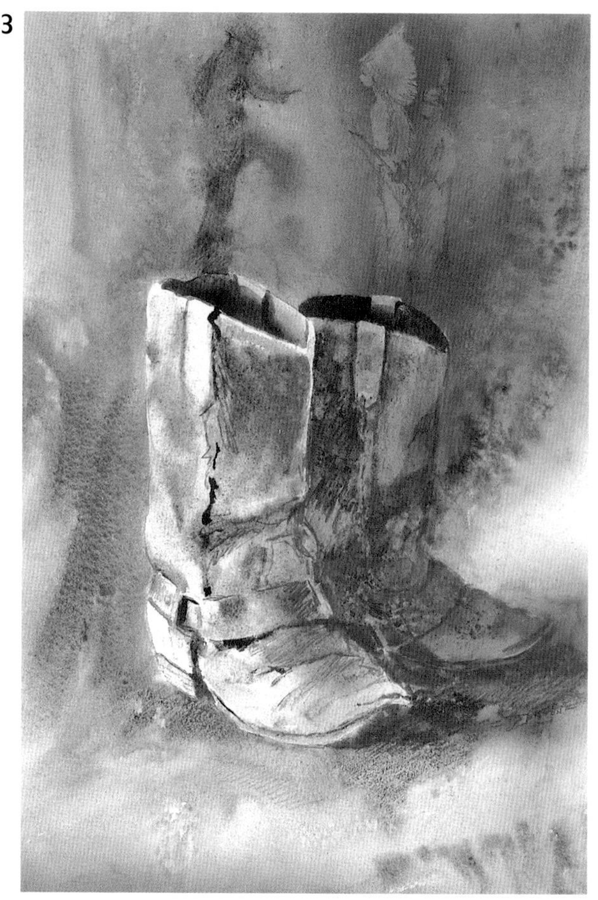

(Facing Page)

Patry Denton

1 *Cat and Mouse*
6 x 17" (152 x 432 mm)
Crescent #115 Watercolor Board
Media: Colored Pencil, Stabillo Pencil, Acrylic

2 *Beach Buddies*
16 x 20" (406 x 508 mm)
100% Rag French Handmade Paper

3 *They Played Cowboys and Indians*
22 x 14" (559 x 356 mm)
100% Rag Crescent #115 Hot Press Board
Media: Colored Pencil, Watercolor, Acrylic

This Page

1 *Minstrel*
22 x 16" (559 x 406 mm)
Crescent #115 Watercolor Board
Media: Water-Soluable Colored Pencil, Watercolor, Airbrush

2 *Jonathan's Bounty*
18 x 14" (457 x 356 mm)
100% Rag Crescent #115 Hot Press Board
Media: Colored Pencil, Watercolor

3 *Jumpin' Rope*
8 x 15" (203 x 851mm)
100% Rag Marble Surface Bainbridge Mat Board
Media: Colored Pencil, Acrylic

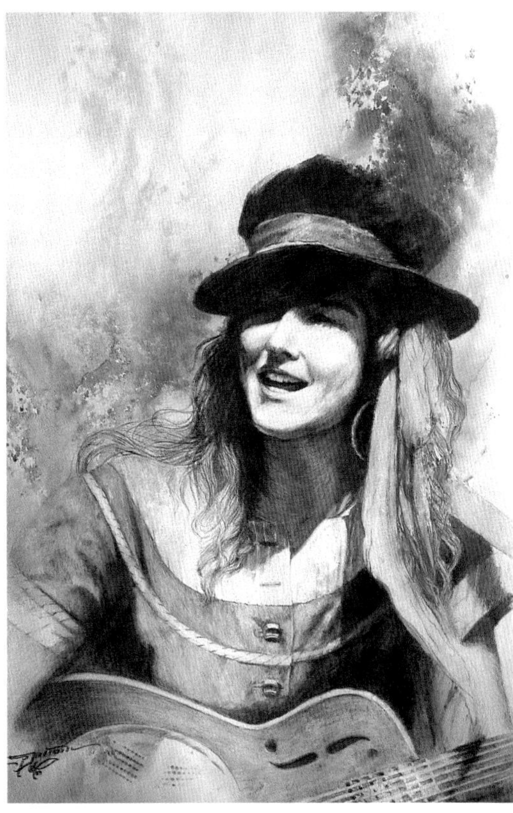

1

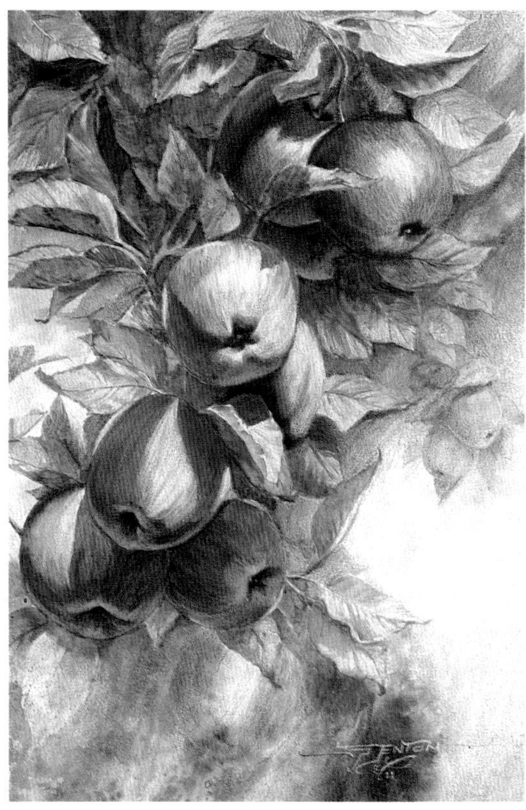

2

3

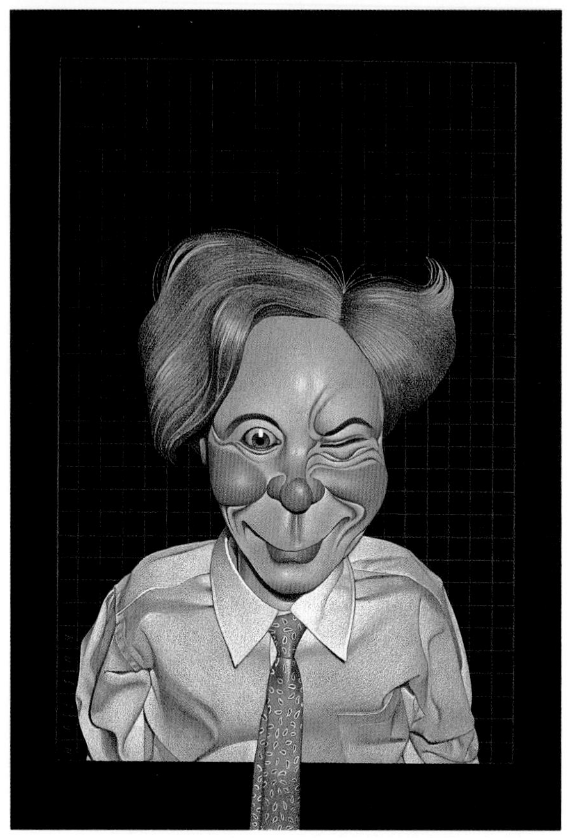
1

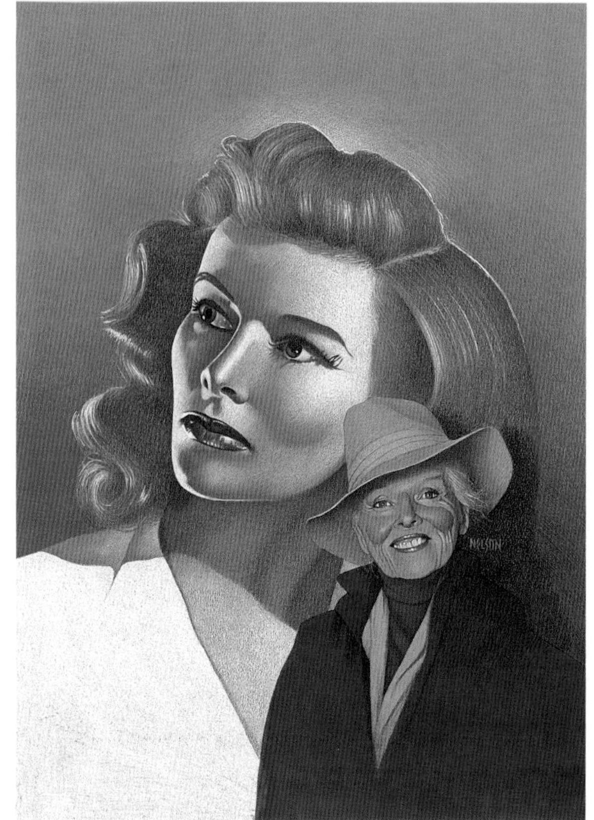

2

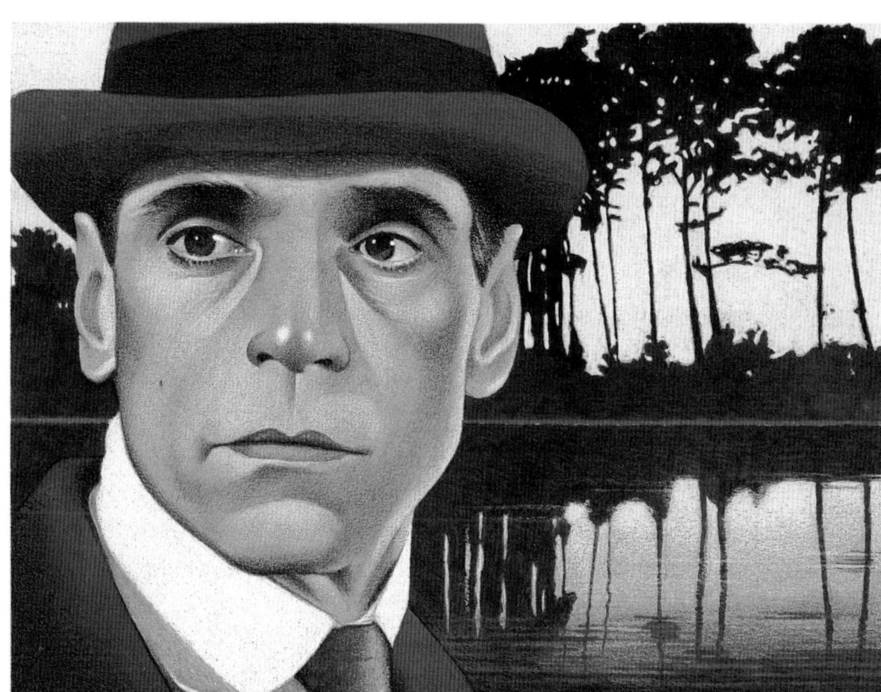
3

Bill Nelson

1 *Froto*
10 x 15" (254 x 381 mm)
Canson Charcoal Paper
Technique: Colored Pencil Collage

2 *Katherine Hepburn*
For the Cover of *Cable News Guide*
12 x 15" (305 x 381 mm)
100% Rag Crescent Mat Board
Media: Colored Pencil, Watercolor

3 *Jeremy Irons*
5 x 8" (127 x 203 mm)
100% Rag Crescent Mat Board
Media: Colored Pencil, Marker Pen

1

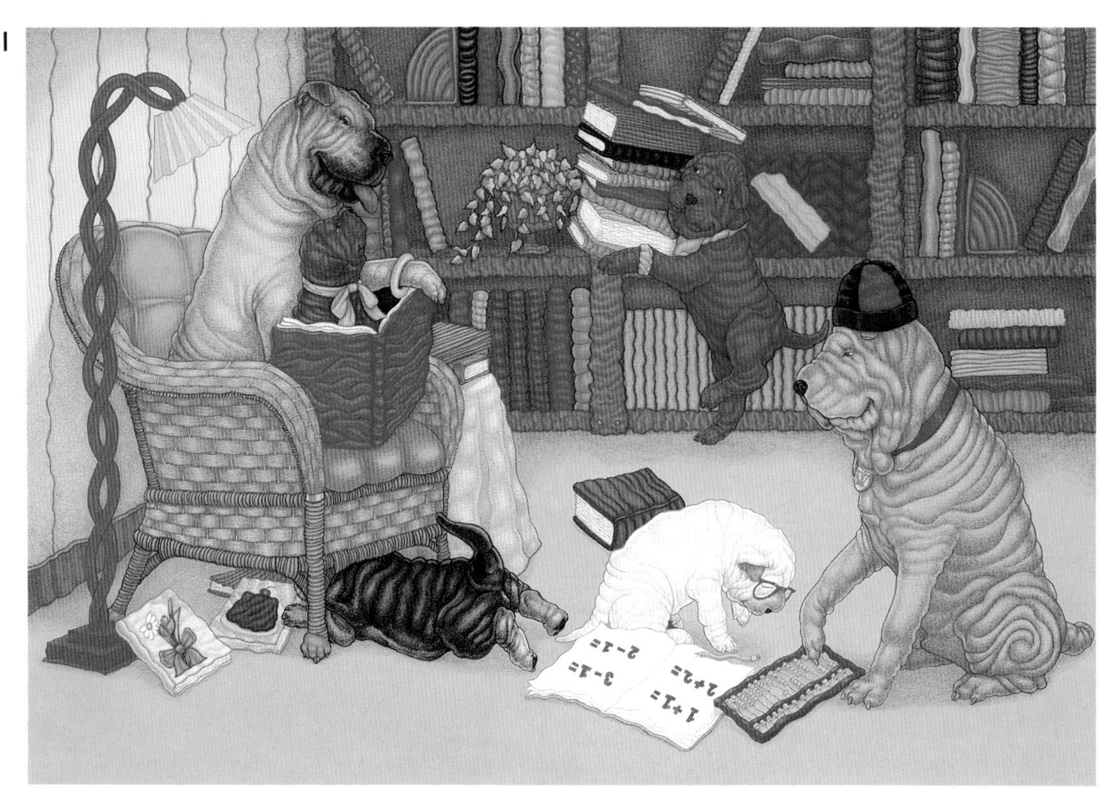

2

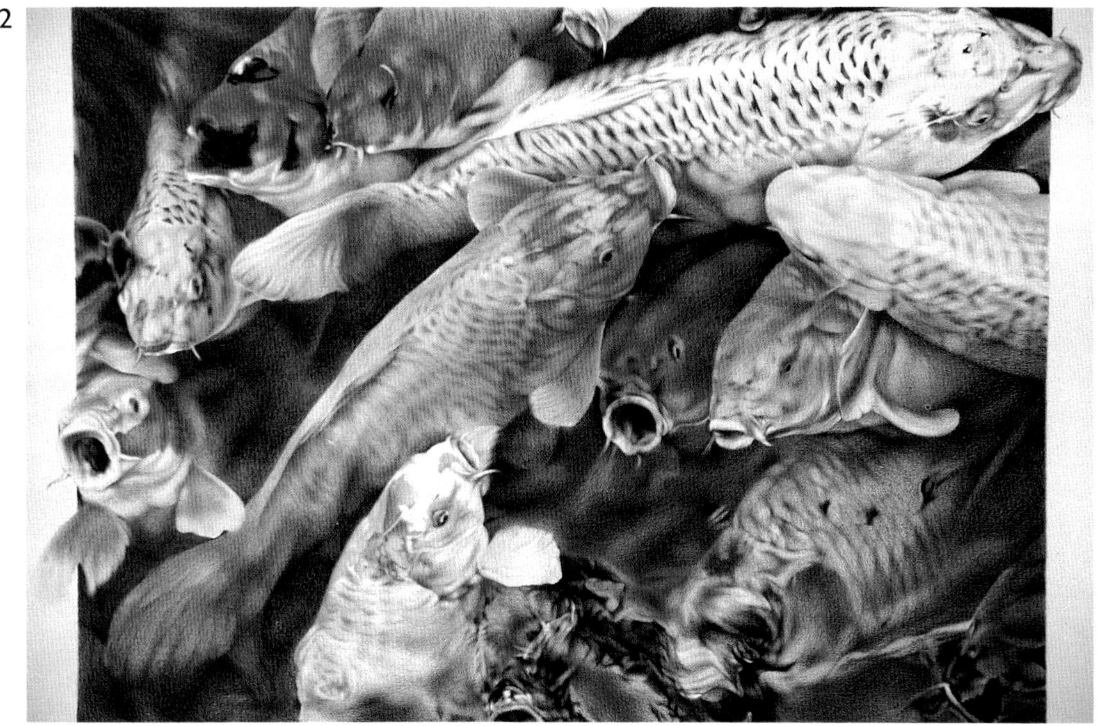

Laura Almada

1 *The Library*
From the Book, *Six Wrinkled Woos*
Media: Colored Pencil, Watercolor

Mike DeRossett

2 *Feeding Time*
24 x 28" (610 x 711 mm)
400 Series Strathmore Bristol
Technique: Colored Pencil , Graphite, Burnishing between Layers

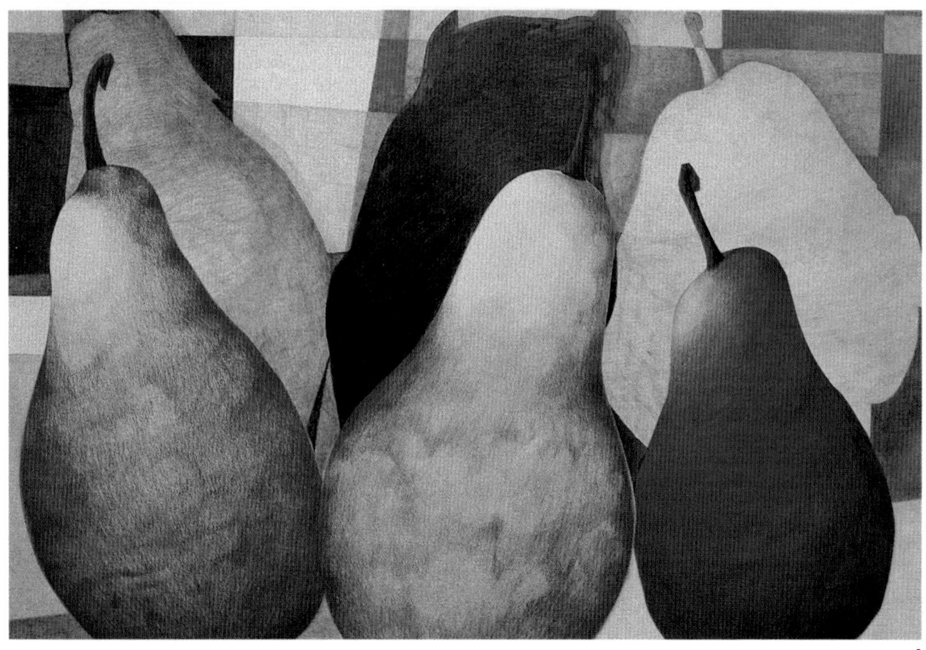

1

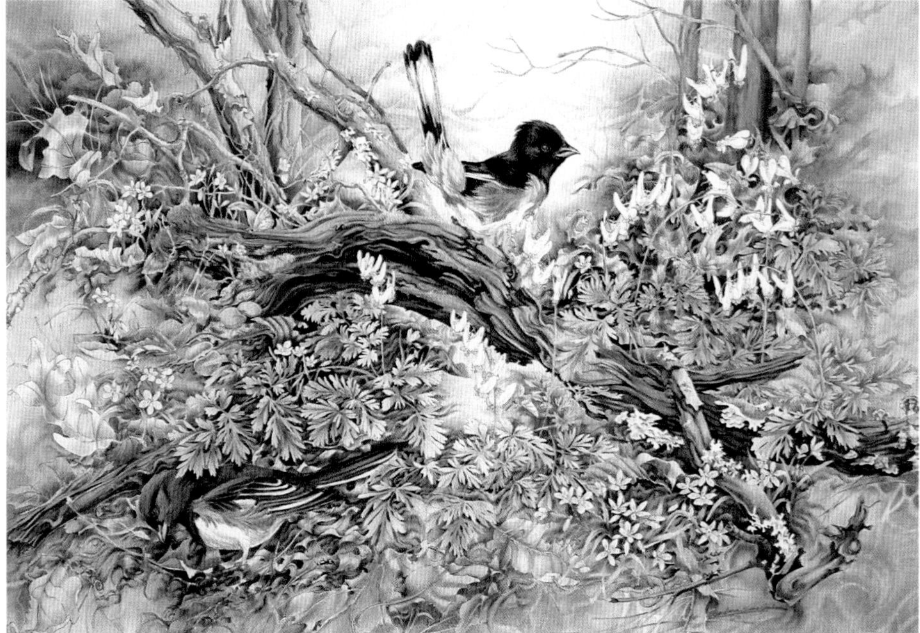

3

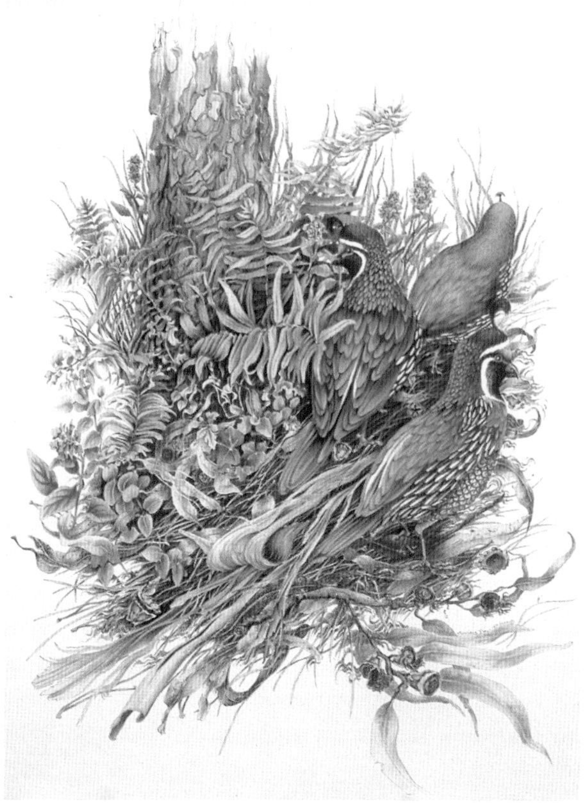

2

Marty Swan

1 *Trio of Pears*
20 x 24" (508 x 610 mm)
Letramax 2000 Bristol Board with Arches 90 Lb.
Hot Press Paper Collage
Media: Colored Pencil, Watercolor, Graphite

Barbara Krans Jenkins

2 *Calfornia Quail*
15 x 12" (381 x 305 mm)
100% Rag Strathmore Watercolor
Crescent Hot Press 115 Watercolor Board
Media: Colored Pencil, Ink

3 *Towhee in Dutchman's Breeches*
14 x 19" (356 x 483 mm)
100% Rag Strathmore Bonded Watercolor
Media: Colored Pencil, Ink

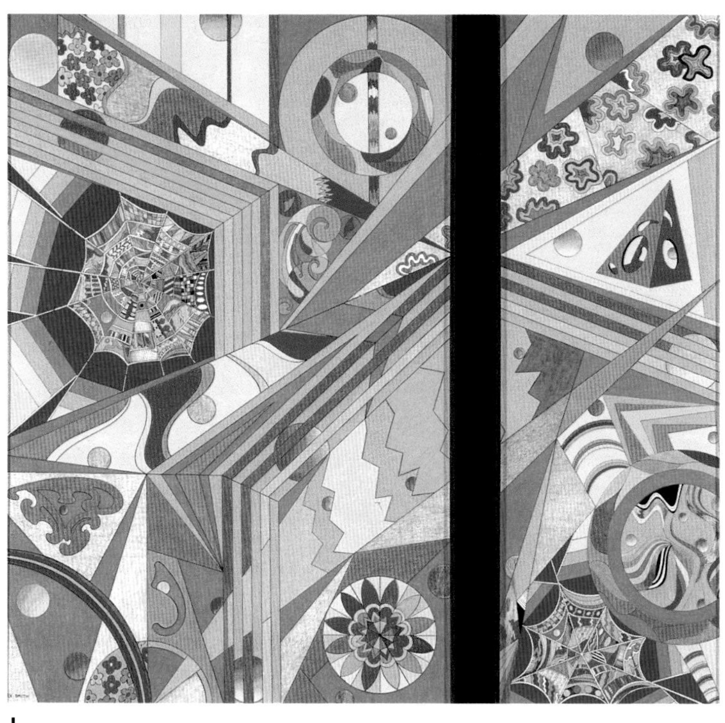

1

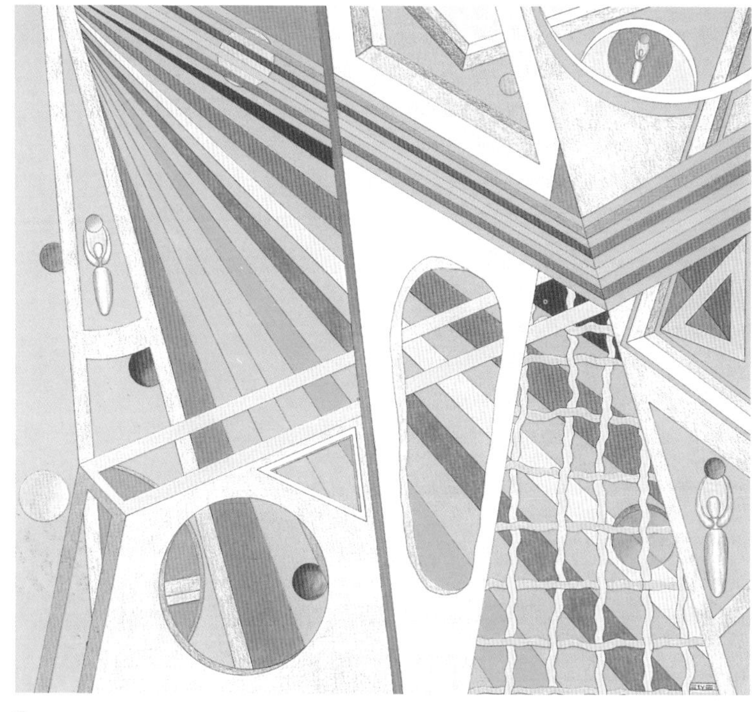

2

Ev Smith

1 *Eclectic Vision* (Diptych)
36 x 24 / 36 x12" (914 x 610 / 914 x 305 mm)
Strathmore 2-ply A/F Bristol Board
Media: Colored Pencil, Ink

2 *Eclectic Vision 93-52*
26 x 29" (660 x 737 mm)
Bainbridge 2-ply A/F Museum Board
Media: Colored Pencil, Ink

Marilyn Gorman

3 *Flying on the Fringes*
23 x 29" (584 x 737 mm)
Strathmore 500 4-ply Bristol, Vellum Finish
Media: Colored Pencil, Pro White, Watercolor

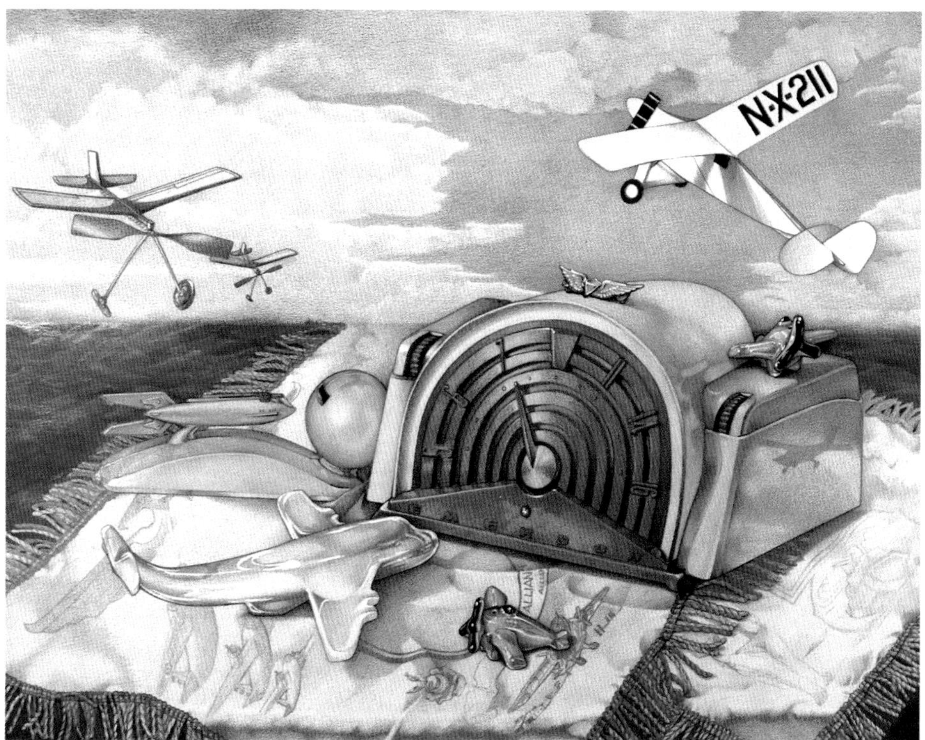

3

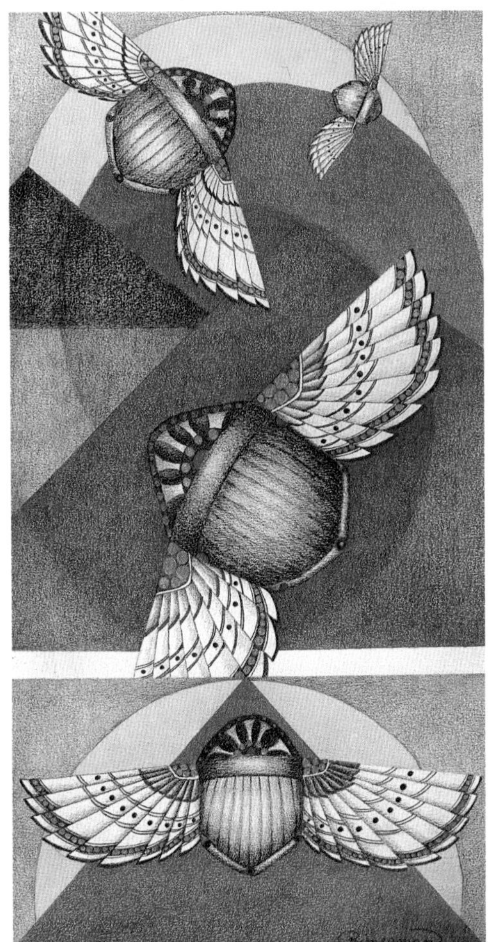

1

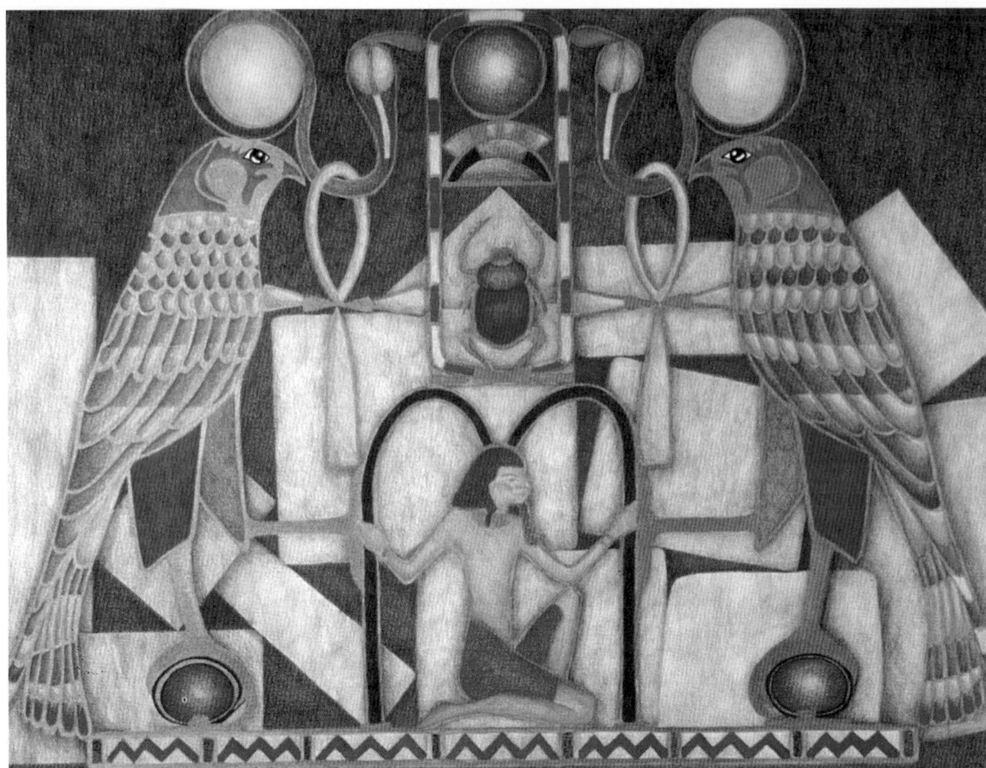

2

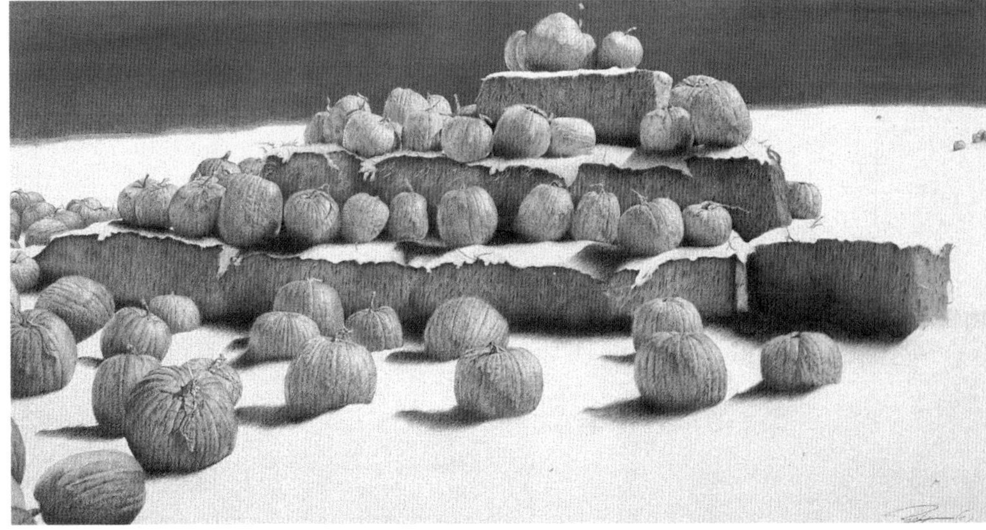

3

Jan Rimerman

1 *Circle of Time*
26 x 14" (660 x 356 mm)
Rising Bristol, 4-ply Vellum Finish
Media: Colored Pencil, Metallic, Watercolor

2 *Treasure of Lahun*
29 x 38" (730 x 953 mm)
100% Rag Board, 8-ply Vellum Finish
Media: Colored Pencil, Metallic, Watercolor

Gilbert Rocha

3 *Pumpkin Pyramid*
11 x 22" (286 x 552 mm)
Fabriano 140 lb. Cold Press Watercolor Paper
Media: Colored Pencil, Watercolor

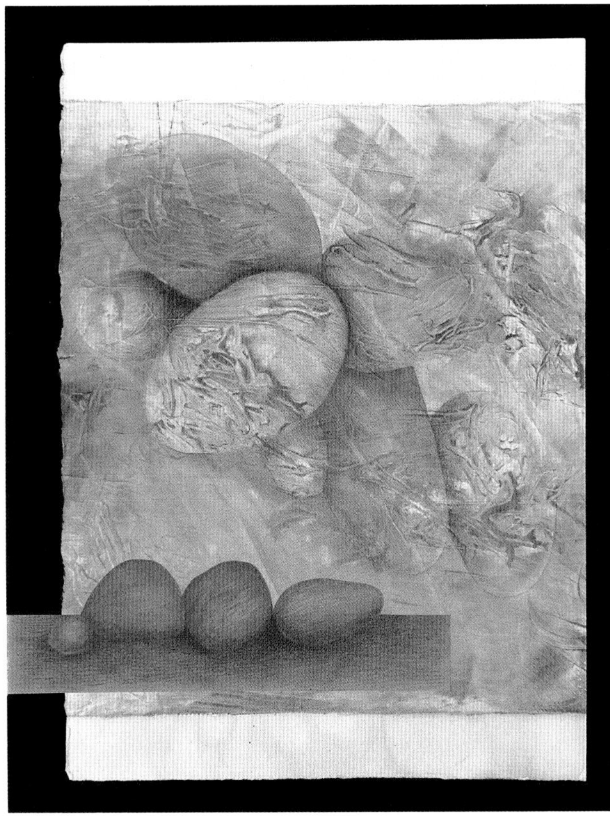

1

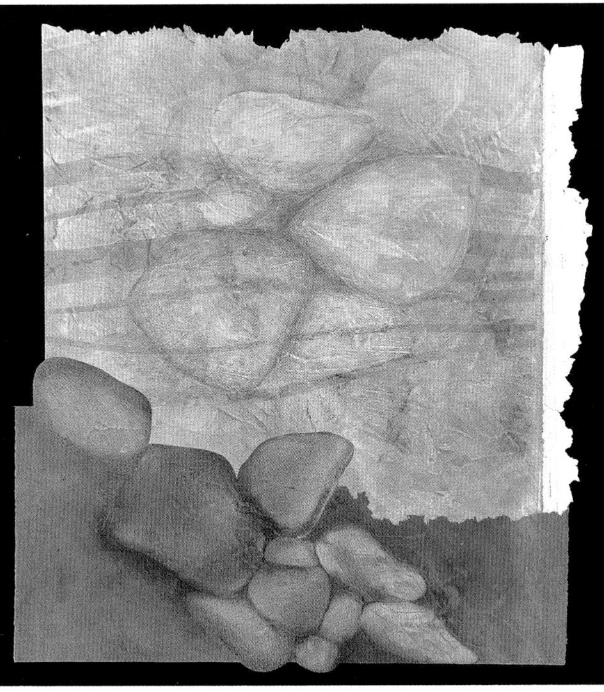

2

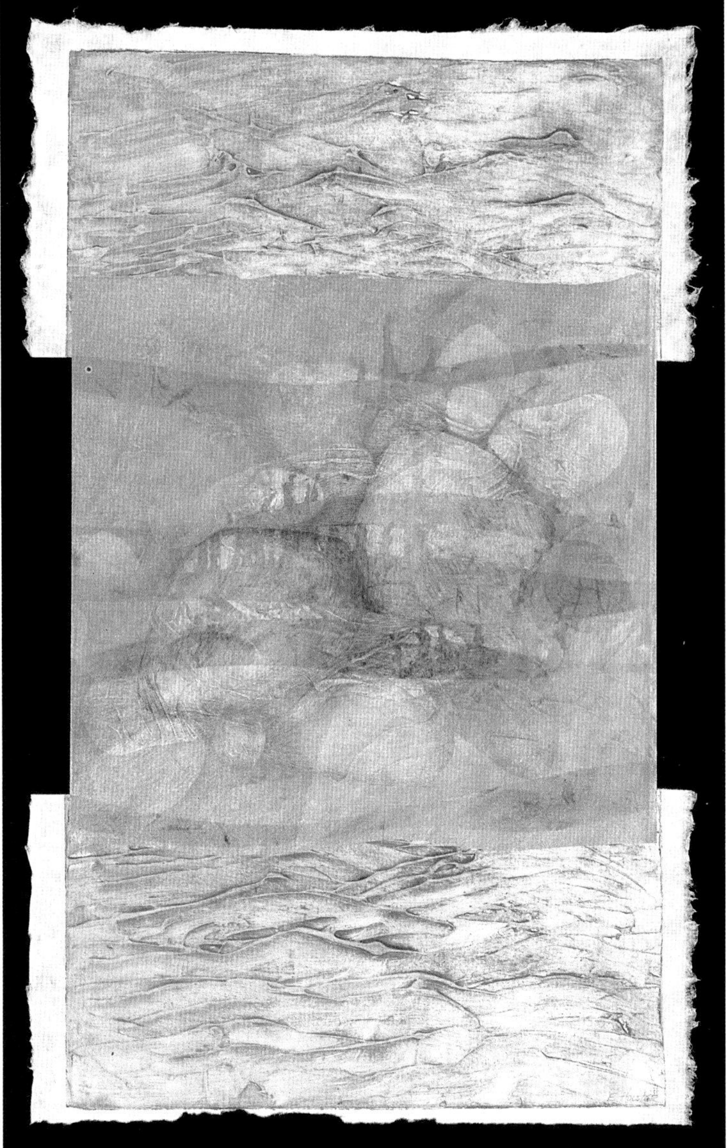

3

Elizabeth Holster

1 *Rocks in Water #17*
25 x 23" (635 x 584 mm)
Handmade Paper
Media: Colored Pencil, Collagraph

2 *Rocks in Water #13*
31 x 23" (787 x 584 mm)
Handmade Paper
Media: Colored Pencil, Collagraph

3 *Rocks in Water #20*
24 x 21" (608 x 532 mm)
Arches Printing Paper
Media: Colored Pencil, Collagraph

Michelle de Alberich

1 *Leeward Lights*
30 x 40" (762 x 1,016 mm)
Arches Cover Black Etching Paper
Media: Colored Pencil, Metallic Ink

2 *Falling Man*
30 x 40" (762 x 1,016 mm)
Arches Cover Black Etching Paper
Media: Colored Pencil, Metallic Ink

3 *Breaking Away from Paradise*
30 x 40" (762 x 1,016 mm)
Arches Cover Black Etching Paper
Media: Colored Pencil, Metallic Ink

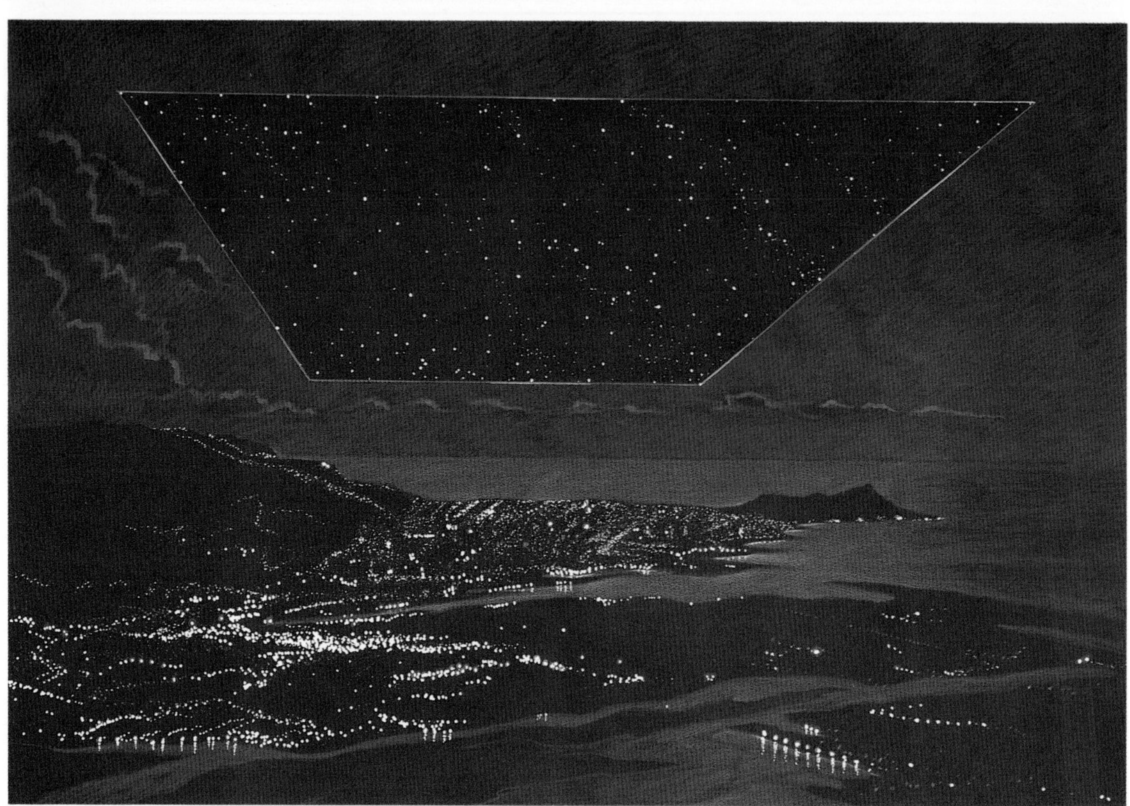

1

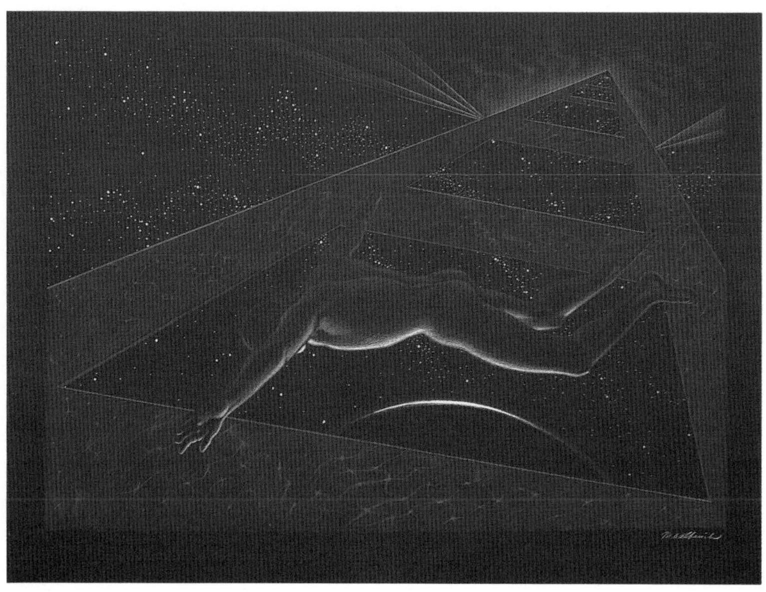

2

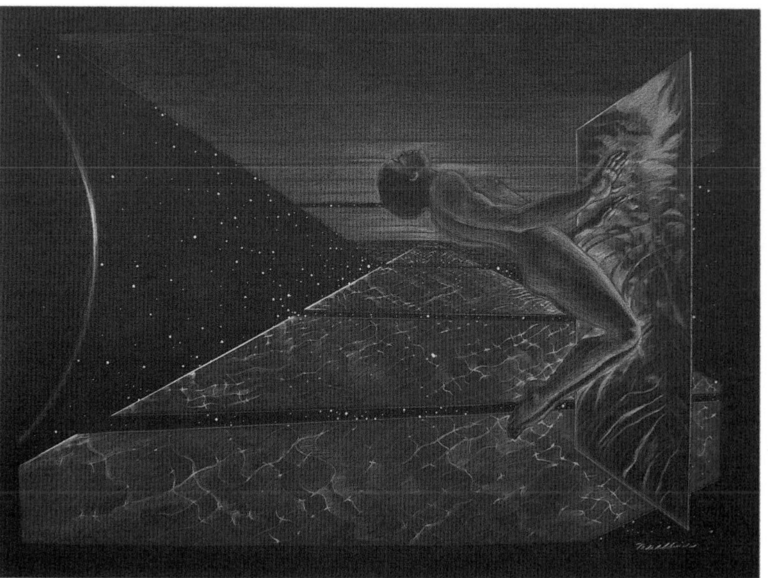

3

Michele Johnsen

1 *Mayan Secrets*
6 x 10" (152 x 254 mm)
100% Cotton Strathmore Illustration Board
Media: Colored Pencil, Watercolor

2 *Mayan Secrets II*
6 x 10" (152 x 254 mm)
100% Cotton Strathmore Illustration Board
Media: Colored Pencil, Watercolor, Ink

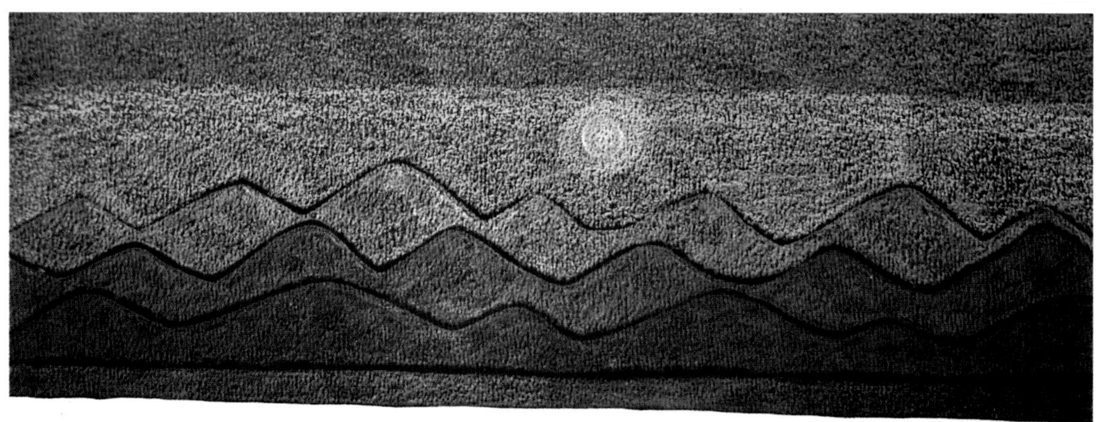

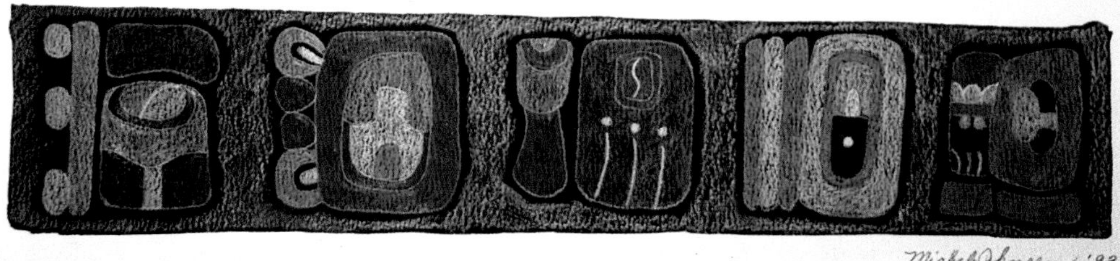

1

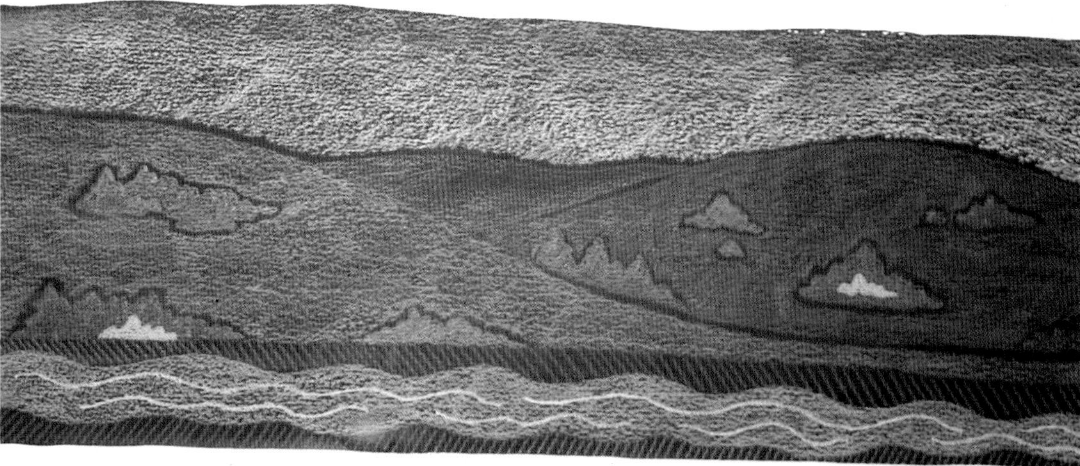

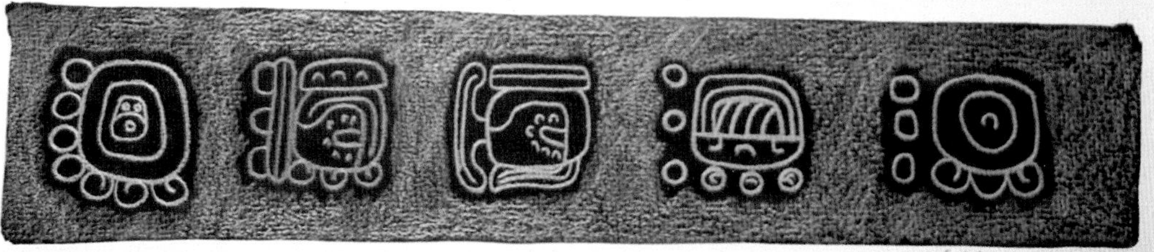

2

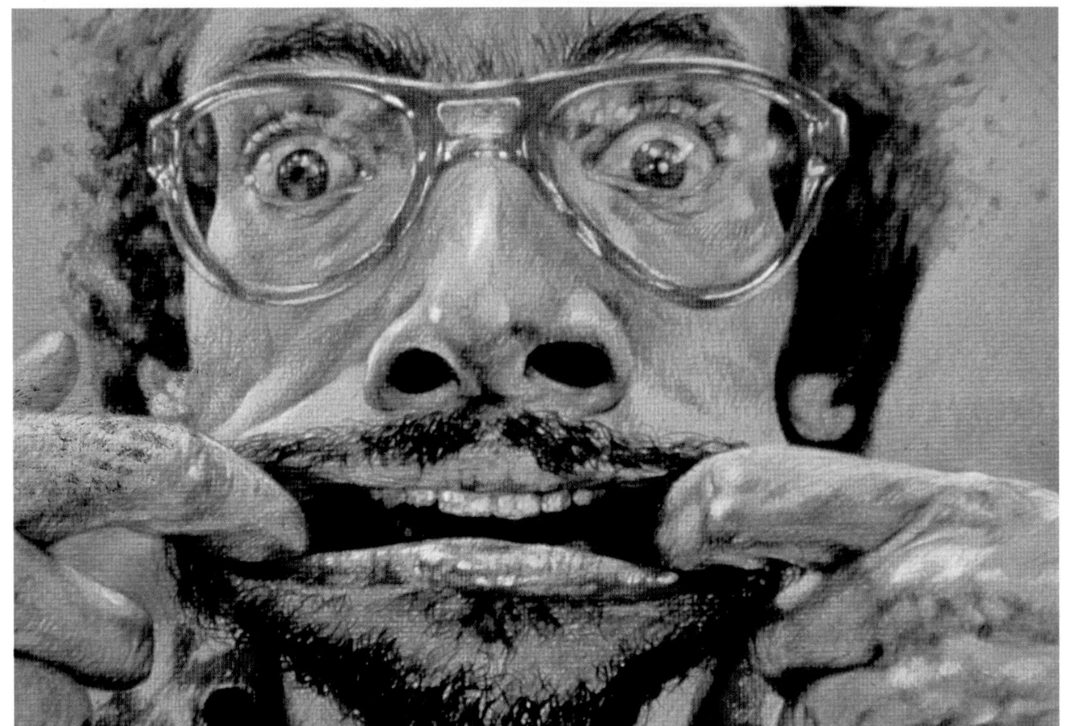

1

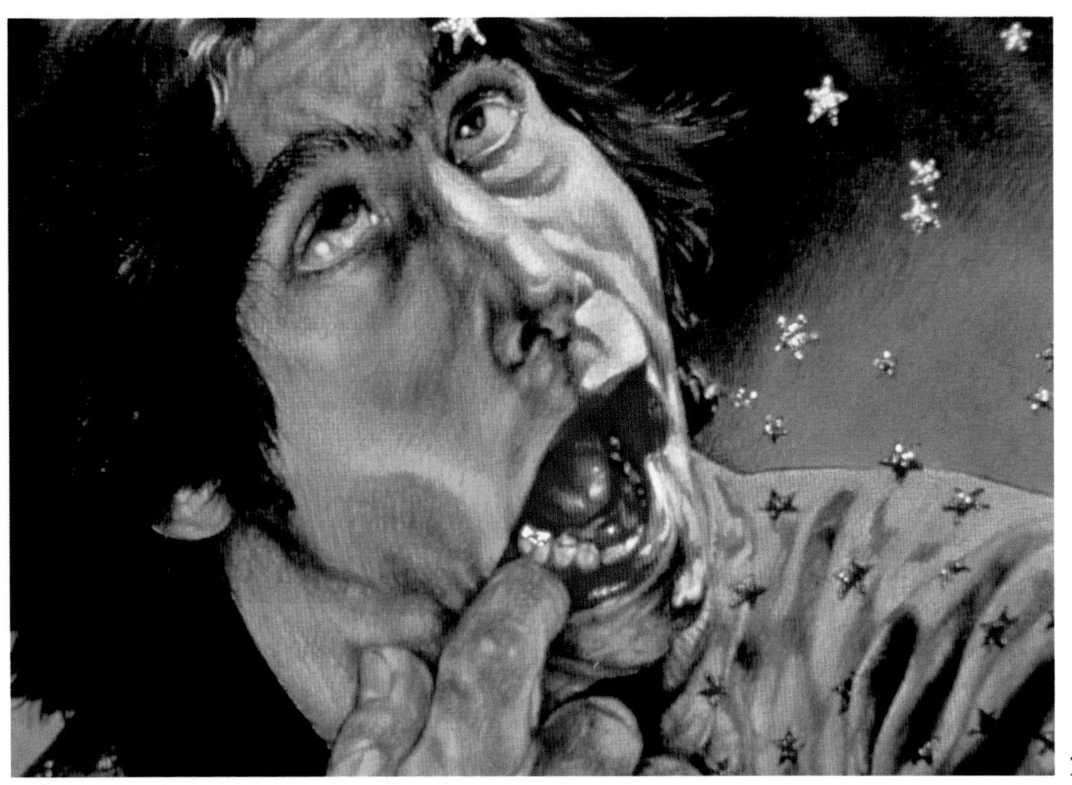

2

Chuck Richards

1 *Dave*
11 x 14" (279 x 356 mm)
Crescent Drawing Paper

2 *Willie*
11 x 14" (279 x 356 mm)
Crescent Drawing Paper
Media: Colored Pencil, Glitter, Foil
Technique: Burnishing

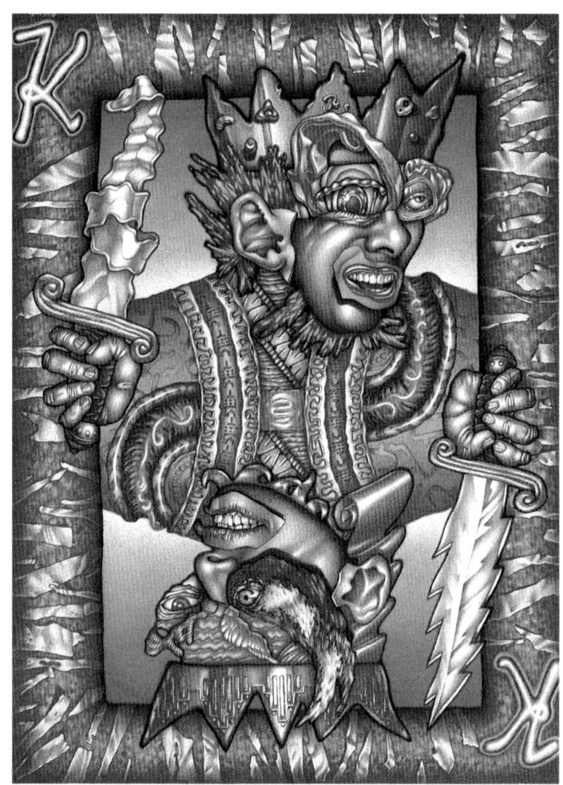

1

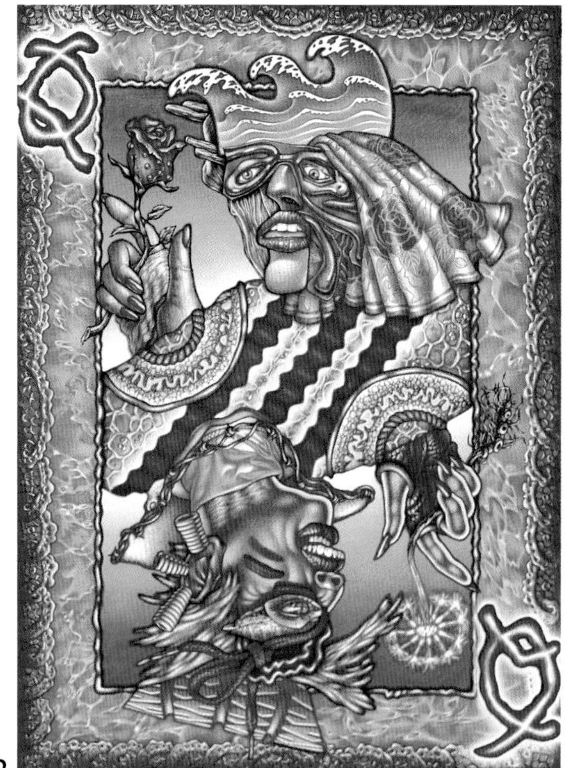

2

Chuck Richards

1 *King*
29 x 21" (737 x 533 mm)
140 lb. Hot Press Arches Paper
Media: Colored Pencil, Watercolor

2 *Queen*
29 x 21" (737 x 533 mm)
140 lb. Hot Press Arches Paper
Media: Colored Pencil, Watercolor

Carla McConnell

3 *Remembrance*
16 x 22" (406 x 559 mm)
Media: Colored Pencil, Etching Ink

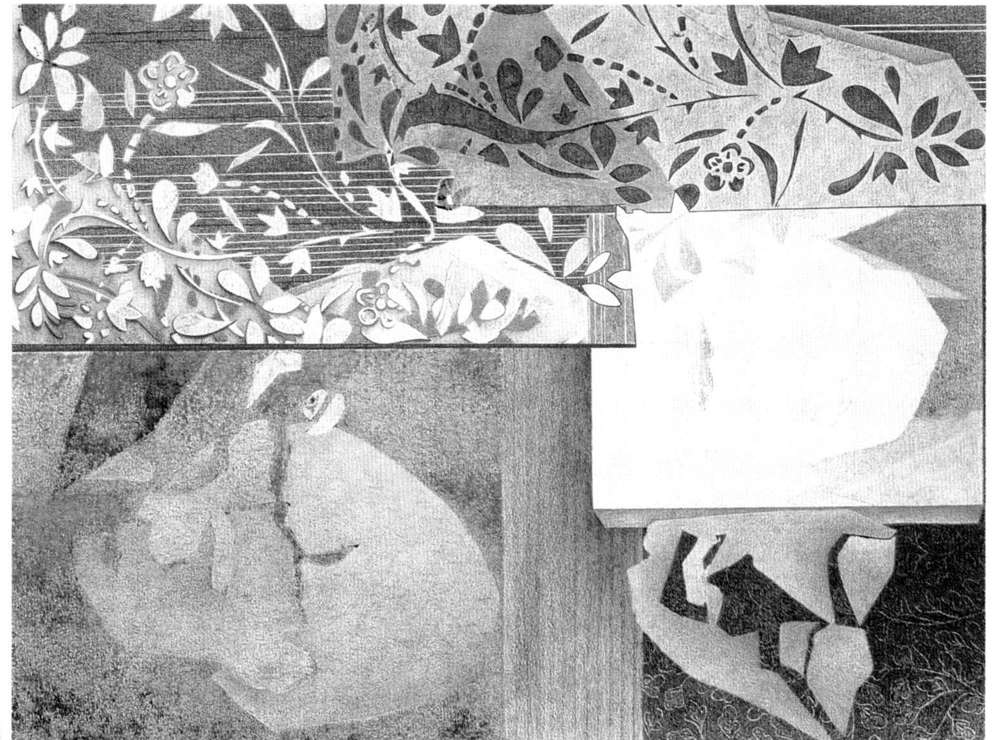

3

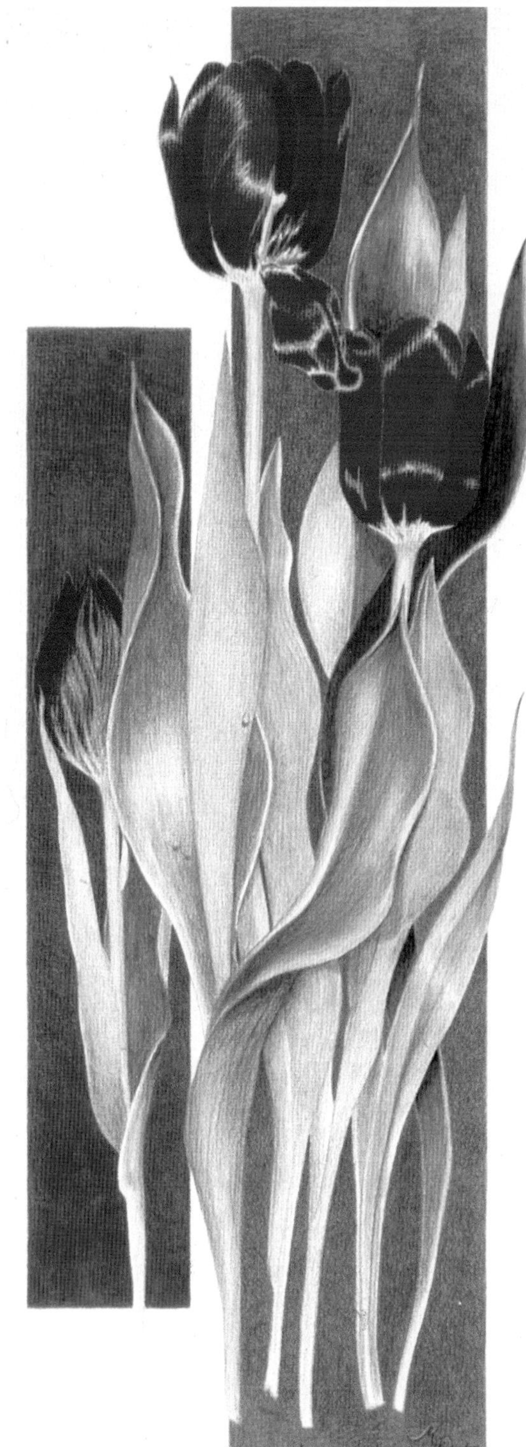

1

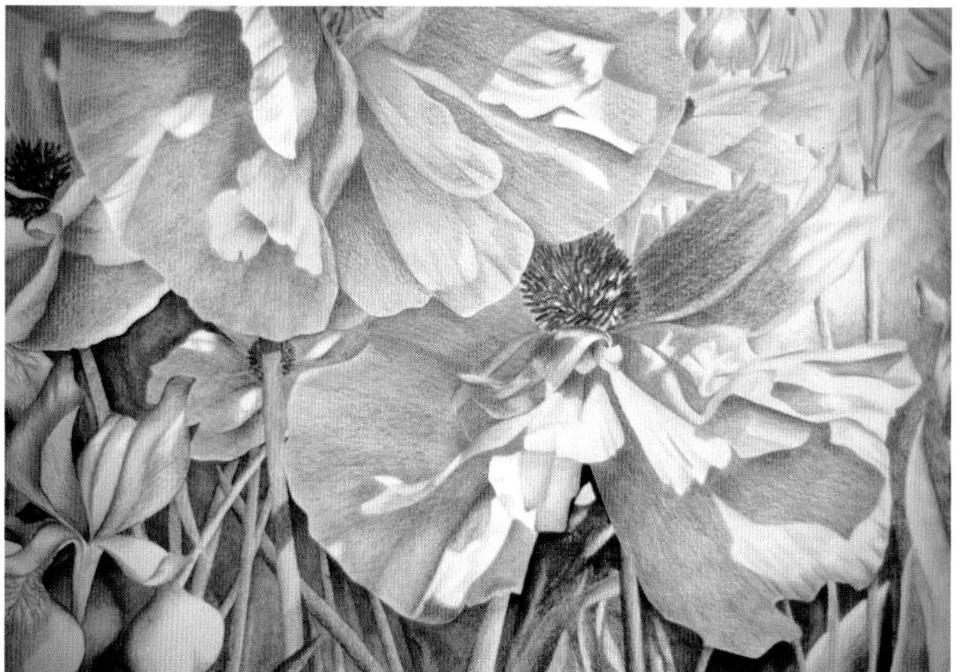

2

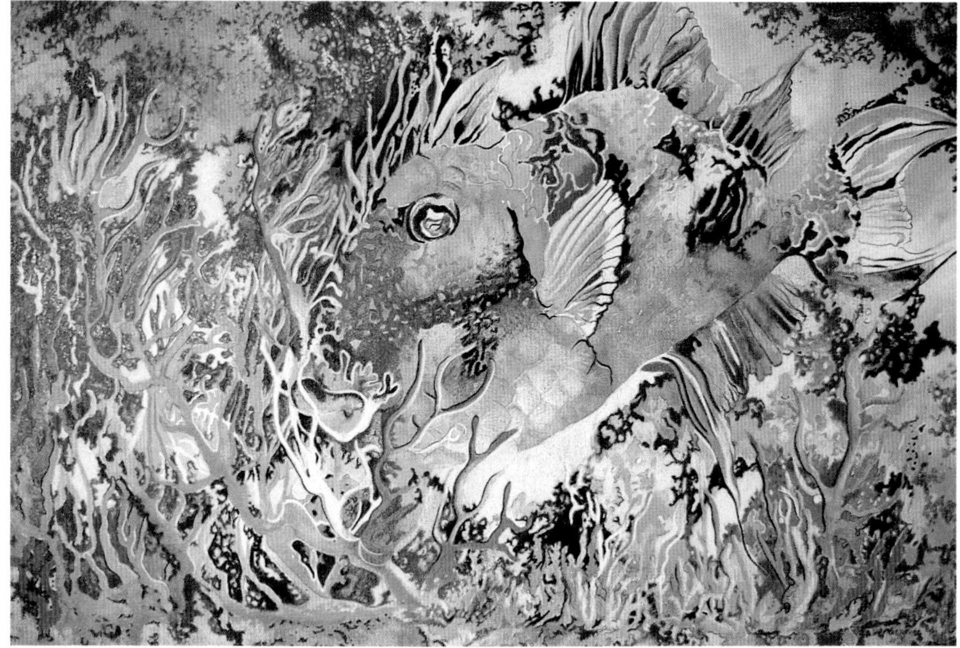

3

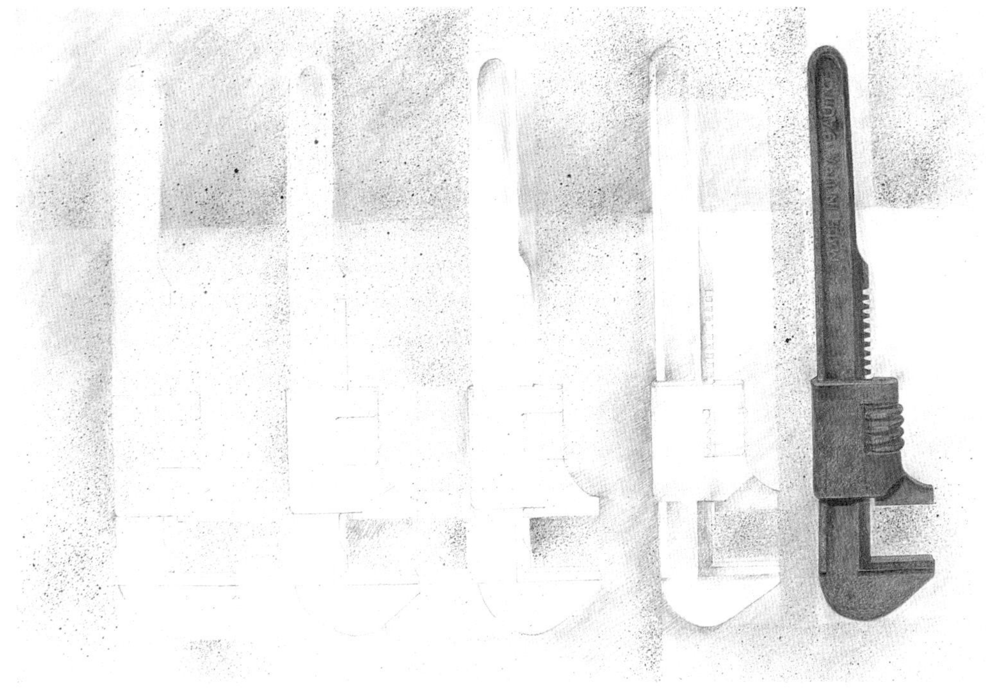

1

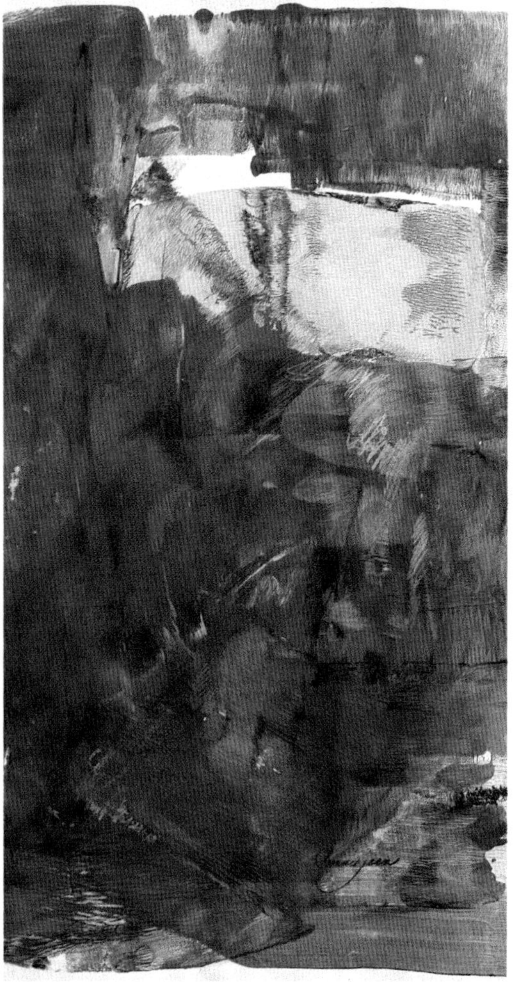

2

Facing Page

Marjorie Post

1 *Red Tulips*
34 x 16" (864 x 406 mm)
Crescent Rag Board
Media: Colored Pencil, Turpentine

Priscilla Heussner

2 *Poppies and Irises (diptych)*
37 x 50" (940 x 1,270 mm)
Colored Rising Stonehenge
Media: Colored Pencil, Watercolor

Dyanne Locati

3 *Camouflage*
15 x 22" (380 x 558 mm)
Media: Colored Pencil, Watercolor

This Page

Kathryn Conwell

1 *Untitled*
22 x 30" (559 x 762 mm)
Buff Stonehenge
Media: Colored Pencil, Graphite, Ink, Pastel

Bonnie J. Ridgeway

2 *Canyon Sunset*
16 x 7" (394 x 105 mm)
Canson Colored Drawing Paper
Technique: Colored Pencil, Tempra applied with a brayer for texture

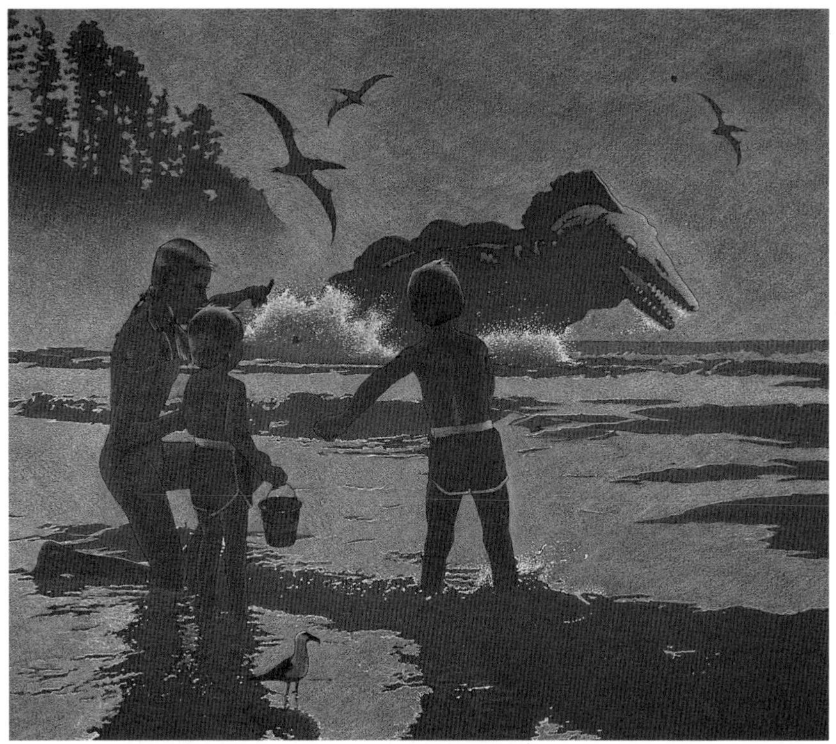

1

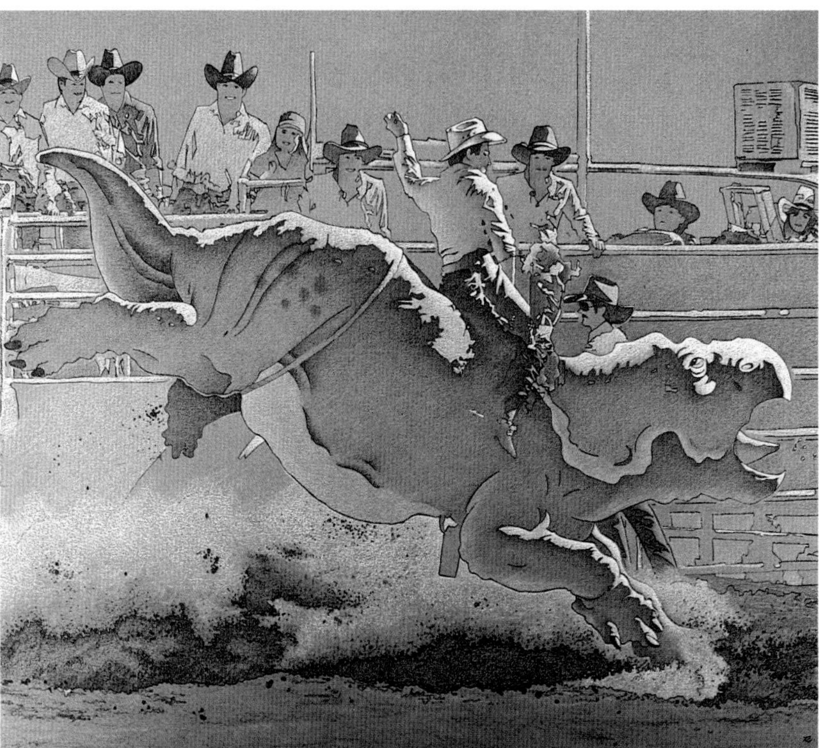

2

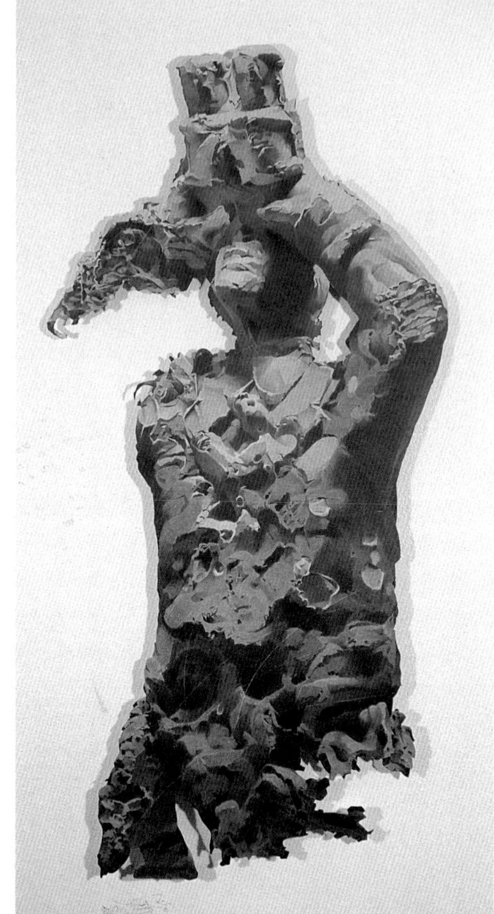

3

Ken Raney

1 *At the Sea Shore*
11 x 13" (279 x 330 mm)
Canson Paper
Media: Colored Pencil, White Ink

2 *Rodeo*
11 x 13" (279 x 330 mm)
Canson Paper
Media: Colored Pencil, Brown Ink

Mike Hill

3 *Watchman*
52 x 26" (1,321 x 660 mm)
1/8" Sheet Styrene, Cut and Shaped
Media: Colored Pencil, Acrylic Enamel

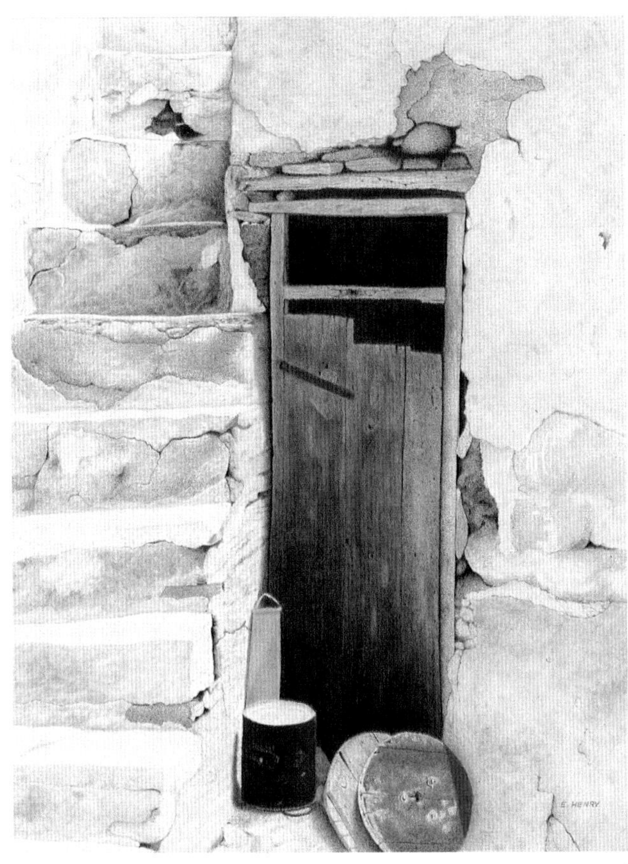

1

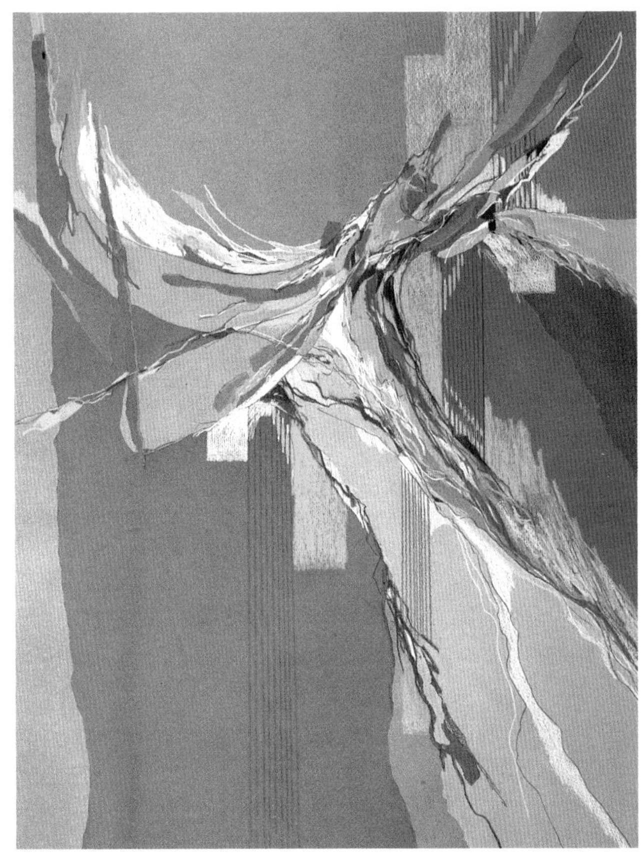

3

Edna L. Henry

1 *Greek Doorway Paros*
11 x 15" (279 x 381 mm)
2-ply Rising Museum Board
Media: Colored Pencils, Art Sticks, Water-Soluble Pencils

Bonnie J. Ridgeway

2 *Orchestrated Color*
23 x 19" (584 x 483 mm)
Canson Drawing Colored Paper
Media: Colored Pencil, Torn Paper Collage

Dara Mark

3 *Above and Below # 1*
31 x 52" (787 x 1,321 mm)
5-ply Bristol Collaged on Lana Roll Paper
Media: Colored Pencil, Gouache

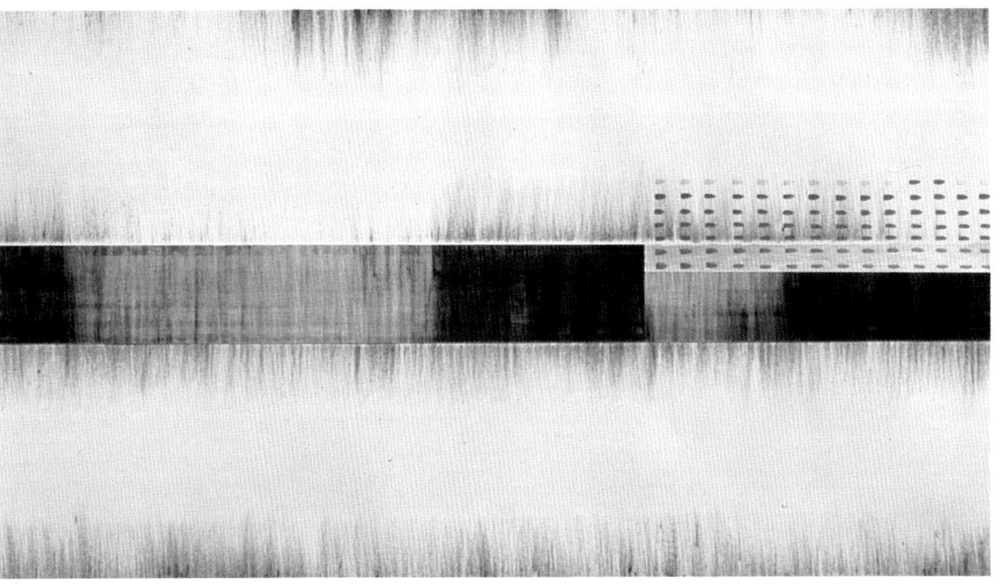

2

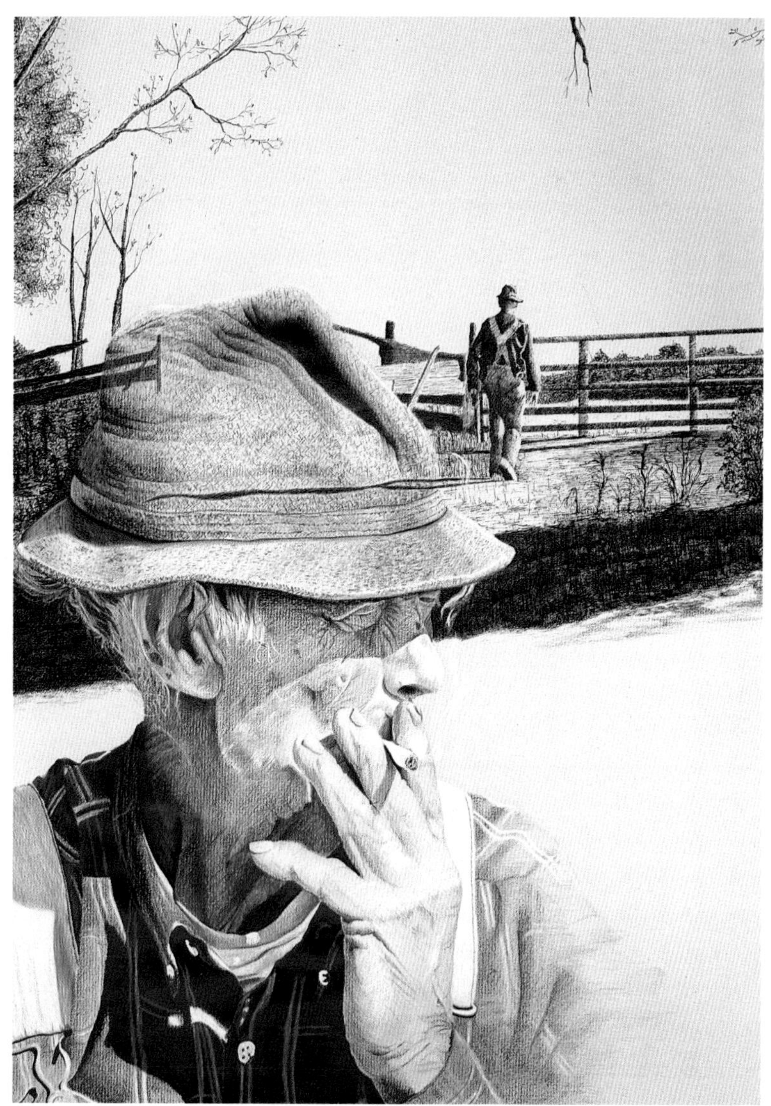

1

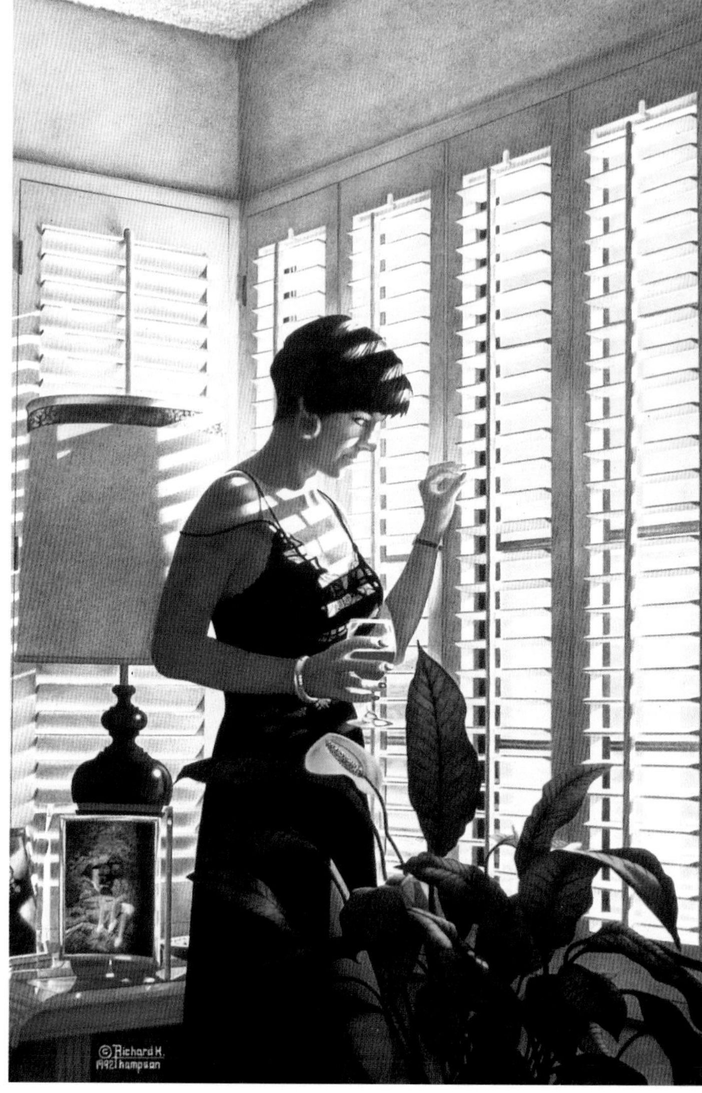

2

Dr. Christine J. Davis

1 *Mr. Ledford: Legacy*
24 x 18" (610 x 457 mm)
Strathmore Charcoal Paper
Media: Colored Pencil, India Ink

Richard K. Thompson

2 *Reflections*
24 x 20" (610 x 508 mm)
#115 Hot Press Strathmore Watercolor Board
Technique: Colored Pencil, Marker Pens

Richard K. Thompson

1 *Sea Rocks*
7 x 9" (179 x 229 mm)
#115 Hot Press Strathmore Watercolor Board
Media: Colored Pencil, Marker Pens

Vicki Visconti-Tilley

2 *Close Watch M'Ladies*
20 x 30" (508 x 762 mm)
Canson Watercolor Paper Rough Finish
Technique: Colored Pencil, Gouache

Charles Aquilina

3 *Hagar Qim*
60 x 40" (1,524 x 1,016 mm)
Strathmore Board (white)
Media: Colored Pencil, Gouache

1

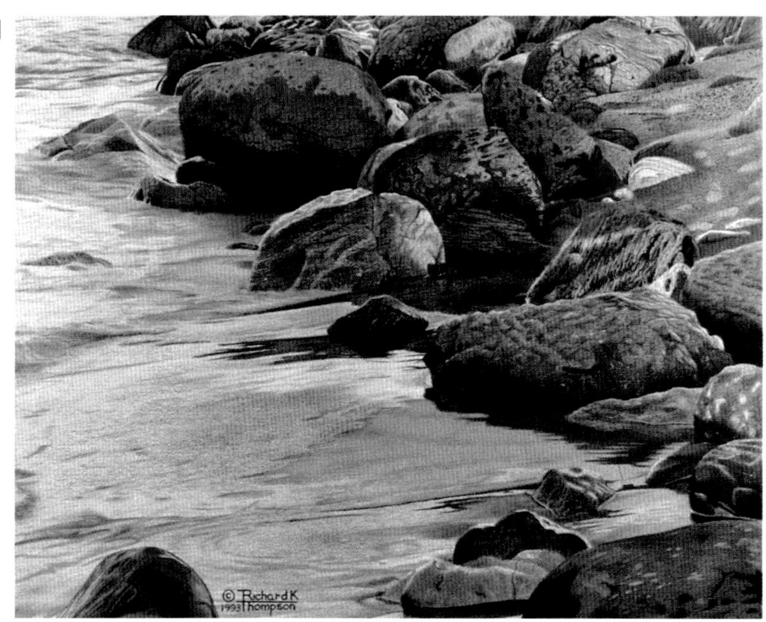

2

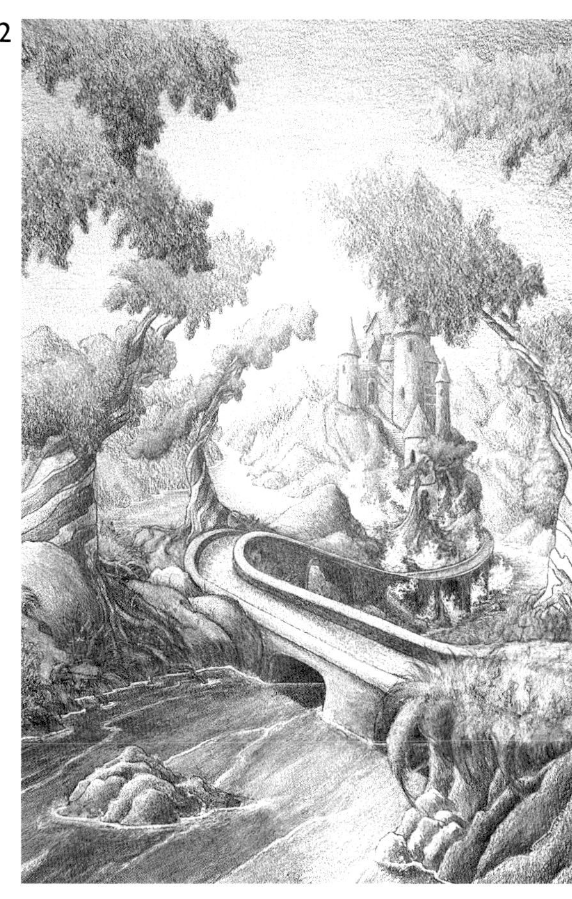

3

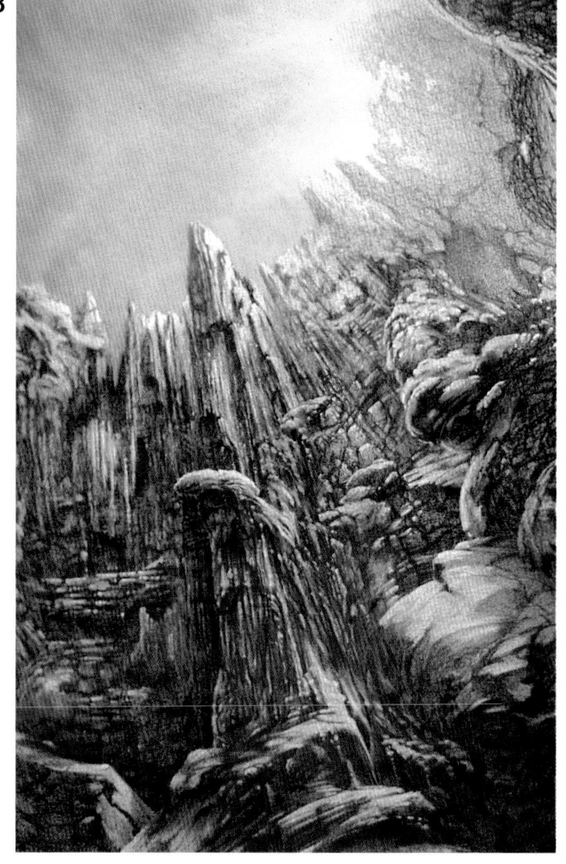

Laura Almada
1730 Catherine St.
Santa Clara, CA 95050
408-243-5089

Charles Aquilina
227 Kentucky St.
Vallejo, CA 94590
707-557-1192

Bonnie Auten
7541 E. Monroe Rd.
Tecumseh, MI 49286
517-423-6184

Pat Averill
640 Ninth St.
Lake Oswego, OR 97034-2221
503-635-4930

Susan Avishai
28 Marlboro St.
Newton. MA 02158
617-969-5451

Jerry L. Baker
4551 Kipling St. #53
Wheatridge, CO 80033
303-425-0141

Pat Barron
6815 Cherry Lane
Annandale, VA 22003
703-914-5078

Brian Bednarek
83 India St.
Brooklyn, NY 11222-1604
718-389-2907

Nancy Blanchard
P.O. Box 243
Erwinna, PA 18920-0243
215-294-9040

Lula Mae Blocton
798 Pudding Hill Road
Hampton, CT 06247
203-455-0820

Brent Bowen
4510 Wormwood Dr.
West Valley, UT 84120
801 963-1744

Ralph Caparulo
122 Montclair Ave.
Montclair, NJ 07042
201-783-4736

Kathryn Conwelll
809 NW 41st St.
Lawton,OK 73505
405-353-7532

June R. Conway
1672 Deer Run Road
Catawba, SC 29704
803-329-3759

Bill Corsick
4810 Brookwood
Eugene, OR 97405
503-686-1995

Vera Curnow
1620 Melrose Ave.
Seattle WA 98122-2057
206-622-8661

Dava Dahlgran
32 Suzanne St. Rt. #1
Washington, WV 26181
304-863-9310

Dr. Christine J. Davis
1071 River Rd.
Greer, SC 29651-8197
803-877-0801

Michelle De Alberich
59-548 Aukanka Pl.
Haleiwa, HI 96712
808-638-72

Chuck Demorat
305 Cornella Dr.
Graham, NC 27253
910-229-7359

Patry Denton
2948 Pierson Way
Lakewood, CO 80215
303-237-4954

Mike DeRossett
421 E. 74th Terrace
KansasCity, MO 64131
816-444-8378

Sheri Lynn Boyer Doty
2801 South 2700 East
Salt Lake City, UT 84109
801-467-6013 / 801- 582-2716

Laura Duis
121 Marson Dr.
Dayton, OH 45405
513-274-5264

Maija L. Earl
18 Westridge Dr.
Simsbury, CT 06070-2916
203-658-0742

Rhonda Farfan
25318 Fereguson Road
Junction City, OR 97448
503-998-3608

Susan Field
14 Asbury Ave.
Farmingdale, NJ 07727
908-938-7355

Mark Frazer
2006 1/2 Cedar St. Apt. I
Holt, MI 48842
906-884-4266

Judy A. Freidel
2382 Hwy 7 North
Hot Springs, AR 71909
501-623-1139

Merren Walker Frichtl
3311 Oberon St.
Kensington, MD 20895
301-946-2974

Susan Lane Gardner
1320 4th St.
Columbia City, OR 97018
503-366-0959

Bruce S. Garrabrandt
1505 Newport Dr.
Lakewood, NJ 08701
908-367-4223

Donna Gaylord
1980 W. Ashbrook Dr.
Tucson, AZ 85704
602-297-6291

Janie Gildow
905 Copperfield Lane
Tipp City, OH 45371
513-335-3570

Jeanne Goodman
1334 Botetourt Gardens
Norfolk, VA 23517
804-627-3113

Marilyn Gorman
739 Lakeview
Birmingham, MI 48009
810-540-8614

Gary Greene
21820 N.E. 156th St.
Woodinville, WA 98072
206-788-2211

Dawn Pierson Guild
1502 W. Anahurst Place
Santa Ana, CA 92704
714-545-5441

Edna L. Henry
29650 SW Courtside Dr. #14
Wilsonville, OR 97070
503-682-8853

Carlynne Hershberger
1016 NE 3rd St.
Ocala, FL 34470
904-622-4943

Priscilla Heussner
916 Whitewater Ave.
Fort Atkinson, WI 53538
414-563-5346

Mike Hill
2509 San Marcus
Dallas, TX 75228
214-328-7525

Joan C. Hollingsworth
2824 NE 22nd Ave.
Portland, OR 97212
503-287-6439

Elizabeth Holster
727 East A St.
Iron Mountain, MI 49801
906-779-2592

Janet Louvan Holt
2768 SW Talbot Rd.
Portland, OR 97201
503-227-7000

Eileen Cotter Howell
3040 Timothy Dr. NW
Salem, OR 97304
503-362-5386

Robert S. Hunter
1224 Marshall Ave.
Colonial Beach, VA 22443
804-224-7166

Barbara Krans Jenkins
580 Megglen Ave.
Akron, OH 44303-2414
216-836-5850

Helen Jennings
872 N. Oxford Ln
Chandler, AZ 85225
602-786-5638

Michele Johnsen
RRI Box 328A
Colebrook, NH 03576
603-237-5500

Karen Ann Klein
4520 N. Woodward
Royal Oak, MI 48073
810-647-7709

Jill Kline
342 Whetstone #6
Marquette, MI 49855
906-228-2769

Ann Kullberg
31313 31st Ave. SW
Federal Way WA 98023
206-838-4890

Kristy A. Kutch
11555 W. Earl Rd.
Michigan City, IN 46360
219-874-4688

Jeanne Lachance
566 Kelly St. Studio 216
Manchester, NH 03102
603-622-2675

Steph Lanyon
83 India St.
Brooklyn, NY 11222-1604
718-389-2907

Viktoria La Paz
2135 NW Flanders St. #206
Portland, OR 97210
503-223-6769/503-497-1252

Dyanne Locati
6720 Doncaster
Gladstone, OR 97027
503-659-6904

Sherry Loomis
P.O. Box 175
Arroyo Grande, CA 93421
805-489-6490

Randy M. McCafferty
305 Edgewood Rd.
Pittsburgh, PA 15221
412-371-4152

CONTRIBUTORS

Lynn McClain
8730 Vinewood
Dallas, TX 75228
214-321-9374

Carla McConnell
729 W Broadway
Montesano, WA 98563
206-249-4810

Judy McDonald
83 N Pinewood Ave.
Agoura, CA 91301
818-991-9303

Patti McQuillin
3611 33rd St. Ct. NW
Gig Harbor, WA 98335
206-858-9361

Patricia Joy McVey
P.O.Box 572
Alta, CA 95701
916-389-2732

Dara Mark
P.O. Box 465
Los Olivos, CA 93441
805-688-0925

Marguerite Dailey Matz
207 Alden Rd.
Carnegie, PA 15106
412-276-0806

Richard Mueller
8530 N Highland Road
Baileys Harbor, WI 54202
414-839-2916

Melissa Miller Nece
2245- D Alden Lane
Palm Harbor, FL 34683
813-786-1396

Bill Nelson
107 E. Cary St.
Richmond, VA 23219
804-783-2602

Bruce J. Nelson
461 Avery Rd. E
Chehalis, WA 98532-8427
206-262-9223

June Bensinger Noone
P.O. Box 224 (Rim Rock Dr.)
Bartonsville, PA 18321
717-629-4463

Barbara Newton
17006 106th Ave. SE
Renton, WA 98055
206-271-6628

Mike Pease
3145 Whitten Drive
Eugene, OR 97405
503-345-8819

Don Pearson
7819 S College Place
Tulsa, OK 74136
918-492-5832

Mary Pohlmann
15398 NE 2nd Ave.
Miami, FL 33162
305-945-8570

Marjorie Post
3475 NE 32 Ave.
Portland, OR 97212
503-335-0743

Bernard Aime Poulin
100 Pretoria
Ottawa, Ont. Canada K1S1W9
613-230-8177

Rita Sue Powell
10193 Bell Road
Elfrida, AZ 85610
602-642-3625

Ken Raney
433 S Ridge Rd.
Hesston, KS 67062
316-327-2669

Marchel Reed
2514 Goshen Rd.
Bellingham, WA 98226
206-966-3009

Valerie Rhatigan
32 Ridgewook Terrace
Maplewood, NJ 07040
201-762-3267

Chuck Richards
1931 Ivywood
Ann Arbor, MI 48103
313-845-6486

Bonnie Ridgeway
1420 Tree Haven Cove
Cordova, TN 38018
901-757-2346

Jan Rimerman
P.O. Box 1350
Lake Oswego, OR 97035
503-635-3583

Gilbert Rocha
153 Hillcrest Dr.
North Platte, NE 69101
308-534-4623

Dawn Rolland
255 Eighth St. #3R
Jersey City, NJ 07302
201-420-0502

Mike Russell
303 Park Ave. South #308
New York, NY 10010
212-598-9707

Steve Schutz
1842 S 17th St.
Lincoln, NE 68502
402-477-2264

Allan Servoss
330 Lincoln Ave.
Eau Claire, WI, 54701
715-832-1758

Jane Shibata
2024 Purdue Ave.
Los Angeles, CA 90025
310-477-1817

Lee Sims
735 Ridge Rd.
Lansing, NY 14882
607-533-7024

Evelyn Smith
243 24th St. SE
Salem, OR 97301
503-581-9345

Timothy Smith
86 Pierre Pont St. #4A
Brooklyn, NY 11201-2720
718-488-9795

Shelly M. Stewart
P.O. Box 296 302 W Fifth St.
Albion, WA 99102
509-332-8926

Bill Stinson
1555 Chapin
Birmingham, MI 48009
810-646-0045

Iris Stripling
4610 Somerset Ct.
Kent, WA 98032
206-854-5704

Marie Sugar
9728 Byeforde Rd.
Kensington, MD 20895
301-949-1074

Judith Surowiec
81 Gallows Hill Rd.
Peekskill, NY 10566
914-736-9689

Don Sullivan
912 S Teluride St.
Aurora,CO 80017
303-671-9357

Marty Swan
300 Brookhaven Court
Slidell, LA 70461
504-641-5581

Thomas M. Thayer Jr.
P.O. Box 5246
Lynnwood, WA 98046
206-778-2988

Margot Van Horn
Box 133
Oxford, MI 48371
810-628-9375

Ronni Wadler
8 Mardon Rd.
Larchmont, NY 10538
914-834-2116

Kristin Warner-Ahlf
P.O. Box 241
South Cle Elum, WA 98943-0241
509-674-5729

Linda Wesner
2834 Honey Tree Dr.
Germantown, TN 38138
901-753-6524

Susan Y. West
5840 Hwy 215
Pauline, SC 29374
803-573-9847

Laura Westlake
129 Weaver Rd.
W. Sayville, NY 11796
516-567-6832

Merle E. Whitley
4611 32nd St. Apt. #7
San Diego, CA 92116
619-284-0691

Brenda Woggon
8785 Sanbur Trail, MW
Rice, MN 56367
612-393-2709

Elly Zadlo
P.O. Box 1597
Sedona, AZ 86339
602-284-0205

Kenneth L. Zonker
703 Ave. J
Huntsiville, TX 77340
409-295-8320

INDEX